MEDICINE
FOR MOUNTAINEERING
& OTHER WILDERNESS ACTIVITIES

Fourth Edition

Edited by

James A. Wilkerson, M.D.

Merced Pathology Laboratory
Merced, California

The Mountaineers
Seattle, Washington

5 4 3
5 4 3 2

Published by The Mountaineers
1011 SW Klickitat Way, Seattle, Washington 98134

Published simultaneously in Canada by Douglas & McIntyre, Ltd., 1615 Venables Street, Vancouver, B.C. V5L 2H1

Published simultaneously in Great Britain by Cordee, 3a DeMontfort Street, Leicester, England, LE1 7HD

Manufactured in the United States of America

Copyedited by Linda Gunnarson
Illustrations by Margorie Domenowske
Cover design by Elizabeth Watson
Layout by Laurie Radin
Typography by Graphics West
Cover Photo: Eldorado Peak and McAllister Glacier, North Cascades National Park, Washington. Bob and Ira Spring.
Cover Insets, from left to right: Cyclist in redwoods, Whakare Warewa Forest Park, New Zealand. Kirkendall/Spring. Snowshoer, Cascade Mountains, Washington. Kirkendall/Spring. Campsite on Norse Peak, Washington. Kirkendall/Spring. Cruising in Puget Sound, Washington. Marge and Ted Mueller.

Library of Congress Cataloging in Publication Data
Medicine for mountaineering & other wilderness activities / edited by James A. Wilkerson.
   – 4th ed.
     p. cm.
    Rev. ed. of: Medicine for mountaineering. 3rd. ed. 1985.
    Includes bibliographical references and index.
    ISBN 0-89886-331-7
    1. Mountaineering–Accidents and injuries. 2. Sports medicine. I. Wilkerson, James A., 1934- . II. Mountaineers (Society) III. Medicine for mountaineering. IV. Title: Medicine for mountaineering and other wilderness activities. (DNLM: 1. First Aid–handbooks. 2. Mountaineering handbooks. 3. Sports Medicine–handbooks. QT 39 M4892)
   RC 1220. M6M4 1992
   617.1'027–dc20
   DNLM/DLC
   for Library of Congress   92-25641
                                         CIP

CONTENTS

Appendixes

CONTRIBUTORS

C. KIRK AVENT, M.D., Professor of Medicine, Infectious Disease Division, The School of Medicine, The University of Alabama in Birmingham, Birmingham, Alabama. (Chapter Nineteen)

EARL E. CAMMOCK, M.D., General Surgeon, Mount Vernon, Washington; Clinical Instructor in Surgery, University of Washington School of Medicine, Seattle, Washington. (Chapter Seven)

FRED T. DARVILL, M.D., Diagnosis and Internal Medicine, Mount Vernon, Washington; Clinical Assistant Professor of Medicine, University of Washington School of Medicine, Seattle, Washington. (Chapter Twelve)

BEN EISEMAN, M.D., Professor of Surgery, University of Colorado School of Medicine; Chairman, Department of Surgery, Rose Medical Center, Denver, Colorado. (Chapters Eleven, Thirteen, and Fourteen)

CHARLES S. HOUSTON, M.D., Internist and Cardiologist, Burlington, Vermont; formerly Professor of Medicine, The University of Vermont College of Medicine, Burlington, Vermont. (Chapter Ten)

HERBERT N. HULTGREN, M.D., Professor Emeritus of Medicine, Stanford University Medical School; formerly Chief, Cardiology Division, Palo Alto Veterans Administration Medical Center, Palo Alto, California. (Chapter Nine)

DRUMMOND RENNIE, M.D., Adjunct Professor of Medicine, The University of California, San Francisco, School of Medicine, San Francisco, California; Senior Editor, The Journal of the American Medical Association. (Chapter Twenty-one)

LAWRENCE C. SALVESEN, M.D., Psychiatrist, Pownal, Maine; Staff Psychiatrist, Outpatient Stress Unit, Veterans Administration Hospital, Togus, Maine; Mental Health Member, Southern Maine and Tri-County Stress Debriefing Teams. (Chapter Four)

JOSEPH B. SERRA, M.D., Orthopedist, Stockton, California; Assistant Clinical Professor of Orthopedics, University of California, Davis, School of Medicine, Davis, California. (Chapter Seven)

JAMES A. WILKERSON, M.D., Pathologist, Merced, California.

Note: The chapter listings indicate the chapters for which each contributor was primarily responsible. However, as in earlier editions of the book, the text has been edited to provide the uniform approach and consistent style desirable for the nonprofessional audience to which this book is directed. The contributors have been most understanding in consenting to such changes in the manuscripts they have submitted.

FOREWORD

Mountaineering: The Freedom of the Hills had been off the press scarcely long enough for copies to traverse the continent to the shores of the Atlantic Ocean when I received a letter from there commenting on a serious imbalance. The writer, a climber completing his medical education at Johns Hopkins, commented that while the chapters on snowcraft and geology were admirably thorough, the chapter on first aid, though expertly written by climber-physicians, was the barest of elementary outlines. The book told more about the snow under climbers' boots and the rocks in their hands than it did about their bodies.

Given this level of instruction, what could the average wilderness traveler do about pyelonephritis, a pulmonary embolism, a retinal hemorrhage? Could he/she cope with snakebite, a flail chest, a "cafe coronary"? Or for that matter, swollen wisdom tooth, fecal impaction, poison oak?

In the Climbing Course of The Mountaineers, and in a companion course in mountaineering first aid, we went a considerable distance into second aid and urged students to enroll, as well, in a Red Cross program. Still, the unspoken rule was: Don't get badly hurt or seriously ill at any distance from civilization unless you have an M.D. in the party. Or, to paraphrase an old Alpine maxim, "When a climber on a weekend trip comes down with the flu or breaks an ankle, he apologizes to his friends. When he gets acute appendicitis three days from the road his friends apologize for him."

Halfway and more through the twentieth century, wilderness mountaineers were recapitulating the frontiering of their nineteenth-century ancestors, settlers of lonesome lands where in emergencies they could turn only to themselves and God, and where, ministers and physicians being equally rare visitors, the family library like as not consisted of two volumes—the Bible and the "doctor book."

Our ancestors were better off than we, because they had a doctor book. Jim Wilkerson's offer to prepare one was welcomed enthusiastically by those of us who had produced *Freedom of the Hills,* yet never in the wildlands been free from submerged anxieties (does that sudden stabbing pain in the abdomen emanate from the appendix? or the salami?), anxieties that erupted as panic when a companion took a hard hit in the head (is it a fracture? a concussion? is blood coming out of the ears? or flowing into them from a cut in the scalp?).

As a nonprofit publisher we had no need to consider the potential sales, if any; we expected to sell fewer copies than we gave away to indigent expeditions unable to recruit an M.D. We were content—if on one climb in one mountain range of the world the book ever saved one life, it was worth doing. We were certain there would be, over the years, many more than one.

Supposing, though, all the wilderness travelers who ever owned copies were guarded by an incredibly lucky star and never experienced or witnessed mortal peril? Even so, the book would be a blessing, for the confidence it gave in "copability." To be sure, it could not help a layman remove an inflamed appendix, but it could help him distinguish a dozen feel-alikes from the real thing, and that would be a comfort. Those travelers under the incredible star might never turn the pages, yet in all their lucky years would gain peace of mind from having the book in their rucksacks.

In the early 1960s we of The Mountaineers book-publishing program took great satisfaction and pride in encouraging Dr. Wilkerson to proceed, and knew the discriminating few would be grateful. What surprised us was that, far from the pages yellowing on the shelves, the book soon was moving out of our warehouse at a rate exceeded only by that of *Freedom* itself. That it has continued to do so and now, after these twenty-five years, comes forth in a state-of-the-art fourth edition shows how wrong publishers can be. Plainly, the merit of the volume has been recognized by the discriminating many.

Harvey Manning

ACKNOWLEDGMENTS

The fourth edition of *Medicine for Mountaineering* has provided an opportunity to update the contents and to include new material. Herb Hultgren, who performed so many of the initial studies of high altitude disorders, has relinquished his role in the compilation of that chapter to Drummond Rennie, who has played an active role in many of the later investigations. Understanding of these disorders continues to progress, and effective therapy is evolving rapidly. Joe Serra, an orthopedist with considerable experience in a variety of wilderness activities, has helped expand the chapter on fractures and related injuries, particularly with a much more thorough discussion of the diagnosis and treatment of dislocations. New vaccines, new therapeutic agents, and even new infectious organisms—Hepatitis C and E, and the human immunodeficiency virus (HIV), for instance—have required greater discussion of preventing, diagnosing, and treating a variety of infectious disorders. Kirk Avent has enlarged that discussion, both in regard to generalized infections and to infections limited to specific organs.

The encouragement of a number of persons, particularly two of the initial contributors, Herb Hultgren and Charlie Houston, and manager of Mountaineers Books, Donna DeShazo, helped overcome the inertia of starting a new edition. All of the contributors have accepted with understanding and grace the editing of their work to provide a uniform approach and consistent style, for which the editor is grateful.

Fred Darvill introduced Margorie Domenowske, who has produced the new drawings for the fourth edition. Her artistic skill, her insight into the problems that needed to be illustrated, and her cordiality have made working with her an unusual pleasure. Linda Gunnarson, the copy editor, has gone through the manuscript with a sharp eye, particularly for word-processor errors. She has made contributions that reflect a considerable knowledge and understanding of the subject, and has even succeeded in decreasing the editor's ignorance of English grammar. The congenial staff of Mountaineers Books has made this endeavor far less onerous than it could have been. Unfortunately, the many other individuals who have contributed to this edition must go unlisted.

With the years, our children have left to live their own lives and I no longer feel guilty about time directed to this book and not spent with them; but the love, support, and understanding of my wife is undiminished, and has made this work possible.

INTRODUCTION

A nyone who partakes in wilderness activities that demand skill, knowledge, strength, and stamina, such as mountaineering, cross-country skiing, or white-water kayaking or rafting, must expect sooner or later to be involved in misfortune—if not his own, then someone else's. The outcome of such misfortune often depends on the medical care the victims receive. For accidents or illnesses that occur at a considerable distance from a physician or hospital, ordinary first aid often does not suffice. If the individuals are to recover with minimal permanent disability, the attitude "Don't do any harm until the doctor comes!" is not adequate, because for many wilderness situations, the doctor is not coming.

In addition to injuries resulting from falls or similar accidents, members of wilderness outings must cope with the problems presented by high terrestrial altitudes and extremes of heat and cold. They must be prepared to provide immediate, appropriate treatment for anaphylactic reactions to insect stings, or to institute cardiopulmonary resuscitation for victims of drowning or lightning strikes. They must avoid the infectious and parasitic disorders that are a constant threat in underdeveloped countries. And they must be prepared to deal with a variety of medical problems usually cared for by physicians. Infectious diseases such as hepatitis and poliomyelitis, noninfectious disorders such as thrombophlebitis or strokes, and surgical problems such as appendicitis have all occurred on wilderness outings in recent years.

The ability to rationally analyze a problem or situation and select and pursue a direct, logical course to a solution is a rare talent sometimes known as "common sense." No ability is more important in caring for individuals with medical disorders in wilderness situations. However, body functions and the intricacies of varied disorders are highly complex, and only those knowledgeable about the principles of diagnosis and therapy can provide optimal medical care for the victims of injury or disease, particularly in remote situations.

Medicine for Mountaineering has been compiled by physicians who actively pursue a variety of wilderness interests, and is intended to provide the information needed to care for medical problems that may be encountered in such circumstances. It is a handbook of medicine—not first aid. The treatment described for some conditions includes potent medications or sophisticated therapeutic procedures. Such remedies are necessary to care for many disorders, but could lead to disaster if used incorrectly. In the years since the publication of the first edition, programs to prepare a variety of emergency medical technicians have emerged and have proven eminently successful. In addition, wilderness enthusiasts who have not taken a formal medical program have demonstrated an ability to assimilate such information and use it appropriately.

To reduce potential complications from the use of medications, the doses of drugs usually are not given in the text but are provided only in the appendix, where the contraindications and side effects have also been listed. By this expedient a warning of the precautions that must be observed whenever a drug is used has been provided without undue repetition in the text. (Most of the medications can only be obtained by prescription from a physician who should make certain the person obtaining the drugs knows their proper use.)

Because no alternate methods for treating some disorders are available, a few procedures have been included that would be impractical or impossible in many wilderness circumstances. Intravenous fluid therapy is an example. Intravenous fluids and the equipment for administering them would almost never be carried by a small wilderness party. Even a large expedition might have difficulty keeping such materials in locations where they could be obtained quickly. However, intravenous fluids are the only means for keeping alive individuals with some disorders, and instructions for their use have been included. (In recent years, large expeditions have left behind a considerable quantity of medical supplies, and on some popular routes a significant supply of items such as intravenous fluids is available.)

The members of wilderness outings should know how to provide basic medical care and should be prepared to administer any treatment that may be needed. The knowledge and medical equipment required depend upon the location and duration of the outing. Traumatic disorders—the injuries produced by physical forces such as falls or falling objects—are most common in wilderness situations, particularly on outings of only a few days. Signs and symptoms of nontraumatic disorders, such as infections or diseases of the heart or lungs, usually develop gradually over a period of several days and often do not become apparent during short trips. On longer trips, the slower onset may permit the victim to be evacuated under his own power before he is incapacitated. Additionally, wilderness enthusiasts tend to be young and healthy and are less susceptible to nontraumatic disorders.

Members of any wilderness outing, regardless of its location or duration should be capable of:

- Caring for soft-tissue injuries, including anticipating and treating hemorrhagic shock
- Anticipating and treating anaphylactic shock, particularly after insect stings
- Recognizing and caring for fractures
- Diagnosing and treating head injuries, including caring for and evacuating an unconscious individual
- Diagnosing and treating thoracic and abdominal injuries
- Recognizing a need for, and performing, cardiopulmonary resuscitation

Potentially threatening environments may call for the capabilities of:

- Recognizing and treating heat or cold injuries
- Recognizing and treating altitude disorders

Members of extended expeditions should, in addition, develop:

- The ability to take a simple medical history and perform a physical examination
- Familiarity with the techniques of patient care, including administration of medications
- Knowledge of the medical disorders, particularly infectious disorders, likely to be encountered on that particular expedition

Every participant in wilderness activities should have regular examinations by a physician knowledgeable about and sympathetic with his interests. Wilderness organizations probably should require such examinations before anyone participates in an outing. (Medical disorders that a physician would recognize during his examination and subsequently treat are too complex for inclusion in a handbook such as this.) For prolonged expeditions into isolated areas, a prior medical examination is essential. Individuals with a peptic ulcer, gallstones, hernia, pregnancy, a history of intestinal obstruction following an abdominal operation, or chronic malaria with an enlarged spleen should be advised of the risk in prolonged isolation where surgical help is not available.

A Note on the Fourth Edition

The editor, contributors, and publisher of *Medicine for Mountaineering* have chosen a title for the fourth edition that reflects the spectrum of medical disorders encountered in the wilderness (and in urban areas of developing countries) this book has always addressed. Of the few additions required to ensure that the new title, *Medicine for Mountaineering and Other Wilderness Activities,* is appropriate, drowning is the most significant. Disorders encountered in marine environments, particularly hyperbaric problems (bends and air embolism) and envenomation by marine organisms, have not been included.

SECTION ONE
GENERAL PRINCIPLES

CHAPTER ONE

DIAGNOSIS

"Disease manifests itself by abnormal sensations and events (symptoms), and by changes in structure or function (signs). Symptoms, being subjective, must be described by the patient. Signs are objective and these the physician discovers by means of physical examination, laboratory studies, and special methods of investigation."[1]

This statement succinctly describes the way medical disorders are diagnosed. Injuries resulting from physical forces (trauma) are identified primarily by physical examination. Symptoms play a greater role in the recognition of nontraumatic disorders. The absence of laboratories, diagnostic radiology, or other facilities should not prevent identification of disorders in the wilderness, particularly common disorders that were being accurately diagnosed before most special investigative methods were available.

Diagnosis is usually the most difficult aspect of care for a person with a nontraumatic disorder. Physicians commonly expend more effort identifying problems than treating them. Outlines are provided below to help care givers recognize the organs that are the site of a disorder. Later chapters contain diagnostic features of the common disorders of specific organs and should be consulted repeatedly.

Effectively examining someone with a medical disorder is not an easy, straightforward procedure. A calm, understanding, and sympathetic manner are essential. The ability to appraise the subject's personality and to adopt an approach that instills confidence is vital. A seriously ill or injured person can not be expected to be cheerful and understanding or, on some occasions, even cooperative.

If an individual has traumatic injuries, an initial cursory examination should identify major problems that require immediate attention, such as bleeding, an obstructed airway, or fractures. Prompt evacuation from a position of imminent danger, such as rockfall, may be necessary, but a complete, unhurried, and uninterrupted examination should be carried out as soon as possible.

THE MEDICAL HISTORY

The individual should be encouraged to describe symptoms in his own words. Leading questions should be avoided, although some prompting or direct inquiries are almost always necessary. A person's failure to describe a symptom must not be considered a reliable indication that the symptom is not present.

The time and circumstances in which symptoms appear and their chronological sequence are significant. The precise location of pain, the time it began, whether the onset was gradual or sudden, the severity of the pain, and the quality of the pain—cramping, stabbing, burning, or other—should be ascertained. Whether symptoms are continuous or intermittent, how they are aggravated or relieved, how they are related to each other, and how they are affected by position, eating, defecation, exertion, sleep, or other activities must be determined. Nonpainful symptoms such as tiredness, weakness, dizziness, and nausea—or their absence—may be highly significant, particularly at high altitude.

An account of any past illnesses must always be obtained, even though in the wilderness the current illness is usually the most significant part of the history. If the person's illness is a recurrence of a previous disease, awareness of that disorder can provide the key to its recognition. Additionally, preexisting disorders that need to be treated, such as diabetes or epilepsy, must be brought to light so that therapy can be continued. Even people with traumatic injuries can have such disorders and should be carefully questioned about them.

Medical History

Past History

Previous Illnesses:	Bronchitis, asthma, pneumonia, pleurisy, tuberculosis, rheumatic fever; any other heart or lung disease; malaria, diabetes, epilepsy, anemia; any other severe or chronic illnesses.
Operations:	Date, nature of operation, complications.
Injuries:	Date, nature of injury, residual disability; wilderness-related injuries, particularly cold injury or altitude illness.
Medications:	Any medications taken regularly, currently or in the past.
Exposure:	Recent exposure to infection or an epidemic.
Immunizations:	When administered, boosters.
Allergies:	Allergy to food, insect stings, or drugs, particularly penicillin and sulfa drugs.

Review of Systems (Including both present and past illnesses)

Head:	Headache, dizziness, hallucinations, confusion, or fainting.
Eyes:	Inflammation, pain, double vision, loss of vision.
Nose:	Colds, sinus trouble, postnasal drip, bleeding, obstruction.

Teeth:	General condition, abscesses, dentures.
Mouth:	Pain, bleeding, sores, dryness.
Throat:	Sore throat, tonsillitis, hoarseness, difficulty in swallowing or talking.
Ears:	Pain, discharge, ringing or buzzing, hearing loss.
Neck:	Stiffness, pain, swelling, or masses.
Heart and Lungs:	Chest pain, palpitations, shortness of breath (greater than that experienced by others following similar exercise at the same altitude), cough, amount and character of material that is coughed up, coughing up blood.
Gastrointestinal:	Loss of appetite, nausea, vomiting, vomiting blood or "coffee ground" material, indigestion, gas, pain; constipation, use of laxatives, diarrhea, bloody or tarry black stools, pale or clay-colored stools, hemorrhoids; jaundice.
Genitourinary:	Increase or decrease in frequency of voiding, color of urine (light yellow, orange), back pain, pain with voiding; passage of blood, gravel, or stones; sores, purulent discharge, venereal disease or sexual contact; menstrual abnormalities such as irregular periods, increased bleeding with periods, bleeding between periods, cramps.
Neuromuscular:	Fainting, unconsciousness from other causes, dizziness or vertigo, twitching, convulsions; muscle cramps, shooting pains, muscular or joint pain; anesthesia, tingling sensations, weakness, incoordination, or paralysis.
Skin:	Rashes, abscesses, or boils.
General:	Fever, chills, weakness, easy fatigability, dizziness, weight loss.

THE PHYSICAL EXAMINATION

If a physical examination is to provide useful information, the examiner must have had some prior experience, particularly in examining the chest and abdomen. For the inexperienced, comparison with a normal individual may be helpful, but nothing can substitute for tutelage by a physician.

A thorough physical examination is essential in the evaluation of anyone with a medical disorder. Even a person with traumatic injuries must be completely examined to ensure no wounds are overlooked, particularly in the presence of an obvious injury. For the examination, the subject should be made comfortable and protected from wind and cold. The examiner's hands should be warm and he must be gentle. Any roughness makes obtaining diagnostic information more difficult and could aggravate the individual's disorder.

To ensure that all areas of the body are examined, a definite routine should always be followed. The outline below is relatively complete and is adequate for both traumatic and nontraumatic disorders. The examination of some anatomical areas, particularly the chest and abdomen, is described in more detail in the chapters dealing with those areas.

Physical Examination

General (Vital Signs):   Pulse rate, respiratory rate, temperature, blood pressure, general appearance.

Skin: Color, texture, rashes, abscesses, or boils.

Head:

  Eyes: Eyebrows and eyelids, eye movements, vision, pupil size and equality, reaction of pupils to light, inflammation.

  Nose: Appearance, discharge, bleeding.

  Mouth: Sores, bleeding, dryness.

  Throat: Inflammation, purulent exudates.

  Ears: Appearance, discharge, bleeding.

Neck: Limitation of movement, enlarged lymph nodes.

Lungs: Respiratory movements, breath sounds, voice sounds, bubbling.

Heart: Pulse rate, regularity, blood pressure.

Abdomen: General appearance, tenderness, rebound and referred pain, muscle spasm, masses.

Genitalia: Tenderness, masses.

Rectum: Hemorrhoids, impacted feces, abscesses.

Back: Tenderness, muscle spasm, limitation of movement.

Extremities: Pain or tenderness, limitation of movement, deformities, unequal length, swelling, ulcers, soft tissue injuries, lymph node enlargement, sensitivity to pin prick and light touch, muscle spasm.

PERSONS WITH TRAUMATIC INJURIES

Individuals with traumatic injuries may have respiratory impairment or severe bleeding that must be cared for immediately. After these emergencies have received attention, however, the care provider must pause and essentially start over from the beginning. An account of the accident and the time and circumstances in which it occurred should be obtained. Frequently the nature of the accident provides clues to injuries that should be anticipated. If the person is unconscious, witnesses must be asked whether unconsciousness caused the accident or resulted from the accident. Witnesses and companions also should be asked whether the individual had any preexisting medical conditions that may have contributed to the accident or that may require treatment.

The subject's pulse and respiratory rate (and blood pressure, if possible) should be measured and recorded immediately and then every ten to fifteen minutes until they are clearly stable. If he is moved, the vital signs should be rechecked immediately; an increase in pulse rate or fall in blood pressure at such times is often an early sign of shock.

Although a few injuries, such as fractures, may have to be cared for first, the person must be completely and thoroughly examined. Concealed injuries must be carefully sought. Injuries of the back are most frequently overlooked, even in hospital emergency rooms. If the individual is lying on his stomach, his back should be examined before he is turned over. At some point his back must be examined, unless suspected fractures of the vertebral column and the absence of bleeding or other evidence of injury dictate that the examination be postponed.

A systematic routine must be followed so that no areas of the body are overlooked. Chest injuries are unquestionably more threatening than hand injuries and deserve prior attention, but failure to recognize and care for a hand injury can result in a permanent handicap. The American College of Surgeons Committee on Trauma has stated: "Many errors in care are due to incomplete diagnosis, to overlooking some serious injury while concentrating on the obvious. A systematic method of examination will obviate such errors."[2]

If evacuation requires more than one day, examinations must be repeated to monitor the subject's condition and to ensure that all injuries have been found. If the individual is unconscious at the time of the initial examination, he must be reexamined as soon as he regains consciousness.

THE MEDICAL RECORD

For disabling diseases or injuries, a written account of the medical history and physical examination findings is an essential element in the person's medical care, particularly when a physician's help is more than a few hours away. In the confusion associated with an accident and subsequent evacuation, a medical attendant may be unable to remember whether a symptom was present or physical changes were detectable, even a few hours after the examination. Memory is not a dependable record of numerical data such as pulse and respiratory rates, temperature, and blood pressure. If any medications have been administered, a written account of the doses and times they were given is essential. Any other treatment must be recorded.

For individuals with nontraumatic illnesses, a written record allows the examiner to systematically review his findings while trying to arrive at a diagnosis. Written records are much easier to use when trying to obtain help by such means as telephone or radio.

Written records of the vital signs (pulse, respiratory rate, blood pressure, and temperature) and other features of the person's illness allow small changes in these signs to be detected. Such changes usually precede more obvious indications that the individual's condition is worsening and allow treatment to be instituted earlier, when it commonly is more effective. These changes may also indicate a response to treatment and presage more obvious improvement in the subject's overall condition, perhaps allowing a difficult evacuation to be delayed until circumstances are more favorable.

When evacuation is prolonged, written records allow more than one person to share in the individual's care. Because all can determine what the signs or symptoms were at any time, all can recognize changes and initiate any therapy that is needed. Written records are also essential for administering medications without omitting or duplicating doses.

If the subject is evacuated, written records are essential for the physician who is to care for him, particularly when his attendants are unable to accompany him. If evacuation has required several days and more than one person has been involved in the subject's care, a written record is the physician's only source of accurate information about the individual's original condition, how that has changed, and the treatment that has been given—particularly medications that have been administered.

Medical records play such a vital role in medical care that they are begun immediately when someone enters a hospital emergency room or physician's office. Such records are subpoenaed at the beginning of any medically related litigation, and omissions are often damaging to the physician's defense, which might be a significant consideration for nonphysicians in an increasingly litigious society.

The outlines provided for the medical history and the physical examination are entirely appropriate for the medical record. Obviously, all abnormalities should be recorded, but the absence of abnormalities is frequently of equal importance, particularly for nontraumatic disorders. Without a specific statement that a sign or symptom was not present, a physician subsequently caring for the individual may be unable to determine whether that change was really absent or was simply not noticed.

For traumatic injuries, an account of the accident should be recorded at the earliest opportunity. All injuries should be carefully described. The absence of injuries, or signs such as swelling or discoloration that are suggestive of injury over major areas of the body—chest, abdomen, head, arms, or legs—should also be noted. The vital signs should be recorded every thirty to sixty minutes for at least four hours if they are stable—more frequently and for longer if they are not stable. After stabilization, vital signs need to be recorded only about every four hours until the person is well on his way to recovery. Any preexisting medical conditions should be described. The dosage, route, and time of administration of all medications must be accurately logged. Notes about any other treatment or changes in the subject's condition must include the time.

The written record must be accessible, not buried away in a pack. Notations of changes in the individual's condition or the administration of medications must be made immediately and not recorded from memory at a later time.

REFERENCES
1. Adams FD: *Cabot and Adams Physical Diagnosis,* 14th ed. Baltimore, The Williams & Wilkins Co., 1958. (Quoted by permission of the author and publisher.)
2. Kennedy RH in Committee on Trauma, American College of Surgeons: *Early Care of Acute Soft Tissue Injuries.* Chicago, 1957. (Quoted by permission of the publisher.)

CHAPTER TWO

BASIC MEDICAL CARE AND EVACUATION

Most individuals injured in accidents or contracting illnesses in the wilderness are evacuated within hours or, at the most, one to two days. Occasionally, however, bad weather, difficult terrain, distance from a hospital or transportation, insufficient personnel for evacuation, or other problems may force an individual to remain in a remote situation. Some persons may not require evacuation if they are expected to recover enough to walk out or resume activity within a relatively short time.

NURSING CARE

Anyone confined to bed (or sleeping bag) by illness or injury has certain needs that require attention. Ministering to those needs is most readily identifiable as "nursing care." The objective of this care is simple: to allow the body to heal itself.

Comfort and Understanding

Comfort and understanding—the essence of nursing—are needed by all, regardless of the nature or severity of their medical problems. Some have a greater need than others; some, particularly young males, try to deny their need. Regardless of the situation, the medical supplies on hand, or the sophistication of available medical knowledge, interest and concern, sympathy and understanding can always be shown; comfort and reassurance can always be provided. All are essential.

Rest

Rest promotes healing in several ways. Exertional and emotional stress are reduced; additional injury to damaged tissues is avoided. Rest can provide improved nutrition, and the nutrients are used for healing instead of muscular effort. Individuals with heart or lung disease and individuals with severe injuries, particularly fractures, may need to be immobilized, but most do not need such confinement. Often, remaining in camp rather than hiking or climbing is all that is required to hasten recovery.

Sedation

In the absence of brain injury or disease, medications that promote sleep may be given at altitudes below 10,000 feet (3,000 m). At higher elevations sleeping medications should not be administered because they lead to reduced blood oxygenation during sleep, which often aggravates symptoms of altitude sickness. The sleeplessness and irregular breathing associated with high altitude can be relieved safely with acetazolamide. (See Chapter Twenty-one, "Medical Problems of High Altitude.")

Analgesia

Analgesics should be supplied liberally, but judiciously, in wilderness situations. The risk of narcotic addiction for individuals with painful injuries or illnesses is essentially nonexistent, particularly when the agents are administered for a week or less. The hazard of strong analgesics consists largely of further depressing cerebral activity in a person whose central nervous system function is already impaired as the result of a head injury or an illness. Depressed cerebral function is manifested by impaired respiration. Breathing becomes slower and shallower, which could result in significant hypoxia, particularly at high elevations. A person with a severe head injury might stop breathing altogether, which usually is catastrophic.

For individuals who do not have a head injury, analgesics can relieve severe discomfort and the associated emotional distress. For many subjects with traumatic injuries, control of pain reduces the severity of shock. Analgesia promotes healing by allowing people with painful injuries or illnesses to sleep restfully. Many individuals are more aware of pain at night when nothing is happening to divert their attention. For three or four days after a major injury—occasionally even longer—strong analgesia may be needed.

Major analgesics have so much sedative effect that a sleeping medication is not needed. Administering a sleeping medication with a major analgesic would be hazardous.

Warmth

Individuals who are ill or injured must be kept warm. At low environmental temperatures, persons with severe illnesses or injuries may not be able to generate enough heat to maintain body temperature, even in a sleeping bag, and like individuals with hypothermia, may require external sources of heat. (See Chapter Twenty-two, "Cold Injuries.")

Lower Altitude

Evacuation from altitudes above 15,000 feet (4,600 m) promotes recovery. Individuals with diseases of the lungs or heart should be taken as low as possible, preferably below 8,000 feet (2,400 m), and provided with supplemental oxygen if it is available.

Coughing

People who are immobilized with a severe injury or illness usually do not breathe deeply, particularly if breathing is painful. As a result of diminished respiratory excursions, their lungs are not fully expanded and fluid accumulates in the immobile segments. These collections are an ideal medium for bacterial growth, which leads to pneumonia. (Such infections are the most common cause of death for elderly persons confined to bed with fractured hips or similar injuries.)

To eliminate the fluid, expand the lungs, and reduce the danger of infection, individuals must be encouraged—or forced—to breathe deeply and to cough at frequent intervals. Coughing may be difficult for someone who is very ill, or very painful for someone with a chest or abdominal injury, but those individuals are the most prone to pulmonary infections and most need to clear their lungs. The practice in most hospitals is to have the person sit up, hold his sides, and cough deeply—not just clear his throat—at least every two hours. A similar routine should be adopted in wilderness circumstances, particularly at higher altitudes where any compromise in pulmonary function could be disastrous.

Elimination of fluid from the lungs can also be increased by postural drainage. If the head and chest are slightly lower than the rest of the body, gravity helps get rid of the fluid. In a tent, such positioning can best be achieved by elevating the abdomen, pelvis, and legs. After the person has recovered to the extent that he is able to be up and walking around, forced coughing and postural drainage are usually no longer necessary.

Ambulation

Anyone confined to bed as a result of illness or injury should be encouraged to get up and walk around several times a day. Such exercise increases the circulation in the legs and helps prevent thrombophlebitis. (See Chapter Ten, "Respiratory System Disorders.") The only major exceptions to this rule are individuals with injuries that prevent walking, and individuals who have already developed thrombophlebitis and should remain as immobile as possible until the disorder has resolved.

Diet

Food is not as important during the acute stages of an illness as an adequate fluid intake. Unless a specific disorder dictates a particular diet, such as the bland diet for peptic ulcer, the person should eat whatever he desires. During convalescence more attention can be given to a nutritionally adequate diet, perhaps with extra protein.

Bowel Care

Difficulties with bowel evacuation are common for persons confined to bed, who repress the urge to defecate, have a low food intake, and become dehydrated. If not corrected, fecal impaction often results. (See Chapter Twelve, "Gastrointestinal Disorders.") Even though stool volume is reduced in the absence of solid food in the diet, bowel movements should occur every three to four days. The best way to ensure normal elimination is to make certain fluid intake is adequate; roughage or fiber in the diet increase stool bulk and are helpful. Laxatives or enemas should rarely be needed to prevent impaction in a bedridden individual.

Convalescence

Although physical activity should be encouraged during convalescence, strenuous exercise too early may delay recovery, particularly at high altitudes. In addition, individuals are more susceptible to other injuries during convalescence. To be certain that recovery is complete, delaying a return to full activity for two or three extra days may be desirable.

FLUID BALANCE

An adequate fluid intake is essential. A person can live for weeks without food, but only for a few days without water. Fluid balance implies an equilibrium between losses (through the kidneys, skin, and lungs—or other routes) and gains (from fluids and foods that have been ingested.) During an illness that increases fluid losses and makes fluid intake difficult or impossible, fluid balance can become critical. Dehydration from massive diarrheal fluid loss used to kill hundreds of thousands during cholera epidemics, and continues to be the leading cause of death of children and adults in many underdeveloped countries.

An adult of average size normally loses 1,500 cc to 2,000 cc of water from his body each day. The "sensible loss" excreted by the kidneys ranges from one to two liters per day. The "insensible loss" through perspiration (even in cold climates) and evaporation from the lungs (to moisten air that is inhaled) is one-half to one liter per day in temperate climates and at low altitudes. Increased fluid losses occur in hot climates or with high fever, when several liters of water may be lost daily through perspiration (which is no longer insensible), or at high altitudes, where four to five liters of water are lost daily through the lungs.

Salt (sodium chloride), potassium, and bicarbonate, known collectively as electrolytes, are vital constituents of body fluids. As with water, a balance between intake and loss must be maintained. The daily salt requirement for an average adult is three grams. When large amounts of salt are lost through perspiration, needs may be considerably higher.

Normally functioning kidneys are very sensitive to changes in the body's fluid balance and react immediately to conserve or eliminate water. The urine volume and color are highly reliable indicators of fluid status. A twenty-four-hour volume of less than 500 cc, or urine that has a deep yellow or orange color, is indicative of fluid depletion; a volume of 2,000 cc of very lightly colored urine is typical of a high fluid intake.

These water and electrolyte requirements represent the needs of a healthy adult. Individuals with heart or kidney disease may be unable to get rid of excess salt and water and can have quite different requirements. The administration of normal quantities of electrolytes and water, particularly salt, to persons with one of these disorders would have serious consequences.

When an illness, such as dysentery or cholera, causes high fluid losses by vomiting and watery stools, the volume of fluid lost should be measured—an unpleasant but necessary task—to stay abreast of the person's fluid status. Insensible losses must be estimated also, taking into consideration fever, environmental temperature, and altitude. The volume of fluid ingested must be measured to ensure enough is consumed. These measurements and estimates must be recorded so the individual's fluid needs can be calculated subsequently.

The urine volume is a good indicator of a subject's fluid balance, but tends to reflect what has already happened. Measuring losses and gains as they occur provides more immediate insight into the condition of someone with a fluid-losing disorder.

Dehydration at Altitude

Higher altitudes tend to produce dehydration, and this tendency becomes progressively greater as the elevation increases and the environment becomes colder. Almost all trekkers or climbers are dehydrated above 18,000 feet (5,500 m). Some investigators have suggested that the depression, impaired judgment, and other psychological and intellectual changes that commonly occur at high altitudes and for which hypoxia has been blamed, may actually be the result of dehydration.

The principal cause of dehydration at high altitude is the increased fluid loss associated with more rapid and deeper breathing of cold air. Air is warmed to body temperature and is saturated with water as it passes through the upper air passages; it has a relative humidity of one hundred percent when it reaches the lungs. The cold air at high altitudes contains little moisture and requires more water for humidification. (The relative humidity might be quite high when the air is cold but can drop to below ten percent when the air is warmed to body temperature. Loss of heat through evaporation of water and through warming inhaled cold air is a significant contributor to hypothermia at high altitudes.)

In cold environments, some of the water that humidifies inspired air is regained during expiration by condensation in upper air passages that have been cooled by the inspired air. However, mouth breathing bypasses the air passages where most condensation occurs and increases water loss. Some individuals are not careful about managing clothing to minimize sweating, particularly with the bulky clothing required to keep warm during periods of immobility at high altitude, and fluid loss from this source is not held to the lowest levels possible.

Decreased fluid consumption often contributes to dehydration at high elevations. Both the need to carry fuel and melt snow to obtain water for drinking or cooking, and dulling of the sensation of thirst that accompanies the loss of appetite, nausea, or even vomiting of acute mountain sickness, tend to reduce fluid intake.

Individuals who are active at high altitudes must consciously force themselves to drink large volumes of fluid. Thirst alone is not a reliable indicator of the need for water. Above 15,000 to 16,000 feet (4,600 to 4,900 m) fluid requirements often exceed four liters per day. The adequacy of fluid intake can best be judged by the urine color and volume. Darkly colored urine—orange snow flowers instead of light yellow—and the absence of a need to void upon awakening from a night's sleep are indicators of significant dehydration.

Fluid Replacement

The easiest and most reliable method for replacing fluids is to drink more. Almost any nonalcoholic liquid is suitable, but since water contains no electrolytes, fruit juices, soft drinks, soups, and similar liquids should be encouraged. (Coffee, tea, and hot chocolate are not as satisfactory because they contain diuretic agents that increase renal fluid loss.)

Seriously ill individuals with very little appetite often refuse liquids as well as solid foods. However, they can often be persuaded to drink small quantities, just two or three sips, at intervals of fifteen to twenty minutes. With tenacity, patience, and gentle encouragement, such persons usually can be coaxed to drink several liters of fluid over a twenty-four-hour period.

Some individuals, particularly those with intractable vomiting or in coma, are unable to take fluids orally. If medical attention can be obtained within one or two days and fluid losses are not increased, the intervening fluid depletion is usually not too severe. However, longer periods without fluid, and disorders that increase fluid loss, can produce severe dehydration if fluids are not given intravenously.

Administering fluids intravenously should be attempted only by knowledgeable persons experienced with such therapy. Fluids suitable for intravenous administration cannot be improvised and would only be carried by a well-equipped expedition, although such fluids might be obtained by air drop. Such fluids are often left behind by expeditions, and in some popular areas a significant supply has accumulated. These fluids come from many nations and their labels are printed in many languages, but the contents are usually in standard chemical symbols or in English.

The volume of fluids to be given intravenously must be determined each day. Fluids are required to replace both normal and abnormal losses. Two liters of five percent glucose and one-half liter of an electrolyte solution (preferably a balanced salt solution, but normal saline if only that is available) usually satisfy the body's daily needs when no abnormal losses are occurring. Fluids lost through vomiting, diarrhea, or excessive perspiration should be replaced with an electrolyte solution. Excessive fluid loss through the lungs due to high altitude should be replaced by glucose since no electrolytes are lost with the moisture in expired air.

Most electrolyte solutions contain little potassium. Individuals with poor kidney function cannot rid themselves of excessive potassium, which may rapidly accumulate to lethal levels. However, persons with normal renal function excrete potassium in the urine. As a result, blood potassium concentrations can fall to dangerously low levels during prolonged intravenous fluid therapy if the potassium is not replaced. Therefore, individuals receiving intravenous fluids for more than two to three days, or losing large volumes of fluid with diarrhea, who have a normal urine volume, should receive an extra 15 to 20 mEq of potassium per liter of electrolyte. (The occasions when such potassium supplements are available in wilderness circumstances must be rare. When available, the supplements are usually supplied in a solution that can be added directly to the electrolyte solution.)

If a person with a healthy heart and normally functioning kidneys is provided with an adequate intake of water (as glucose) and electrolytes (balanced salt solution), the kidneys compensate for any imbalance. The inevitable inaccuracies inherent in measuring fluid intake and output are fully corrected. However, an individual with preexisting heart disease, particularly congestive heart failure, a person with kidney disease, or someone with acute renal failure as a result of his disease or injury requires much more precise therapy, which can only be provided with hospital facilities. For such individuals, any error in administering fluids must be on the side of not giving enough.

CARE FOR TRAUMA VICTIMS

Traumatic injuries are by far the most common medical problems encountered in the wilderness.

Emergencies

True medical emergencies, in which a delay of a few minutes in providing care can significantly affect the outcome, are rare. In wilderness accidents the opportunity to provide such treatment may pass before anyone is able to get to the individual. Nonetheless, wilderness users must be familiar with the procedures for treating traumatic medical emergencies if they are to deal with them successfully when the rare opportunities do occur. True emergencies do not allow time for referral to a textbook.

If immediate action is necessary to prevent loss of life following an accident, the order in which problems should receive attention is as follows:

1. Cardiopulmonary function. An open airway must be established first; interference with breathing by chest wounds must be quickly corrected. If needed for persons who have drowned, been struck by lightning, or received minor head injuries, cardiopulmonary resuscitation (CPR) should be started.
2. Bleeding. After the subject is breathing or being resuscitated, bleeding should be controlled by direct pressure at bleeding sites, not by tourniquets or pressure points.
3. Shock. After cardiac and respiratory function have been established and bleeding has been controlled, attention should be directed to treating or preventing shock. Treatment given in anticipation of shock is more effective than treatment instituted after shock has developed.

Although the order of the first two problems may appear reversed because control of severe bleeding should take only seconds but CPR can be prolonged, in reality they are not. Anyone whose heart has stopped does not bleed. Therefore, CPR must take first priority. Furthermore, anyone who has bled so severely that his heart has stopped can not be resuscitated. The combination of cardiac arrest and severe hemorrhage is essentially always lethal.

Other Injuries

All injuries should be treated as completely as possible before the person is moved. Open wounds are always contaminated to some extent; further contamination should be avoided. Soft-tissue injuries should be covered with voluminous dressings that apply pressure to the wounds to control bleeding, provide immobilization, minimize swelling, and control infection. Even when no fractures are present, severely injured extremities should be immobilized and elevated slightly to aid blood circulation. If the lower extremities are injured and evacuation requires the person to walk or climb, he should stop periodically to lie down and elevate his feet. Splinting fractures before the subject is moved is particularly important. "Splint 'em where they lie" is a time-proven adage.

The equipment necessary for the treatment of some injuries, such as injuries of the chest, is not available on most short outings. However, this equipment should always be available in popular wilderness recreation areas and should be a part of the emergency gear of all wilderness rescue organizations.

SPECIFIC ACCIDENTS

Avalanches

Most avalanche victims are killed by the impact of large blocks of hard-packed snow or ice. Others are suffocated by densely packed snow. Almost no one buried more than three feet below the surface by an avalanche survives. The following outline can be followed in caring for individuals caught in an avalanche immediately after they have been found:

1. Obviously lethal injuries should be identified so that attention can be directed to the living. Evacuation of bodies can be delayed until the hazard of additional avalanches has passed.
2. The subject should be assumed to have a broken neck if he is unconscious and no lethal injuries can be found. Appropriate splinting must be continued as long as he remains comatose.
3. An open airway must be established, chest injuries must be covered, and resuscitation must be initiated if the person is not breathing. Movement of his neck must still be avoided, which is not easy.
4. After the individual is breathing, his injuries should be treated rapidly so he can be protected from cold and moved out of the avalanche path at the earliest possible moment.

Lightning

In the United States between 150 and 300 persons die from lightning strikes every year; in 1943, 430 lightning deaths occurred. However, the number who die is less than one-third of those who are hit. Since only the individuals with more severe lightning injuries are reported, the true fatality rate is probably between ten and twenty percent. Most survivors have no significant residual disabilities.

Because the voltage in a bolt of lightning is so high (200 million to 2 billion volts of direct current), it typically "flashes" over the outside of the body, particularly if the body is wet. Electricity does penetrate the body enough to disrupt the electrical functions of the brain and heart, but lightning injuries are not usually associated with the extensive burns produced by manmade voltages (up to 200,000 volts of alternating current, usually less than 30,000 volts). Since the current flows around the outside of the body (just as electricity tends to flow along the outside of a conductor), the electrical energy can instantly vaporize moisture on the body surface and blow away the person's clothing, resulting in some unusual incidents.

The most significant effects of lightning are on the brain. The electricity does shock the heart, causing it to arrest, but the heart's intrinsic tendency to contract rhythmically causes it to resume beating, just as it sometimes does after being shocked to stop ventricular fibrillation. However, the brain requires significantly longer to recover from the effects of the electrical current, and because the brain controls respiration, the person does not breathe. Although the heart has resumed beating, it can not function without oxygen and subsequently goes into ventricular fibrillation, resulting in death.

Clearly the emergency treatment for someone struck by lightning consists of immediate, and sometimes prolonged, artificial respiration. (Cardiac resuscitation should be given only if needed; the heart most often resumes beating on its own.) More than seventy percent of the individuals struck by lightning have enough disruption of brain function to lose consciousness. Recovery of enough function to resume breathing commonly takes as long as twenty to thirty minutes, and rarely takes hours.

If more than one person has been struck, which commonly occurs, attention should be directed first to the ones who are not breathing and appear dead. Those who are groaning or rolling around, although unconscious, are breathing and do not require immediate attention.

After the subject is breathing on his own, he should be evacuated to a hospital. Other problems are common. Occasionally and unpredictably, heart failure, which requires intensive care, develops several hours later, apparently as the result of electrical damage to the heart muscle. Most individuals who have been struck by lightning lose their short-term memory for two to five days and can never recall the circumstances of the accident. Emotional or psychiatric problems are common but usually clear up with time and appropriate treatment. Various types of paralysis appear but are usually transient. The extremities may appear blue and pulseless, as if the arteries were obstructed. This change usually is the result of intense spasm of the muscles in the walls of the arteries and passes after a few hours. More than fifty percent of the people struck by lightning have one or both eardrums ruptured, possibly as the result of incredibly loud thunder. Superficial burns are common and typically have a feathery or fernlike pattern.

Delayed problems sometimes occur. Neurologic problems have developed three to twelve months after injury. Cataracts can appear as long as two years later.

Drowning

Drowning is by far the most common fatal accident among participants in outdoor activities, even though relatively few drownings occur in circumstances that would be considered wilderness, and most of the victims are children. In the United States more than 8,000 deaths occur annually. Drowning is the second most common cause (after motor vehicle accidents) of accidental death in children between the ages of one and fourteen, and the third most common cause of death overall. Forty to fifty percent of drowning victims are four years old or younger; the only other large group is teenage males.

Alcohol plays a major role in many adult drownings by causing the accident that results in submersion and by impairing the ability of the individuals to get out of the water or contrive some type of flotation device. (The term "near-drowning" is used for submersion incidents survived for at least twenty-four hours, but also can be defined as two fishermen in a flat-bottomed boat with a case of beer.)

Some drowning victims, such as white-water boaters and kayakers, get pinned or trapped underwater. A few people dive into shallow water, strike their heads on the bottom or on submerged objects, and are knocked unconscious or suffer cervical fractures. Individuals competing to determine who can stay underwater the longest or swim the greatest distance underwater may lose consciousness, particularly if they have hyperventilated beforehand and lowered their blood carbon dioxide concentration, a major component of the drive to breathe.

The mechanism of death for others is less obvious. Many drowning victims dive or jump into cold water and simply do not come up. No struggle of any kind is witnessed. In many accidents of this type, the sudden contact with cold water apparently prompts a sudden, uncontrollable gasp or inspiration that results in inhalation of water. This response has been labeled the "gasp reflex" and is essentially universal, although it usually can be controlled. Many have observed a similar response upon stepping into a cold shower.

Many individuals temporarily trapped underwater have experienced an overwhelming compulsion to breathe. (The time anyone can hold his breath when submerged in cold water is much shorter than when submerged in warm water or on land—usually one-fourth to one-third as long.) Apparently some individuals give in to this urge, perhaps thinking they can safely take a single breath to relieve the respiratory drive until they reach the surface.

One inhalation or gasp of water may stop all efforts to reach the surface; complete asphyxia apparently is not necessary. Possibly the water passes without delay through the lungs into the blood, and the reduced osmotic pressure or some other altered characteristic of the diluted blood has an immediate effect on the brain. Individuals who have been resuscitated after drowning have described the sensation as enjoyable. This hypothetical mechanism would explain the drowning of individuals after water washes over their heads in a turbulent stream or ocean surf, but does not explain the deaths of individuals who suffer laryngeal spasm and can not inhale any water, approximately fifteen percent of all drownings.

Reviving drowned individuals requires cardiopulmonary resuscitation, which does not differ significantly from CPR given for other disorders. If the subject has entered the water head first, particularly by diving, measures to splint a cervical fracture should be instituted before he is removed from the water. CPR should be initiated without delay as soon as the individual is out of the water. Attempts at chest compression while the person is still in the water are ineffective and delay extraction. Efforts to remove water from the lungs, particularly with the Heimlich maneuver, are a waste of time. Water in the lungs passes immediately into the blood, even after saltwater drowning, can not be removed, and can not interfere with oxygen transport. Efforts to relieve laryngeal spasm in that fifteen percent of drowning victims are not needed.

No other specific treatment can be administered outside a hospital, although some individuals require treatment for immersion hypothermia. Therapy for pulmonary and other complications produced by the aspirated water is often needed, but can only be administered in a hospital. Although dissimilar effects from drowning in fresh water and salt water, due to their chemical and osmotic differences, have been anticipated, little substantive variation has been found.

A few individuals, mostly children but some adults, have been successfully resuscitated after prolonged submersion. Most have been submerged less than thirty minutes in water colder than 50°F (10°C). The longest submersion followed by successful resuscitation was sixty-six minutes. CPR was started for that two-and-one-half-year-old girl by an experienced, professional rescue team as soon as she was retrieved from 41°F (5°C) water. She was transported without delay to a hospital (that was prepared for her arrival) and was immediately rewarmed with cardiopulmonary bypass.

Apparently, when some submerged individuals aspirate cold water, the cooled blood is selectively transported to the brain, which begins to cool immediately and can tolerate oxygen deprivation that would be disastrous at normal temperature. Animal studies have demonstrated such immediate cooling, but not all investigators are willing to accept this explanation for the well-documented survival of a few individuals following prolonged submersion.

Such successes are uncommon. Relaxation of surveillance or other protective measures for individuals engaged in water sports can not be justified. Submerged individuals should be located and retrieved as quickly as possible; if submersion has lasted less than thirty minutes, CPR should probably be attempted. However, unjustifiable expectation of success can lead only to frustration, anger with no suitable target, and the emotional consequences of such responses.

EVACUATION

An effective wilderness rescue requires a good stretcher and enough people to carry it without further injury to the subject or the rescuers. Basket stretchers are the best available in most areas. Leg dividers interfere with splinting broken legs and packaging of the subject and should be removed if that can be accomplished without destroying the structural integrity of the stretcher. Better stretchers have been developed but are rarely found in wilderness areas within the United States. The McInnes stretcher can be transported over the roughest terrain by only two people.

Few circumstances can justify rolling someone with fractures of the legs, pelvis, back, or neck onto a makeshift stretcher and bouncing him along over a rough descent simply because a rigid support, such as a basket stretcher or a body board, and enough people to carry it are not immediately available.

If bad weather makes evacuation urgent, the person rarely needs to be carried very far below tree line before personnel and equipment are obtained to complete the evacuation with minimal risk of further injury. The rescue may be easier and the outcome better if equipment and supplies for an overnight stay are carried to the party and the evacuation is delayed until the following morning or even until the weather improves.

"Four dozen" stretcher bearers are essential too. Transporting an injured person over rugged terrain is physically demanding. Fewer than six ordinary individuals can not carry well a basket stretcher containing an adult and tire rapidly.

If the party is small, deciding who should go for help and who should stay with the injured may be a problem. If the group has signed out with a park ranger or similar official, the wisest course may be to wait until search efforts locate the entire party. In wooded areas a fire may be built to attract attention and to provide warmth. Since at least one person must stay with an injured individual, small parties should always register.

The safety rules for wilderness activities are the same after an accident as before. Further injuries or loss of life as the result of ignoring these rules simply because one accident has occurred can not be justified. One person must not go for help alone over terrain (such as a snow-covered glacier) that he would not cross by himself under normal circumstances. The fundamental soundness of this policy was pointed out in a Pacific Northwest accident in which a climber died from hypothermia while attempting to go for help, but the accident victim and an uninjured climber who remained with him were subsequently rescued by a search party.

Helicopters

The use of helicopters for wilderness rescues has greatly reduced the time needed to get an injured or ill individual to medical care and has reduced the number of stretcher bearers to four or six, most of whom can be brought in by the helicopter along with a stretcher and needed medical supplies.

Working effectively with helicopters requires knowledge of their capabilities and limitations. Although landings have been made at altitudes above 20,000 feet (6,100 m) by turbine (jet) helicopters, most helicopters can not land or take off above 8,000 to 10,000 feet (2,400 to 3,000 m). The maximum altitude at which a helicopter can operate is determined by air density. Because cold air is more dense, a helicopter can operate at higher altitudes at lower temperatures. Conversely, the altitude at which a helicopter can land or take off can be reduced by several thousand feet by high air temperatures.

Helicopters usually can not make absolutely vertical ascents or descents. Some space for an approach and departure is needed. The most level spot that is free of obstructions, particularly electrical or telephone wires, which are difficult to see from the air, should be selected. The wind direction should be indicated to the helicopter pilot, preferably by smoke, which also indicates the wind speed, or with an easily seen article of clothing.

Helicopters are hazardous. The downward thrust from the main rotors can produce winds ranging from 60 to 120 miles per hour. Obviously, a person helping to guide a helicopter to a landing should not be standing on the edge of a sheer drop. Eyes must be protected from flying dirt and debris. Personal equipment must be stored where it can not be blown away. Strong rotor winds can tumble full packs over the ground and over a drop or into a crevasse. Burning embers from fires can be blown about, causing injuries to rescuers or starting fires in surrounding brush or forests.

The danger from the tail and main rotors would seem to be obvious, but a surprising number of people walk into spinning rotors every year. While the helicopter is on the ground the main rotors may be higher than a person's head, but a sudden gust of wind or slowing of their speed can bend them downward to an amazing extent. No one should stand beneath the tips of the rotors. Rescue personnel should approach the helicopter from the front, where they can be seen by the pilot, and in a crouched position.

CHAPTER THREE

SPECIAL PROBLEMS

Fever and chills are well-known signs of infection, but are signs of other illnesses as well. Shock, unconsciousness, and the need for airway maintenance are associated with widely varying disorders. These problems are discussed only in this chapter instead of with all the disorders with which they might occur.

FEVER

Human body temperature in normal individuals averages 98.6°F (37°C) when measured orally, ranges from 96.5°F (35.8°C) to 100°F (37.8°C), and usually varies 1.25° to 3.75°F (0.7° to 2.1°C) daily. The lowest temperature occurs between 3:00 A.M. and 5:00 A.M. and the highest in the late afternoon or early evening in individuals who are active during the day and sleep at night. The temperature of a woman of child-bearing age rises about 1.0°F (0.5°C) at the time of ovulation and remains elevated until menstruation begins. During vigorous exercise, a healthy, well-conditioned athlete's temperature can climb as high as 104°F (40°C) if he is generating heat faster than it can be lost.

In a moderate or hot wilderness environment, a person should not be considered to have a fever until his temperature at rest exceeds 100°F (38°C) orally or 101°F (38.5°C) rectally. In a cold environment, hypothermia can mask a fever, sometimes a very high fever, by reducing the body's temperature to normal or subnormal levels.

Oral temperatures are easier to measure but are affected by recently consumed food or beverages, smoking, or mouth breathing and talking. Oral temperatures should not be taken for at least ten minutes after eating or smoking, and the person should preferably have been sitting or lying quietly. Rectal temperatures are more reliable and usually are about one degree Fahrenheit (one-half degree Celsius) higher than oral temperatures. If rectal measurements are necessary, a rectal thermometer is preferable. It should be lubricated, gently inserted about one and one-half inches into the rectum, and left for three minutes.

If the subject is delirious or thrashing about, he must be watched carefully and perhaps restrained to prevent his breaking the thermometer and injuring himself, regardless of where the temperature is measured. Taking the temperature may have to be postponed until he is calmer.

As long as an illness persists, the temperature and pulse rate should be recorded every four hours (a soundly sleeping individual rarely needs to be awakened just to have his temperature taken). Fevers sometimes follow specific patterns that are diagnostically helpful. The temperature may go up and stay up, gradually coming down at the termination of the illness, or it may spike to high levels and then fall to normal or below normal every day or every second or third day. A record is essential for such patterns to be recognized.

A moderate fever, although it may make the person uncomfortable, does not produce lasting harmful effects. In contrast, temperatures above 106°F (41°C) can cause irreversible damage if not promptly lowered. In hot or temperate climates such high fevers should be reduced by covering the individual's body and extremities with wet cloths (or wetting the clothes he is wearing) and fanning him to increase evaporation and cooling. A person with a life-threatening fever in an environment of ice and snow may only require removal of a portion of his clothing.

Cooling should be continued until the person's temperature is below 103°F (39.5°C). Aspirin may be given orally if the individual is fully conscious or rectally if he is stuporous or comatose. His temperature must be watched very carefully for at least twenty-four hours after cooling because high fevers frequently recur quite rapidly.

Although his fever must be lowered, the subject must be protected from environmental extremes of heat or cold. He must be redressed in clothing similar to that being worn by everyone else. In a warm environment, he should not be closed up in a sleeping bag that traps the heat and can cause his temperature to go up again; however, if sleeping bags are necessary for everyone else to keep warm, he may need one as well.

CHILLS

An individual with a chill shivers uncontrollably and feels cold and miserable. These symptoms are produced by the entry of showers of microorganisms into the blood stream. In comparison with the usual chills resulting from exposure to cold, chills caused by infection are much more severe and produce violent, uncontrollable shaking of the entire body. Teeth chatter, the lips and nails turn purple, and the skin becomes pale and cold. (In years past, a chill could be diagnosed when a patient was shaking hard enough to make his bed rattle.) The cold feeling persists in spite of blankets and heating pads until the chill has run its course, usually five to fifteen minutes. Typically, a chill is followed by a fever that may reach high levels.

A chill is almost always the first sign of an infection, and treatment consists of caring for the underlying disorder. Pneumonia, meningitis, and "strep throat" are frequently introduced with a single shaking chill. Malaria, infections of the kidneys or liver and bile ducts, and generalized bacterial infections are characterized by recurrent chills.

SHOCK

Shock is a sign of severe disease and is most commonly caused by a sudden reduction in the blood volume, typically as a result of hemorrhage. Blood volume can also be reduced by disorders in which only fluid is lost. Large volumes of serum pour into the damaged tissues following a severe burn. Dehydration causes a reduction in blood volume and is lethal if severe and uncorrected.

When the blood volume is reduced, regardless of the cause, the arteries in the skin and muscles constrict, diverting blood to the vital organs. The heart pumps at an increased rate to circulate the remaining blood faster and enable a smaller volume of blood to carry more oxygen. When these mechanisms can no longer compensate for the reduction in blood volume, blood pressure falls. If untreated, severe shock eventually becomes irreversible in spite of therapy and the person dies.

Shock also occurs in disorders not associated with an evident reduction in blood volume. Severe infections or heart attacks are often associated with shock. A period of shock of varying duration is characteristic of the terminal stages of any fatal disease. The mechanisms by which shock is produced in those conditions is poorly understood, and efforts at treatment, other than therapy directed toward the underlying disease, are frequently unrewarding.

Diagnosis

The severity of shock following hemorrhage depends upon the volume of blood lost and how fast it is lost. Signs of shock are usually more severe when blood loss is rapid than when loss is gradual, even though the amounts lost are identical. Estimating the volume of blood loss is not easy, and most individuals tend to overestimate. A small amount of blood can cover an amazingly large area.

Individuals of different sizes have roughly proportional blood volumes. A person 6 feet (180 cm) tall and weighing 175 pounds (80 kg) who is normally hydrated has a blood volume of about 6,000 cc. A person 5 feet 2 inches (155 cm) tall and weighing 110 pounds (50 kg) has a blood volume of about 4,000 cc.

Mild shock results from loss of ten to twenty percent of the blood volume. The person appears pale and his skin is cool, first over the extremities and later over the trunk. As shock becomes more severe, the subject often complains of feeling cold and is often thirsty. A rapid pulse and reduced blood pressure may be present. However, absence of these signs does not indicate shock is not present since they may appear rather late, particularly in previously healthy young adults.

Moderate shock results from loss of twenty to forty percent of the blood volume. The signs characteristic of mild shock are present and may become more severe. The pulse is typically fast and weak or "thready." Blood flow to the kidneys is reduced as the available blood is shunted to the heart and brain, and the urinary output declines. A urinary volume of less than 30 cc per hour is a late indication of moderate shock. In contrast to the dark, concentrated urine observed with dehydration, the urine is usually a light color.

Severe shock results from loss of more than forty percent of the blood volume and is characterized by signs of reduced blood flow to the brain and heart. Reduced cerebral blood flow produces restlessness and agitation initially, but confusion, stupor, and eventually coma and death follow. Diminished blood flow to the heart can produce abnormalities of the cardiac rhythm.

Treatment

Treatment for shock is much more effective if begun before the typical signs appear. The first measures instituted after controlling bleeding and ensuring adequate respiration should be for shock. Shock would obviously be expected after a severe hemorrhage, but some fractures of the spine, pelvis, or thigh, and many injuries to the internal organs, are associated with severe bleeding that produces no external evidence of hemorrhage. Shock should be anticipated with such injuries and with other disorders, particularly those that result in severe fluid loss, such as severe diarrhea.

Successful treatment of shock depends largely upon treating the cause. However, several measures should be taken regardless of the underlying disorder. The subject should be supine with his head at the same level or lower than the rest of his body and his feet elevated ten to twelve inches (twenty-five to thirty centimeters). This position helps the venous blood in the legs to return to the body, making that blood available for more vital tissues. In severe shock, a lower position of the head may aid circulation to the brain.

The individual's body temperature must be maintained. Blankets or sleeping bags are not adequate in severe shock because the person can not produce enough heat to warm himself. An external heat source is needed, particularly in a cold environment. Warmth should be supplied before the body temperature has begun to fall.

Any impairment of respiration must be corrected; oxygen should be administered if it is available.

Pain, movement, or unpleasant emotional stimuli such as fear or the sight of blood often increase the severity of shock. If severe pain is present (someone in moderate or severe shock usually does not feel much pain), the person does not have a head injury or other contraindication to such medication, and evacuation is going to be prolonged, a strong analgesic should be administered.

Circulation to the skin and muscles of the extremities is impaired in shock, and injected drugs may not be absorbed. When the patient recovers from shock and the circulation is restored, all of the injected medication could be absorbed at once, which would produce a severe overdose. Analgesics can be injected intravenously if an attendant is familiar with such therapy.

Morphine also helps to allay anxiety. With or without its use, the individual should be given all possible comfort and reassurance to minimize emotional turmoil. (See Chapter Four, "Psychologic Responses to Accidents.")

The person may have to be moved from the path of falling rock or a potential avalanche or carried a short distance to a helicopter, but transport for greater distances, particularly evacuation by stretcher, should not be attempted until all injuries have been treated, shock has been controlled as well as possible, and he appears to be in a stable condition.

Low blood volume can be temporarily corrected to a considerable extent by the intravenous administration of a balanced salt solution. Blood plasma or plasma expanders are more effective but have potentially harmful side effects and should only be given by an individual knowledgeable about their use. The red blood cells necessary for carrying oxygen are not replaced by these fluids, and such therapy does have limited benefits. Blood is the optimum replacement for blood loss, but preservation, cross-matching, and transfusion are impossible without a blood bank.

Intravenous fluids should be given in anticipation of shock, particularly after injuries such as extensive burns or major fractures. (Accessing a vein suitable for inserting a needle for intravenous fluids is difficult once shock has appeared.) Fluids should be administered in amounts that approximate the volume of lost blood. (Blood loss is difficult to estimate accurately, particularly with injuries where most of the blood loss is hidden from view.)

A healthy adult with no heart disease is rarely harmed by under- or over-replacement of fluids by as much as one or two liters. For such individuals, as much as three to four liters of fluids may be administered fairly rapidly until the heart rate begins to slow and the patient appears to be responding to treatment. Thereafter, fluids should be given at a much slower rate, and no more than four liters should be given within the first eight-hour period. If blood loss is so great that more fluids are needed, the administration of a balanced salt solution alone probably would not be adequate treatment. (Individuals with extensive burns may need larger volumes and should receive them whenever they are available. See Chapter Eight, "Burns.")

If the subject does have heart disease, any error in fluid administration must be on the side of under-replacement. Excess fluids could lead to heart failure.

The adequacy of treatment can be determined by measuring the pulse rate, the blood pressure, and the urinary output. Pulse and blood pressure should return to levels close to normal within a few minutes to a few hours after replacement of the lost blood volume. A low urinary output and increasing pulse rate indicate the need for further therapy. Pulse rates, blood pressure, urinary output, and all therapy that has been administered must be carefully recorded so the individual's course can be accurately followed and his precise status known when care is assumed by a physician.

The treatment of shock associated with nontraumatic disorders is less clear cut, and the results are often less satisfactory. Individuals in shock from peritonitis or similar disorders may benefit from one or two liters of balanced salt solution per day, but more should not be given. Anyone who has suffered a heart attack, but has sustained no blood loss, must not be given fluids as they increase the work load on his already damaged heart.

UNCONSCIOUSNESS

An unconscious individual requires attention to four needs: protection from the environment, specific treatment for the cause of his unconscious state, replacement of fluids, and maintenance of an open airway. The nature of the first two requirements depends upon the circumstances in which the person is found and the cause for his condition. Fluid requirements are discussed under fluid balance in Chapter Two, "Basic Medical Care and Evacuation." Anyone with a disorder so severe that breathing ceases can rarely be kept alive by manual artificial respiration for more than a few hours. Therefore, the only specific care for unconscious individuals in wilderness circumstances is the maintenance of an open airway to permit unimpeded respiration.

If unconsciousness is the result of trauma, the subject must also be treated as if he had a broken neck. Fifteen percent of all head injuries that result in prolonged unconsciousness are associated with cervical fractures. Medications for sleep or pain are completely unnecessary, would further depress brain function, and must not be administered.

Maintaining an open airway is simple, but vitally important. Skilled treatment of other injuries or heroic rescue efforts would be completely wasted by five minutes of airway neglect. No matter how precarious the situation, no rescue efforts can be justified until means for keeping the air passages clear during the entire evacuation have been established. It should be obvious that an injured person must be left in an exposed and dangerous situation if rescue attempts would cause certain death by airway obstruction.

AIRWAY MAINTENANCE

The mouth and nose, throat, larynx (voice box), trachea, and bronchi form the passages through which air moves into the lungs and are known collectively as the airway. The mouth, throat, and tongue are constructed so that the base of the tongue moves backward and closes off the opening to the trachea during swallowing to prevent food or fluid from entering the lungs. Partial obstruction of the larynx by the tongue during sleep results in snoring. However, the larynx is only partially blocked during natural sleep because the muscles that hold the tongue and structures of the throat are not totally relaxed (fig. 3-1). In contrast, disorders resulting in unconsciousness produce such complete relaxation of these muscles that the tongue totally obstructs the passage of air (fig. 3-2).

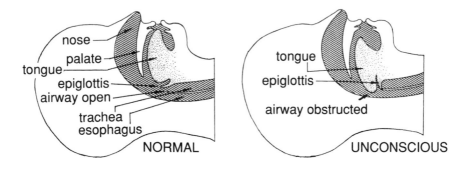

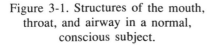

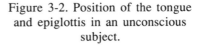

Figure 3-1. Structures of the mouth, throat, and airway in a normal, conscious subject.

Figure 3-2. Position of the tongue and epiglottis in an unconscious subject.

The easiest way to prevent such airway obstruction is to tilt the person's head back by placing one hand on the back of his neck and lifting while pushing down on his forehead or pulling up on his chin with the other hand. When the head is in this position, the tongue is pulled forward and can not fall back far enough to produce obstruction (fig. 3-3). If the individual has no injuries that might be aggravated by turning him, particularly a broken neck or back, he may be placed on his side with his head facing downward. In this position his tongue tends to fall forward instead of backward and does not block the throat. However, his head should also be extended to help keep the airway open.

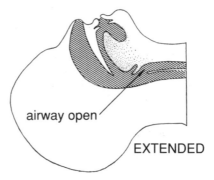

Figure 3-3. Position of the tongue and epiglottis in an unconscious subject with the head and neck extended to relieve airway obstruction.

The adequacy of the airway is easily checked. If breathing is quiet, the airway is open. Snoring or noisy breathing, labored respirations, or the absence of respiratory movements indicate partial or complete airway obstruction.

If a broken neck is suspected, the airway can be opened by placing the fingers at the angles of the person's jaws and pulling forward. Alternately, a finger or thumb can be hooked behind the teeth of his lower jaw and the jaw pulled forward. His neck should not be moved.

Disorders that produce unconsciousness are also frequently associated with vomiting. The vomitus may be aspirated, completely obstructing the air passages or producing severe, often lethal pneumonia. To prevent such accidents, the unconscious person's head must be lower than his chest and turned to the side whenever he is vomiting or appears likely to vomit. If there is no reason not to do so, he can be placed on his side to help keep his airway open and prevent aspiration. (Unconscious persons must never be given food, liquids, or medications by mouth.)

If the individual does not recover consciousness within a few hours and evacuation requires a long stretcher carry over rough terrain, the maintenance of an open airway would be difficult. A plastic airway or tracheostomy is necessary. Many first aid kits contain plastic airways (oropharyngeal airways), which are flattened curved tubes that fit over the base of the tongue and allow air to enter the larynx (fig. 3-4). (If the subject starts to regain consciousness and the tube causes him to gag and cough, he no longer needs it, and it can safely be removed.)

Another method of keeping the airway open is to insert a large safety pin through the meaty part of the tongue and hold the tongue forward by taping the pin to the chin or anchoring it in a similar manner. Although this technique sounds and appears brutal, it is simple, highly effective, and produces no permanent damage.

In rare circumstances a tracheostomy may be required.

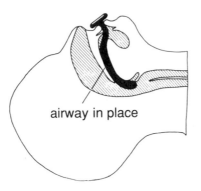

airway in place

Figure 3-4. Oropharyngeal airway in place in an unconscious subject.

Tracheostomy

A tracheostomy is an opening into the trachea through which a person can breathe if the upper air passages are obstructed. Although tracheostomies are commonly performed in hospitals, the occasions when one would be needed in the wilderness are rare. Accidents that produce such severe facial fractures that the person is unable to breathe through the nose or mouth are probably the most common disorders for which a tracheostomy is needed. A crushing blow to the larynx also can produce airway obstruction.

A tracheostomy is simply a hole in the trachea, and any reasonable technique for creating the hole and keeping it open is acceptable. The site for the tracheostomy must be selected carefully to minimize scarring and to avoid damage to other structures in the neck, particularly large blood vessels that could produce massive hemorrhage. (The location of the opening has little to do with how well the tracheostomy functions except that it obviously must be below any obstruction.) Most hospital tracheostomies are placed just above the sternum at the base of the neck. This site must not be used by inexperienced individuals for tracheostomies because the thyroid and the common carotid arteries (two of the body's largest) may be encountered. Instead, an opening should be made in the cricothyroid membrane.

The thyroid cartilage forms the Adam's apple. The cricoid cartilage is the large cartilaginous ring just below the thyroid cartilage. The cricothyroid membrane connects these two structures (fig. 3-5). (A physician's help in identifying this structure should be obtained before such knowledge is needed to care for someone.)

If possible, the person should be lying on a flat surface with his head extended backward to stretch the structures of his neck. The skin should be cleaned with soap and water and an antiseptic applied if time is available. The space between the thyroid and cricoid cartilages should be precisely identified. A one-quarter-inch skin incision can be made in the midline of the neck over the cricothyroid membrane with a scalpel or similar sharp blade, but is not essential. The device being used should be inserted through the membrane into the trachea.

Several devices for cricothyroidostomy are commercially available, but the technique for using them must be learned before they are needed. An eight- to ten-gauge needle is suitable for this purpose and easy to use; a fifteen-gauge needle can provide an adequate airway for most individuals if nothing larger is available. Air can be heard moving in and out immediately.

The opening in the trachea collapses unless something is inserted to keep it open. Commercially available devices have a tube for this purpose. If a large needle is used to perform the tracheostomy, the needle can be left in place to provide an opening. The device must be anchored to keep it from falling out or from being jammed into the back wall of the trachea and obstructed.

The needle or tube should be left in place until the individual is under a physician's care. If, during a prolonged evacuation, an unconscious person should recover enough to not need the tracheostomy, the needle or tubing can be plugged so that it can be easily opened again, or removed. The wound almost always closes and heals with no further attention.

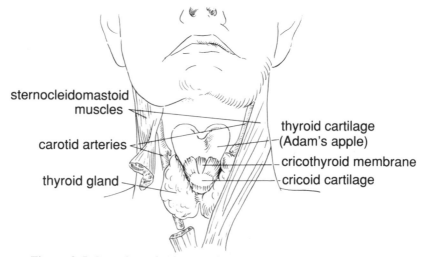

Figure 3-5. Location of cricothyroid membrane and carotid arteries.

FOOD ASPIRATION ("CAFE CORONARY")

A common cause of respiratory obstruction is the aspiration of food, most often meat. Prior to the development of the Heimlich maneuver, a procedure that usually dislodges the food and was named for its originator, an estimated 4,000 people died each year from this type of accident in the United States alone. Alcohol consumption is commonly associated with such events. Surprisingly large food fragments can be impacted in the larynx. Whole radishes or chunks of poorly chewed food similar in size are typically found. The food plugs the larynx and obstructs the passage of air, usually completely. Since no air can move through the larynx, the individual can not speak, cough, or breathe.

While eating, the person suddenly indicates that he is choking, usually rises out of his chair, and after a brief struggle collapses. Since the food is jammed into his larynx he can not speak. A signal has been devised for the individual to indicate that he is choking and consists of thrusting the "V" between the thumb and first finger of the hand against the throat (fig. 3-6).

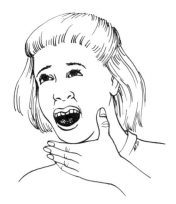

Figure 3-6. Signal that a person has choked on aspirated food, can not speak, and needs assistance, usually the Heimlich maneuver.

Attempts to dislodge the food by inserting a finger or a special device developed for that purpose through the mouth are rarely successful and may only force the food farther down. Pounding on the back is usually fruitless. Such measures may be tried, but no more than a few seconds should be spent this way. Airway obstruction by aspirated food is a true emergency, and only three or four minutes are available to correct the problem.

The Heimlich maneuver is a method for suddenly forcing the diaphragm upward by thrusting a hand or fist into the upper abdomen. The abrupt pressure on the diaphragm forces air out of the lungs and usually pops the obstructing food out of the larynx. The food is commonly ejected completely out of the person's mouth. The maneuver is so effective it can be used to evacuate aspirated pills or similar objects that do not completely obstruct the airway.

The subject can be stood up if he is still conscious. Without delay, the rescuer's arms should be extended around him and one fist placed in the top of the "V" formed by the ribs just below the sternum. The second hand should be placed on top of the first, and both should be pulled inward and upward as sharply as possible (fig. 3-7). Several attempts may be required to expel the food.

When performing the maneuver in this manner, little pressure should be placed on the subject's ribs. (Some is unavoidable.) Squeezing the ribs does not expel the food; thrusting against the diaphragm does. Squeezing the ribs has led to fractures—in a few cases, multiple fractures.

If the individual is unconscious or obese, he should be placed on his back on the flattest surface that can be found. The rescuer should straddle the person (not kneel beside him) and place both hands, one on top of the other, on the upper abdomen just below the sternum. Pressing downward and toward the head briskly forces the diaphragm upward and dislodges the food (fig. 3-8).

Figure 3-7. Position for Heimlich maneuver with the subject standing.

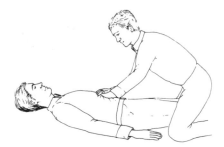

Figure 3-8. Position for Heimlich maneuver with the subject lying down.

If the Heimlich maneuver is not successful after several tries, a tracheostomy must be performed. It should be done as quickly as possible. Artificial respiration through the tracheostomy may be necessary for a short time if the subject has stopped breathing. However, most poor outcomes have not resulted from lack of success with the Heimlich maneuver but failure to use it in time to prevent permanent brain damage.

CARDIOPULMONARY RESUSCITATION

Occasions for effective cardiopulmonary resuscitation (CPR) in wilderness circumstances are rare. Resuscitative efforts for individuals with cardiac problems are futile unless advanced life support (ALS) can also be provided. However, individuals who have been struck by lightning can definitely be revived, if efforts are begun promptly, and resuscitation should be attempted. Persons who have drowned can sometimes be revived, particularly if they have drowned in cold water and have been submerged for thirty minutes or less. A few individuals buried by avalanches can be successfully resuscitated. Even a person knocked unconscious in a relatively minor accident may temporarily stop breathing and require artificial respiration.

Resuscitation is usually not effective if the disorder that has caused breathing to stop or the heartbeat to cease is not corrected. Lung diseases such as pneumonia or high altitude pulmonary edema, severe infections, extensive trauma—particularly severe head, chest, or abdominal injuries—and severe shock of almost any origin are disorders for which cardiopulmonary resuscitation is not effective, particularly in wilderness situations.

Resuscitation takes time and energy; an unsuccessful attempt extracts a heavy emotional toll. Such expenditures may affect the survival of other members of the party in a threatening situation.

Attempts to resuscitate anyone who has a normal body temperature after fifteen minutes has elapsed without respiratory or cardiac action are futile. At a normal temperature, the brain can survive only about five minutes without oxygen before suffering permanent damage. After this period, deterioration is rapid, and by ten to twelve minutes death is inevitable. (Much longer periods without breathing—even as long as an hour—are survivable if the body has been cooled.)

Individuals must be thoroughly familiar with resuscitative techniques and must have perfected them with practice before if efforts to apply them are to have a reasonable chance for success. Excellent CPR educational programs are widely available. Because those programs are so much more effective than the brief instructions provided in previous editions of *Medicine for Mountaineering,* such instructions have not been included in this edition. (Instructions for other sophisticated procedures have been included because they are not so widely available.)

Other Considerations

After a person has responded to resuscitation, he must be watched closely. A prolonged period of unconsciousness usually follows, even though he is breathing on his own. The airway must be kept open. Most individuals vomit and must be placed with the head lower than the chest and turned to the side to avoid aspiration. Shock must be anticipated and treated appropriately. The person should be evacuated as quickly as possible.

One of the most difficult questions concerning resuscitation is when to give up. The final decision in every case must be based on consideration of the circumstances in which the accident has occurred, the extent of injuries, the treatment required and administered, the people available for care of the victim, and the possibility of obtaining medical assistance within a short time. Artificial respiration must be continued for anyone whose heart is beating. On the other hand, anyone with a normal body temperature who requires cardiac massage has a much poorer prognosis. After thirty minutes, if spontaneous heart action has not resumed, and if the pupils are widely dilated and do not contract when exposed to light, the person is beyond further help. In contrast, resuscitative attempts for hypothermic individuals should be continued for a significantly longer time, preferably until the individual has been rewarmed to a body core temperature above 92°F (33°C).

In major medical institutions less than five percent of the patients who receive cardiopulmonary resuscitation survive. Usually the injury or disease is too severe to begin with, or resuscitation is initiated too late. However, rescuers are often reluctant not to make the effort, even if the prospects for success appear remote. The rare individuals saved may make the efforts expended on others worthwhile, but the physical and emotional costs of unsuccessful attempts are high.

CHAPTER FOUR

PSYCHOLOGIC RESPONSES TO ACCIDENTS

E motional responses to traumatic accidents by accident victims and by their rescuers should be expected. Most reactions are normal and tend to be consistent. Many are beneficial; only a few are not.

Anyone involved in an accident can benefit from attention to his psychologic responses. For some individuals, care for emotional needs is as essential as care for physical needs in order to return to a functioning role in society.

PSYCHOLOGIC RESPONSES OF RESCUERS

Psychologic reactions by first responders have been well recognized by police, fire, and emergency medical services, many of which have professional counselors on their staffs or on call to help with such reactions. In most situations critical-incident stress debriefing is provided for humanitarian reasons, but financial considerations provide valid justification for counseling because individuals leave their jobs when their cumulative response to psychologic trauma becomes overwhelming and training replacements is expensive.

The potential magnitude of personnel losses was dramatically illustrated by the response to the crash of American Airlines Flight 191. This wide-bodied jet, a DC-10, lost the hydraulic system in one wing when the engine ripped away during takeoff, rolled upside-down, and crashed. No one survived. The city of Chicago had staged a rescue drill only weeks before this accident, and 351 rescuers were at the accident scene within twenty minutes. The impact of the hundreds of mutilated bodies was devastating, but no program to alleviate the emotional impact on the responders was established. One year later, 275 had left their positions for jobs in which they performed no emergency services!

Wilderness rescuers also respond psychologically to accidents, and their reactions require attention, but this need has not been as well recognized as the needs of police, fire, and ambulance service members. Such problems, labeled "rescue trauma," are well known to many rescuers, but few discuss them with their colleagues, possibly from fear of appearing unmanly or even unbalanced.

Dissociation

Performing well in rescue situations requires a high level of objectivity. The rescuer's emotional response to those involved in an accident and to their injuries must not interfere with caring for them. To maintain objectivity, most rescuers dissociate, or "split," their intellect from their feelings and deny, or "block out," the emotional shock of the events surrounding them. Such defensive dissociation, or "splitting," is effective, but can not be kept up indefinitely. Eventually the "mental circuits" become overloaded and rescuers develop symptoms of decompensation.

The symptoms are highly variable. Some rescuers become withdrawn and appear dazed, apathetic, forgetful, or tired. Some become openly expressive and are irritable, irrational, destructive, or violent. Some shut off their feelings and become less able to experience intimacy with their families and friends. Some rescuers become increasingly reliant on alcohol or drugs.

Overload may come on suddenly after a major disaster that produces many casualties and mutilating injuries, or it may come on insidiously from the accumulated stress of a series of less distressing accidents. A rescuer's susceptibility to overload, his "rescue trauma threshold," may change from day to day as the result of events or circumstances entirely unrelated to the rescue, such as poor health, family problems, or insufficient sleep.

Sources of Stress

The many causes of rescue stress are interrelated, but can be categorized as overt and covert. Overt sources of stress are immediately related to the accident. The senses may be assailed by sights or smells at the scene. The person to be rescued may be dead or die during the rescue. Rescue equipment may be so inadequate and personnel so insufficient that greater effort is demanded of fewer people. Wilderness accident casualties frequently must be evacuated over miles of difficult and dangerous terrain, often at night, which requires hours of exhausting labor. (Rescues require an average of twelve hours in the White Mountains of New England, for example, and can require days in more remote areas when helicopters are not available.)

The rescuer may be weakened by fatigue or illness, or preoccupied with financial, legal, or family problems, which are covert sources of stress. The attitude of other participants, or their lack of ability, can be stressful. Rescuers may have high expectations of success at the start of an operation, only to be frustrated by the death of the accident victim, by their fallibility or their co-workers', and by lack of appreciation for their work, including inaccurate, critical, or even censorious reports in the media.

Another source of stress is the enforced inactivity a portion of the rescue team experiences after arriving at an accident scene. Dozens of stretcher bearers are required to carry a loaded litter through difficult terrain, but only a few can administer medical treatment. While the rest wait, their energy and enthusiasm ebb; some sink so low they need to be "psyched up" to evacuate the subject. The stress of this "middle period" is often overlooked and appears to result from feeling unneeded, from the setting in of fatigue, and sometimes from newness of the rescue experience.

Normal Reactions to Stress

Reactions to stress may be immediate or delayed. Immediate reactions among rescuers at the accident site include anxiety and apprehension, doubts about their abilities, and hopelessness and despair, which are often mixed with denial or "splitting." All are normal. Some rescuers experience cognitive difficulties, forgetting where they put things and finding decisions hard to make. Rescuers in all types of incidents report nausea, a pounding sensation in their hearts, muscle tremors, cramps, profuse sweating, chills, headaches, and muffled hearing. These symptoms tend to dissipate within one to three days, but if the underlying emotions are not recognized as normal and allowed to surface within a reasonably short period of time, they eventually work their way into the rescuer's daily life and can cripple him emotionally, cognitively, and physically.

Delayed stress reactions appear hours to weeks—sometimes months to years— after an accident and may be directed inward or outward. Inward reactions include depression, apathy, or feelings of guilt for not having helped or for having further injured the subject. Nightmares, insomnia, or occasional visual flashbacks, or physical symptoms such as headache, loss of appetite, or nausea may be experienced. Outward reactions typically include irritability, explosiveness, and in some cases anger with others who contributed to the stress of the incident, particularly with the press for inaccurate or distorted reporting. Like the immediate stress reactions, these delayed reactions are entirely normal.

Preventing Adverse Stress Reactions

Rescuers, whether amateurs or professionals, must be emotionally prepared for the worst casualties—the dead, dying, and mutilated—and for the worst situations, such as watching helplessly while someone dies because he is inaccessible, equipment is inadequate, or he just does not respond to the best possible medical care. In preparing for the worst, participants must be aware of their limitations and must balance their expectations with reality.

Rescuers must be prepared to serve under leaders who do not have time for explanations or who are not aware of the needs of their crew members. They must expect sparse recognition and abundant criticism from others and should not be surprised when rescue work turns out to be ninety percent drudgery and ten percent terror.

Despite training and experience, rescuers must withdraw from situations they find particularly stressful, such as accidents that involve family or friends, injuries to children, and some specific injuries. This sensitivity must be respected by the rescuer and his leader and associates.

Rescuers must realize that stress overload is virtually inevitable regardless of training and experience if their accumulated emotional stress is not relieved by sharing it with others. To ensure the emotional health of rescuers, established preventive or therapeutic programs, such as the following, are essential.

- Within twenty-four hours after a rescue, team members engage in vigorous exercise to relieve tension and achieve greater muscular relaxation.
- Within twenty-four to seventy-two hours after a stressful rescue, a *mandatory* "emotional debriefing" is held for the entire team. Effective sessions require an hour or more and promote expression and sharing of emotional reactions to the rescue—specifically the pain, sadness, terror, guilt, or feelings of helplessness experienced by each rescuer in different ways. These emotions must be expressed and accepted without shame or embarrassment. The participants must share their humanity and support each other.

The session must be entirely nonjudgmental. There can be no right or wrong, correct or incorrect, as long as emotions did not interfere with the rescue. To ensure absolute confidentiality, no records should be kept.

Although some groups can manage this process quite well by themselves, such exercises frequently are more effective when guided by someone experienced in stress management who was not directly involved in the rescue. Completely resolving the stress may require more than one meeting, but all meetings should be conducted as close to the event as possible, preferably within three days. Delays of a week or more increase the risk of converting early, tenuous emotional reactions into entrenched, chronic disorders. The debriefing must be conducted without any alcohol; to maximize the benefits, the minds of all must be fully functional.

- After debriefing, rescuers must eat and rest well, rounding out the recovery of the entire organism.
- Only after physical and emotional recovery has been assured should the rescue team critique the rescue objectively, learning from successes as well as mistakes, and planning for the future.

Case Study One

A professional rescuer, who was a member of a wilderness medical educational organization, was on a Himalayan trek with that group when a close friend became seriously ill and clearly needed to be evacuated. The leader decided to split the party—most continuing to their objective while the rescuer and two physicians stayed behind with the person who was ill. After the main party had moved on, that person's condition deteriorated catastrophically, and over a period of days the three rescuers worked virtually to the point of exhaustion to save him.

During this ordeal, the rescuer became aware of several strong feelings. He found that attending for a close friend aggravated normal feelings of inadequacy and guilt, particularly guilt for not having more forcefully cautioned the person before he became so ill. He also felt guilt for not having resisted more vigorously the decision to split the party, which left the person who was ill with a support team barely able to provide for his care.

In retrospect, the rescuer realized that he had deferred to the leader because the leader was a physician, despite the rescuer's own considerable judgment and experience. During and after the subsequent vigil, the rescuer began to question his confidence in the leader, in his associates, in himself, and even in the categories of people (doctors and nurses) who were members of the group. His confidence was further eroded following reuniting of the party when "significant" people "acted like nothing had happened."

The rescuer kept these feelings hidden for some time, not realizing that others were experiencing the same emotions. Only months later, when he made an offhand comment that he was considering dropping out of the educational organization, did he have an opportunity to share his pain and begin to reconstruct relationships. Since then he has made a variety of recommendations, particularly that the emotional residue of stressful situations be discharged through debriefings.

He also observed that even though support from associates is helpful, in the long run the benefits fade unless the rescuer recognizes the value of his efforts and learns from his mistakes, rather than wallowing in destructive self-criticism. To grow, everyone must accept responsibility for his actions, both good and bad.

Post-Traumatic Stress Disorder

Should rescuers not work through their normal reactions, they risk developing a more severe abnormality. This condition has been repeatedly described during the past century and, depending on its origin, has been given widely varying names, including accident neurosis, shell shock, traumatic neurosis, combat fatigue, combat exhaustion, post-Vietnam syndrome, and neurasthenia. The term "post-traumatic stress disorder" unites these conditions under one label.

The features of post-traumatic stress disorder are:

- The individual has undergone a recognizable stressful experience that would evoke significant symptoms of distress in almost everyone.
- The individual reexperiences the event in one or more ways:
  - recurrent and intrusive recollections
  - recurrent dreams of the event
  - sudden acting or feeling as if the traumatic event were recurring due to the stimulus of an environment or thought associated with the event
- The individual has numbed responsiveness to or reduced involvement with the external world that began some time after the event and is manifested by one or more of the following:
  - markedly diminished interest in one or more significant activities
  - feeling of detachment or estrangement from others
  - constricted affect
- The individual usually has two or more of the following symptoms that were not present before the event:
  - hyperalertness or exaggerated "startle" response
  - sleep disturbances
  - guilt about surviving when others have not, or about the behavior required for survival
  - memory impairment or difficulty concentrating
  - avoidance of activities that arouse recollections of the traumatic event
  - intensification of symptoms by exposure to events that symbolize or resemble the traumatic event

Post-traumatic stress disorder has been subclassified as acute when symptoms appear within six months of the trauma and last less than six months; chronic when symptoms appear within six months and last longer than six months; and delayed when symptoms appear six months or more after the trauma.

Diagnostic studies suggest that with sufficient unrelieved stress, anyone would develop a post-traumatic stress disorder. Vietnam veterans who developed this disorder shared five characteristics that correlate with experiences of wilderness rescuers (table 4-1).

Treating post-traumatic stress syndrome is the province of professional therapists. However, the earlier the disorder is recognized, the faster and more successful is the outcome of therapy. Recognizing stressful events, taking measures to relieve the emotional pressures they engender, and recognizing the symptoms of emotional disorders are certainly within the abilities of rescuers and their friends and should be the responsibility of their leaders.

TABLE 4-1.
Comparison of Stress Sources for Vietnam Veterans and Wilderness Rescuers

Vietnam Veterans	Wilderness Rescuers
■ Positive attitudes toward the war before engaging in combat	■ Unrealistic expectations
■ High levels of combat exposure	■ High levels of exposure to hazardous terrain or weather, and to massive trauma
■ Immediate separation from the military service upon returning to the United States	■ Infrequent opportunities to share emotional experiences; "suffering in silence"
■ Negative perceptions of family helpfulness upon returning home	■ Lack of support or appreciation
■ Feelings that forces beyond their control were directing the course of their lives	■ Feelings that uncontrollable factors such as weather, timing, inadequate personnel or equipment, communication failures, or accidents involving members of the rescue group determined the outcome of the rescue

---

PSYCHOLOGIC RESPONSES OF ACCIDENT VICTIMS

The emotional responses of accident victims are similar to the bereavement or grief that follows loss of a loved one. Since many more individuals have experienced such grief than have been involved in wilderness accidents, the emotional reactions to accidents may be more understandable when compared with grief reactions. This comparison also illustrates the normality of psychologic reactions to accidents, which may seem abnormal to individuals who have not experienced such phenomena.

Grief Reactions

The period of mourning that follows loss of a loved one can be lengthy and painful, but if his grief is properly worked through, the survivor reconciles himself to the loss and resumes his life. Like other emotional states, bereavement is more easily resolved when shared with others.

Grief evolves through several stages, and the boundary between normal and abnormal reactions is often blurred. A bereaved person commonly displays attitudes, beliefs, and behavior that smack of irrationality. The first stage of his emotional response, which has been labeled the protest phase, is characterized by stunned shock and denial. ("He can't be dead!") Anger commonly follows and illogically may be directed at the person or circumstance that caused the loss, at the deceased, or at the bereaved person himself for not having prevented the loss —even for surviving. The bereaved frequently manifest emotional pain by crying, weakness, loss of appetite or even nausea, or sleep disturbances. Survivors may search for their loved ones or for mementos of their loved ones.

After days or weeks, bereaved individuals move into a stage dominated by despair. They experience anguish, grief, and depression, think slowly, display emotional pain, and continue to search for loved ones and remembrances of them. After weeks or months, they move slowly into the detachment stage, during which they lose interest in life and want to withdraw and give up. They appear bland, lack spontaneity and social energy, and behave like robots or "zombies" (fig. 4-1).

Normally the cycle of protest, despair, and detachment takes six to eighteen months. The bereaved finally work through their loss, say their final good-byes, and restructure their lives and personalities, reconciled with their loss. The success with which a bereaved individual can resolve his grief is proportional to his capacity to face the finality of death, whether the death of others or himself.

Sometimes grief can not be handled successfully. When the bereaved's relationship with the deceased has been an ambivalent mixture of love and hate, and hostile feelings have been denied, the bereaved may be tortured with guilt. His grief may go on indefinitely at great emotional cost.

Normal Responses by Accident Victims

The normal emotional state of an individual involved in any sudden, unpredictable, and overwhelming crisis is similar to an acute grief state. If the incident was traumatic, the overwhelming emotion for the person involved results from experiencing the possibility of death and fearing for his life. An accompanying

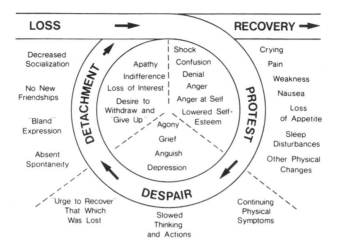

Figure 4-1. Diagram of reaction cycle associated with grief. (From William M. Lamers, M.D. Reproduced by permission.)[1]

sense of helplessness, of having lost control over his survival, adds to the impact. He is aware of seeking to escape and of being weak, vulnerable, and helpless. His self-esteem and sense of competence have been assaulted, and he sees himself as unable to keep out of harm's way or as having acted with poor judgment.

Hours to weeks after the incident, depending upon the individual and the nature of the incident, the accident victim is subjected to secondary stresses such as the prospect of being immobilized and isolated without food or shelter, the prospect of being totally dependent upon strangers for rescue, or the more distant prospect of not being able to go back to work or to other valued activities.

Five "phases of disaster" for accidents have been identified:

1. Preimpact (threat)
2. Warning
3. Impact
4. Recoil
5. Postimpact

The preimpact or threat phase occurs months or years before the incident and is characterized by a failure to take appropriate measures to minimize the possibility of an accident. The warning phase takes place immediately before the incident and usually consists of ignoring obvious hazards such as avalanche paths. Since both of these phases take place before the accident, rescuers are not involved.

The impact phase refers to the time during and immediately after the accident. During accidents, one-eighth to one-fourth of the people involved react effectively. They are often "too busy to worry." About one-half to three-fourths are stunned and bewildered. They show no emotion, are inactive or indecisive, and are usually docile. They may be totally unresponsive or behave in an automatic, robotlike manner. Manifestations of fear such as sweating, palpitations, tunnel vision, or a dry mouth may be present. This type of reaction is known as "psychologic shock" but should not be considered an abnormal reaction. A final one-eighth to one-fourth of people involved in accidents react inappropriately, with incapacitating anxiety or hysteria.

The recoil phase occurs a few minutes to a few hours after the accident, and is the period during which psychologic responses that are similar to the stages of the grief reaction occur. During the early protest or denial stage of the recoil phase the person may not be able to deny that a problem exists, but refuses to admit the magnitude of the problem. The problem is understood intellectually but not emotionally, and the individual is blasé and unconcerned.

Some individuals are stunned and confused; others are vigilant and cool. Some are emotionally expressive, displaying anxiety, anger, sobbing, a sense of relief, or a tendency to blame others. Others are controlled, exhibit little distress, and appear composed. Both behaviors reflect denial and emotional exhaustion or "shock." Both reactions are normal, but the individuals need acceptance and assurance of the normality of their responses. They may be vulnerable to damaged self-esteem if they perceive their behavior as inadequate or abnormal.

A person may say, "This will hit me later." He should be reassured (or informed) that indeed it will hit him later and that his emotional responses may take time and talking out.

During the second stage of the recoil phase, ninety percent of the individuals involved in accidents become aware of problems, but regard them as overwhelming and unbearable. Strong emotions are manifested by tightening of muscles, sweating, restlessness, difficulty in speaking, sadness and weeping, irritability and anger, or passive dependency and childlike behavior. Some persons develop a "zombielike" gaze—the "1,000-mile stare"; many need to tell and retell the experience.

During the third stage of the recoil phase, the individuals begin to return to normal, accept their problems, and make efforts to solve them. They are more hopeful and confident, and emotions from the second stage are less intense.

The final phase of a disaster, the postimpact phase, takes place six to twelve months after the incident and may last a lifetime. The source of stress is the personal and social aftereffects of the incident. The normal reaction, after recovery from the accident, is to return to normal activities. A sense of well-being returns, and the individuals are able to make decisions and act on them. Grief that was encountered is successfully worked through. Many survivors develop altered attitudes toward life and death and display a definite philosophic mellowing and growth.

Abnormal reactions occasionally occur and have been labeled the "delayed stress syndrome." The characteristics of this disorder include post-traumatic stress disorder, psychosomatic or physical illness, depression, accident proneness, accidental death, or suicide. Professional counseling is often needed to work out the problems of this syndrome. However, proper emotional support during rescue can significantly reduce the severity of such disorders or prevent them altogether.

Abnormal Responses by Accident Victims

Abnormal psychologic reactions to trauma may affect four functional areas:

- Orientation to time, place, events, and person
- Observable motor and physical behavior
- Verbal behavior
- Emotional or affective expression

Since typical abnormal behavior patterns are rather easily recognized, they are outlined without further discussion.

I. Orientation

    A. Mild derangement (adequately aware of time, place, events, and person)
      1. Dazed, confused
      2. Minor difficulty understanding what is being said
      3. Minor difficulty thinking clearly or concentrating
      4. Slow or delayed reactions

    B. Severe derangement (confused about time, place, events, and person, but may gradually respond to information and reassurance [unlike individuals with brain trauma, which must be considered])
      1. Forgetful of own name and names of associates
      2. Unclear about date—year or month
      3. Unable to state clearly his location
      4. Unable to recall clearly events of the previous twenty-four hours
      5. Regresses to an earlier period of life
      6. Complains about memory gaps of thirty minutes or more
      7. Confused about who he is or what he does
      8. Appears unaware of what is happening around him

II. Motor Behavior

    A. Mild derangement
      1. Wringing hands or clenching fists; stiff and rigid appearance; continuously sad expression
      2. Some restlessness; mild agitation and excitement
      3. Difficulty falling asleep or keeping down food
      4. Rushing about trying to do many things at once, but accomplishing little
      5. Feelings of fatigue inconsistent with previous and concurrent activity
      6. Halting or rapid speech that is out of character; difficulty getting words out

    B. Severe derangement
      1. Agitated movements; inability to sleep or rest quietly
      2. Grimacing or posturing of recent onset
      3. Markedly reduced activity; sits and stares; remains immobile for hours
      4. Incontinence
      5. Mutilation of self or objects for no reason

    6. Repeated ritualistic acts of no functional significance; attempts to prevent the acts create resistance and excessive emotion

    7. Excessive use of drugs or alcohol

    8. Inability to carry out simple functions such as eating, dressing, or organizing equipment

III. Verbal Behavior

  A. Mild derangement

    1. Verbalizes hopelessness: "It's no use," "I can't go on"

    2. States he cannot make a decision; doubts his ability to recover

    3. Overly concerned with small things and neglectful of more pressing, major problems

    4. Denies any problems; overconfident; claims he can do everything without help

    5. Blames the problems on others; has difficulty making plans or discussing future actions

  B. Severe derangement

    1. Hallucinations, auditory or visual, unverifiable by others

    2. Verbalizes fear of losing his mind; claims the world seems unrecognizable and unreal; claims his body feels unreal and completely different

    3. Preoccupied with an event or idea to the exclusion of anything else

    4. Unrealistic claims that an agency, object, group, or spirit is out to harm him and others such as his family or friends

    5. Expresses inability to make a decision to carry out familiar activities

    6. Expresses a real fear of killing or harming himself or others; far exceeds simple statement of anger or hopelessness

IV. Emotional Expression

  A. Mild derangement (significantly different from most individuals but largely appropriate to situation)

    1. Frequent uncontrolled tearing and weeping; rehashing of traumatic events

    2. Blunted expression of feelings; apathetic; seemingly withdrawn emotionally and unable to react with feeling to what is happening

    3. Unusual laughter and gaiety

    4. Overly irritable; quick to get angry over trivia

  B. Severe derangement (markedly unusual affect or emotion)

    1. Excessively flat emotionally; virtually no expression of feeling

    2. Excessive emotional expression; inappropriate joy, anger, fear, or sadness for situation

Trauma or Disease Simulating Psychologic Abnormalities

A number of disorders, particularly those that reduce the availability of oxygen to the brain or cause metabolic derangements, produce abnormal behavior that simulates abnormal psychologic reactions. Hypoxia is common, can result from altitude, but also is produced by pneumonia, chest injuries, shock, and other disorders. Hypothermia typically produces changes ranging from forgetfulness and slow thought processes, through loss of coordination and greater mental dullness, to irrationality and finally coma. Hyperthermia can cause headache, irritability, agitation, and mental dullness before progressing to stupor and coma. Hypoglycemia (low blood glucose or sugar) produces restlessness, irritability, lethargy, poor judgment, agitation, disorientation, and finally coma. Severe hypoglycemia is almost always a complication of diabetes, but milder glucose depletion occurs in normal individuals who are exhausted and have not maintained an adequate food intake. Dehydration can produce similar abnormalities.

Head injuries may result in immediate or delayed changes that include drowsiness, apathy, and irritability; disorientation; forgetfulness and wandering off; bizarre behavior including homicidal or suicidal mania; or convulsions and finally unconsciousness. Signs such as unequal pupils or abnormal reflexes may be present. Severe infections of the nervous system can produce such signs, as can pneumonia or severe generalized infections. Intoxication by drugs (including alcohol) or drug withdrawal (particularly from alcohol, tranquilizers, and barbiturates) can have similar effects.

Generally, personality changes such as silliness, irritability, agitation, belligerence, and lethargy occur first. Loss of cognitive functions, which progresses from mild mental dullness through disorientation to time, place, events, and person (in spite of frequent reminders), loss of calculating ability and specialized knowledge, to loss of judgment and memory appear next. Eventually, obvious confusion with anxiety or hallucinations supervenes and may be associated with staggering and slurred speech, tremors, convulsions, and unconsciousness progressing to deep coma and eventual death.

If sedation is essential for evacuating a person whose behavior is uncontrollable, a tranquilizer is preferable. Barbiturates or narcotics complicate the neurologic abnormalities, depress respiration, and should be avoided.

Psychologic Aid for Accident Victims

Persons injured in an accident, uninjured members of the party, and rescuers must cope with the reactions of the impact phase at the scene of the accident or during evacuation. Assistance provided at that time can greatly diminish the emotional aftereffects. Rescue leaders and their crew members must be prepared to provide as much psychologic help as possible with constructive, understanding listening.

The essence of psychologic care is listening effectively and creatively. The subject must be allowed to express his feelings openly and freely; the counselor must understand that such expression is the major purpose of the conversation. The counselor can not judge what the person should feel, and he certainly must not convey any such opinion to him. The counselor must look directly at the person who is speaking, giving his complete attention, and only asking questions or paraphrasing statements to emphasize his attentiveness or to make certain he fully understands what is being said.

Preferably, the counselor should be the same gender as the injured person. The counselor should remain in constant contact and should stay at the subject's head throughout the evacuation.

Some goals rescue leaders and counselors should strive for are:

- To create acceptance of an injured person's feelings as normal reactions to stress
- To reduce feelings of guilt by not assessing blame for the accident
- To reduce panic and rage; to allow ventilation of feelings and to accept them
- To give realistic, honest answers balanced with judicious omissions
- To be aware of the special needs due to the person's sex when immobilized and dependent (as in a litter)
- To restore a feeling of well-being with food and water, warmth, attention to injuries, physical restraint when necessary, analgesia when indicated, and comfort and support through listening and touching
- To restore a sense of hope and of belonging through quiet, firm, and knowledgeable leadership with clearly understood goals and sensitivity to the needs of injured or ill individuals and rescuers
- To maintain awareness that supposedly unconscious individuals often hear some of what is said around them

A person's self-esteem and sense of mastery are also based on his judgment of how well he responds to problem situations. Success heightens self-esteem; failure lowers it. The rescuer must constantly seek ways to help a person involved in an accident preserve his dignity, particularly ways in which he can help in the rescue operation. Participation is essential for restoring and preserving self-esteem and a sense of mastery and control and for minimizing psychic trauma, guilt reactions, and delayed stress reactions. Rescue leaders must be aware of this need and do all they can to ensure it is met.

Some attitudes or actions rescue leaders and counselors must try to avoid are:

- Callousness or flippancy—the "M*A*S*H" syndrome
- Lying to provide unrealistic optimism and reassurance
- Talking around a subject without talking to him
- Authoritarian style—telling the subject how to feel or imposing ideas on him; not really listening
- Expecting a subject to function at top level too quickly
- Expecting too little of a subject, damaging his chances to salvage self-esteem
- "Chicken soup"-style; oversolicitousness that interferes with a subject's recovery of self-esteem
- "Democratic" leader(less)ship—floundering by committee, with no definitive leader, goals, plans for achieving goals, or communication within the party

Case Study Two

Some insights into the psychology of individuals involved in accidents and helpful recommendations for rescuers have been made by Ray Smutek in his account of his own mountaineering accident and rescue. When describing his fall he recalls "accelerated mental activity, the detached overview of the situation, the recollection of past events. Most amazing was the absence of pain, coupled with a very acute awareness of the damage being done."[2]

He observes that potentially the most dangerous stage of an accident is immediately afterward, "not necessarily to the victim . . . I think the natural tendency in a situation like this is to rush to the victim, perhaps unbelayed. Action! Do something! Don't just stand there!" But Smutek continues, "this is not the time to rush; few situations require that immediate an action. There is only one thing that you should do immediately and that is to think."

He describes directing his immediate rescue and first aid to the extent that he was conscious and able to state what his injuries were and what he was capable of doing. Further, he says that the long wait for rescue "psychologically was the worst part of the entire episode. There was nothing to do but worry." He was very happy to have the company of a fellow climber and thinks everyone in a similar situation should have an "official comforter."

When rescue did come, some of the rescuers were "over their heads," and Smutek states, "nothing is more devastating to a person's morale than an obviously incompetent rescuer." Finally, he reports that administration of a pain killer muddled his mind and increased his anxiety because he could not understand the procedures to which he was being subjected. He feels that rescuers should use pain medication on a highly selective basis, particularly if that medication may interfere with a person's need to feel in control and be aware of what is going on. These feelings clearly reflect Smutek's need to maintain a sense of self-efficacy. On the other hand, some people are not used to being in control and may be more comfortable being medicated or being told that everything is being cared for.

Case Study Three

In *The Breach,* Rob Taylor traces the various phases of his devastating accident on Kilimanjaro, his almost miraculous rescue, his prolonged recovery, and his reactions to these events. Following a fall in which he suffered a severe compound fracture of his lower leg, he subsequently descended a perilously steep snow slope on his own and survived a solitary, exposed, life-threatening bivouac that lasted several days. During this ordeal his thoughts and behavior were strikingly organized. His self-control becomes more understandable when he says, "unrestrained emotions and unbridled feelings in the end, after the fact, are fine, but during the crisis they are illusory defenses."[3]

Nonetheless, while on the mountain Taylor experienced grief over the loss symbolized by the injury to his leg. He also felt anguish over the days of waiting for the unknown, but was preparing for and accepting the worst. He writes of "the need to relive the event" during his recovery and of becoming "daily more aware of the positive aspects of the pilgrimage . . . and [of a] renewal of a reverence and deep appreciation of the gift of life." Finally, he speaks of a heightened sense of self-definition, of altering his concept of death, and of coming to realize that he "must make the most of each encounter, each meeting" as a result of his experience.

Taylor recommends to rescuers the therapeutic use of concern, small talk, encouragement, and infectious optimism.

SELECTION OF RESCUERS

Enthusiasm alone is not an adequate qualification for wilderness rescuers. In addition to good physical condition, technical expertise, and support persons who are the same gender as the individuals involved in the accident, members of rescue teams should have the following characteristics:

- Reasonable personality that is not excitable, impulsive, or prone to harbor anger
- Ability to take the initiative
- Ability to cooperatively follow others
- Attentiveness to details of procedure and equipment
- Sense of humor
- Empathy and ability to feel for another's plight without being overwhelmed
- Optimism, although prepared for the worst
- Ability to minimize or shelve worry or fear, yet accept those feelings as normal

PSYCHOLOGIC REACTIONS TO DEAD BODIES

When faced with the dead bodies of intimates or strangers, many people experience emotional difficulties. In *The Hour of Our Death,* Aries states that people have long resisted believing that death deprives the body of all life.[4] He says, "belief in the sensibility of the cadaver has the support of the people, and what we would call folklore . . . though scientists consider such to be superstition." Reinforced by recent descriptions of out-of-body, life-after-death experiences, many believe that the body still hears, feels, and remembers after death and treat the dead gently for fear of hurting them or, in some cases, for fear of angering them.

Other reactions to dead bodies include anxious discomfort, horror and panic, fear of the unknown or of one's own death, and fear of contamination. A few people react with intellectual or morbid fascination and curiosity. Defensive behavior such as indifference, joking, hostility, or detachment are more commonly encountered.

In nursing and medical students the fear of the dying and death of others decreases with increasing academic preparation and experience. However, the fear of their own death and dying remains the same or increases as they near the age where their death is more likely.

Professional rescuers encounter death so commonly that they lose any feeling of discomfort when near a body, at least when near the body of someone they do not know. For amateur rescuers, who have fewer encounters with death, two methods for reducing the emotional shock of the experience have been suggested: desensitization through gradual, nontraumatic exposure to death; or coming to terms with their own death by experiencing it in fantasy, discovering what is really essential for them to have accomplished during their lives, and taking steps to leave as little unfinished as possible. Anticipatory grief as a buffer for sudden and serious loss has demonstrated value.

Many individuals have come to accept death as another stage of life, but that crosses into the purview of religion.

ACKNOWLEDGMENT

The author wishes to acknowledge his indebtedness to Grady P. Bray, Ph.D., Jeffrey Mitchell, Ph.D., George Everly, Ph.D., Herbert Benson, M.D., Roger Zimmerman, Ph.D., and William Moss, EMT, for their professional expertise.

REFERENCES

1. Lamers W: Death, dying and bereavement. Symposium, Stockholm, Sweden, 20 June 1982.
2. Smutek R: Good morning, I'm your guest victim for today. *Off Belay,* February 1978. (Quoted by permission of the author and publisher.)
3. Taylor R: *The Breach: Kilimanjaro and the Conquest of Self.* New York, Coward, McCann, and Geoghegan, 1981. (Quoted by permission of the author and publisher.)
4. Aries P: *The Hour of Our Death.* New York, Alfred Knopf, 1981.

CHAPTER FIVE

IMMUNIZATIONS, SANITATION, AND WATER DISINFECTION

In underdeveloped countries infections, particularly gastrointestinal infections, are a constant threat. Preventing illnesses in wilderness areas, where disease is coupled with inaccessibility, has obvious advantages. Many infections can be prevented by immunizations and by sanitation measures, particularly water disinfection. (Immunization for rabies is discussed in Chapter Twenty-four, "Animal Bites and Stings"; the prevention of malaria and some other infections for which immunization is not possible is discussed in Chapter Nineteen, "Infections.")

IMMUNIZATIONS

Immunization is the easiest and most reliable method for preventing infections. Only a few effective vaccines are available, but those that are only partially effective can significantly reduce the likelihood of infection and lessen the impact should the infection occur. (The immunologic principles upon which immunizations are based are discussed in Chapter Twenty, "Allergies.")

Recommendations for immunization change frequently. The Centers for Disease Control annually publishes a list by country of the immunizations and other preventive measures advisable for travel or required for entry. This bulletin, "Health Information for International Travel," can be purchased from the Superintendent of Documents, U.S. Government Printing Office, Washington, DC 20402. Most local health departments have a copy that can be consulted, sometimes by telephone.

The International Association for Medical Assistance to Travelers (IAMAT) is a volunteer, nongovernmental organization of health care centers and physicians that provides travelers with access to physicians who speak their language and who meet IAMAT's standards, which are similar to U.S. standards. Membership in IAMAT and a directory of its affiliated institutions in more than 115 countries are free. The address of the U.S. affiliate is IAMAT, 736 Center Street, Lewiston, NY 14092. Also free from that organization is its World Immunization Chart, which lists the potential risks for more than a dozen diseases, country by country, in a quick reference format.

An International Certificate of Vaccination is a convenient means for keeping a record of all immunizations and is required for entrance into some countries.

Scheduling Immunizations

Foreign travel is usually preceded by months of planning and preparation. Immunizations are a critical part of such preparation and must not be put off until the last minute.

Viral vaccines, including hepatitis B, and toxoid for tetanus and diphtheria can be given six months or more before departure because such immunizations persist for years. Bacterial immunizations, such as for typhoid fever and cholera, are not as enduring and should be given closer to the date of departure. Pooled immune globulin to help prevent hepatitis A should be given as close to departure as possible.

Immunizations such as those for typhoid fever or hepatitis B must be administered four weeks or more apart. Live virus vaccines such as yellow fever and oral polio vaccine must be given at the same time or one month apart. Immune globulin should not be given for three months before and for at least two weeks after any live viral vaccine.

Smallpox

Smallpox has been eliminated worldwide by a vigorous vaccination campaign carried out by the World Health Organization—a medical triumph! The last reported case of smallpox outside of a laboratory was in Somalia in 1977. Most countries have eliminated the entry requirement for recent smallpox vaccination. The vaccine is now considered more hazardous than the risk of contracting the infection and should not be administered.

Rubella

Rubella (German measles) is one of the most widely documented causes of birth defects. The Centers for Disease Control recommends that everyone, not just women, be vaccinated unless he has been previously vaccinated or has laboratory evidence of immunity. A single injection of live rubella virus vaccine provides lasting immunity.

Measles

Measles can be a severe disease, particularly in adults. Many of the cases occurring in the United States are contracted in other countries. Individuals born after 1956 who have not had a documented vaccination or a physician-diagnosed infection, or who do not have laboratory evidence of immunity, should receive measles vaccine, whether or not they plan to travel.

Poliomyelitis

Poliomyelitis (polio) is now almost entirely preventable by immunization. Trivalent oral live virus (Sabin) vaccine provides effective immunity for much longer than the inactivated virus (Salk) vaccine. The oral vaccine should be taken even though prior inactivated virus immunization has been carried out. A booster should be obtained in preparation for a trip to an underdeveloped country. Many countries can not afford routine polio immunizations and infections are common.

Tetanus

The organisms producing tetanus are ubiquitous, and infections can result from trivial wounds. Because no effective treatment for tetanus is available, the mortality rate is high, and immunization provides highly reliable protection, inadequate protection against this disease is inexcusable. The initial series of tetanus toxoid immunizations consists of two injections four to eight weeks apart. A third inoculation should be obtained six to twelve months later. A booster should be obtained at least every ten years thereafter. However, if a booster has not been received within five years, one should be obtained before departing on a wilderness outing or following a contaminated wound.

Typhoid

Typhoid immunization is estimated to be only about seventy percent effective in preventing typhoid infection, but it does significantly reduce the severity of infections. Such immunization is recommended, sometimes strongly, for travellers outside of major cities in underdeveloped countries. A live oral typhoid vaccine has recently become available and is preferable to injected vaccine because it produces fewer side effects. It is more expensive. The live vaccine is administered in four capsules that are taken every other day.

Cholera

Cholera immunization is only about fifty percent effective for preventing infection, lasts for only six months, and is not recommended. However, cholera immunization within the previous six months is required for entry into some countries for travelers from areas where the infection is widespread. A single inoculation at least six days before departure satisfies entry requirements. Protection is maximal when injections are obtained shortly before going to the endemic area, but immunizations can not substitute for meticulous water disinfection.

Yellow Fever

Yellow fever is endemic in the equatorial regions of Africa and South and Central America. The possibility of a resurgence in the Caribbean has appeared as the carrier mosquito, *Aedes aegypti,* has developed resistance to insecticides. Yellow fever has never been recognized in Asia, and its introduction could result in disastrous epidemics. For that reason, yellow fever immunization is required to travel in many Asian countries, particularly for persons arriving from countries where yellow fever is endemic. A single inoculation provides effective immunization; boosters are needed only every ten years. Immunizations must be obtained from a World Health Organization Yellow Fever Vaccination Center, the locations of which can be obtained from local health departments.

Meningococcus

Outbreaks of meningococcal infection occur sporadically in underdeveloped areas. Major epidemics occur in sub-Saharan Africa. Individuals traveling to countries in which such outbreaks are occurring should receive meningococcal vaccine before departure. Vaccination is required in Saudi Arabia and is recommended in other countries, such as India and Nepal. Vaccination appears to be effective for three years.

Hepatitis A

Hepatitis is caused by a number of completely different viruses. Prevention of all types is essential because no specific medical treatment is available for any of them. (These infections are discussed in Chapter Twelve, "Gastrointestinal Disorders.")

Hepatitis A is produced by a simple RNA virus that is most commonly transmitted by fecal contamination of water. Although the virus has been grown in culture, no vaccine is available. The only available immunoprophylaxis for hepatitis A is pooled immune globulin. The protection provided by this agent is incomplete and transient, but it is probably advisable for backcountry travel in underdeveloped countries. Diligent water disinfection more effectively prevents this infection.

Hepatitis B

Hepatitis B is caused by a large, complex DNA virus that is quite different from the hepatitis A virus and is primarily transmitted by body fluids, particularly blood and semen. However, it can be transmitted by contaminated water or food. A safe, effective vaccine is available.

Hepatitis B vaccination should be obtained by everyone traveling into backcountry areas of underdeveloped countries, although individuals who have previously come into contact with this virus and developed natural immunity do not need to be vaccinated. Such subclinical infections are common and can be detected with a blood test that is less expensive than the vaccine, which costs approximately $120 in the United States for a course of three injections.

Hepatitis D, or delta agent, infection only occurs in association with hepatitis B infection and can be prevented by vaccination against hepatitus B virus.

Hepatitis C and E

Although hepatitis C and E infections are common, the viral agents causing these disorders have only recently been isolated. No vaccines are available. Pooled immune globulin may help prevent these infections as it does for hepatitis A, but its efficacy has not been proven.

SANITATION

Sanitation plays a vital role in preventing infections. Many inhabitants of underdeveloped countries have not even heard about the most rudimentary sanitation procedures, such as washing their hands after defecating. Even when they follow such practices, many do not understand their purpose and consider them idiosyncrasies of foreigners. When local inhabitants are employed as cooks or in similar roles, hand washing, disinfection of water for drinking, cooking, or even washing dishes, and sanitary preparation of food must be vigorously enforced to prevent a lapse into old habits.

Locally obtained food must be regarded with the same distrust as the water supply. The only food that can be regarded as safe from contamination is that which has been thoroughly cooked under supervision. The plates on which it is served and the utensils are almost never washed in water hot enough to kill bacteria. Soap may not have been added to the water. The most common practice is to simply rinse these items with water that has not been disinfected. However, well-cooked food usually is safe—and often delicious—if the traveler provides his own plate, cup, and spoon.

Fruits that have been picked above ground level, cleaned, and peeled or sliced by the eater should be safe because bacteria can not enter the fruit as it is growing. However, fruits that have been previously sliced for display often have been cut with contaminated knives and sprinkled with undisinfected water to keep them attractive for potential buyers. Melons sold by the pound may be injected with undisinfected water to increase their weight. Leafy vegetables are often fertilized with human feces (night soil) and can not be adequately disinfected by washing. Even soaking in strong chlorine solutions is not completely effective.

All other foods must be assumed to be dangerous, particularly custards, cakes, bread, cold meats, cheeses, and other dairy products. Milk is a potential source of tuberculosis. Bottled carbonated drinks—water, sodas, and beer—are generally safe, but a few infections have resulted from drinking bottled noncarbonated water. Ice is often made from undisinfected water.

Sites for garbage disposal and latrines should be downstream, downhill, downwind, and as far as possible from water sources. However, latrines that are too far away are not used, which can make campsites unpleasant and unsafe. Local inhabitants often must be instructed to use latrines. Nepal suffers an epidemic of cholera at the beginning of each monsoon season because the rain washes human feces from the streets into the streams that serve as the water supply.

WATER DISINFECTION

As the popularity of outdoor recreation has grown, microbial contamination of backcountry water sources has increased. Even though travel to all areas of the world has also increased, underdeveloped countries have been unable to build reliable water systems that supply uncontaminated water for drinking, cooking, and food preparation, or sewage systems that prevent contamination of the water supply.

Desirable Characteristics of Water Disinfection Systems

A water disinfection system for wilderness use must be:

• Simple and convenient
• Fast
• Small and lightweight
• Dependable

Wilderness users tend to be young and impatient; many will not use a system that is not simple and convenient or wait for a slow process. Water that is clear and appears uncontaminated will be consumed without disinfection. A system that is not small and lightweight will not be carried. A system that is not reliable should not be used by anyone.

Disinfection systems suitable for wilderness use are also suitable for urban use in countries with an unsafe water supply. However, long-term residents usually develop a more convenient system, most commonly a system that combines a filter with chemical treatment.

Goal of Water Disinfection

The goal of water disinfection is the elimination of infections by waterborne microorganisms. Unlike urban systems, the techniques used to disinfect small quantities of water usually kill all organisms.

Three types of microorganisms must be eliminated: parasites, bacteria, and viruses. Some parasites are single-cell organisms such as amoebae and *Giardia;* others are larger, multicellular organisms such as tapeworms or roundworms. Single-cell parasites often form thick, tough walls around themselves when they are eliminated from the body. Such structures—cysts—are much more resistant to chemical agents or heat than the unprotected organism. More complex parasites lay eggs that are excreted by the host.

Bacteria, which are smaller than parasites but larger than viruses, make up most of the bulk of feces and produce a wide range of infections, many of them potentially lethal.

Viruses are much smaller than bacteria and also produce a wide variety of infections. Evidence that many cases of "traveler's" diarrhea result from viral infection, particularly the Norwalk agent, is accumulating. Hepatitis A has long been known to result from fecal contamination of water. The newly identified hepatitis E, which is associated with a ten percent mortality in pregnant women, is predominantly transmitted by water.

Most travelers know that water supplies in underdeveloped countries are contaminated, but often are not aware of the many ways in which they can consume that water. Tap water is usually contaminated, even in the best hotels, although many establishments provide insulated pitchers of disinfected cold water for drinking. Tap water should not be used for brushing teeth. Ice used to chill drinks may be unsafe. Even in remote areas, small wilderness streams are often contaminated by herdsmen and their cattle or sheep.

TECHNIQUES FOR WILDERNESS WATER DISINFECTION

Water disinfection methods suitable for wilderness employ heat, microfiltration, or chemicals.

Heat

Heat is reliable; simply bringing water to a boil provides adequate disinfection. Even though water boils at a lower temperature at higher altitudes, the boiling temperature and the time required to reach that temperature are adequate to kill disease-producing microorganisms, including parasitic cysts, bacteria, and viruses (table 5-1). (Milk is pasteurized by heating it to 160°F, or 71°C.)

Boiling is inconvenient and time-consuming, particularly for large quantities of water. Fuel must be carried, particularly above tree line. If a fire is built, an unsightly residue is unavoidable without heavy, bulky firepans. Pressure cookers save time and fuel at all elevations. No additional disinfection can be achieved by distillation.

TABLE 5-1.
Boiling Temperature of Water at Various Altitudes

Altitude	Temperature
Sea level	212°F/100°C
10,000 ft/3,000 m	194°F/90°C
14,000 ft/4,300 m	187°F/ 86°C
19,000 ft/5,500 m	178°F/82°C
29,000 ft/8,800 m	160°F/71°C

Microfiltration

Microfiltration is a technique for water disinfection that effectively removes bacteria and larger organisms such as *Giardia*. However, the filter pores are much too large to remove viruses, and filtered water still must be chemically treated to destroy them, which is the major shortcoming of such systems (table 5-2). Some manufacturers claim, directly or indirectly, that their filters remove hepatitis A virus, but no basis for such claims is cited. No statements are made about other hepatitis viruses, rotavirus, the Norwalk agents, and other viruses that produce gastrointestinal infections.

Filters are bulky and expensive. Sediment produces obstruction that can be relieved in many systems only by replacing the filter. Replacements can cost almost as much as the entire system. One ceramic filter is sold with a brush for scrubbing away sediment; others come with prefilters that remove the sediment.

Because they remove parasitic ova and cysts so effectively, large ceramic filters are frequently used by residents of underdeveloped countries. The water must be chemically disinfected after filtration, but much smaller quantities of

TABLE 5-2.
Size Comparison (Micrometers) of Organisms and Filter Pores

Katadyn® filter pore	0.2 μm
Giardia cysts	6.0 μm
Bacteria (diameter)	0.3–1.5 μm
Viruses	0.004–0.06 μm

disinfectant can be used. Many sophisticated disinfection systems have been developed for yachts and for other situations and users for whom size, weight, and cost are not major considerations. These are not suitable for backpacking.

Chemical Disinfection

Only chemical disinfection systems meet the criteria of simplicity, speed, small size and weight, and reliability. Although many systems are effective, only halide (chlorine or iodine) systems are simple and inexpensive, readily available in the United States, and proven by extensive use. A silver-containing compound is widely used in Europe but has not been approved by the FDA for sale in the United States.

CHLORINE DISINFECTION SYSTEMS

The effectiveness of chlorine for water disinfection is well documented. Most municipal water systems in North America use chlorine. However, the disinfectant action of chlorine is pH-sensitive. In water that is even slightly alkaline the antimicrobial activity of chlorine is greatly reduced. Furthermore, if organic residues are present, chlorine combines with ammonia ions and amino acids to form chloramines, which release chlorine slowly, inconsistently, and unreliably. In municipal systems, free chlorine levels in the water must be constantly monitored to ensure they are adequate for reliable disinfection. Monitoring is not possible in the wilderness, or in urban situations in underdeveloped countries.

The water disinfection action of chlorine is much slower than that of iodine; two to three times as much time is required. Furthermore, most chlorine compounds are unstable and of questionable reliability for wilderness water disinfection. Household bleach should be used only when nothing else is available and only by individuals who are allergic to iodine or have thyroid dysfunction (table 5-3).

Halazone®

Halazone® contained p-dichlorosulfamoyl benzoic acid, which releases chlorine when dissolved in water, but it was unstable. Studies of iodine as a water

---

TABLE 5-3.
Chlorine-based Water Disinfection Systems

Unavailable: Halazone® tablets

Questionable: liquid bleach

Reliable: Sierra Water Purifier®

---

disinfectant were initiated during World War II because Halazone® was so unsatisfactory. The tablets are no longer available; Abbott Laboratories, the manufacturer, discontinued production in 1989.

Household Bleach

Household bleach, a source of chlorine that is commonly recommended, has shortcomings as a water disinfectant. Agitating the solution, which is unavoidable when it is carried in a pack, accelerates chlorine loss. Since these products are not intended for use as water disinfectants, the manufacturers apparently have not performed or have not released the findings of studies to determine the speed of chlorine loss with agitation or the loss of antimicrobial effect that would result.

Calcium Hypochlorite

The Sierra Water Purifier® is a chlorine-based system that adds far more chlorine to water than is needed for disinfection (superchlorination). In the presence of such excessive amounts of chlorine the problems of pH inactivation or organic binding are not significant. After disinfection has been completed, the chlorine is driven off with a concentrated solution of hydrogen peroxide.

Superchlorination is achieved by adding to each gallon (four liters) of water 27 grams or more of calcium hypochlorite. (A measuring scoop is provided or the crystals can be counted out.) After a few minutes the water develops a strong smell of chlorine as the result of a chlorine concentration of 27 to 30 parts per million, far more than is required to kill all organisms. After allowing enough time for all organisms to be killed—ten to thirty minutes depending upon the water temperature—approximately six drops per gallon of a thirty percent solution of hydrogen peroxide is added to dechlorinate the water.

This system is more suitable for disinfecting relatively large quantities of water—five to ten gallons, or twenty to forty liters—than the one or two liters that would be carried in a backpack. Additionally, the concentrated hydrogen peroxide is caustic. (Thirty percent hydrogen peroxide is used in cosmetic dentistry to bleach teeth.) Avoiding contact with this agent is difficult, and some individuals employing this system have experienced burning in their fingers that lasted thirty to sixty minutes (although it produced no visible injury) almost every time it has been used.

Superchlorination is reliable; the presence of a "strong smell of chlorine" should be unmistakable. Additionally, the system is small, lightweight, and relatively simple, although two compounds must be added to the water instead of one. It is more expensive than iodine-based systems, but still is relatively cheap. The hydrogen peroxide that drives off the chlorine not only removes all halogen taste, but imparts a sparkle to the water.

IODINE DISINFECTION SYSTEMS

When a search for a simple, reliable water disinfectant was instituted because chlorine-based systems were unreliable, the investigating team found that diatomic iodine (I^2 and the various ions resulting from the reaction of molecular iodine with water) consistently and reliably disinfected grossly polluted water. The effectiveness of iodine as a disinfectant was demonstrated on raw sewage from the Cambridge, Massachusetts, sewage system.

Iodine acts faster than chlorine, resists inactivation by organic compounds, is active over a wide pH range, and is available in stable preparations. In clear water the eradication of bacteria, viruses, parasites, and parasitic cysts by an iodine concentration of 8 mg/l (8 parts per million) in ten minutes has been repeatedly demonstrated. The recommended contact time already includes a considerable margin of safety. (Such high iodine concentrations are needed primarily to destroy parasitic cysts. A concentration of 0.5 mg/l is adequate for other microorganisms.)

Several precautions must be observed when iodine is used for water disinfection. In cold water (or 32°F to 41°F, or 0°C to 5°C), the chemical activity of iodine is slower, just as all chemical reactions are slower at lower temperatures. Contact time must be increased to twenty minutes to ensure complete disinfection. Cloudy or colored water requires more iodine or a longer contact time to compensate for binding of the disinfectant by organic compounds; however, doubling the iodine concentration to 16 mg/l or doubling the contact time is sufficient.

For individuals who find the iodine taste strongly objectionable, several methods for eliminating the iodine or masking its taste are available. (Such procedures must be instituted only after enough time has elapsed for microorganisms to have been destroyed.) Artificial flavorings hide the taste but usually contain ascorbic acid, which reacts with iodine and blocks its antimicrobial activity. The iodine can be converted to tasteless (and microbiologically inactive) sodium iodide with an equal weight of sodium thiosulfate. The water can be filtered through activated charcoal, which by adsorption physically removes the iodine (and some microorganisms, but not enough to make the water suitable for consumption.)

If more time is available for disinfection, lower concentrations of iodine can be used. In clear water, the rate at which microorganisms are destroyed by halogens is dependent on contact time and iodine concentration. Half the standard concentration of iodine is an equally effective disinfectant if allowed to act for twice the usual time; one-fourth the standard concentration is an equally effective disinfectant if allowed to act for four times the usual time. Lower concentrations are not needed because such small amounts of iodine can not be tasted.

Persons with known thyroid dysfunction should not rely on an iodine disinfection system in the wilderness until they have determined how they react to water disinfected with iodine at home. The uncommon individuals who are allergic to iodine, including iodine-containing compounds in radiographic contrast media, must not use iodine for water disinfection. For such individuals a filtration system to physically remove bacteria, parasites, and parasitic cysts followed by chlorine to kill viruses is a reliable alternative.

Several publications have decried the use of iodine for water disinfection, claiming that it is dangerously toxic. The skull-and-crossbones symbol on bottles of tincture of iodine is quite familiar. However, iodine is not highly toxic. The third edition of Goodman and Gilman's textbook of pharmacology states " . . . that iodine is highly toxic, however, is a popular fallacy." The generally accepted lethal dose is two to three grams, but survival after ingestion of ten grams has been reported. Iodine in such large quantities is a strong gastrointestinal irritant and causes immediate vomiting, which eliminates most of the iodine. That remaining in the gastrointestinal tract is largely neutralized by the intestinal contents. (The immediate treatment for iodine poisoning is administration of starchy food.)

Accidental iodine poisoning is rare, and almost all fatalities are suicidal; even successful suicide is uncommon if the individual receives medical care. No deaths occurred among 327 patients attended at Boston City Hospital between 1915 and 1936 following attempted suicide with iodine.

In an investigational program, inmates of three Florida prisons were given water disinfected with 0.5 to 1.0 mg/l of iodine for fifteen years. No detrimental effects on the general health or thyroid function of previously normal persons were detected with careful medical and biochemical monitoring. Of 101 infants

---

TABLE 5-4.
Iodine-Based Water Disinfection Systems

Reliable

Tetraglycine hydroperiodide (Potable-Aqua®, Globaline®, EDWGT®)

Saturated aqueous iodine solution (Kahn-Visscher, Polar Pure®)

Alcoholic iodine solution (Polar Pure *Plus*®)

Tincture of iodine

Questionable

Povidone-iodine (Betadine®, Povidone®, Pharmadine®, and others)

Lugol's solution

Resin-bound iodine (Water Tech Travelmate Water Purifier®)

born to inmates who had been in prison for 122 to 270 days, none had detectable thyroid enlargement. However, all four individuals with hyperthyroidism encountered during these studies became more symptomatic while consuming iodinated water.

These studies indicate that individuals with normal thyroid function, including pregnant women, can consume water disinfected with 8 mg/l of iodine for several months with no ill effects. For longer periods, a system that incorporates a filter to remove parasitic cysts and requires only 0.5 to 1.0 mg/l of iodine to kill all other microorganisms would eliminate the risk of iodide goiter.

A wide variety of iodine sources are available. Some are of questionable reliability and are not recommended; several are highly reliable, and a selection must be based on availability and convenience.

QUESTIONABLE IODINE-BASED WATER DISINFECTANTS

Povidone-Iodine Solutions

"Three to four drops" of a ten percent solution of povidone-iodine, an organic iodine complex sold as Betadine®, Povidone®, Pharmadine®, and other trade names, has been recommended for water disinfection in a widely publicized letter to a medical journal. Apparently no studies demonstrating its effectiveness have been published. Until the effectiveness of povidone-iodine for water disinfection has been established by careful, controlled investigation, these agents should not be used for this purpose.

Lugol's Solution

Lugol's solution has been recommended as a source of iodine for water disinfection, but iodine concentrations cited for Lugol's solution range from one to eight percent. Sodium or potassium iodide must be added to Lugol's solution for the iodine to dissolve, which adds to the solution extra iodine that has no antimicrobial action. Furthermore, although Lugol's solution used to be used to treat thyroid disorders, it is no longer readily available, even to pharmacists. Better sources of iodine are available.

Resin-bound Iodine

Quaternary ammonium anion exchange resins combined with iodine are used in a water disinfection system known as the Water Tech Travelmate Water Purifier®. As water is filtered through the resin, microorganisms come in contact with the iodine and are destroyed. Careful studies have demonstrated the ability of the resin-bound iodine to destroy all types of microorganisms.

A major attraction of this system is the small quantity of iodine released into the water, which imparts no iodine taste. Additionally, the cup would be convenient for disinfecting water in public dining places in underdeveloped countries.

However, this system has significant shortcomings. It has no indicator that the resin has been exhausted. The filter releases so little iodine that no taste or visible color is produced. The Water Tech Travelmate Water Purifier® is claimed to have the capacity for disinfecting 100 gallons of water, but few users would keep the records needed to determine when that quantity had been filtered.

Apparently the filters are fragile, and damage that allows water to flow through unimpeded is not uncommon. A backup system that is absolutely dependable would have to be available in case the filter is damaged. Carrying two water disinfection systems is inconvenient at best; the reliable system is the only one really needed.

A minor disadvantage is the time required for filtration with the six-ounce cup—thirty seconds for one cup, or more than three minutes for a liter of water.

RELIABLE IODINE-BASED WATER DISINFECTANTS

Tetraglycine Hydroperiodide

Tablets containing tetraglycine hydroperiodide are widely sold under the trade names Globaline®, Potable-Aqua®, and EDWGT®. One fresh tablet dissolved in a liter of water provides an iodine concentration of 8 mg/l. The major advantage of tetraglycine hydroperiodide tablets is their convenience. A small bottle of fifty tablets can be carried easily. Sealed bottles can be stored for months with little loss of iodine.

The principal disadvantage of tetraglycine hydroperiodide is its tendency to dissociate after exposure to air. In studies to document their stability, tetraglycine hydroperiodide tablets placed in a single layer in an open dish at 140°F (60°C) lost forty percent of their iodine in seven days. At room temperature and 100 percent humidity, the tablets lost thirty-three percent of their iodine in four days. Studies to determine the rate of dissociation of tablets in a small bottle opened several times a day for one or two weekends a month, the pattern of typical weekend use by outdoorsmen, have not been reported.

Because 8 mg/l of iodine produces a definite brown color, the potency of tetraglycine hydroperiodide tablets can be roughly determined.

Tightly capping and refrigerating bottles of the tablets may help retard iodine loss, but they probably should be discarded a few months after opening.

Saturated Aqueous Iodine Solution (Kahn-Visscher)

In 1975 Kahn and Visscher described a procedure for disinfecting water with a saturated aqueous solution of iodine. Iodine crystals (2 to 8 g, U.S. Pharmacopoeia [USP] grade, resublimed) are placed in a 30-cc (1-oz) clear-glass bottle with a paper-lined bakelite cap. (These details are significant.) The bottle is filled with water, shaken vigorously, and allowed to stand for at least one hour to produce a saturated solution. One half of the supernatant solution (15 cc) is poured into one liter of water to be disinfected. If the water in the 30-cc bottle has a temperature of 68°F (20°C), which can be achieved easily by carrying it in a shirt pocket, the iodine concentration in the disinfected water would be about 9 mg/l.

The Kahn-Visscher method has two distinct advantages: compactness and reliability. The small bottle can contain enough iodine to disinfect 250 to 500 liters of water, and if crystals can be seen in the bottom of the bottle, enough iodine for disinfection is known to be present.

This technique for water disinfection has been denounced, even in terms such as "it can kill you," because in decanting the supernatant, iodine crystals could be poured into the water to be consumed. This hazard appears insignificant. Iodine is so weakly toxic that three or four crystals would not be expected to produce any symptoms. Individuals who have used this technique extensively have found that small flakes of iodine are commonly caught by surface tension in the small bottle, poured into the large bottle, and ingested without producing any detectable ill effects. A jar with a sleeve in its neck to prevent decanting the iodine crystals (Polar Pure®) is available. (On its label this jar also has a temperature indicator and data for calculating the volume in capfuls of saturated iodine solution that would contain 8 mg of iodine.)

A saturated aqueous solution of iodine has been singled out as being uniquely ineffective at low temperatures for eradicating *Giardia* cysts. However, all of the disinfectants tested in that study produce their antimicrobial effects by releasing diatomic iodine. A difference in effectiveness when all act through the same mechanism appears unlikely, and extensive use of this system has not been associated with parasitic infestations.

One real problem with the Kahn-Visscher system is the tendency for the small glass bottle to break, particularly if the water within it freezes. (Such a small amount of iodine is dissolved in the water, even when the solution is fully saturated, that the freezing temperature of the solution is depressed very little.) The bottle can be kept warm in a sleeping bag, or it can be left half empty after its last use in the evening so the water can expand as it freezes without breaking the bottle. Unfortunately, glass is the only satisfactory container for aqueous iodine solutions.

The Kahn-Visscher disinfection method is widely used because it is convenient and reliable. For informed adults, particularly for members of prolonged expeditions or urban residents of undeveloped countries, the method is safe. Children must not be entrusted with a potentially lethal quantity of iodine.

Concentrated Alcoholic Iodine Solutions

A concentrated solution of iodine in ninety-five percent ethanol can provide a compact source of iodine for disinfecting larger quantities of water. A solution of 8 g of iodine in 100 cc of ethyl alcohol contains enough iodine to disinfect 250 gallons (1,000 liters) of water. The 8 mg of iodine needed to disinfect one liter of water is present in only 0.1 cc of the solution; enough iodine for 5 gallons (20 liters) is contained in 2 cc. This preparation is reliable because the concentration of iodine could only increase if the alcohol evaporated. In addition, alcoholic solutions do not freeze. This system has no major disadvantages.

A concentrated alcoholic solution of iodine, Polar Pure *Plus*®, has been developed by the retailer in Saratoga, California, who produces the Polar Pure® system and who is in the process of obtaining approval for his product from the EPA. The opening in the tip of the bottle delivers drops that contain 2.5 mg of iodine.

Tincture of Iodine

The principal advantage of tincture of iodine for water disinfection is its wide availability. It can be found throughout the world when other water disinfection preparations are not available.

The disadvantages of iodine tincture are its taste, its iodide component, and possibly a need for precisely measuring the amount added to water—none of which is a major problem. Many individuals find the iodine taste imparted by the tincture to be much stronger than that of other preparations containing equivalent quantities of iodine. The USP standard tincture of iodine solution is two percent iodine and 2.4 percent sodium iodide in fifty percent ethanol. The iodide has no disinfectant activity, but does increase total iodine intake. Dispensing exactly the volume of tincture that would contain 8 mg of iodine requires a measuring device such as a tuberculin syringe. Many individuals simply add several drops per liter of water, and look for a brown color or check for a distinctive iodine taste to ensure that a sufficient quantity for disinfection has been added.

Although the USP tincture of iodine is a two percent solution, preparations with different concentrations are sold as "tincture." All are effective for water disinfection, but the concentration of the solutions must be checked to determine how much iodine is being added to the water.

Tincture of iodine resists freezing. It can be used to disinfect skin, but aqueous solutions are just as effective and do not sting. Adding 0.4 cc of a two percent solution to a liter of water provides an iodine concentration of 8 mg/l. Iodine tincture is rarely sold by pharmacies in quantities larger than one ounce. Larger

---

TABLE 5-5.
Comparison of Reliable Preparations for Water Disinfection

Method	Advantages	Disadvantages
Tetraglycine hydroperiodide	Convenient	Undetectable iodine loss
Crystalline iodine	Compact	Freezes and breaks container
Concentrated alcoholic iodine solution	Compact; resists freezing	None
Tincture of iodine	Available; resists freezing	Strong taste of iodine; extra iodide
Calcium hypochlorite	"Sparkling" taste; no iodine	Requires two agents; 30 percent H_2O_2 is caustic

volumes are available from chemical suppliers, but other preparations for water disinfection can be obtained just as easily. Tincture of iodine is used primarily when nothing else is available. The tincture must be stored in glass bottles, which can break.

Editor's Note: Since completion of this text, two developments have occurred. The manufacturer of the saturated aqueous iodine solution Polar Pure® has decided to discontinue that product after EPA approval for the alcoholic solution Polar Pure *Plus®* is received, probably in spring 1992.

Secondly, a recently introduced filter, PŪR®, incorporates a triiodine resin to destroy the viruses and small bacteria, particularly vibrios, that pass through the filter. These resins release so little iodine into the water that it can not be tasted. Other resin-based products have not included an indicator that the resin has been exhausted. However, the PŪR® filter has been designed to become plugged so that it must be replaced well before the resin has been exhausted. Because water passes through the resin rather rapidly, cold water should be filtered twice.

TRAUMATIC AND NONTRAUMATIC DISORDERS

CHAPTER SIX

SOFT-TISSUE INJURIES

L acerations, abrasions, bruises, and blisters are the most common injuries occurring in the wilderness. They are called "soft-tissue" injuries to distinguish
them from injuries to bones and ligaments.

The treatment of soft-tissue injuries has four objectives:

• Control of bleeding
• Control of infection
• Promotion of healing
• Preservation of function of the injured part

CONTROL OF BLEEDING

Direct pressure is the only effective means for controlling bleeding from a
soft-tissue wound. The severed blood vessels must be collapsed to obstruct blood
flow and permit clots to form. The pressure must be applied directly over the
wound. Pressure points are not worth considering. Tourniquets are dangerous and
are essentially never needed or even justifiable.

Bleeding from most skin wounds is from veins and capillaries. The pressure in
these vessels is so low that simply holding a dressing on the wound for two to
five minutes allows the blood to clot and plug the vessels. Deeper lacerations may
cut larger veins, such as the veins visible beneath the skin of the arms and legs.
Bleeding from these vessels is more profuse, but can be easily controlled by
compression because all veins have thin walls and the pressure within them is low.

Arteries have much thicker walls and are rarely cut. However, arterial blood
is under much higher pressure, and blood loss is harder to control when these
vessels are damaged. The only reliable way to identify arterial bleeding is to see
blood spurting from the wound with each heartbeat. The color of the blood is not
a reliable indicator of its source. Arterial bleeding also must be controlled by
direct pressure.

With severe wounds, bleeding may persist, even after direct pressure has been
applied for fifteen to twenty minutes, particularly when an artery has been cut.
Such wounds must be packed with sterile gauze and wrapped snugly with a
continuous bandage.

Bandages that completely surround a limb may obstruct circulation to the rest of the limb. Absent pulses, bluish discoloration of the skin or nails, tingling sensations, or pain indicate that the blood supply to the tissues beyond the bandage is inadequate. Since swelling at the site of the wound can greatly increase the pressure beneath a circumferential bandage, the limb beyond the bandage must be carefully examined for circulatory impairment every two to three hours. If the bandage initially is too tight, or later becomes too tight, it must be loosened; after bleeding has been controlled, the circumferential bandage should be removed.

Movement may cause bleeding to recur, even after it has been controlled. To avoid further blood loss, severely injured limbs should be immobilized before the individual is evacuated. In expedition circumstances, delaying evacuation for two to three days to allow the clots within severed vessels to become more firmly anchored may be desirable.

CONTROL OF INFECTION

Wound infection results from contamination, and all open wounds are contaminated to some extent. Preventing infection by minimizing contamination and eliminating conditions that promote bacterial growth is far preferable to treating an established infection.

Wound Cleansing

After bleeding has been controlled, further contamination of soft-tissue injuries must be avoided. The person caring for the injured individual should wash his hands, preferably with an antibacterial agent such as PhisoHex® or a povidone-iodine preparation. Sterile gloves, if available, should be used, but only after the hands have been scrubbed. The skin around the wound should be vigorously cleaned, preferably by scrubbing with the same antibacterial agent. Washing dirt, dried blood, or other contaminants into the wound must be avoided.

Finally, the wound itself must be cleaned. A 20-cc or 50-cc syringe with a large bore needle, or even without a needle, is ideal for this purpose, because a jet of water can be directed into the wound with sufficient force to rinse out any foreign material. Such rinsing produces little pain and does not damage the tissues. Obviously, only disinfected water is suitable for such cleansing. Any foreign material, dead tissue, or even clotted blood left in the wound virtually ensures infection. Wound cleansing must be complete. The syringe must be repeatedly refilled and emptied into the wound. Sterile forceps should be used to remove any embedded debris that cannot be rinsed away; small tags of dead tissue may be snipped off with sterile scissors.

For puncture wounds, bleeding should be encouraged to help remove bacteria and debris. The depths of such wounds are not reached by air, and anaerobic bacteria that thrive in such conditions, such as those that cause tetanus and gas gangrene, produce devastating infections.

Antiseptics

Antiseptics have surprisingly little value in the control of wound infections. They can not compensate for negligent wound cleansing and, for wounds that are thoroughly cleaned, provide little additional bacterial control. However, the informed use of antiseptics is prudent, particularly for animal bites or other heavily contaminated wounds.

Antiseptics placed in a wound must be able to kill bacteria without injuring the tissues. Minimizing tissue damage is essential because no agent can kill all of the bacteria, and injured tissue provides an excellent media for the growth of the remaining organisms. Only two readily available antiseptics meet this qualification: a 1:750 aqueous solution of benzalkonium chloride (Zephiran®) and a ten percent solution of a povidone-iodine preparation. Povidone-iodine has two advantages over benzalkonium chloride: it is ideal for scrubbing hands and the skin around a wound (and is routinely used by surgeons), and it can be packaged in polyethylene bottles rather than glass. Benzalkonium chloride is not readily available in a form suitable for wilderness use.

Povidone-iodine can be used undiluted for cleansing skin prior to needle punctures; for rinsing a wound it should be diluted with ten to twenty times its volume of clean water. The wound should be flooded with the solution.

Antiseptics such as alcohol, tincture of iodine, or mercurial preparations damage tissues and should not be placed directly in an open wound.

Wound Closure

In the wilderness, soft-tissue wounds never need to be sutured. If a wound is left open, purulent material from infected areas drains to the outside. This purulent material cannot escape from a sutured wound and is extruded into the surrounding tissues, spreading the infection. In hospitals, soft-tissue wounds are sutured under sterile conditions to promote healing and minimize scarring. However, the conditions available in hospitals can not be duplicated in the wilderness, and the damage that would be produced by an infection in a sutured wound would greatly prolong healing and lead to far greater scarring and deformity. Furthermore, if an unsutured wound is not infected, skin edges tend to fall together, healing is rapid, and scarring is minimal.

Minor wounds that appear to present little risk of infection can be held together with "butterflies" or tape that has been sterilized by flaming. Such devices can be removed easily and the wound opened and drained should infection develop. Wounds that are too large to close with tape should not be closed by anyone but a surgeon, who knows how to obliterate any space beneath the surface and how to avoid further damage by the sutures.

The danger of introducing infection, and the far greater destruction of tissue that results from infection in a wound that has been sutured, far outweigh any benefits that might be obtained from early closure.

Diagnosing Wound Infections

If infection occurs in spite of preventive measures, early detection minimizes tissue damage and the threat to the person's health. In order to look for signs of infection, the dressing over any wound except a burn should be changed daily, at least until healing is clearly under way. The person's overall condition should also be monitored, particularly his temperature.

The signs of infection around the wound itself are primarily the signs of inflammation—pain, redness, swelling, heat, and limitation of motion. These signs can be found with every wound but are much more severe in the presence of infection. Pain from soft-tissue injuries usually begins to subside by the second or third day after injury. Persistence of severe pain beyond this period, or an increase in pain, suggests infection. Redness is usually limited to the margins of a wound. More extensive discoloration, particularly the presence of streaks extending upward along a limb, indicates infection. Severe swelling around a wound, particularly a simple cut with which swelling would not be expected, is a sign of infection, as is a detectable increase in the skin temperature. Swelling and pain combine to limit voluntary and involuntary motion, which is more obvious in the presence of infection.

An oral temperature of 100°F to 101°F (37.8°C to 38.3°C) can be expected for one or two days after any severe injury. A temperature elevation after a minor injury, a higher temperature, or an elevation persisting for a longer time is suggestive of infection.

Located throughout the body are collections of lymph nodes that trap bacteria and the debris from a localized infection and become enlarged and tender (fig. 6-1). Tissue destruction occurs with any injury, and the regional lymph nodes often

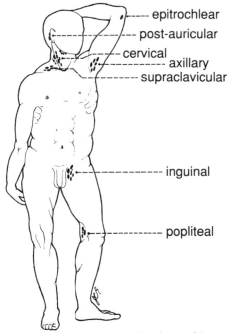

epitrochlear
post-auricular
cervical
axillary
supraclavicular
inguinal
popliteal

Figure 6-1. Location of the major collections of lymph nodes.

become enlarged, but in the presence of infection the nodes become more enlarged and painful. Lymph nodes in more than one area often are enlarged and tender with an infection.

The diagnosis of a wound infection is confirmed by the finding of purulent material—"pus"—in the wound or on the dressings. The discharge may be cream-colored, green, or even pink or reddish in color depending upon the infecting organism. Occasionally the discharge may be clear and straw-colored. A foul odor is often—but not always—present. Rarely, an infected wound produces a very scanty discharge. A diagnosis of infection is not necessarily wrong just because little purulent drainage is present.

The skin edges of an infected wound are sometimes sealed by coagulated serum, in which case exudate from the infection can not escape onto the dressings. If other signs of infection are present, the edges of the wound should be spread apart and the wound gently probed with a pair of sterile forceps. (This process is less painful if the coagulum is first softened by soaking the wound in warm, disinfected water.) If an infection is present, pus usually pours out when the wound is opened. If no infection is present, opening the wound usually does little harm except for the discomfort, which is of little consequence when compared with the damage that could result from an undiscovered infection.

Treating Wound Infections

Treatment for an infected wound consists of drainage and antibiotic therapy. The wound should be opened by prying apart its edges with a pair of sterile forceps. Since pus in an infected wound tends to collect in pockets, the deeper parts of the wound must be probed to ensure that all such pockets are drained. If one is found, others should be expected. After drainage, gauze should be placed in the wound to keep it open. The gauze, preferably impregnated with petroleum jelly, should be changed whenever the wound is dressed. The edges of the wound should not be allowed to reseal as long as any evidence of infection is present.

Infected wounds covered by a crust of coagulated serum and pus, particularly on the extremities, benefit from soaking in warm, disinfected water. Moisture softens the crust and permits more thorough drainage. Heat causes the blood vessels to dilate, increasing the flow of blood to the tissues, which promotes healing and the eradication of infection. For small infected wounds on the extremities—or for large wounds if the subject cannot be evacuated—the dressing should be removed and the wound immersed in warm, sterile water for periods of twenty to thirty minutes three or four times a day. An antiseptic such as povidone-iodine should be added to the water. Afterward, the skin should be carefully dried and a fresh dressing applied.

Antibiotics should not be given routinely to individuals with soft-tissue injuries because the probability of infection is low, antibiotics have only a limited ability to prevent soft-tissue infections, and the risk of allergic reactions and other adverse side effects is significant. However, for severe soft-tissue injuries or badly contaminated wounds, antibiotics should be administered prophylactically before signs of infection appear. In a remote situation, antibiotics should also be given to persons with major wound infections with the understanding that the major benefit is inhibiting spread of the infection and not eradicating the infection within the wound.

If antibiotics are administered as a preventive measure, they should be given in large doses for only two days; such a brief course of antibiotics does not allow the emergence of resistant bacterial strains. If a significant, established soft-tissue infection is being treated, however, high doses of antibiotics should be given for at least five days, or until all signs of infection are gone. If the subject is not allergic to penicillin, he should be given a penicillinase-resistant penicillin or a cephalosporin. If he is allergic to penicillin, erythromycin or some other antibiotic must be used.

BANDAGING

A bandage is usually composed of three layers, each with different functions.

Inner Layer

The inner layer of a bandage should be a thin layer of material, such as gauze impregnated with petroleum jelly, or a plastic material, such as Telfa®, that does not stick to the wound and allows the bandage to be changed relatively painlessly without aggravating the injury. Obviously, this material must be sterile.

Dressings

The middle portion of a bandage is referred to as dressings and has five different functions:

- Prevent contamination in order to prevent infection or limit the infection to organisms already present
- Absorb wound drainage, which must not be allowed to contaminate clothing or other wounds
- Keep the skin adjacent to the wound dry to prevent maceration and infection
- Apply pressure on the underlying wound to aid in the control of bleeding and swelling
- Protect the wound from further trauma

In order to perform these functions, dressings must be sterile and bulky. Although special dressing materials are available, simple gauze pads that have been opened and crumpled to increase their bulk work almost as well and are easier to transport into wilderness areas.

Dressings that have been contaminated by purulent drainage should be handled with forceps or similar instruments that can be sterilized. Such dressings should never be touched with the fingers and should be disposed of by burning. If more than one wound or more than one accident victim must be cared for, attention to the infected wounds should be put off until last, and the attendant must scrub his hands thoroughly after dressing each wound to prevent the spread of infection.

Outer Wrapping

The outer portion of a bandage also has more than one function:

- Hold the dressings securely in place
- Keep the dressings from becoming wet with water or perspiration, which would inevitably carry along bacteria
- Apply pressure to help control bleeding and swelling
- Splint and immobilize portions of the body, particularly the hand

Materials that have some elasticity are easier to use and stay in place better than plain gauze. Such materials also compress the wound slightly, but an elastic bandage is more satisfactory if significant compression is needed. If the wound must be kept dry, it should be covered with waterproof tape, plastic, or some other waterproof material. However, moisture accumulates beneath waterproof tape, lifting it from the skin surface. If protection from water is not needed, porous tape should be used to hold the bandage in place. When the bandage is changed, the tape should be clipped off at the skin edges and new tape placed on top of the old to avoid the skin irritation that results from repeatedly stripping off the tape.

SPECIFIC INJURIES

Lacerations

Lacerations are slicing injuries that may be clean and straight or quite ragged. Such wounds commonly bleed. Infections are also a threat, particularly when small tags of dead tissue are present in ragged wounds. Blood vessels, nerves, or tendons may be damaged, but attempts to repair such structures outside of a hospital would often cause further damage and increase the risk of infection. Individuals with such severe injuries should be evacuated.

Puncture Wounds

A puncture wound may extend deeply into underlying tissues. Hidden structures may be damaged and infection is always a threat. Bleeding—to wash out dirt and bacteria—should be encouraged. Foreign bodies should be removed. A small wick of gauze can be inserted into the opening of the wound to prevent sealing and to allow the exudate from any infection to drain to the outside. In remote areas, antibiotic therapy is probably a justifiable precaution.

The greatest danger from such wounds is tetanus, which should be prevented with tetanus toxoid inoculations well before an outing is even contemplated.

Abrasions

Abrasions are scraping injuries produced by forceful contact with a rough surface. Severe bleeding is rare, and the objectives of treatment are to control infection and promote healing. Before bandaging, large fragments of foreign material should be removed from the wound with sterile forceps. Removing numerous small, embedded particles usually aggravates the injury and does more harm than good. Many such particles are extruded during healing; the rest should be removed under more propitious circumstances.

The wound should be covered with a layer of nonadherent material, such as gauze impregnated with petroleum jelly, over which should be placed a bulky dressing to absorb drainage and cushion against further trauma. During dressing changes, the inner layer should not be removed until it spontaneously separates from the wound surface. Similarly, crusts that form during healing should not be removed.

Infected abrasions usually produce purulent exudate, but the entire wound is open and drainage is not impaired. Dressings should be changed frequently and should be thick enough to absorb the exudate.

Skin Flaps and Avulsions

Forces roughly parallel to the skin surface tend to lift or tear out chunks of tissue. If the tissue is completely torn away, the injury is considered an avulsion. (A limb may be completely severed or avulsed, but few survive accidents in which such powerful forces are generated.) If the skin along one side of the wound remains intact, a skin flap is created. Small skin flaps are rather common, but occasionally larger flaps are produced.

If the full thickness of the skin is avulsed, the injury should be bandaged like an abrasion. As a general rule, wounds of this type that are more than one inch in diameter require skin grafting, so the subject eventually will have to be hospitalized. Large avulsions are incapacitating.

If a thick flap of tissue with fat or muscle attached to the undersurface has been produced, the individual must be evacuated. Such injuries heal poorly and tend to become infected. The wound should be thoroughly cleaned and the tissue flap replaced in its original position. If the tissue flap is large, a strip of gauze should be placed along the lip of the wound so that the edges do not seal and purulent exudate can escape if the wound becomes infected. The wound should be bandaged with a bulky compression dressing, and the entire limb should be immobilized. The flap, which must not be allowed to move or shift its position, is in essence a skin graft. If the wound is to heal, the flap must remain stationary while new blood vessels grow into the tissues.

The subject must be closely watched for signs of infection, and any wound infection that does occur must be promptly drained. Antibiotic therapy should be started at the time of the injury.

In expedition situations, evacuation may not be necessary if the wound appears to be healing satisfactorily without infection, particularly if the flap consists only of skin. The tissue flap is much less likely to be moved inadvertently while the individual is lying in a tent than when he is walking or being carried over rough terrain. However, such wounds usually do not heal without infection, and evacuation of a person with a severe injury that is heavily infected may be much more difficult. (When such wounds are treated in a hospital, the fat, muscle, or other tissue on the undersurface of the flap—the tissue that typically dies or becomes infected—is usually trimmed away, and only the skin is preserved.)

When the flap does not survive, it first acquires a dusky appearance and then becomes progressively darker until it eventually is totally black. Uninfected flaps are dry and hard; infected flaps are usually moist, foul-smelling, and soft. Surgical excision and grafting are required for both, but the infection can be life-threatening.

Small skin flaps with little or no fat on the undersurface are an entirely different matter. The wounds must be cleaned and the flaps held securely in position by bulky bandages just as larger flaps are, but such wounds often heal with no complications or severe infection. The skin flaps commonly do not "take," or attach to the underlying tissue, but they protect the delicate new skin that grows in from the sides and allow it to cover the wound. By the time the wound is covered, the flap usually has dried up and fallen off. The new skin may need to be protected for a few days, but no further therapy is required.

Contusions

Contusions, or bruises, are crushing injuries that cause bleeding into the damaged tissues. Usually the subcutaneous tissue and muscle are injured without a break in the overlying skin. Most contusions are minor, almost insignificant injuries, but rarely the damage can be great enough to severely incapacitate the individual.

The ideal treatment for a severe contusion is immediate application of cold and rest until bleeding has ceased. However, such treatment may be impractical—even life-threatening—in some circumstances. Cessation of bleeding usually requires six to eight hours, but by that time the muscles may be so stiff and sore the person is unable to walk. Anyone with a severe contusion in a remote area may need to walk out, or at least back to his camp, while he is still able to do so. After the muscles have stiffened, they often are too painful for vigorous exercise for three or four days, and weeks may be required for complete recovery.

If circumstances do not require immediate evacuation, the injured area should be elevated and cooled with wet towels or clothing, snow, or ice, which causes the blood vessels in the area to constrict, reduces bleeding into the tissues, and tends to reduce pain. (Cooling can hasten disabling muscle pain and stiffness and should not be used for lower extremity injuries if the subject must be able to walk.) If extensive swelling develops, the extremity may be wrapped with an elastic bandage that applies mild pressure. The wrapping should encompass the entire limb, from the toes or fingertips to well above the area of injury, and must not occlude the circulation.

After twelve to eighteen hours, movement of the injured area may be resumed, if tolerated, in order to speed resorption of the blood. After three days, heat may be applied to accelerate blood resorption and to relieve some of the muscle pain.

Stiffness persisting for more than two to three weeks in a muscle that has been severely bruised may herald the onset of calcium deposition in the injured tissue. Rarely, this process can continue until the entire clot has been transformed into bone—about twelve to eighteen months. The amount of muscle damage varies and is sometimes significant, so the condition should be recognized and treated to minimize disability. Diagnosis requires x-ray demonstration of the calcium deposits.

Wounds of the Hands and Feet

Wounds of the hands and feet are of special importance because these structures are anatomically complex. All wounds in these areas must be thoroughly cleaned, but no tissue should be trimmed away unless it is unmistakably dead. If these members are enclosed in a large bandage, the fingers or toes must be separated by gauze to prevent maceration of the skin from the dampness produced by perspiration. Such bandages should splint the hand in the "position of function," which is the position the hand assumes when holding a pencil (fig. 6-2). The color and sensation in the fingertips must be checked frequently to ensure the bandage is not too tight (fig. 6-3). For severe injuries, antibiotic therapy should be instituted at the time of injury and evacuation begun immediately.

Figure 6-2. "Position of function" of the hand.

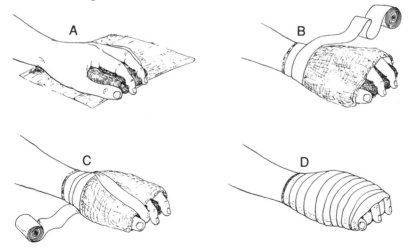

Figure 6-3. Technique for bandaging the hand in the "position of function."

Blisters

Traumatic blisters are caused by friction that pulls the skin back and forth over underlying tissues. Eventually a cleft or tear develops in the midportion of the epidermis, the most superficial portion of the skin, and fluid collects in this cleft.

For a blister to develop, the epidermis must be thick and tough enough to resist destruction by the friction, which otherwise would produce an abrasion. Also, the skin and subcutaneous tissues must be bound to the underlying bone to some extent, or the friction would just move the skin and no shear stress would develop. Finally, the skin must be moist enough for the object producing the blister to adhere to the skin surface instead of sliding back and forth. Only the last condition can be modified to prevent blisters, but the first two conditions explain why blisters usually form at only a few specific sites, such as the heels.

The most common cause of blisters is new or ill-fitting boots. Boots that are too loose in the instep allow the foot to slide forward when going downhill, producing "downhill blisters," usually on the toes or front part of the foot. "Uphill blisters" are most common over the heel or the Achilles tendon at the back of the ankle.

Boots should fit properly and should be broken in slowly and thoroughly. Areas prone to blister should be protected with adhesive tape or moleskin. Adherence between skin and boot should be minimized by keeping the feet dry with powder and by wearing a thick outer sock and a thin inner sock that allows slippage between the two socks. As soon as the pain or heat of an early blister—a "hot spot"—has been detected, the area should be covered with tape or moleskin. (Well-fitting boots do not provide enough space for thicker coverings, such as rings of padded material.)

Healing is faster, pain is diminished, and the risk of infection is greatly reduced when the blister roof is preserved. Blister fluid may have to be drained to allow the roof to adhere to the base. To drain the fluid, the skin should be cleaned, preferably with an agent such as povidone-iodine, and a sterile needle inserted underneath the skin and into the blister from a point three to five millimeters beyond its edge.

If the roof of the blister has been torn away, the injury should be treated like an abrasion: covered with a nonadherent inner layer and protected with a thicker outer layer. Second Skin® is a proprietary product developed to cover unroofed blisters that reportedly is effective. The feet should be kept as clean as possible to reduce the risk of infection.

CHAPTER SEVEN

FRACTURES AND RELATED INJURIES

Wilderness accidents often result in broken bones or joint and tendon injuries. The care for victims of such accidents demands an understanding of these injuries and their potential complications. The diagnosis of a fracture—or the absence of a fracture—without x-rays is particularly challenging.

Fractures vary widely in severity. Fractures of a small bone in the hand or foot may produce little pain or disability. The bone ends of a fractured hip may be driven into each other (impacted) in such a manner that the fracture is stable, produces little deformity, and causes little damage to the surrounding tissues. In contrast, a bone can be so shattered that the limb feels as if no bone is present.

Fractures with a single, clean break are called "simple." If the bone is broken into one or more fragments, the fracture is "comminuted." Fractures in which the bone simply collapses are called "compression" fractures. When the surrounding skin is intact, the fractures are "closed." If the skin has been penetrated, the fracture is called "open" or "compound."

Many bone or joint injuries are of major significance, particularly in wilderness situations where immobilization without food or shelter is life-threatening. Laceration of major blood vessels can produce severe hemorrhage; vascular obstruction can cause gangrene; breaks in the skin can lead to chronic infections; damage to nerves may result in paralysis.

DIAGNOSIS

The principal signs of a fracture are:

- Pain and tenderness
- Swelling and discoloration
- Deformity

Most fractures are painful, the pain is aggravated by movement or manipulation, and the fracture site is sensitive. Swelling and discoloration are usually present. However, these signs are not diagnostic and may occur with sprains or occasionally with simple contusions.

Obvious deformity is diagnostic of a fracture; grating of the ends of the broken bones is also diagnostic. One or both ends of the bone can be seen occasionally in open fractures. A common sign of a fractured hip is shortening of the extremity by one to two inches and outward rotation of the foot.

Loss of function of the injured extremity is not a reliable sign of a fracture. Loss of function can be an emotional response to an injury. A few injuries are so painful that function is lost without fracture. Function may persist even though a fracture is present, particularly with compression fractures of vertebrae and fractures of small bones in the feet and hands.

In a wilderness situation, ascertaining that a fracture is present is not essential. If a fracture is suspected, its existence should be assumed until x-rays prove otherwise. Occasions commonly arise, particularly with ankle injuries, in which an extremity is severely injured but does not appear to be fractured. In a remote area, delaying evacuation until the character of the injury becomes evident may be desirable. If a fracture is present but the extremity has been immobilized and elevated, the delay would rarely have an adverse effect on healing. If no fracture is present, the injured person may be able to walk out.

TREATMENT

Immobilization

The basic treatment for any fracture is immobilization, which minimizes further tissue damage by the bone ends, reduces pain, decreases shock, and ultimately allows the fracture to heal.

Immobilizing a fracture in a wilderness setting can be challenging if splints must be improvised. Any material that stabilizes the fracture can be used. A folded newspaper, magazine, or map is particularly effective for splinting fractures of the forearm and wrist. (Cardboard arm and leg splints have been used in downhill ski areas.) Ensolite pads can be used to splint forearms or lower legs and make excellent cylindrical splints for knee injuries. Cross-country skis or ice axes can be used for lower leg splints. Pillows, heavy clothing, or sleeping bags can be used to splint ankles. Metal pack frames can be used for splints, and the pack straps can be used to hold the splint in place.

Bony prominences at the wrist, elbow, ankle, and knee must be padded to prevent discomfort and nerve damage from hard splint materials. The subject must be given the responsibility for reporting any symptoms, or any change in existing symptoms, that may herald nerve or vascular compression.

A large and well-prepared outing probably should carry splints. Padded aluminum splints (Sam Splint®) are lightweight and relatively small and can easily be molded to form stable splints for fractures of the arms, wrists, lower legs, or ankles.

Inflatable splints are most suitable for immobilizing fractures of the lower leg and ankle (fig. 7-1). These splints are lightweight, easy to apply, and help control hemorrhage by applying pressure over the leg when the splint is inflated. (The air pressure in the splint may need to be briefly lowered every one to two hours to ensure the blood supply to the skin is not impaired.) Inflatable splints must be

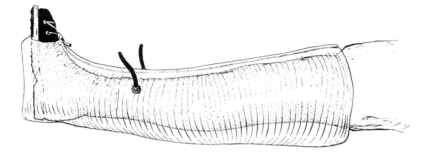

Figure 7-1. Inflatable splint for fractures of the lower leg and ankle.

protected from puncture during evacuation. Changes in air pressure within the splint with changes in altitude and environmental temperature must be anticipated. Heavier splints with zipper closures and screw-type air locks seem to work better than lighter, self-sealing splints, which are affected by large temperature changes.

To achieve immobilization, both the joint above and the joint below a fracture must be splinted. For a fracture of the forearm, the wrist and elbow should be immobilized. For a fracture of the lower leg, the knee and ankle must be stabilized.

Fractures of the thigh (femur) are often associated with severe bleeding and usually are very painful, particularly a few hours after injury when the surrounding muscles go into spasm. Immobilization of such fractures, particularly during evacuation, requires traction, which is described in more detail in the specific discussion of such injuries.

To apply a splint or pack the injured person in a basket stretcher, a fractured extremity must be straightened, which can be accomplished most readily immediately after the fracture has occurred. Later, muscle spasm and the person's diminished tolerance for pain make manipulation more painful and more difficult.

A definite indication for manipulation of a fractured limb is loss of the blood supply to the limb beyond the fracture site. If the ends of fractured bones obstruct blood flow by pressing on an artery, or have lacerated the artery, the result is severe pain, numbness, and coldness in the affected limb, which typically is cyanotic or pale. If the bone ends are only pressing against the artery or vein, straightening the limb may relieve the obstruction. If the vessel is actually torn, manipulation is usually not helpful. (Loss of sensation may also result from injury to a nerve.)

Bleeding

Some bleeding occurs with all fractures. Broken bones with sharp ends can cause extensive destruction of the surrounding soft tissues and profuse blood loss. Fractures of the pelvis or thighs are usually associated with severe bleeding. The hemorrhage often causes shock and can be lethal and yet produces little or no external evidence of bleeding. Anyone caring for an accident victim with either of these injuries—or multiple fractures of other bones—must be aware of the threat of shock and should institute treatment in anticipation of its appearance.

Open Fractures

The danger of infection makes open, or compound, fractures much more serious problems. Osteomyelitis, an infection of bone, can produce extensive bone destruction, may prevent healing of fractures, and occasionally leads to permanent deformities—even amputation. The infection may be difficult to eradicate with antibiotic therapy and rarely can persist for years, producing general debilitation as well as local destruction.

Any fracture is considered open if the skin is broken, regardless of whether the skin was damaged by the bone ends or in some other way. A fracture produced by a penetrating injury, such as a gunshot wound, is considered open because the skin is no longer able to keep bacteria away from the injured bone.

If the bone ends protrude through a break in the skin, they should be rinsed with disinfected water until all visible foreign material has been removed before any attempt to straighten the extremity is made. Manipulation causes the bone ends to retract beneath the skin, and foreign material carried with them greatly increases the severity of the subsequent infection. The wound should be left open and should be covered with a bulky bandage. The individual should be evacuated as rapidly as possible. If evacuation can be completed in a few hours, antibiotics should not be administered unless they can be given intravenously. If evacuation must be delayed, high doses of oral or intravenous antibiotics should be given. A cephalosporin is the drug of first choice; a penicillinase-resistant penicillin or erythromycin are second choices.

Control of Pain

Pain from a fracture is greatly reduced by immobilization. If a fracture is splinted shortly after injury, pain medications often are not needed. However, analgesics may be required for the inevitable jolts of a prolonged evacuation over rough ground.

If needed, morphine or meperidine should be injected intramuscularly every four hours. However, absorption of the drug from the injection site will be reduced if the person is in shock, and repeated injections can lead to an overdose when normal circulation is restored. Therefore pain medications usually are inadvisable for accident victims who are in shock. If such persons do require analgesia, morphine should be injected intravenously in small amounts (two to four milligrams every fifteen to thirty minutes) until any necessary manipulation has been completed or the pain has been reduced to a tolerable level.

TRANSPORTATION

Immobilization of fractures and treatment for other injuries must be completed before the individual is moved unless his location is threatened by hazards such as falling rock, an avalanche, or an electrical storm. After obvious injuries have been treated, but before evacuation is begun, the person must be examined slowly and thoroughly to ensure that no additional injuries have been overlooked in the initial evaluation. Attention must be directed to the person's back, which is often neglected. If not treated, such injuries could be seriously aggravated during evacuation.

Individuals with fractures of the upper extremities, collar bone, or ribs and some persons with head injuries are able to walk. Such individuals must be closely attended because weakness and instability can result from the injury or from drugs given for pain. Subjects with fractures of the lower extremities, pelvis, or vertebral column and persons with severe head injuries usually must be carried. Considerable resourcefulness and sheer determination are required to successfully evacuate individuals with these injuries, particularly in bad weather.

SPECIFIC FRACTURES OF THE UPPER EXTREMITIES

Hand and Fingers

Fractures of the fingers are usually obvious; fractures of the hand may be difficult to diagnosis. If pain persists for several days, a fracture is probably present. The hand and fingers should be immobilized by bandaging the hand in the position of function with a wad of material in the palm (figs. 6-2 and 6-3). An elastic bandage or rolled-up pair of socks serves nicely for this purpose. If the fracture is adjacent to the wrist, a splint should be applied to the palm and the underside of the forearm. A forearm sling should be used to keep the hand elevated (fig. 7-2).

Forearm

Forearm and wrist fractures are usually obvious. To stabilize wrist and forearm fractures, the hand and elbow must be included in the splint. After splinting, the injured arm should be suspended in two slings as with fractures of the upper arm.

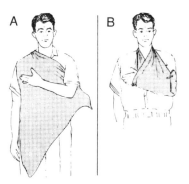

Figure 7-2. Application of a forearm sling.

Elbow, Upper Arm, and Shoulder

Fractures of the upper arm and shoulder can be distinguished from dislocations of the shoulder because the arm is held snugly against the chest. (When the shoulder is dislocated, the forearm can not be brought into contact with the chest.) In addition, the bone in the upper arm (humerus) is palpable throughout its entire length on the inner surface of the arm. Undisplaced fractures can be detected by gently running a finger along this bone.

Immobilization of fractures of the elbow, upper arm, and shoulder is best achieved with two slings. One supports the elbow, forearm, and hand. The second is tied around the body and holds the upper arm against the chest, which serves as the splint (fig. 7-3). The elbow should not be flexed more than ninety degrees to avoid impairment of circulation. Should numbness of the little and ring fingers develop, the elbow should be padded to relieve pressure on the nerves located there. If only one triangular bandage is available, webbing or similar material can be substituted for one of the slings. A sling can be improvised by pinning the shirt sleeve to the front of the shirt with safety pins.

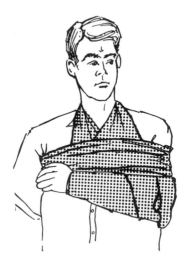

Figure 7-3. Forearm sling with an upper arm binder.

Collar Bone

Fractures of the collar bone (clavicle) usually can be felt by running a finger along the bone. Such fractures are less uncomfortable if the shoulders are held back. The shoulders can be splinted in this position by webbing or rope that is passed over the shoulder and under the armpit on opposite sides, forming a figure eight (fig. 7-4). The strapping should be applied over the subject's clothing, and the shoulders and armpits must be padded. The straps should be just tight enough for the person to be able to relieve pressure on his armpit by holding his shoulders back.

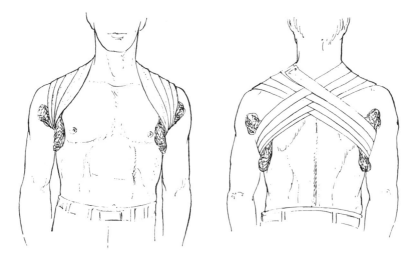

Figure 7-4. Figure-eight bandage for splinting a fractured collar bone.

SPECIFIC FRACTURES OF THE LOWER EXTREMITIES

Foot and Toes

Fractures of the small bones in the foot may be difficult to diagnose. Some fractures result from accidents that seem insignificant, such as stepping off a curb, and are associated with relatively little pain. If pain persists for several weeks, the injured person should consult a physician. Injuries of the toes and foot can be splinted by a well-fitting shoe or boot. Since they are usually wearing a boot when injured, fractures below the ankle are uncommon among climbers or skiers.

Fractures of the heel (calcaneus) result from a jump or fall when the individual lands flat-footed or on his heels on a hard surface. Pain usually prevents bearing weight on the injured foot during evacuation.

Ankle

Fractures of the ankle may be difficult to differentiate from sprains if the ankle is not dislocated. Swelling is often more severe with sprains. If pain in an injured ankle does not begin to subside in two or three days, the presence of a fracture should be assumed until x-rays can prove otherwise.

Ankle fractures can best be immobilized with a U-shaped splint that passes around the bottom of the foot and extends up along both sides of the leg. A flexible splint such as a Sam Splint® is ideal. Straightening may be necessary before a displaced or dislocated fractured ankle can be splinted and can best be achieved by applying gentle traction on both the heel and front part of the foot while rotating the foot and ankle into a more normal position.

A person with a minor injury, such as a fracture of the bony protuberance on the outside of the ankle (lateral malleolus) or a fracture of the bone in the foot just below the malleolus (fifth metatarsal), may be able to walk a considerable distance with a walking aid such as an ice axe after immobilization. An individual with a more severe injury may be able to hop short distances on the uninjured leg, but evacuation for distances greater than a few hundred yards usually requires a stretcher.

Lower Leg and Knee

Fractures of the lower leg are usually obvious if the tibia (the larger bone) or both bones are broken. Fractures of the fibula (the small bone on the outer side of the leg) may not be so apparent. Some individuals with a fibula fracture can walk gingerly on their injured leg.

Lower leg fractures should be immobilized in the same manner as fractures of the ankle, with a splint on either side of the leg or with an inflatable splint (fig. 7-1). Fractures that involve the knee require immobilization of the ankle and knee.

Kneecap

A fracture of the kneecap (patella) may be difficult to distinguish from a severe bruise. Occasionally the fracture severs the tendons that pull the leg forward. To immobilize such fractures, a splint that extends from the ankle to the hip should be applied. A cylindrical splint is best, but if material to make one is not available, a straight splint should be applied to the back of the leg. With his knee well splinted, the individual may be able to walk short distances.

Thigh

Fractures of the thigh (femur) are usually readily apparent due to pain and deformity. Adequate immobilization of a fractured thigh requires traction to control bleeding. The strong thigh muscles cause the bone ends to override and damage the surrounding tissues, resulting in severe hemorrhage. Traction stretches the muscles to their normal length and compresses the blood vessels—particularly veins—within them, limiting the bleeding. Compression over the fracture site with a circumferential dressing, such as an elastic bandage, also helps to control bleeding.

Traction is also required to control muscle spasms, which usually begin within an hour after the fracture, move the bone ends, and can be very painful.

Traction splints consist of a padded ring or half-ring attached to a metal frame. The ring fits snugly against the buttock and is held in place by a strap that passes over the front of the leg at the groin. The frame is composed of metal rods that extend along both sides of the leg and are joined by a crosspiece beyond the foot (fig. 7-5).

When a splint of this type is to be applied, the individual's shoe or boot should be left in place, the ankle should be carefully padded to prevent obstruction of the blood supply to the foot, and a figure-eight bandage similar to that used for

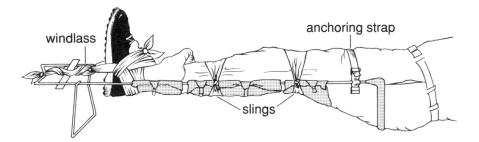

Figure 7-5. Fractured thigh immobilized by a Thomas splint.

sprained ankles should be placed over the boot and padded ankle. The leg should be gently lifted by pulling on the foot, and the splint should be slipped into place and secured at the groin. A hitch slipped under the figure-eight bandage should be looped over the crosspiece of the metal frame and tied. A rod inserted through this hitch can be twisted to apply traction on the leg. The pull should only be strong enough to prevent the foot and leg from sagging when the splint is lifted, but the hitch has to be tightened periodically as the thigh muscles relax and lengthen.

Bandages should be used as hammocks to support the leg in the splint, and one bandage must completely surround the leg to prevent swinging from side to side. The lower end of the splint should be elevated so that no pressure is on the person's heel. The individual is more comfortable, particularly during a long evacuation, if the knee is flexed five to ten degrees.

Pain in the foot after the splint has been applied indicates that the blood supply to the foot has been impaired. The figure-eight bandage must be disassembled at once and the ankle more carefully protected. Permanent injury, which may be more crippling than the fracture, can result if the circulation is not adequately protected. Such injury is more likely when traction splinting lasts overnight or longer. In a cold environment careful attention to the circulation is required to avoid frostbite.

Well-equipped rescue groups and wilderness expeditions should probably carry one or more Kendrick traction devices or Sager traction splints. However, a makeshift traction splint can be made from two ski poles. The wrist straps can be hooked together and slipped up against the buttock like the half-ring of a manufactured splint. A handkerchief or strap can be used to tie the hand grips together across the front of the thigh like the belt on a standard splint. Bandages tied between the poles support the leg, and the hitch around the ankle is hooked to the baskets or ends of the ski poles.

Other materials can be used similarly to improvise a traction splint. Ordinary splints that do not apply traction, such as those for fractures of the ankle and lower leg, should not be used for fractures of the thigh because they do not control bleeding or prevent muscle spasms. If materials to improvise a nontraction splint are available, they can be used for a traction splint.

An individual with a fractured thigh must be evacuated, preferably in a basket stretcher and by mechanical means, such as a helicopter. Since the basket stretcher must be carried to the injured person, a traction splint can be carried along. If avoidable, improvised splints should not be used during evacuation.

Hip

Fractures of the hip or its socket may be very difficult to diagnose. Shortening of the leg and rotation to the outside, the typical signs of a fractured hip, may not be present if the fracture is not displaced. If a fracture is suspected, the individual must not be permitted to walk on the injured leg.

Such fractures require no splinting other than binding the legs together.

SPECIFIC FRACTURES OF THE TRUNK

Pelvis

Fractures of the pelvis should be suspected following violent accidents, particularly if side-to-side or front-to-back pressure over the pelvis causes pain. Blood loss of major proportions is inevitable with pelvic fractures, is rarely evident when the subject is examined, but commonly produces shock and may be lethal. Therapy for shock should be instituted if a pelvic fracture is suspected.

Splinters of bone from pelvic fractures frequently damage the organs within the pelvis, particularly the urinary bladder. This complication should be suspected if the individual fails to void or passes only a few drops of bloody urine after the injury. (Injuries of the bladder are discussed in Chapter Fourteen, "Abdominal Injuries.")

No splinting is required for pelvic fractures because the muscles around the pelvis hold the bone fragments in place. The subject should be placed on a stretcher in a supine position and should be evacuated without being permitted to sit up or stand.

Vertebral Column Fractures

Fractures of the vertebral column (spine) in the back and neck are always accompanied by the possibility of injury to the enclosed spinal cord. The higher the level at which the fracture occurs, the greater is the risk of serious nervous system damage.

Pain or tenderness along the spine or anywhere in the neck following a fall should arouse concern about a vertebral fracture. Occasionally such fractures present areas of swelling or discoloration similar to fractures elsewhere. Unusual prominence of one of the vertebral spines is sometimes found. However, pain alone demands that the existence of a fracture be assumed.

If an accident victim is unconscious, the presence of a cervical fracture must be assumed. Approximately fifteen percent of accident victims with a head injury severe enough to produce prolonged unconsciousness have fractures of the cervical vertebrae.

Spinal cord damage is often associated with pain that typically radiates to the front of the body or down the arms or legs. Numbness, tingling, and partial or complete paralysis may also be present. However, the vertebral column is commonly fractured without injuring the underlying cord, and the absence of symptoms of spinal cord damage is by no means evidence that a fracture has not occurred. Cord damage resulting from inadequate fracture precautions would turn an unfortunate accident into a genuine catastrophe. Paralysis resulting from a spinal cord injury is usually permanent.

The American Red Cross recommends that "amateurs" not try to evacuate a person suspected to have a vertebral fracture. Transportation should be delayed until a cervical collar, a body board, a basket stretcher, and emergency medical technicians experienced with their use have been brought to the scene of the accident. Within North America and Europe such advice is excellent and should be followed if at all possible. However, in most of the rest of the world emergency medical technicians and the necessary equipment are not available.

During evacuation, a person with a confirmed or suspected vertebral fracture must be secured so that his body does not roll or twist as it is moved over rough terrain. A rigid support such as a metal basket or a broad wooden board is essential. A rolled-up jacket or similar object should be placed under the small of the back to support the spine in that area. With injuries of the neck, a cervical collar must be installed or padding must be placed on both sides of the head and neck to prevent the head from rolling from side to side (fig. 7-6).

An individual with spinal cord damage and paralysis requires special attention during evacuation, particularly when evacuation takes more than twenty-four hours. Special care must be given to the areas that support the body's weight—heels,

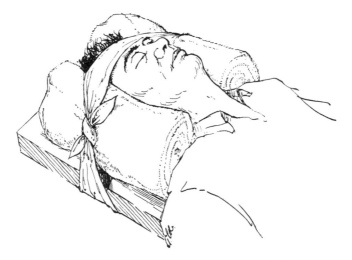

Figure 7-6. Technique for immobilizing the head for a subject with fractured cervical vertebrae.

buttocks, shoulders, and elbows. Pressure on these areas does not allow blood to circulate through the tissues. Normally such deprivation of the blood supply results in pain and the person shifts his position. Individuals with spinal cord injuries may not be able to feel pain and may not be able to shift position. After a few hours of being deprived of blood the tissues in these areas die, eventually resulting in ulcers known as "bed sores." To avoid this complication, the pressure points, particularly the heels and buttocks, must be carefully padded. Furthermore, this padding must be rearranged every two hours, day and night. The prevention of bed sores, which heal very poorly and are difficult to cure, requires diligent and devoted nursing care.

Most vertebral fractures that damage the spinal cord paralyze the urinary bladder and large intestine. Bladder care requires repeated catheterizations at least every eight hours or the insertion of an indwelling catheter.

OTHER FRACTURES

Rib fractures are discussed in Chapter Eleven, "Chest Injuries"; skull fractures and fractures of the face and jaw are discussed in Chapter Sixteen, "Head and Neck Injuries."

DISLOCATIONS

A dislocation is an injury in which the normal relationships of a joint are disrupted. The bone may be forced out of a socket, as occurs in dislocations of the shoulder, elbow, or hip. But some joints, like those between the bones in the fingers, have no socket, and the joint surfaces are simply displaced. Bones may be fractured and adjacent nerves, blood vessels, and supportive structures may be injured.

The signs of dislocation are similar to those of a fracture: pain that is aggravated by motion, tenderness, swelling, discoloration, limitation of motion, and deformity of the joint. The findings are localized to the area around a joint, but comparison with the opposite, uninjured joint may be necessary to be certain that a definite abnormality is present. Frequently, the dislocated joint appears larger than normal due to overlapping of the bone ends. Pain and muscle spasm usually prevent use of the extremity for physical activities.

Dislocations should be reduced. The risk of causing additional damage is quite small, and any existing fractures of the joint surface will be better aligned after reduction. Furthermore, dislocations should be reduced as quickly as possible. The muscles surrounding a dislocated joint go into spasm quickly. The chances for successful correction of the dislocation decrease and the risk of further injury increases with the passage of time after injury.

Other advantages of early reduction of a dislocation are:

- Pain relief is often dramatic.
- The risk of circulatory or neural damage is reduced.
- Immobilization of the joint is easier.
- Transportation of the victim is easier.

Pain, pallor or cyanosis, swelling, numbness, or the absence of pulses beyond the dislocation are indicative of obstruction of the blood supply. Entrapment or compression of arteries is particularly likely to occur with dislocations of the elbow or knee. Prompt action may be required to save the limb from gangrene.

The individual performing the reduction should use other members of the party if they can help. He must ensure that the subject understands and agrees with what he is attempting, why, and the technique he plans to use. Strong analgesics (intramuscular or intravenous morphine or meperidine) are helpful; diazepam (Valium) promotes relaxation of the muscles and the subject. Traction must be gentle and steady; forceful, jerking maneuvers must be avoided.

After any dislocation is reduced, the extremity should be splinted in the same manner it would be for a fracture. It may need to be immobilized for two to three weeks—sometimes longer.

Fingers

Dislocations of the fingers most commonly are displaced in an anterior-posterior direction, occur most commonly at the second joint, are usually obvious, and may be corrected quite easily immediately after the injury. Reduction is best accomplished by holding the digit in a slightly flexed position and applying traction to the tip while pushing the end of the dislocated bone back into place (fig. 7-7).

Figure 7-7. Technique for reducing a finger dislocation.

Dislocations at the base of the index finger and at the base of the thumb may not be reducible. With such injuries, the end of the bone is often entrapped by surrounding ligaments and tendons, and surgery is required for reduction. An initial effort to reduce such dislocations should be made, but if unsuccessful, the hand should be splinted in the position of function and the patient evacuated.

After reduction, an injured finger can be splinted effectively by taping it to an adjacent uninjured finger.

Elbow

Dislocation of an elbow is usually obvious, particularly when compared with the uninjured elbow. Most dislocations are posterior, and the tip of the dislocated ulna is very apparent. Movement of the joint is restricted.

Elbow dislocations may be difficult to reduce. The slightly flexed forearm should be pulled downward while the upper arm is pulled upward by an assistant. A considerable amount of force is usually needed. As the joint separates, any sideways displacement of the bones should be corrected first. The forearm may need to be rocked back and forth very gently. If the joint is not fully reduced, gentle bending of the elbow may complete the correction. The ability to flex the elbow to ninety degrees or more is proof of reduction.

Immediately after the dislocation has been reduced, the pulse at the wrist should be checked. If the pulse is absent but the color of the hand is normal and pain is diminished, the absence is probably the result of arterial spasm for which nothing needs to be done. If the pulse is absent, the hand is dark or cyanotic, and pain is increasing, the artery to the forearm may have been entrapped when the bones of the elbow slipped back into position. The joint should be slightly separated again with traction (not dislocated again) and gently rocked back and forth to free the entrapped structures.

The arm and hand should be splinted, with the elbow at a ninety-degree angle. Pulse and sensation should be checked again after the splint is applied. The elbow must not be wrapped circumferentially with tape or bandages because swelling does occur and, if confined, compresses blood vessels and nerves. Fracture of the bones of the elbow commonly occurs with the dislocation. A physician should be consulted as soon as possible, particularly if pain persists.

Shoulder

Shoulder dislocations result from strong jerks when the arm is rotated outward and held away from the body. A typical situation is a kayaker thrusting back and downward with his paddle (fig. 7-8). Many individuals have recurrent dislocations, can readily identify the injury, and often are helpful with reduction.

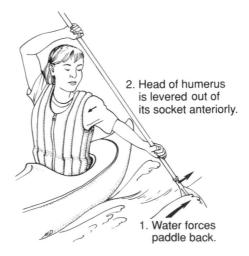

Figure 7-8. Mechanism of shoulder dislocation by a kayaker.

Most shoulder dislocations are anterior (fig. 7-9). Subjects are in pain and hold the upper arm and forearm away from the body in various positions, but the arm can not be brought into contact with the chest. (With a fractured humerus, the arm is usually held snugly against the chest.) The absence of the end of the humerus in the joint, which is located just lateral to the collar bone and below the tip of the shoulder, may be most easily recognized by loss of the normal roundness or fullness, particularly when compared with the opposite shoulder (fig. 7-10).

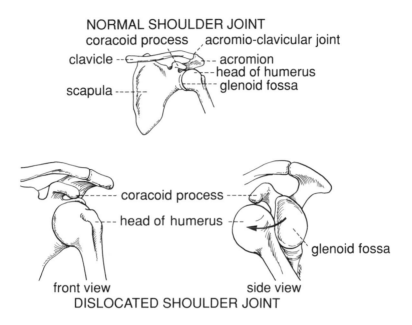

Figure 7-9. Normal and dislocated shoulder joints.

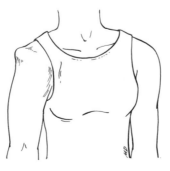

Figure 7-10. Appearance of a shoulder after anterior dislocation.

Posterior shoulder dislocations are rare and are often difficult to diagnose. The forearm and upper arm are typically held across the chest in contact with the chest wall. The forearm can not be externally rotated away from the chest. A defect is usually present in the normal contour of the deltoid muscle, which forms the outer point of the shoulder, and the head of the bone in the upper arm (humerus) sometimes can be palpated posteriorly.

Of the many methods for reducing a dislocated shoulder, two appear to combine the best chance for success with the least risk of additional injury.

The first requires traction applied by someone else. The subject should be lying flat with the injured arm held straight out from the side of the body. (A table for the subject to lie on would provide the best positioning, but a wilderness situation requires improvisation.) The subject's arm should be flexed at the elbow and the forearm held in a vertical position. A loop of webbing, clothing, or similar material that has been tied loosely around the attendant's waist should be slipped over the arm and down to the elbow. After padding the elbow, the attendant standing just beyond the elbow and facing the subject can apply traction by simply leaning backward. A second person must hold the subject, preferably with a loop of clothing around the chest, to prevent movement of his entire body by the traction (fig. 7-11).

Communication with the subject helps him achieve maximal relaxation. The humerus may be gently rotated by moving the forearm from side to side, and the head of the humerus may be gently pushed toward the socket with the fingers of the opposite hand. After a few minutes, reduction can be recognized by the palpable settling of the humeral head into its fossa and is heralded by the relief of the subject, who is immediately more comfortable. If the forearm can be swung across the body and placed in contact with the chest wall, reduction has been achieved.

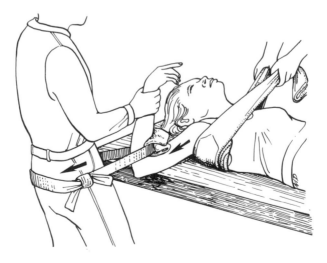

Figure 7-11. Technique for reduction of a shoulder dislocation
with active traction.

A second method to restore the dislocated bone to its normal position is to attach a ten- to fifteen-pound weight to the individual's forearm or wrist (fig. 7-12). The person must be lying face downward on a flat surface with the injured arm dangling straight down. After a somewhat longer time than required by the first technique, the constant pull by the weight tires the muscles surrounding the shoulder, causing them to relax and permit the bone to slip back into its socket.

If a dislocated shoulder is not corrected within an hour, traction should be discontinued, the arm splinted, and the subject evacuated.

Following reduction of a shoulder dislocation, the arm should be immobilized for at least two weeks, preferably three, with two slings, one supporting the forearm and hand and the other holding the upper arm against the body. A recurrent dislocation of the shoulder may not require such long immobilization. The ultimate treatment of repeated shoulder dislocations is surgical repair of the lax ligaments that allow the dislocation, which may occur with disabling frequency after insignificant trauma until reparative surgery is performed.

Dislocated shoulders sometimes can not be reduced, and the discomfort makes rapid evacuation necessary. When the shoulder is dislocated, the arm is held in an awkward position that makes splinting difficult. Successful techniques use a strap or bandage to anchor the hand on top of the head. Sometimes the hand is held close to this position spontaneously, but the muscles soon tire, producing increased pain in the muscles and in the shoulder. On ski slopes, effective splinting has been achieved with a rolled-up blanket secured in a figure-eight position like the splint for a fractured clavicle, with the bulk of the blanket in the armpit to support the upper arm (fig. 7-13). In more remote wilderness settings, a similar splint would have to be devised.

Figure 7-12. Technique for reduction of a shoulder dislocation with passive traction.

Figure 7-13." Technique for reduction for splinting a dislocated shoulder that cannot be reduced."

Hip

Most hip dislocations are posterior and result from falls with the hip flexed. The force of impact transmitted longitudinally through the knee and femur drives the hip backward out of its socket. Strong forces are required to produce such injuries. Impact of the knees with the dashboard in an automobile accident is a common cause. Anterior hip dislocations are most commonly produced by falls in which the individual lands directly on the outer aspect of his hip.

With a posterior dislocation the hip is bent and the leg is rotated so that the knee is pulled upward and inward over the opposite leg. With an anterior dislocation the hip may be bent backward or forward, but the leg is rotated so that the knee is turned outward and pulled away from the body (fig. 7-14). The key diagnostic clue with both types of dislocation is that returning the leg to a normal position for splinting or transportation in a stretcher is impossible. The position of the leg helps differentiate dislocations from fractures of the hip or thigh, with which the leg lies flat. Reducing a dislocated hip is difficult and painful for the subject, but is worth attempting because reduction relieves pain, improves circulation to the femur, and greatly facilitates placement of the person in a basket stretcher and evacuation.

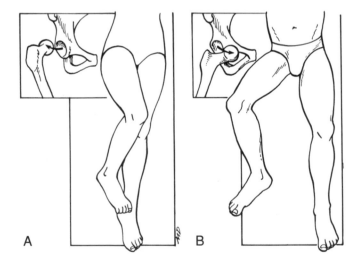

A   B

Figure 7-14. Posterior and anterior hip dislocations.

The technique for reduction is the same for anterior and posterior dislocations. Two attendants are required. One holds the subject flat on the ground with his hands on both sides of the subject's pelvis. The other straddles the injured leg and gently flexes the knee and hip to ninety degrees. After bending his knees and locking his hand behind the subject's knee, the second attendant can apply strong upward traction by simply straightening his legs (fig. 7-15). The weight of the subject and the first attendant provide countertraction. Rotating the hip by moving the lower leg gently from side to side may help with reduction.

After reduction, the injured leg must be splinted to the opposite leg. Gentle traction is beneficial if available; the subject should be transported in a supine position.

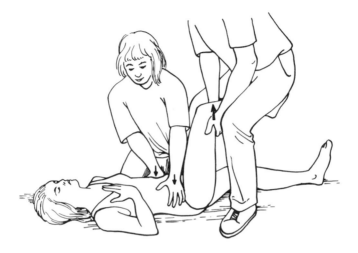

Figure 7-15. Technique for reducing a hip dislocation.

Knee

Knee dislocations are major, sometimes disastrous injuries that result from forceful impact with the knee bent. In most instances, the ligaments and tendons around the knee are so extensively torn that the dislocated knee pops back into position spontaneously. The nature of the injury can be recognized by the pain and instability of the knee. If the knee remains dislocated, reduction can usually be achieved quite readily with traction on the lower leg. Pulses and sensation in the foot must be checked. Injury to the large vessels behind the knee occurs frequently. Such damage is suggested by painful swelling behind the knee developing immediately or hours after correction of the deformity and is confirmed by the absence of pulses. The leg should be splinted as securely as possible, although care must be taken not to interfere with circulation. Dislocated knees are too unstable for walking over rough terrain.

Kneecap

Dislocations of the kneecap (patella) frequently are recurrent, much like shoulder dislocations. The kneecap is usually displaced to the outside, and the knee is held in a flexed position for comfort. Comparison with the opposite knee typically makes the abnormality obvious.

To reduce the dislocation, the leg should be gently straightened while the kneecap is pushed back into place. Straightening alone may be adequate.

The leg should be splinted as if the patella were fractured, but individuals are usually able to walk on the injured leg.

Ankle

Dislocated ankles are usually associated with fractures of the adjacent bones. They should be reduced and treated the same as fractures.

Jaw

An individual can become so completely relaxed while asleep that his jaw falls downward and slips out of its socket. When the subject awakens he finds that he can not close his mouth. In a remote situation, the resulting inability to swallow could lead to serious difficulties. Usually such complete relaxation follows the use of sleeping pills or overindulgence in alcohol.

Dislocations of the jaw can be safely reduced, usually rather easily. Both thumbs should be inserted over the molars of the subject's lower jaw and pressed directly downward (fig. 7-16). Considerable force is required to overcome the spasm in the jaw muscles, which are quite strong, but the jaw should slip back into place without too much difficulty. (The thumbs should be padded to prevent bites as the jaw pops back into its socket.) After reduction, persistent pain in the joint, which is located just in front of the ear, may be indicative of a fracture, and a physician should be consulted. If dislocations recur, the individual can wear a bandage to hold his mouth closed when he is asleep. The bandage should cover the tip of the chin and should be tied over the top of the head and around the back of the neck.

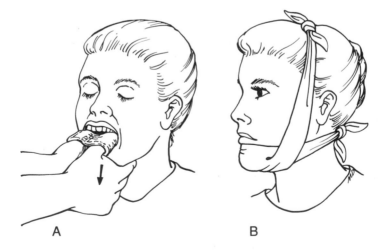

A   B

Figure 7-16. Technique for reducing a jaw dislocation and bandaging the jaw to prevent recurrence.

OTHER INJURIES OF BONE AND RELATED STRUCTURES

Contusions of Bone and Subperiosteal Hematomas

A blow that does not produce a fracture or dislocation may still cause sufficient damage to produce swelling in the fibrous bone sheath (periosteum) or bleeding between that tissue and the rigid portion of the bone (subperiosteal hematoma). The injured person complains of pain, the area is tender, and the bone may appear or feel larger than normal.

Treatment for the first twenty-four hours following injury consists of cooling, a pressure bandage, and immobilization. After twenty-four hours, local heat should be applied, and activity can be allowed to the limits of pain tolerance. However, if a fracture or dislocation can not be ruled out, immobilization should be continued.

Sprains and Strains

Sprains and strains are stretching, tearing, or avulsing injuries of ligaments around a joint and often can not be differentiated from fractures without x-rays. They can be as disabling as broken bones. The signs are similar to a fracture, although grating of broken bone ends and deformity are not present. Swelling is often quite marked, and discoloration may also be present. If an injury is obviously severe, the wisest course is to treat it as a fracture.

The treatment for sprains is summarized in the acronym "RICE," which stands for rest, ice, compression, and elevation. Applying cold immediately after an injury reduces hemorrhage and swelling. An elastic bandage can partially immobilize a small joint such as an ankle and applies compression that helps limit swelling. Absorption of blood and edema fluid can be promoted by elevating the injured area. Later, heat may be helpful, but it should not be applied until at least three days after the injury. Motion and use may speed recovery, but only when resumed after the initial swelling and hemorrhage have subsided.

Sprained ankles are the most common injuries of this type, and circumstances frequently require the subject to walk (hobble?) from the injury site. In most situations the ankle should be supported by a figure-eight bandage put on over the shoe or boot. Loops of the figure eight should pass around the back of the heel and under the sole of the foot, crossing on top of the foot. Support must be snug but must not obstruct the circulation. The individual can no longer rely on the injured ankle, and the risk of further damage is significant.

If the ankle is to be taped, alternate interlacing layers of tape should be placed under the heel and straight up the leg, and around the back of the heel and straight out over the foot (fig. 7-17). Tape must not completely surround the leg, or swelling (which could result just from immobilization) would impair blood circulation to the foot.

One of the most common downhill skiing injuries is a strain or tear of the ligaments of the knee. Occasionally the cartilage that covers the joint surfaces is injured also. The knee should be splinted as if it were fractured, but the person may be able to walk after the knee has been immobilized. If standing or walking

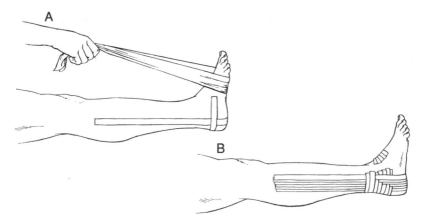

Figure 7-17. Technique for taping a sprained ankle after healing has begun. (The foot should be held perpendicular to the leg while the tape is being applied. The ankle should be taped only for the first three or four days of use after healing is under way.)

is painful, the individual should be evacuated by sled or stretcher. Such injuries frequently require a cast and four to six weeks or more to heal.

Muscle and Tendon Tears

A sudden, strong jerk with the bones and joints fixed in position, as occurs at the end of a fall, may rip a muscle from its insertion or may partially or completely tear the body of the muscle or tendon. Muscle tears or "pulls" can also result from vigorous activities such as sprinting at top speed and from sudden movements or changes in direction. A penetrating injury may sever a muscle or tendon. Complete separation of the muscle, or its tendon and attachments, results in loss of its function. Incomplete separation seldom produces complete loss of function, but is painful and does predispose the structures to subsequent injury.

Insertions are the points at which muscles or tendons are attached to bone. The most common sites at which insertion injuries occur are the fingertips behind the nails, the shoulder, the elbow, and the ankle. Rupture of muscles and tendons more commonly occurs in the calf, the front and back of the thigh, and the upper portion of the arm and shoulder. Pain, tenderness, swelling, and loss of motion are the usual findings. Sometimes a defect in the muscle or tendon can be felt.

Prehospital treatment should include applying cold, immobilization, and rapid evacuation. Definitive repair of such injuries is most successful if performed within twenty-four hours of the accident.

Muscle Compartmental Syndromes

Some muscles are enveloped in a fibrous sheath, or "compartment," that is only slightly distensible. Swelling of the muscles as the result of unaccustomed exercise or trauma can raise the compartmental pressure to a level that impairs blood flow to the muscle. When deprived of its blood supply, the muscles die, usually crippling the extremity.

Compartmental syndromes are uncommon, but because they can produce permanent disability, they should be recognized and promptly treated. The anterior tibial muscle, which is located on the outside of the shin, is the muscle most commonly involved by compartmental compression. Most subjects have an obvious leg injury, typically a crushing injury. However, compartmental syndromes are insidious because they can develop following unaccustomed exercise. Occasionally pressure on the leg during a period of unconsciousness, or injuries such as burns, can produce this disorder. A few individuals have experienced previous episodes of milder pain, particularly following vigorous exercise.

The initial symptom is pain in the involved muscles, which typically is much more severe than would be expected from the injury or exercise by which it was preceded. Passive movement or stretching of the muscles is also painful. Usually the muscles are obviously swollen and the overlying skin is tense and glossy. However, the most diagnostic feature is severe weakness or paralysis of the involved muscles. A person with an anterior tibial compartmental syndrome can not flex his foot upward or resist pressure forcing it down. The foot may be cold and numb and the pulses may be weak, but such signs are inconsistent and their absence is not an indication that a compartmental syndrome is not present.

Outside of a hospital two maneuvers may be beneficial: any constricting clothing or bandages should be removed, and the extremity should be positioned at or above the level of the heart. However, the only effective treatment is surgically opening the compartment to relieve the pressure. Since surgeons alone are familiar with the technique and the anatomy, individuals with this disorder must be evacuated to a hospital.

Evacuation is urgent. Treatment must be prompt to avoid permanent paralysis. Only thirty-one percent of one group of subjects treated within twelve hours had residual disability; ninety-one percent of those decompressed later had permanent functional deficits, and twenty percent required amputations. The usual functional deficit is an inability to flex the foot upward, called "foot drop," which usually requires a brace to support the foot when walking on a flat surface. On a wilderness trail disability would be much greater.

Bursitis, Tendinitis, and Shin Splints

Bursitis, tendinitis, and shin splints are caused by inflammation of tendons or the flattened, cystlike spaces (bursae) that cushion the movement of tendons. These disorders are characterized by pain and stiffness that has a gradual onset, usually following unaccustomed use of a muscle for an extended length of time. The pain can be quite severe and frequently is first noticed the morning after such activities.

Splinting may relieve the immediate discomfort but often prolongs the problem. Moist heat and a mild analgesic may provide some relief; sometimes cold is more effective. The pain, which is rarely disabling, may persist for days, weeks, months, or years. Continued use of the joint through its full range of motion helps to prevent stiffness.

Tenosynovitis

Inflammation and infection of the sheaths that surround tendons and lubricate their movements may result from unaccustomed overuse or a penetrating injury. In the field, such infections may develop several days after a small cut or puncture wound that did not appear significant at the time, particularly on the hands, fingers, or feet. Pain with motion of the involved tendon is the diagnostic finding. When infection is present, painful swelling, increased warmth, and redness are apparent. A crackling sensation in the affected tissue may be felt with pressure or movement of the tendon. Although sterile inflammatory episodes caused by overuse usually subside with rest, an infected tenosynovitis requires the attention of a physician, who sometimes must surgically drain the tendon sheath. If infection is suspected, broad-spectrum antibiotics should be started and the subject evacuated without delay. Failure to obtain surgical treatment can result in permanent loss of mobility of the tendon, or extension of the infection to adjacent tendons and body spaces and even greater loss of function.

Joint Effusion

Swelling, mild discomfort, increased warmth, and redness may appear in a joint after an injury—sometimes without any preceding trauma. The knee is most commonly involved, but other joints, particularly the elbow or wrist, can be involved. The cause may be outside the joint, as with "tennis elbow" or a similar condition involving the insertion of the tendons just below and to the side of the kneecap. Within the joint, effusions often result from deterioration of the cartilage following repeated injury. If inflammation is present with no signs of infection, the discomfort and swelling may respond to rest, wrapping with an elastic bandage, moist heat, and a mild analgesic. An infected joint—manifested by more obvious redness, greater pain and swelling, and fever that is sometimes high— requires immediate care by a physician, particularly when the subject is febrile.

Ingrown Toenails

Ingrown toenails are best prevented by trimming the toenails straight across, without rounding the corners, and by wearing well-fitted boots and socks. If pain and redness occur during an outing, a wedge can be cut from the outer third of the nail. The offending sharp corner must be removed. Warm soaks hasten recovery; elevating the new corner of the nail with a pledget of gauze as it regrows may prevent recurrence.

Corns and Calluses

Corns and calluses should be prevented by wearing well-fitted shoes, but if they cause discomfort on an outing, they can be shaved flat with a razor blade after they have been softened by soaking in warm water.

BACK INJURIES

Strain and Spasm

Back pain is produced by a wide variety of disorders, such as carrying heavy loads, working in an unaccustomed stooped position, or sleeping in an awkward position. However, treatment is frequently frustrating. The measures that provide the greatest relief are sleeping on a firm support, such as a mattress with a sheet of plywood underneath, and applying heat to the affected area. When sleeping outdoors, a mat that provides insulation but little padding is best. Heat may help relieve muscle spasm. Mild analgesics may mask the pain, but codeine may sometimes be necessary. A few individuals have severe, incapacitating pain from muscle spasms.

Ruptured Disc

The vertebrae of the spinal column are separated by cushions of cartilaginous material. A ruptured disc is an extrusion of this semisolid material into the spinal canal so that it compresses the spinal cord or the nerves coming from the cord. The basic defect is degeneration and weakening of the ligaments that normally hold this cushion in place. Trauma is only the final incident. Unless the basic defect is present, trauma alone usually fractures the vertebrae instead of causing the disc to rupture.

Symptoms of a ruptured disc in the lumbo-sacral area are highly characteristic. Pain begins in the lower back, radiates to one side, and passes through the buttock and down the back of the leg. The pain may involve the outside of the leg but is rarely felt in the front or inner portion of the leg. The individual frequently walks with a decided limp. Pain when moving to and from a supine position is also characteristic.

As a result of the pain associated with movement, muscles in the lower back go into spasm. The vertebral column in the lower back is immobilized and does not bend when the person leans to either side, which can be seen when he is examined from behind. This muscle spasm can usually be palpated by an examiner's fingers. Loss of sensation to pin prick or to the light touch of a wisp of cotton may be present over the foot and lower leg on the affected side.

The treatment for a ruptured disc is the same as for strain of the back muscles. However, the two conditions should be differentiated since each has a quite different outlook. Strain usually clears up in a few days, or perhaps a few weeks, with rest and proper treatment. Although the pain of a ruptured disc sometimes disappears in a similar time with rest, it may be more prolonged and may be relieved only by surgery. Furthermore, a ruptured disc can produce permanent nerve injury and muscle weakness. Finally, even though symptoms disappear rather promptly, a recurrence is likely at any time.

In expedition circumstances these prognostic factors must be considered. Individuals with a previous history of a disc problem should consult an orthopedist or neurosurgeon before undertaking remote wilderness activities, particularly if evidence of sensory impairment is present.

CHAPTER EIGHT

BURNS

B urns can be divided into minor and major categories. Minor burns, such as burns of the hands or fingers by hot pots or stoves, are common, and their care is straightforward—although they must not be neglected. Major burns are rare in the wilderness. Possibly the greatest risk is at high altitudes when stoves are being used inside a tent. In these situations, fuel spills and even explosions occur, due both to the notoriously poor performance of stoves at high elevations and to hypoxic impairment of the individuals using them. Such accidents can be catastrophic if destruction of tents, sleeping bags, and clothing leaves people with severe burns exposed to a bitter environment.

Successful rescue of individuals with major burns from this kind of situation requires an incredible combination of medical knowledge, evacuation skills, dedication and determination, and sheer luck. The intravenous fluids and other supplies needed just to keep these individuals alive for the first twenty-four hours are almost never available in such circumstances. However, severe burns can occur in less remote circumstances, and few wilderness users would not try to provide the best care possible. Therefore, a discussion of the basic principles of medical care for subjects of major burns appears worthwhile, even though few opportunities for its successful application can be expected.

EVALUATING BURN SEVERITY

The severity of a burn is determined by its depth, size, and location. In the past, burns have been classified according to their depth as first, second, or third degree. First-degree burns were superficial, did not kill any of the tissues, and only produced redness of the skin. Second-degree burns damaged the upper portion of the skin, resulting in blisters. Third-degree burns destroyed the full thickness of the skin and could extend into the underlying tissues. This terminology has been modified, and first- and second-degree burns are currently lumped together as "partial thickness" because generally they are treated in the same manner. Third-degree burns are labeled "full thickness."

The area covered by the burn is of critical significance. Before the development of burn centers, few individuals survived full-thickness burns that covered more than fifty percent of their body surface. In contrast, few burns covering less than fifteen to twenty percent of the body are lethal when given proper care.

Location of the burn is also important. Burns of the face and neck, hands, or feet are more incapacitating due to the specialized organs and complex anatomy of these areas. Burns of the face may be associated with burns of the air passages or lungs, which often are lethal. Burns of the genitalia or buttocks are difficult to keep clean and usually develop severe infections.

BURN SHOCK

The life-threatening problem associated with major burns is shock—specifically "burn shock." When tissues are burned, the damaged capillaries allow blood serum to pour out into the burned tissues. This fluid loss reduces the blood volume and produces shock just like a major hemorrhage. A person with a major burn usually dies in shock within twelve to eighteen hours unless appropriate fluid therapy is instituted. Such fluids almost always must be administered intravenously. Individuals with severe burns are often unconscious or too stuporous to swallow fluids; if they can swallow, they often vomit anything taken by mouth; and if they are not vomiting, the fluids often remain in the stomach and are not absorbed. Since appropriate fluids are rarely available in wilderness situations, a major burn in a remote area usually requires immediate evacuation by the fastest means available.

EVACUATION

As a general rule, all full-thickness burns larger than one inch in diameter eventually require surgical therapy—debridement and skin grafting. Therefore the only decision that must be made for individuals with burns of that size or larger is how urgently they should be evacuated. Help with this decision can be obtained from the following criteria for the classification of burn injuries established by the American Burn Association and the American College of Surgeons:

Major

- Blistering partial-thickness burns of more than twenty-five percent of the body surface.
- Full-thickness burns of more than ten percent of the body surface.
- Significant burns of the critical areas: face, eyes, ears, hands, feet, or perineum (genitals and buttocks).
- Significant associated trauma or coexisting disease.

Moderate

- Blistering partial-thickness burns of fifteen to twenty-five percent of the body surface, with less than ten percent full-thickness burns, and no involvement of critical areas.

Mild

- Blistering partial-thickness burns of less than fifteen percent of the body surface, with less than two percent full-thickness burns, and no involvement of critical areas.

Individuals with moderate or major burns require hospitalization and must be evacuated. If intravenous fluids are not available, emergency evacuation is needed.

If any question exists about the severity of the burn, the person should be evacuated. Experts have difficulty determining whether a burn is partial or full thickness immediately after it occurs, and inexperienced persons almost always underestimate both the depth and the area. Persons with major burns are often deceptively alert for several hours until fluid losses become severe.

Many individuals with less extensive burns must also be evacuated, particularly with burns of the hands or face, but speed is not as crucial. Fluid loss occurs with all burns, both partial and full thickness, but in previously healthy young adults does not achieve life-threatening proportions if the burns cover less than ten to fifteen percent of the body surface.

Care of a seriously burned individual demands a major commitment of time and personnel. Only a large group would have enough members for some to continue the expedition while others took care of even one burned individual.

BURN WOUND CARE

Immediate Treatment

Immediately after the burn, all clothing and jewelry around the injury should be removed. If the burn is small and is not full thickness, immediate application of cold helps reduce the pain. Holding a towel soaked in ice water against the burned area or immersing the wound in cold, soapy water usually is effective. More extensive partial-thickness burns and full-thickness burns should not be treated in this manner. Full-thickness burns are usually painless because the nerves in the skin have been destroyed.

The burn, like any other open wound, should be cleaned and covered with a dressing. In the field, cleaning can best be done with sterile cotton, liquid soap, and warm, disinfected water. If these materials are not available, the burn should be cleaned in the best way possible. All debris, dirt, and fragments of loose skin must be removed. These measures are surprisingly painless if carried out gently.

The burn should be covered with a thin layer of an antibacterial ointment such as silver sulfadiazine in a petroleum jelly base (Silvadene®), over which should be layered gauze, a thick bulky dressing, and a snug bandage that applies pressure but does not interfere with blood circulation. The dressing or slings can be used to immobilize a burned extremity and reduce pain. Burned hands should be splinted in the "position of function," the position the hand assumes when holding a pencil.

Ointments or creams that do not contain appropriate antibacterial agents increase the risk of infection and should not be used.

Subsequent Care

The bandage should be left undisturbed for six to eight days. Changing the dressing increases the risk of introducing dirt and bacteria that could produce an infection. Furthermore, an accurate distinction between partial- and full-thickness burns can be made only about a week after the injury. If the burn is very superficial and no blisters are found when the bandage is removed, no further treatment is required. Subsequent bandaging would be needed only to protect a sensitive area from trauma.

Unbroken blisters generally should be left intact. However, the blister fluid is an ideal medium for bacterial growth, and blisters larger than eight centimeters (three inches) in diameter probably should be opened (without contamination) to reduce the potential for infection. A protective dressing should be applied to prevent rupture of smaller blisters and infection and should be changed every three or four days until healing is complete.

Full-thickness burns six to eight days old are covered by a thick, leathery layer of parched, dead skin that may range in color from white to dark brown or black. The dead skin is usually insensitive to touch. If the depth of the burn—whether it is partial or full thickness—is uncertain, gentle probing with a sterile needle or pin is a good way of testing.

If the burn is full thickness, it should be rebandaged and the subject evacuated. Even under ideal conditions these wounds almost always become infected. They require operative care, including skin grafting, which can be provided only in a hospital.

FLUID REPLACEMENT

The most urgent aspect of treatment for a major burn is the administration of fluids to prevent or treat shock.

Calculating Fluid Volumes

A convenient formula for determining the volume of intravenous fluids to be administered during the first twenty-four hours following a major burn is:

Weight (kg) × Percent Surface Area × 3 = Volume of Fluid to be Administered

The body weight in kilograms (2.2 pounds = 1 kilogram) multiplied by the percentage of the body surface covered by the burn, and that product multiplied by three equals the volume (in cc) of fluids to be given. The percentage of the body area covered by the burn can be estimated from figure 8-1.

The fluid requirements for the first twenty-four hours after a burn for an 80-kilogram (176-pound) man with a thirty percent body surface area burn (approximately one arm and one leg) would be:

80 (kg) × 30 (%) × 3 = 7,200 cc

Approximately half of this fluid should be given in the first eight hours of treatment; the remainder should be given over the next sixteen hours. Although opinions

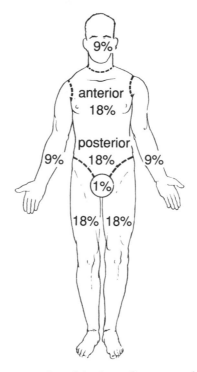

Figure 8-1. Percentage of total body surface area of various portions of the body.

differ about the ideal composition of the fluids, in a wilderness situation saline or Ringer's lactate are almost certain to be the only fluids available.

MONITORING

The calculations above illustrate the tremendous volume of fluids required, but such exact volumes can not be given indiscriminately because the severity of the vascular injury produced by the burn and the functional capacity of the subject's heart and kidneys vary widely. (In some burn centers, the product of body weight times burn area is multiplied by four instead of three.) Careful monitoring of the response to the fluids is just as essential as the calculations. Failure to give enough fluid can lead to shock; administering too much can overload the cardiovascular system and lead to heart failure, particularly in older individuals who already have reduced cardiac reserve. A fine line separates inadequate fluid replacement and overload, and at high altitudes the margin of safety is even narrower.

If the person remains confused or stuporous (in the absence of a head injury), his blood pressure is below normal, his pulse is weak and rapid, and his urinary output is below 50 cc per hour after several hours of treatment, fluids must be administered more rapidly and perhaps in larger quantities. Excessive fluid administration is indicated by a urinary output greater than 75 cc per hour; subcutaneous fluid accumulation causing swelling in unburned tissues, particularly in the legs or over the sacrum; or a pooling of fluid in the lungs that produces unusual shortness of breath. If these signs are present, the rate of fluid administration must be slowed, occasionally drastically. An indwelling urinary catheter is helpful for monitoring urinary output.

Other Considerations

Fluid requirements for individuals with burns covering more than fifty percent of the body surface should be calculated as if the burn were limited to a fifty percent area. Larger fluid volumes overload the heart if given within twenty-four hours.

A severely burned person is usually thirsty, as are most individuals in shock, but thirst should be controlled with intravenous fluids, because fluids given orally usually cause vomiting and still greater fluid loss. (Fluids lost by vomiting must also be replaced with Ringer's lactate or saline.)

Subsequent Fluid Therapy

During the first twenty-four hours after a burn, Ringer's lactate or saline solutions should be used to replace the fluid and sodium lost into the burned tissues. Thereafter, five percent glucose should be used for fluid replacement. (Few expeditions carry such fluids, but in some popular trekking areas, such as the southern approach to Everest, some fluids left behind by expeditions are available.)

Once shock has been prevented or corrected, fluid requirements are somewhat greater than normal, but not on the enormous scale of the first day after the burn. Also, the subject may be able to take fluids by mouth, with only small (one- or two-liter) intravenous supplements. As always, urine volume is an excellent indicator of fluid status.

By the second or third day after the burn, the blood vessels in the burned tissues begin to recover and the fluids lost into those tissues are reabsorbed and excreted by the kidneys. Large volumes of urine may be passed, but in this recovery stage, fluid intake should not be restricted because the urinary output is high. Fruit juices that have a high potassium content may be particularly beneficial at this time.

Control of Pain

Inexperienced persons often are horrified by the appearance of a major burn and mistakenly administer unneeded pain medications, thinking the wound must be painful. However, the pain from a burn is quite variable. Superficial burns hurt initially but are usually relatively painless once they are covered and not exposed to air. Full-thickness burns are usually less painful because they destroy the nerves and produce anesthesia in the area of injury. In addition, shock tends to dull the pain. If the individual complains, pain should be controlled with as little medication as possible. Drugs stronger than a moderate analgesic are rarely needed. If a strong analgesic is necessary, a smaller dose (one-half to three-fourths the usual dose) should be tried before resorting to a full dose. Strong analgesics may aggravate the general effects of the burn and are almost never needed. Furthermore, if the individual is in shock when the drugs are administered, they are poorly absorbed; if they are absorbed later, when the shock is corrected, an overdose can result.

Facial Burns

Burns around the face and neck are particularly dangerous because the flames and hot smoke may be inhaled, damaging the lungs. Persons with such injuries must be evacuated with extreme urgency. Burns of the face, nose, mouth, and upper respiratory tract cause swelling and obstruction of the airway. Treatment requires intubation with an endotracheal or nasotracheal tube or creation of an alternate airway by tracheostomy or crichothyroidostomy. If the flames and smoke reach the lower portion of the respiratory tract and the lungs are seared, no effective treatment is possible outside of a hospital. If the subject survives the initial injury, the burn and smoke cause fluid to collect in the lung in quantities that are often lethal. Subsequently, severe pneumonia is common. Fortunately such injuries are rare.

Burns of the upper airway should be anticipated after any facial burn, particularly if the skin around the nose and mouth is burned or the nasal hairs are singed. The subject typically becomes hoarse and begins to have difficulty breathing. Wheezes may be heard when listening to his chest. The most critical sign of an airway burn is coughing up black, sooty material, which should be considered diagnostic. Sometimes these signs do not become detectable until twenty-four to forty-eight hours after the injury, so individuals with facial burns must be closely watched.

Oxygen

Oxygen, if available, should probably be administered immediately to all individuals with severe burns at high elevations. Burns can reduce respiratory effectiveness, and at high altitudes such persons may not be able to breathe rapidly and deeply enough to compensate for environmental hypoxia. A fire in enclosed quarters such as a small tent, in which air circulation may be further reduced by a covering of snow, produces large amounts of carbon monoxide. An individual burned in such circumstances may have to cope with a reduced oxygen-carrying capacity of his blood due to carbon monoxide poisoning regardless of the altitude. Oxygen may be life-saving until the subject can be evacuated to lower altitudes, particularly for the first hour or two after the burn while the carbon monoxide is being eliminated.

Additional Measures

To prevent secondary streptococcal infection, penicillin G should be administered to individuals with major burns every six hours until they are in the care of a physician.

Individuals with burns covering more than twenty to twenty-five percent of their body surface usually develop paralysis of the stomach and intestine. Since they continue to swallow air and saliva, the paralyzed stomach becomes distended, and they vomit. To avoid these problems, a nasogastric tube should be inserted, if one is available, and gastric suction should be instituted. (See Appendix B, "Therapeutic Procedures.") Fluids lost through the nasogastric tube should be replaced with intravenous Ringer's lactate or saline solution.

Dehydration following a burn, caused by the outpouring of fluids into the tissues, greatly increases the risk of thrombophlebitis (see Chapter Ten, "Respiratory System Disorders"). This complication should be anticipated and appropriately treated if it occurs. However, prevention—by administering the required fluids and avoiding dehydration—is far more desirable.

CHAPTER NINE

HEART AND BLOOD VESSEL DISORDERS

The heart and blood vessels circulate blood, which transports oxygen and nutrients to the body tissues and carries away carbon dioxide and "wastes." The heart consists of a four-chambered pump: right atrium, right ventricle, left atrium, and left ventricle. Blood travels from the left ventricle through the aorta and through repeatedly branching smaller and smaller arteries until it enters capillaries barely large enough to permit passage of single red blood cells. In the capillaries, oxygen, carbon dioxide, and other substances are exchanged between blood and tissue. From the capillaries, blood flows through larger and larger veins to return through the right atrium into the right ventricle. Blood is then pumped from the right ventricle through the lungs, where it replaces the oxygen it has lost and gives off carbon dioxide. It returns through the pulmonary veins and the left atrium to the left ventricle (fig. 9-1).

Four valves permit the heart to function as an efficient pump. The tricuspid and mitral valves in the right and left ventricles close during cardiac contraction (systole), preventing reflux of blood into the atria. Simultaneously the pulmonic and aortic valves open, permitting blood to be pumped into the pulmonary artery and aorta. After systole has been completed and the heart muscle relaxes (diastole), the pulmonic and aortic valves close, preventing reflux of arterial blood into the ventricles, and the tricuspid and mitral valves open, allowing the ventricles to fill.

Valves are also located in veins. Compression of peripheral veins by contracting muscles, and low pressure within the chest produced by inspiration, produce a pressure gradient that moves blood from the extremities toward the heart. Venous valves prevent backflow when pressures change.

Delicate receptors sense blood volume, as well as oxygen and carbon dioxide concentrations, and adjust cardiac output (heart rate and the volume of each heartbeat) and the amount of blood supplied to different areas of the body.

PHYSICAL EXAMINATION OF THE CARDIOVASCULAR SYSTEM

Simple methods for examining the functions of the heart and circulatory system can provide highly significant information, even for inexperienced examiners.

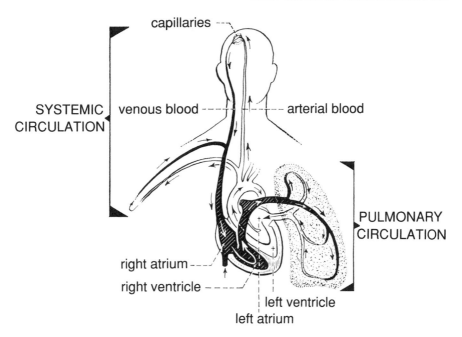

Figure 9-1. Diagram of the circulation of the blood.

The examination should include:

- Determining heart rate and rhythm
- Judging arterial and venous pressure
- Evaluating the peripheral circulation
- Listening to the heart and lungs

Heart Rate and Rhythm

The heart rate can be measured most conveniently in the wrist at the base of the thumb, where pulsations in the radial artery can be felt. The pulsations are usually counted for fifteen or twenty seconds and multiplied by four or three to obtain the rate per minute. (Longer counts, sometimes as long as two or three minutes, may be needed for individuals with irregular rhythms.)

In some subjects, particularly those in shock, radial artery pulsations may be too weak to count, and the carotid or femoral pulse must be sought. The carotid pulse can be found on either side of the neck in the groove between the thyroid cartilage (Adam's apple) and the prominent muscle that extends from behind the ear to the top of the sternum (breastbone.) The femoral pulse can be found in the fold where the leg meets the abdomen about midway between the center of the pubic area and the lateral bony edge of the hip. Clothing must be removed before the femoral pulse can be palpated.

If shock is so severe that no pulses can be felt, the heart rate can be determined by listening with a stethoscope placed between the left nipple and the sternum. Each heartbeat is accompanied by two heart sounds of slightly different tone (lub-dup, lub-dup). Occasionally a faint third sound may be heard (lub-dup-dup, lub-dup-dup). Although heart sounds in normal subjects can be heard with the unaided ear pressed against the chest, the heart sounds are usually faint in shock and a stethoscope is often needed. A little prior practice by the examiner—even listening to his own heart—is useful.

The normal resting heart rate ranges from fifty (in a few well-conditioned individuals) to ninety beats per minute. The heart rate is slower during sleep. At high altitude the resting heart rate may be as high as 100 beats per minute during the first few days of acclimatization.

Normally the heart rhythm is regular, but in young individuals may change with respiration—speeding up during inspiration and slowing during expiration. Such variation is normal; having the subject hold his breath causes the rhythm to become completely regular.

Arterial and Venous Pressure

When the pulse is barely palpable, the blood pressure is usually low. Strong, "bounding" pulses usually indicate a normal blood pressure and normal heart action. Arterial pulses are usually equal in both wrists, both sides of the neck, and both sides of the groin. Absence of a pulse on one side indicates arterial obstruction or injury.

When healthy persons are lying flat, the partially or fully filled neck veins can be seen extending from the middle of the clavicle (collar bone) to just below the lower jaw. When the subject is sitting upright or even partially upright (semirecumbent), filled neck veins should not be visible above the clavicle. Visible, distended neck veins in an upright position are abnormal and usually indicate heart failure or obstruction of venous blood flow to the heart.

Accurate measurement of blood pressure requires a blood pressure cuff (sphygmomanometer) and stethoscope. The cuff should be wrapped snugly around the arm above the elbow and inflated to a pressure of about 180 mm (Hg) or until the radial pulse disappears. The stethoscope bell should be placed over the inner aspect of the elbow crease with the arm extended. The pulsations of the brachial artery can often be felt here, and the best position for the stethoscope is over the artery. As the pressure in the inflated cuff is allowed to fall by slowly releasing air through the valve on or near the bulb, a thumping sound synchronous with the pulse appears. The pressure indicated when the sound first can be heard is the systolic blood pressure. The pressure at which the sound completely disappears as the cuff pressure continues to fall is the diastolic blood pressure. If the radial pulse can be felt and a stethoscope is not available, the systolic blood pressure can be approximated by inflating the cuff and allowing the pressure to fall until the radial pulse first appears. This pressure is 10 to 20 mm lower than the pressure determined by a stethoscope, but the method is reliable in an emergency. Normal blood pressure ranges from 105 to 140 mm systolic and from 60 to 80 mm diastolic.

Peripheral Circulation

The lips, tongue, and fingernails (nail beds) are normally pink, but when the oxygen concentration in the blood is low, they become blue or purple. This discoloration (cyanosis) is commonly noted at high altitude and is usually severe in high altitude pulmonary edema. At lower elevations cyanosis usually indicates inadequate oxygenation of the blood by the lungs and is caused by disorders such as airway obstruction, pneumonia, or chest injuries.

When the blood pressure is low and blood flow to the extremities is decreased, the nail beds and lips may be cyanotic even though oxygenation of the blood in the lungs is normal. This type of cyanosis is commonly seen in shock.

Edema is an accumulation of excess water in the tissues and is not uncommon in women during the first few days at high altitude due to retention of salt and water. The face may be puffy in the morning and the feet or ankles may be mildly swollen. More severe edema, particularly if progressive and lasting for more than week, suggests heart failure or kidney disease and should be investigated.

Individuals who become short of breath with mild exertion, or who experience shortness of breath when lying flat that is relieved by sitting up, usually have fluid accumulations in the lungs (pulmonary edema). In young individuals at high elevations, high altitude pulmonary edema should be suspected. In older individuals at lower elevations heart failure is a common cause. When listening to the chest of someone with pulmonary edema from any cause, crackling or bubbling sounds (rales) can be heard with each breath. (Asthma usually produces wheezes, or squeaking or groaning sounds, particularly during expiration. Auscultation of the lungs is discussed further in Chapter Ten, "Respiratory System Disorders.")

Written records are vital in the care of anyone suspected to have heart disease. All observations, including the time of the observations, must be recorded. Examinations should be repeated at frequent, regular intervals, such as every two to four hours. Such records are needed by physicians when the individual is evacuated and may make possible a prompt, accurate diagnosis by radio.

HEART DISEASE IN THE WILDERNESS

Heart disease is common in individuals over the age of fifty, particularly men. However, many persons with heart disease live long and useful lives; modern therapy, including surgery and medications, has extended life expectancy with reduced symptoms. Modern management of heart disease encourages physical activity within specified limits, particularly among older people, and many of these individuals participate in wilderness activities.

In general, heart attacks, heart failure, or other cardiac emergencies are rare among individuals who maintain their physical fitness by regular exercise. Acute heart problems are much more common in individuals who only occasionally participate in vigorous activity, such as hunters or anglers who are largely sedentary most of the year and participate in their sport only when it is in season. When they engage in strenuous outdoor activities for which they are not physically conditioned, such as forcing their way through heavy underbrush, or carrying a heavy pack or deer, heart attacks are much more likely to occur.

The Physician's Role

A person who partakes in wilderness activities without consulting his physician not only risks his own health, but imposes upon his companions an unjustifiable responsibility for his care they may not be prepared to provide. Individuals more than fifty years old who are likely to have coronary disease, or who have evidence of heart disease, should have an electrocardiogram, a chest x-ray, and an exercise test to evaluate their cardiac status and determine the risk of moderate to severe exertion at some distance from medical facilities. An informed decision to accept that risk can only be made with the assistance and recommendations of a concerned physician who understands the lure of wilderness recreation.

The individual must follow his physician's instructions and obtain prescribed medications. The outing leader should be familiar with the treatment the person is receiving and must be alert for complications that require additional care or evacuation. However, the person's physician is responsible for his medical management, not the trip leader. For longer trips or expeditions, the leader should be supplied by the physician with a detailed description of the individual's condition, restrictions on activity that should be observed, medications to be taken, and the anticipated signs or symptoms that could require additional therapy or evacuation.

THE HEART AND ALTITUDE

High altitude poses no threat to a normal heart. The level of exercise an individual can maintain is limited by the tissue oxygen supply. (Only highly motivated individuals can exercise so vigorously that their tissues are not fully supplied with oxygen, and lactic acid and other unoxidized metabolites temporarily accumulate—anaerobic exercise.) During severe exertion at sea level, oxygen supply is limited by cardiac output. To increase tissue oxygen to a maximum, the heart is pushed to work as hard as possible.

At high elevations, the oxygen supply to the tissues is limited by the smaller amount of oxygen in the atmosphere, not by cardiac output. As a result, the heart is not pushed to work at a maximum level. In fact, during maximal exercise at high altitude, the heart rate, which is a rough guide to the cardiac work being performed, is lower than at sea level. If cardiac performance during exercise is normal at sea level, it will be normal at high altitude.

MAJOR HEART DISEASES

Coronary artery disease is the most common form of heart disease in men and women over fifty. Progressive narrowing of the arteries that supply the heart results from deposits of cholesterol and other fats on the inner surface of the arteries (arteriosclerosis, or "hardening of the arteries") and can produce chest pain (angina pectoris), a heart attack (myocardial infarction), heart failure (cardiac dyspnea), or sudden death. Rupture of one of these fat deposits, or thrombosis where an artery is narrowed by such deposits, further impairs the cardiac blood supply and may cause angina, increase the severity of preexisting angina, or produce an acute myocardial infarction.

Angina Pectoris

Angina pectoris (or simply angina) is a sensation of pressure or deep-seated pain beneath the sternum that characteristically appears during exercise and disappears after a few minutes of rest. The discomfort may be described as crushing, a sensation of being squeezed, a feeling as if a weight were on the chest, a feeling as if a band were around the heart, or a deep, burning sensation. It may be felt in the neck, jaws, or arms as well as in the chest. If exercise is continued, the discomfort increases; pain is relieved by rest and nitroglycerine. The discomfort is predictable and rarely occurs at rest except during periods of emotional stress. The duration is short, rarely longer than fifteen to thirty minutes. Angina is frequently accompanied by shortness of breath, which subsides as the discomfort eases.

Individuals with only mild angina at sea level may experience increased symptoms during the first few days at higher altitudes. A decrease in physical activity, additional medications, and oxygen usually control the symptoms. If the person has medications such as beta blockers or calcium channel blockers, the dose may be cautiously increased. However, if symptoms persist, the individual should descend.

Individuals with mild angina may safely take part in mildly strenuous outdoor activities if they follow their physicians' instructions, do not overexert, and carry nitroglycerine tablets to relieve episodes of pain. Their low risk for catastrophic cardiac events must be established by appropriate studies, including an exercise test. They should be able to carry out moderately strenuous, continuous exercise, such as hill walking, for several hours a day with minimal or no symptoms. Trips to remote areas far from medical facilities or prompt evacuation are not advisable.

Individuals who develop angina for the first time, or who experience unusually frequent or severe attacks of angina, should lie down, completely at rest, and should take nitroglycerine if it is available. Absolute rest, preferably with sedation, should be continued for at least six to eight hours—longer if the anginal episodes persist—after which the person should be evacuated with as little exertion as possible, preferably transported if that can be arranged. Angina is an indication of severe heart disease and often is a prelude to a more serious event, such as an infarct.

Myocardial Infarction

Myocardial infarction may occur in someone who has had angina, or it may occur in an individual who has never had chest pain. It is caused by obstruction of one of the arteries to the heart, usually by a blood clot, that results in death (necrosis or infarction) of part of the heart muscle.

Myocardial infarction is a common cause of sudden death and is a major medical emergency. Chest pain is the most common initial symptom and may appear at rest or during exercise. The pain resembles angina pectoris, but is usually more severe, may last one to six hours, and usually is not relieved by nitroglycerine. Other frequent symptoms and signs are nausea, vomiting, difficulty in breathing, weakness, sweating, pallor, cyanosis, and cold extremities. The blood pressure may be low; the heart rate may be slow and irregular. (Elderly individuals may have an acute infarction with minimal or no chest pain.)

The person should lie down immediately and rest completely. Nitroglycerine should be tried, although it usually is ineffective. If the pain is not relieved in ten to fifteen minutes, a strong analgesic should be administered every two hours until the pain is relieved. If the individual is agitated, a tranquilizer should be given. If oxygen is available, it should be administered with a face mask at a flow rate of four to six liters per minute. If the person is short of breath, coughing, and can breathe more easily in that position, he should be permitted to sit up, preferably supported by a back rest. (Administration of oxygen should be continued.) Prompt evacuation, preferably by helicopter, is essential. A physician or advanced emergency medical technician should accompany the helicopter; cardiac resuscitation may be necessary at any moment.

Cardiac Dyspnea

Cardiac dyspnea is undue shortness of breath caused by heart disease and is indicative of heart failure. Such dyspnea occurs with exercise but sometimes develops at night. The person awakens with a sense of suffocation and feels compelled to sit up or move out into fresh air to obtain relief. He is usually anxious, is breathing fast, and has a rapid heart rate. Rales or crackling sounds indicative of fluid in the lungs may be heard when listening to the chest.

Questioning usually discloses a history of high blood pressure, angina, a prior heart attack, or a heart murmur. In the few individuals who have no history of cardiac disease, the heart failure may be the result of an asymptomatic (silent) myocardial infarct or a marked rise in blood pressure. Nitroglycerine may be helpful, particularly if the blood pressure is high. Complete rest, sedation, oxygen, and a diuretic are the usual methods of treatment. The subject should be evacuated after twelve to twenty-four hours of rest with as little effort on his part as possible. If the dyspnea is severe, oxygen and a strong analgesic should be given even though no pain is present.

At high elevations, high altitude pulmonary edema should be considered, particularly if the subject has no history of heart disease and has recently ascended to that elevation. If high altitude pulmonary edema is suspected, rest, oxygen, and assisted descent to a lower altitude are necessary.

Sudden Death

Sudden death—instantaneous or within a few minutes of the onset of symptoms—is very rare in well-conditioned wilderness users who have never had symptoms of heart disease. The underlying cause in most cases is arteriosclerotic coronary artery disease, which may not have been suspected by the subject or the physician. Individuals who have a family history of sudden death, have high blood pressure, smoke, have high blood cholesterol concentrations, or have a sedentary lifestyle are predisposed to coronary disease. Investigation of sudden death during jogging or running has revealed that most of the individuals were known to have coronary artery disease or had experienced episodes of chest pain during exercise. Had they obtained a treadmill exercise test, the underlying coronary disease would probably have been detected.

Valvular Heart Disease

Many persons who have deformities of heart valves that cause heart murmurs are capable of strenuous physical effort without difficulty. However, with some types of valvular heart disease such activities may produce complications such as cardiac failure, atrial fibrillation, or stroke. Anyone with a heart murmur or valvular heart disease should consult a physician to determine whether or not he should take part in wilderness activities. Leaders of an outing must be informed of that person's activity limits, medications to be taken, and complications that might be expected.

Noncardiac Chest Pain

Chest pain in most individuals is not a sign of heart disease, although an unfortunate number fear it is. Several common types of chest pain not related to heart disease are:

- Aching and soreness due to muscular effort. After unaccustomed physical work involving the arms and shoulders, such as climbing, cross-country skiing, carrying a heavy pack, or cutting wood, pain may be present in the upper chest muscles for two to three days. The ache is usually constant, may be aggravated by motion, and the muscles may be tender. Aspirin, codeine, and rest are effective treatment. Reassurance should be provided.
- Chest discomfort due to anxiety. Nervous, anxious, or fearful individuals may notice a sensation of pressure in the chest that is associated with a sense of suffocation, trembling, dizziness, and occasionally numbness of the lips and fingers. The heart rate may be increased. Reassurance, rest, and mild sedation are usually the only measures needed. (See Hyperventilation Syndrome in Chapter Ten, "Respiratory System Disorders.")
- Aching pain over the heart. After heavy exertion some individuals note an aching pain over the area of the left nipple. The pain may be constant or intermittent and is often worse at night. Reassurance, rest, and a mild analgesic are all that is usually needed.
- Heartburn. A burning pain below the end of the breastbone, sometimes extending upward into the throat or jaw, may be noted after a meal, excessive consumption of spicy foods, coffee, tea, or alcohol, or the use of carbonated beverages. The discomfort is not related to effort and may last for one to three hours. Heartburn should not be mistaken for angina. Antacids or milk, smaller meals, rest, and reassurance are the most appropriate management. (See Chapter Twelve, "Gastrointestinal Disorders.")

DISORDERS OF CARDIAC RHYTHM

Paroxysmal Tachycardia

Paroxysmal tachycardia is characterized by a very rapid heart rate, sudden in onset, that is associated with a sensation of pounding in the chest, weakness, dizziness, and shortness of breath. True syncope (unconsciousness) is rare. The heart rate is very rapid (150 to 220 beats or more per minute) and completely regular. The pulses may be so weak that listening to the heart with a stethoscope is necessary to determine the rate. (When beating so rapidly, the heart does not have time to fill between contractions and the amount of blood pumped with each heartbeat decreases). Individuals may have previously experienced similar attacks.

Preferably, the subject should rest and let the episode stop spontaneously. However, if the tachycardia does not stop within ten to fifteen minutes, a few simple maneuvers may be tried. The person can try forcefully blowing up a paper bag or an air mattress. He can try holding his breath as long as possible. Inserting a tongue blade or a spoon handle in the back of the throat and making him gag may stop the attack. Immersing his face in water for as long as he can hold his breath sometimes works. A sharp blow over the heart with the edge of the hand (a karate chop) may help. (The person obviously should be warned in advance, and the blow must not be heavy enough to fracture ribs!) In some instances standing the person on his head has terminated episodes of tachycardia.

If these measures fail, the right carotid artery can be massaged, gently at first, but firmly if necessary. The subject usually is immediately aware that the attack has ended. Digitalis may prevent recurrent attacks. Since episodes of tachycardia tend to recur, the individual may require evacuation, particularly if the attack is his first and control has been difficult. However, paroxysmal tachycardia is almost never a sign of imminent cardiac disease.

Atrial Fibrillation

Atrial fibrillation is a rapid, but irregular heartbeat. The heart rate may be 100 to 180 beats per minute, and the onset may be sudden and resemble paroxysmal tachycardia. The important difference is the totally irregular rhythm of atrial fibrillation. Careful palpation of the pulse and listening to the heart may be necessary to be sure of the irregularity. At rates exceeding 160 beats per minute, irregularities are difficult to detect. Rest and sedation should be instituted. Normal heart action frequently returns spontaneously after a few hours. Maneuvers that stop paroxysmal tachycardia are of no value for atrial fibrillation. If the attack does not respond to rest and sedation within twelve to twenty-four hours, the subject should be evacuated. Atrial fibrillation is a more significant disorder that may be a sign of serious heart disease.

Digitalis may be advisable if evacuation of a person with uncontrollable rhythm disturbances is difficult or unavoidably delayed. If the cardiac rhythm has not returned to normal within twelve to twenty-four hours, 0.25 mg of digoxin may be given every two hours until a total dose of 1.5 mg (six 0.25-mg tablets) has

CARDIAC ARRYTHMIAS

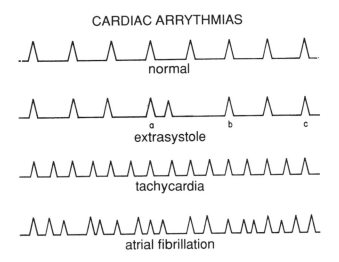

Figure 9-2. Diagrammatic comparison of normal and abnormal cardiac rhythms. (Note: interval ab = interval bc.)

been administered. (The subject must not have taken digitalis during the previous week.) If irregularities persist and evacuation is impossible, 0.25 mg of digoxin may be given once daily. The individual must rest; he should be sedated if necessary. Adequate fluids must be given to prevent the formation of clots that could cause embolism or a stroke in the irregularly beating heart. If nausea or vomiting appear, or the heart rate slows to below sixty per minute—these are signs of an overdose—digoxin should be discontinued.

Syncope (Fainting)

Syncope is a transient loss of consciousness commonly referred to as fainting. Two general varieties are encountered.

- True syncope is complete loss of consciousness. The individual falls down, cannot be aroused, and may display seizure activity. The duration may be seconds or minutes.
- Partial syncope is a condition in which the person feels "weak" or "faint" and slumps to a chair, a bed, or the floor, but consciousness and communication are maintained. After a few minutes the subject recovers but remains weak and unsteady for several minutes more.

True syncope is present in only ten to twenty percent of the individuals referred to physicians with that diagnosis. Partial, or near, syncope makes up the rest. True syncope is a serious symptom, particularly if it has occurred more than once and without warning and should be investigated in a hospital where sophisticated diagnostic studies can be performed. Many serious conditions, including brain tumors, heart tumors, and cardiac arrhythmias may cause true syncope.

Most instances of partial syncope—and some cases of true syncope—are vascular, or "vasovagal," in origin and also are situational. Common provocations are a crowded, overheated room, the sight of blood, recent arrival at high altitude, a large meal, or prolonged standing. In rare instances, partial syncope may occur during or immediately after heavy exertion, but in the absence of cardiac disease most such episodes are vasovagal also.

An individual with partial syncope typically becomes pale, sweaty, weak, and anxious. His pulse is usually slow and regular but may be weak. A history of similar episodes in the past may be obtained.

Partial syncope can be avoided by having the person sit down with his head between his knees or lie down with his legs elevated. Fresh air and a cold, wet towel for his face usually aid recovery. If the individual has no history of cardiac disease or episodes of true syncope, hospitalization is not necessary. Precautions to prevent subsequent episodes should be observed.

Partial syncope may occur as a result of postural, or orthostatic, hypotension, a fall in blood pressure upon assuming an erect posture. The individual experiences faintness upon standing after a prolonged period of lying down or sitting, such as upon arising in the morning or after a large meal, particularly when alcoholic beverages have been consumed. The diagnosis is made by measuring the blood pressure in a supine position and in a standing position. A fall in systolic pressure of more than 20 mm upon standing is abnormal. Postural hypotension is a common problem in persons who are receiving drug therapy for high blood pressure or coronary artery disease. Reassurance and a decrease in the medication dose are usually the only necessary measures.

Individuals more than sixty years old have a higher incidence of true syncope resulting from cardiac disease and are less likely to have benign, vasodepressor syncopal attacks. Such persons also are more susceptible to postural hypotension, particularly if medications for hypertension are being taken.

Cardiac Syncope

Cardiac syncope is a loss of consciousness caused by heart disease and is usually a form of true syncope. Two forms are recognized: exertional and arrhythmic. Exertional syncope occurs during a burst of heavy effort such as walking fast uphill. Unconsciousness may occur suddenly or may be preceded by a "gray out" sensation, severe dizziness, or weakness. Convulsive movements may occur. Exertional syncope most frequently occurs in individuals with aortic stenosis (narrowing of the outlet valve from the left ventricle) but is occasionally seen in people with other forms of heart disease. Most affected individuals have a history of similar episodes.

Arrhythmic syncope occurs as the result of an abnormal cardiac rhythm—either a sudden increase in heart rate (tachycardia) or a marked slowing or temporary cessation of the heartbeat (heart block). The episode may occur suddenly, without warning, and the person may fall and be injured.

The blood pressure should be measured, the heart rate should be determined, and the rhythm should be evaluated. The individual should rest, with sedation if needed, for six to twelve hours and then be evacuated to a physician's care.

Cardiac syncope may be an early warning of heart disease that can cause sudden death.

MINOR DISTURBANCES OF CARDIAC RHYTHM

Sinus Tachycardia

An anxious individual, after heavy exertion or at high altitude, may become aware of the pounding in his chest of a rapid, forceful heartbeat and fear he has heart disease. If the heart rate does not exceed 120 beats per minute and gradually slows with rest and sedation, a diagnosis of harmless sinus tachycardia may be made. No specific treatment except rest and reassurance is necessary.

Extrasystoles ("Skipped Beats")

Healthy individuals may notice occasional irregular thumping or "fluttering" sensations in their chests, particularly at rest or during the night. They may feel their pulse and notice occasional pauses between beats. Such irregular beats are called extrasystoles and are of no significance unless the person clearly has heart disease manifested by angina, myocardial infarction, or cardiac dyspnea. Rest and reassurance are usually the only measures needed. Avoiding stimulants such as coffee and tea, and avoiding tobacco often entirely eliminates the extrasystoles.

If a bothersome irregularity of the heartbeat persists, if the skipped beats occur more than five times per minute, or if such irregularities have never been experienced before, evacuation to a physician's care may be desirable.

HIGH BLOOD PRESSURE (HYPERTENSION)

Ten to twenty percent of the over-forty population of the United States has elevated blood pressure, and many individuals with high blood pressure pursue wilderness activities. For such individuals to be safe, the following guidelines should be observed:

- Persons with mild or drug-controlled hypertension should partake in wilderness activities only after consulting sympathetic physicians. On an outing, such individuals must supply their own medications and follow their physicians' recommendations carefully. Fluid intake should be adequate, and their diet should be low in salt and protein.
- Individuals with severe, uncontrolled hypertension or complications of hypertension should not venture into remote wilderness areas. The complications of uncontrolled hypertension—strokes, heart failure, coronary artery disease, decreased visual acuity, and kidney failure—could be disastrous in such situations.

Individuals with moderately high blood pressure may experience complications with which wilderness outing leaders should be familiar. These complications include cardiac dyspnea, angina pectoris, stroke, and severe headache, any of which is an indication for prompt evacuation.

Some persons with only moderate hypertension have periodic episodes of severe blood pressure elevation. Such episodes are typically associated with severe headache, confusion, forgetfulness, visual impairment, slurred speech, and other neurologic signs and symptoms. The blood pressure should be measured if such symptoms appear. If the systolic pressure exceeds 200 mm, the individual should be forced to rest, with sedation if needed, and nitroglycerine should be given every hour to reduce the pressure. Evacuation should be arranged after six to twelve hours.

Some hypertensive persons experience an increase in pressure at high altitudes. The rise in pressure, which may not be detectable unless the blood pressure is measured, is usually evident within one to two days at even moderate altitudes such as 6,000 feet (1,800 m). If an individual has a significant rise in pressure at such moderate altitudes, he should consult his physician, who may advise him to increase his medications when he is at high altitudes or may advise him not to go to high elevations at all.

Individuals taking certain types of medication for high blood pressure (such as propranolol, a beta blocker) may not experience the usual increase in heart rate at high altitude. Some develop orthostatic (postural) hypotension. Individuals on diuretics must continue to take potassium supplements if that has been recommended by their physicians. Diuretic-induced potassium depletion can result in muscular weakness but is relieved by potassium-rich foods such as dried fruits, nuts, soups, and fruit juices.

VASCULAR DISEASE

Claudication

Older individuals with arteriosclerosis of the arteries in their legs may experience pain in their calves, hips, buttocks, or thighs while walking uphill, particularly when carrying a heavy load. The pain occurs during effort, becomes more severe as effort is continued, and is relieved by rest. The medical term for this condition is claudication. When severe, it can appear while a person is strolling on level terrain.

Claudication should be distinguished from common leg cramps, which occur at rest or during the night, are characterized by painful contraction of the muscles—not just pain—and usually involve the calf or foot.

If claudication is mild, a slower pace and a lighter load may permit the individual to continue. Smoking increases the severity of claudication and should be avoided. If claudication suddenly becomes severe or appears for the first time in the wilderness, the person should be evacuated with minimal effort on his part.

Varicose Veins

The veins of the extremities have numerous small valves within them to ensure that blood flows only in the direction of the heart. The blood pressure in veins is so low that the increase in intrathoracic or intra-abdominal pressure associated with straining or strenuous exercise would reverse the direction of the venous blood flow if these valves were not present.

In some individuals the valves in the leg veins become incompetent, the direction of blood flow is no longer controlled, and the veins become dilated and tortuous (varicose). The return of venous blood from the limb to the heart may be impaired, causing persons with varicose veins to complain of aching in their legs, particularly after they have been on their feet for a prolonged period. The condition should be corrected surgically (by removing or ligating the affected veins) because it can lead to ulceration of the skin and other complications. The results are more satisfactory when surgical therapy is instituted early.

The greatest significance of varicose veins in the wilderness lies in the tendency for this disorder to increase fatigability of the legs and limit endurance. A second problem is the greater tendency for veins in the legs to thrombose as the result of stasis associated with the reduced venous blood flow typical of varicose veins. A less common problem is caused by the presence of greatly enlarged blood vessels just beneath the skin. Minor injuries that ordinarily would go unnoticed can penetrate one of these veins and produce relatively severe bleeding. Although the hemorrhage can be controlled easily, a person with varicose veins should be aware of this danger.

Individuals with varicose veins should consult a physician about proper management of their condition.

In the wilderness, a person with painful varicose veins should be encouraged to elevate his legs on pillows or a soft pad during rest stops to decrease the pressure within the veins. Relief may be obtained with smooth elastic bandages or elastic stockings, which should applied when the person is lying on his back and the veins are collapsed. (The bandages or stockings should be removed at night.) A hard knot or cord that is inflamed and tender indicates the blood in one or more of the enlarged veins has clotted. Thrombosis of such superficial veins is rarely a problem except for the discomfort. However, swelling of the foot or ankle beyond the area where clotting has occurred is indicative of associated clotting of the deeper veins. To avoid pulmonary embolism, the individual should be treated as described in Chapter Ten, "Respiratory System Disorders."

ACKNOWLEDGMENT
Howard B. Burchell, M.D., provided valuable advice and suggestions in the preparation of this chapter.

ADDITIONAL READING
Hultgren H: Coronary heart disease and trekking. *J. Wild Med* 1990; 1:154-161.
Rennie D: Will mountain trekkers have heart attacks? *JAMA* 1989; 261:1045-1046.
Selzer A: *The Heart: Its Function in Health and Disease.* Berkeley, University of California Press, 1966.
Sokolow M, McIlroy M, and Cheitlin M: *Clinical Cardiology.* Norwalk, Conn.: Lange, 1990.

CHAPTER TEN

RESPIRATORY SYSTEM DISORDERS

The respiratory system moves air in and out of the lungs to provide oxygen for the body and to eliminate carbon dioxide. The components of this system are:

- The upper airway: the nose and mouth, trachea, bronchi, and bronchioles, which form the passages through which air moves. These are lined with mucous membranes that remove foreign material, saturate the air with water, and raise or lower the temperature of the air to that of the body.
- The gas exchange area: the alveoli, or air cells, which make up the major portion of the lung tissue and in which oxygen and carbon dioxide are exchanged between blood and air.
- The bellows: the chest wall and diaphragm, which expand and contract to move air in and out of the lungs. A thin membrane, the pleura, covers the lungs, lines the inner surface of the chest wall, and eases the movement of the lungs within the chest.
- The control system: sensing cells that detect chemical changes in the circulating blood (chemoreceptors); other sensing cells that detect movements of the chest wall, diaphragm, and lungs (neuroreceptors); and the network of nerves that carries information from these receptors to the brain, which controls the rate and depth of respiration.

Respiratory movements are controlled by a complex system of receptors, transmitters, and effectors throughout the body. Chemical receptors respond to oxygen deficiency, increase or decrease of carbon dioxide, or a change in the acidity of the blood, which normally is maintained at the slightly alkaline pH of 7.4. These receptors signal the brain to increase or decrease the rate and depth of breathing (ventilation). Two collections of special cells (the carotid bodies) are in the neck; others are situated deep within the brain (the respiratory center) and respond to blood circulating through the brain and also to the spinal fluid that bathes the brain.

Under ordinary resting conditions approximately a half-liter of air is inspired with each breath. The normal respiratory rate is ten to twelve breaths per minute, and the corresponding normal ventilatory volume is five to six liters per minute. This volume is called the tidal air. After inhaling as deeply as possible, the total

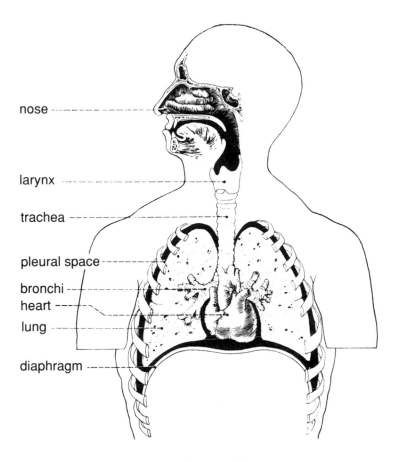

nose

larynx

trachea

pleural space

bronchi

heart

lung

diaphragm

Figure 10-1. Anatomy of the respiratory system.

volume of air that can be exhaled is called the vital capacity, a commonly used measure of ventilatory function. In addition, some air that cannot be exhaled remains, the residual volume.

The respiratory volume is decreased as much as twenty to thirty percent during sleep, which further decreases oxygenation of the blood at high altitude and aggravates the symptoms of mountain sickness. Exertion greatly increases ventilation because it increases the need for oxygen and for elimination of carbon dioxide. These demands stimulate the respiratory center in the brain to increase the respiratory volume to as much as 150 liters per minute during vigorous exercise. Even at rapid respiratory rates, oxygen is taken up by the blood and carbon dioxide given off with extraordinary efficiency and precision, thanks to the sensitivity of the control mechanisms.

A variety of disorders centered in a number of different locations can affect the function of the respiratory system. Breathing is usually slowed or stopped by head injuries or diseases of the brain, but occasionally it is increased. Airway obstruction can result from aspirated material or from injuries to the throat; it is usually sudden and may halt effective breathing. Injury of the chest, with or without fracture, can impair the bellows action of the chest wall and diaphragm. Air, blood, or fluid within the chest cavity compresses the lungs and prevents expansion during inspiration. An injury that damages a lung in such a way that inhaled air continuously leaks into the space between the lung and chest wall but can not be exhaled (tension pneumothorax) is life-threatening. Collections of fluid in the alveoli due to edema or infection can block the exchange of gases between inhaled air and blood.

The control system may malfunction due to a tumor in one of the carotid bodies, injury to the respiratory center, or an infection of the brain. A congenital defect in the ventilatory response to oxygen deficiency, or a weakening of this response by a long stay at altitude, severe stress, or starvation, may blunt the normal increase in ventilation at altitude. However, many fail-safe mechanisms protect from failure of these controls.

Biochemical changes in the blood due to kidney disease, uncontrolled diabetes, certain inhaled or ingested agents or drugs, or rare metabolic defects usually increase the rate and depth of breathing and must be considered when evaluating breathing abnormalities.

SYMPTOMS

The principal symptoms produced by diseases of the lungs are shortness of breath (or air hunger), cough, pain, and fever. Each must be considered in order to diagnose the disorder that has caused them.

Shortness of Breath

- How and when did it begin?
- How is it affected by position?
- What makes it worse—or better?

Cough

- Is the cough dry or productive (sputum is coughed up)?
- What kind of material is coughed up?
- Does it contain blood, pus, or foreign material?

Pain

- Where is the pain? Did it begin suddenly or gradually?
- Is the pain mild or severe? What makes it worse?
- Is the pain stabbing, sharp, dull, or crushing?
- Is the pain constant or intermittent? How is it related to breathing?
- How is it related to other symptoms?

Fever

- How high is the temperature?
- Did it rise suddenly or gradually?
- Have chills or sweating occurred?

Shortness of breath can be caused by many illnesses or injuries. At any altitude above 8,000 feet (2,400 m), particularly if the individual has ascended rapidly, shortness of breath, with or without cough, may indicate early high altitude pulmonary edema (HAPE). Since this disorder may progress rapidly to a life-threatening problem, early detection is important.

A persistent, dry, hacking cough is common at high altitude due to drying and irritation of the throat, but may indicate lung disease or the presence of fluid in the lungs. Usually such fluid is reabsorbed, but it may develop into high altitude pulmonary edema. The sputum is usually thin, watery, and pink or bloody with this disorder. (See Chapter Twenty-one, "Medical Problems of High Altitude.") The cough due to infections of the lung is deeper and usually produces sputum that is green, yellow, or rust-colored, and thick and stringy. With pulmonary embolism (see below) the sputum is usually bloody.

Pain caused by diseases of the lung or pleura or injuries of the chest wall changes with respiratory movements; deep inspiration typically causes sharp, stabbing pain. Pain that is dull or crushing is more typical of heart disease. (See Chapter Nine, "Heart and Blood Vessel Disorders.")

PHYSICAL EXAMINATION

The entire individual must be examined even though his problem appears to be in the lungs. A rapid, hard pulse and fever are indicative of significant disease. Fever is usually a sign of infection but may occur with pulmonary embolism or high altitude pulmonary edema. Serious infection anywhere causes fever, rapid pulse, and shortness of breath.

The first step in examining the chest is careful observation. Breathing difficulty, irregularities of respiratory rhythm, and differences in movement of the two sides of the chest are important. Obvious signs include rapid or labored breathing; shallow, irregular, or noisy breathing; and cyanosis of the lips, nails, or skin. Flaring of the nostrils and tensing of the neck muscles are signs of severe respiratory difficulty. Efforts to breathe that do not move the chest indicate upper airway obstruction.

The respiratory rhythm should be observed while counting the rate. Minor changes of rhythm are of no significance; important irregularities are hard to overlook. In contrast, differences in movement of the two sides of the chest may be subtle and should be watched for during quiet respiration as well as during deep breathing.

Auscultation consists of listening to the sounds made by air passing in and out of the lungs. A stethoscope makes the sounds easier to hear and is more convenient, but the sounds can be heard by pressing the unaided ear against the bare chest. Clothing must be removed or important sounds and signs may be missed.

Quiet breathing by normal lungs produces sounds so faint that they are barely audible. The person being examined must be told to breathe deeply through his mouth during the examination to amplify these sounds. All portions of the lungs should be examined to be sure no abnormalities are missed and the extent of any diseased area is recognized.

Many diseases of the lung cause fluid to collect in the small bronchi and alveoli, producing bubbling or crackling sounds known as rales. Fluid accumulation is typical of infection or edema of the lungs. Wheezing is more indicative of asthma or some other form of small airway obstruction. Wheezing that can be cleared by a single cough is rarely significant. With severe pneumonia or pulmonary embolism a portion of the lung is often consolidated or airless due to fluid and inflammatory exudate in the alveolar sacs. Over this area, the breath sounds are harsher and louder.

Infection or an embolus often produces inflammation of the pleura overlying the involved lung, which makes the pleural surface rough. Since the pleural surfaces no longer slide smoothly over each other, movement of the lung during respiration produces a squeaking sound like two pieces of leather being rubbed together. This sound is called a "friction rub" or simply a "rub." Pain with a rub means pleurisy, but does not define its cause.

If no sounds whatever are heard over a portion of the chest, fluid or air is usually in the space between the lung and the chest wall. Rarely, the absence of breath sounds may be due to obstruction of a large airway leading to that portion of the lung.

Auscultation of the lung, although it requires practice and experience, is not too difficult to learn and can be a valuable diagnostic aid, particularly in a remote, wilderness situation.

CHRONIC LUNG DISEASE

The most common chronic lung diseases are chronic obstructive lung disease and emphysema, which often occur together. Both result from long exposure to many types of air pollution, most often cigarette smoking. Emphysema, which is characterized by destruction of the walls of alveoli and the formation of numerous cystlike areas, is the result of chronic irritation or infection of the smaller air passages. Asthma also may lead to emphysema if severe and present for many years. Bronchitis causes an irritative and often productive cough and after years may lead to obstructive disease and emphysema.

Most individuals with chronic lung disease are aware of the problem and are not likely to venture into the wilderness. However, the early stages of these diseases may be detectable only during strenuous exertion or at altitude. The first sign of chronic obstructive lung disease or of emphysema is often decreased vital capacity, which reduces the extra breathing capacity that is called on at high altitudes, during exertion, or whenever infection of the lungs, shock, or loss of blood decreases the availability of oxygen to the rest of the body. Persons who know they have impaired respiratory reserve should be cautious about altitude, particularly about exertion at altitude.

Less common chronic lung disorders include slowly growing tumors, fibrosis or scarring of the lung, and tuberculosis, which is now rare in the United States.

DISORDERS OF RHYTHM

Cheyne-Stokes Respiration

Above 10,000 feet (3,000 meters) almost everyone has Cheyne-Stokes respiration (periodic breathing) during sleep; it is not rare as low as 8,000 feet (2,400 m), and can occasionally be observed in resting individuals who are awake, particularly children. The typical pattern begins with a few shallow breaths, increases in depth to deep, sighing respirations, and then falls off rapidly. Respirations can cease entirely for a few seconds, leading an observer to fear that the person is dead. Then the shallow breaths resume and the pattern is repeated (fig. 10-2).

During the period when breathing has stopped, the person often becomes restless and sometimes wakes with a frightening sense of suffocation. Acetazolamide relieves the periodic breathing seen at altitude. Sedatives are harmful in such situations and should be avoided. An aminophylline rectal suppository at bedtime may help if respiratory irregularity prevents adequate rest.

This type of irregular breathing is so common at altitudes above 9,000 feet (2,700 m) that it should not be considered abnormal. Cheyne-Stokes breathing may be present on some occasions and not on others. However, it may be a sign of a serious disorder if it occurs for the first time during an illness or after an injury, particularly a head injury.

Some persons have intermittent upper airway obstruction (manifested by snoring) that may cause an unpleasant morning headache and lethargy at altitude. This problem is not relieved by acetazolamide.

Central apnea is another form of irregular rhythm that has been recently recognized. Some defect in the respiratory control center in the brain causes alarming periods of absent breathing, followed by increasing respiration that rises to a peak and then decreases. This disorder is congenital, tends to be familial, and may

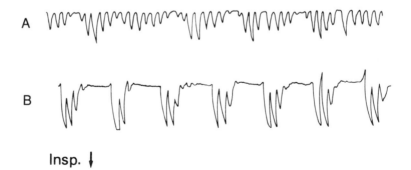

Figure 10-2. Actual tracings of Cheyne-Stokes respirations. A, increasing and decreasing depth of respirations. B, two to three deep inspirations followed by total cessation of respiration for about twelve seconds.

be responsible for some "crib deaths" in infants. It resembles periodic breathing but occurs at any altitude and is not relieved by acetazolamide.

Hyperventilation Syndrome

Hyperventilation (overbreathing) is common. The subject begins to breathe more rapidly and deeply than is appropriate and appears to be suffering from serious disease. However, this syndrome is almost entirely emotional in origin. Individuals who hyperventilate tend to be nervous, tense, and apprehensive, although the disorder can occur in apparently stable persons. Among beginning climbers, for example, apprehension about hazards or fear of exposure might initiate this reaction. Knowledge of the person's emotional status, particularly unusual anxiety, helps establish the diagnosis.

When a person breathes too rapidly and deeply for more than a short time, an abnormally large amount of carbon dioxide is exhaled, altering the acid-base balance and increasing the pH of the blood, which produces the characteristic symptoms.

The first and most prominent symptom is a sense of suffocation, described as shortness of breath, which is accompanied by a rapid pulse, dizziness, faintness, sweating, and apprehension. The person often complains "the air doesn't go down far enough." He, or more frequently she, breathes in gasps or takes frequent deep sighs. As the blood becomes more alkaline, numbness or tingling around the mouth and in the fingers appears. If hyperventilation persists, these symptoms increase to painful cramps or spasms of the fingers, hands, and forearms that are particularly frightening to the subject.

The feeling of shortness of breath is puzzling since the mechanisms that control breathing so well would be expected to correct the overbreathing as the carbon dioxide in the blood decreases and the blood becomes more alkaline. However, in this condition, these mechanisms are overridden for reasons that are not understood.

Even though hyperventilation syndrome is suspected, the individual should be examined to ensure no other problem is present. If none is found, reassurance and explanation are usually enough to reverse the disorder. The subject should be instructed to deliberately slow or stop his breathing, or to breathe gently into and out of a bag held over the mouth and nose. This permits carbon dioxide to reaccumulate, which usually relieves symptoms promptly. If these measures are not effective, a tranquilizer may be necessary. Once recovered, the individual may feel weak and shaky and may have a headache. The disorder should be explained in some detail to help prevent recurrences. It appears to be one component of "chronic fatigue syndrome."

INFECTIOUS DISORDERS

Tracheitis

The trachea is the large airway leading from the throat to the middle of the chest, where it divides into the two main bronchi. This structure sometimes becomes inflamed and occasionally infected. Usually the person has pain in his throat below his tonsils or beneath his sternum that becomes worse with breathing. Coughing may cause pain in the same area and may produce thick sputum. The treatment for tracheitis is the same as for bronchitis.

Bronchitis

Bronchitis, or more properly tracheobronchitis, is an infection of the major air passages to the lungs. Such infections are rarely disabling but can progress to pneumonia. This disease frequently comes on during or after a cold and may be called a "chest cold." Although the trachea and bronchi may be infected by the same viruses that cause the common cold, bronchitis is more often caused by secondary bacterial infection. Bronchitis also occurs without a preceding viral infection.

Some individuals, particularly those with asthma, tend to develop tracheobronchitis following a cold. Preventing this type of infection, particularly on an extended wilderness outing, is one of the few reasons to administer antibiotics to someone with a cold. Such individuals should confer with their physicians about the antibiotic therapy preferable for prevention.

The predominant symptom of bronchitis is a persistent, irritating cough that may be dry but frequently becomes productive after one or two days. The sputum is usually green or yellow and is thick and tenacious. Slight pain may be associated with the coughing and easy fatigability may be present, particularly at high altitudes. However, the subject usually does not appear severely ill and has only a slight fever or none at all. If the infection involves the larynx (voice box), he may be hoarse (laryngitis). A few wheezes and rales may be heard throughout the chest, but these tend to disappear with coughing.

The treatment for tracheitis or bronchitis begins with adequate hydration. The subject must drink lots of warm fluids that do not contain caffeine. If he can sit or lie in a tent with a boiling kettle or pot to humidify the air, his airways can be moistened and the material in his bronchi liquified so that it can be coughed up more easily.

Many physicians advocate administering a broad-spectrum antibiotic if laboratory facilities are not available for specific diagnosis. Others prefer to withhold antibiotics except for severe infections. At high altitude, where progression of the infection to pneumonia could be disastrous, antibiotics probably should be administered. Ampicillin is effective for many infectious agents. For individuals allergic to penicillin, tetracycline or erythromycin are the drugs of choice. Newer broad-spectrum antibiotics are more expensive and are not needed except for laboratory-diagnosed specific infections, or when other measures seem ineffective.

Rest, warmth, and aspirin are helpful. The subject does not need bed rest but should refrain from strenuous exercise. If the condition persists for more than two or three days, descent to a lower altitude may be necessary.

Although hard proof is not yet available, increasing evidence suggests that even a mild upper respiratory infection increases the risk of high altitude pulmonary edema.

Pleurisy

Pleurisy is an inflammation of the thin membranes that cover the lungs and inner chest wall, usually due to an infectious process in the underlying lung. Injury to the chest wall, or irritation due to pulmonary embolism, can produce similar symptoms. Viruses occasionally cause an infection called epidemic pleurodynia or Bornholm disease in groups of healthy young persons. These disorders are of short duration and are rarely disabling, although they are uncomfortable, particularly at high altitudes, where individuals are required to breathe more rapidly and deeper than at sea level.

The principal symptom—usually the only symptom—is pain with respiration. The pain is usually sharp and stabbing and is limited to a rather small area on one side of the chest. Deep inspiration elicits a particularly severe twinge. Physical signs are mild or absent. Motion of the affected side may be limited, and a few wheezes or rales may be heard over the involved area. Sometimes a leathery, rough, rubbing sound can be heard over the area where pain is worst. This "friction rub" is diagnostic of pleurisy but does not indicate its cause. The person may be more comfortable when lying on the affected side, limiting the motion of that part of the chest.

The general appearance of the person is important. If pleurisy alone is present, the individual rarely appears seriously ill. If the fever is high, the pulse rapid, or the subject seems quite sick, pneumonia or embolism should be suspected.

Pleurisy unaccompanied by another disease, although painful, usually clears in three or four days and requires little treatment other than rest. Only if pneumonia is suspected should antibiotics be given and the person taken to a lower altitude.

Taping or splinting the chest increases the risk of pneumonia or collapse of part of the lung, but if the pain of pleurisy (or broken ribs) is severe, temporary splinting may be unavoidable. Both sides of the chest must not be splinted at the same time. Wide strips of tape should be placed from a point one to two inches beyond the vertebral column to beyond the sternum over the painful area. (It is helpful to paint the skin with tincture of benzoin before applying the tape.) The tape should be removed after three days but can be replaced if necessary.

Pneumonia

Bacterial and viral pneumonia are infections of the lung tissue, notably the alveoli. Persons weakened by fatigue, exposure, or disease elsewhere in the body are particularly susceptible. Infected fluid accumulates in the alveoli, and the exchange of carbon dioxide and oxygen is impaired. Fever increases the body's need for oxygen as the infection itself decreases the supply. If a large amount of lung is involved, hypoxia combined with toxic substances released from the bacteria may cause death. Pneumonia should always be taken seriously.

Anyone with any type of pneumonia is oxygen-deficient above 8,000 feet (2,400 m). When oxygen is available, it should be given freely while transportation is arranged. Individuals should be evacuated to a lower altitude as soon as possible whenever pneumonia is suspected.

The symptoms of pneumonia vary with the causative organisms and the severity of the infection. All pneumonias usually cause a fever of more than 102°F (39°C) orally and rapid pulse and respiratory rates. Bacterial pneumonias are often ushered in by shaking chills, followed by a high fever. The individual looks quite sick and may be very weak.

Coughing is a prominent symptom of all lung infections. The cough may be dry at first but usually becomes productive after one or two days. The sputum, which is usually green or yellow but sometimes has a rusty color, is thick and mucoid and frequently resembles pus.

Some bacteria tend to localize in a single segment of the lung that becomes consolidated. The physical signs are limited to that area of the lung. The overlying pleura is often involved, and stabbing pain with each breath may be severe. Not infrequently, pleuritic pain is an early—sometimes the first—indication of underlying infection. Since the pain varies with the depth of respiration, the chest is often splinted by involuntary muscle spasm, and respiratory movement on the affected side is reduced, which may be apparent on inspection.

Lobar pneumonia, which is limited to one or two lobes of the lung, has be-

TABLE 10-1.
Features of Various Pulmonary Disorders

	PNEUMONIA	HIGH ALTITUDE PULMONARY EDEMA	PULMONARY EMBOLISM
Onset	Gradual, 24 hours	Gradual, 12 to 36 hours after ascent	Sudden
Chills	Frequent at onset	Absent	Absent
Fever	Usual; often high	Absent or low	Moderate; may be absent
Sputum	Thick, stringy; green, yellow, or rusty	Frothy; white or pink	Frothy; later bloody
Pain	Pleuritic; may be absent	None	Pleuritic; may be absent
Fluid (Edema)	Localized or diffuse, often mild	Usually diffuse	Localized if present
Physical Findings	Crackling rales; rub; loud, harsh breath sounds	Crackling rales; bubbling	Rub; harsh or absent breath sounds
Other	May follow a cold or bronchitis	No history of heart disease; recent ascent to 8,000 feet (2,400 m) or above	Signs of thrombophlebitis

come much less frequent in recent years. Lung infections by viruses, fungi, yeasts, and other microorganisms are more common now than several decades ago. Each of these infecting organisms produces a somewhat different type of disease with different signs and symptoms. Most cause small, widely scattered areas of infection that rarely produce signs of consolidation or pleurisy. Diagnosis of pneumonia due to rarer organisms usually requires laboratory facilities.

Patchy infections, called bronchopneumonia, viral pneumonia, or diffuse pneumonitis, often begin rather insidiously and become severe only after a longer period than lobar or bacterial pneumonia. Consequently they are harder to diagnose and often are unsuspected. So-called "walking pneumonia" is generally due to a virus. It begins insidiously, is difficult to treat because the organisms are resistant to most antibiotics, and usually is disabling for a longer time.

"Legionnaire's disease" received extensive publicity two decades ago but has been around for a long time. It is caused by a family of organisms that live in water in association with blue-green algae and may be transported in spray. One strain causes signs and symptoms resembling viral pneumonia. The mortality rate is high. If this disease is suspected, erythromycin should be administered at once and evacuation begun.

If an individual is seriously ill, the onset has been rapid, and signs suggest lobar pneumonia, antibiotics should be started immediately. If he is not allergic to penicillin, then penicillin or ampicillin should be given four to six times a day, usually after an initial "loading" of twice the usual dose. If the person is allergic to penicillin, erythromycin or tetracycline should be given; "loading" should be followed by a regular dose every four hours. Whatever antibiotic is given should be continued for at least seven and preferably ten days. Stopping sooner can lead to a relapse with organisms that have become resistant to the antibiotic.

The antibiotic may prevent identification of some less common infectious organisms once the subject has reached a hospital. Consequently, some physicians urge that no treatment be given until the organism has been identified. Despite these reservations, if hospitalization must be delayed for more than two or three days, or the individual is quite ill, treatment should be started at once.

Recovery depends on the severity of the infection and the organism. Rarely can a person who has had pneumonia resume strenuous activity in less than two to three weeks.

OTHER PULMONARY DISORDERS

High Altitude Pulmonary Edema

Although high altitude pulmonary edema was clearly described eighty years ago, only in the last thirty years has it been recognized as a major problem. Prior to 1960 this disorder was usually mistaken for pneumonia, and acute pulmonary edema and pneumonia do have similarities. This potentially serious problem can occur, and has been lethal, as low as 8,000 feet (2,400 m), but it is unusual below 9,000 feet (2,700 m). It is more fully described in Chapter Twenty-one, "Medical Problems of High Altitude."

Asthma

Asthma is a disease of the bronchi caused by allergy. Inhaling the substance to which the individual is allergic (the allergen) increases the secretion of mucus into the bronchi. Simultaneously, the muscles in the walls of the bronchi go into spasm, constricting these air passages. The narrowed bronchi filled with excess mucus obstruct the passage of air.

A few persons develop typical asthma in very cold weather—so-called "cold allergy"—and others have bronchospasm during strenuous exertion. Although called "asthma," neither is allergic in nature.

Asthma may be mild, severe, or—rarely—fatal. Although a first attack may occur at any time, most individuals are aware of their susceptibility long before engaging in wilderness activities.

Asthma is a recurring disease. Most people with this problem have suffered previous attacks and are under the care of a physician, who should provide the medications that should be taken on any outing. Fortunately, individuals with mild asthma are not particularly limited in the wilderness activities in which they can participate; some may breathe more easily at moderate altitude, where the air is thinner and cleaner.

The most significant sign of asthma is difficulty in breathing, particularly during expiration. The expiratory phase of respiration, which normally requires less time than inspiration, is considerably prolonged and may require conscious effort.

An incessant, irritating cough is often present. Toward the end of an asthmatic attack considerable quantities of very thick mucus may be coughed up. Fever is usually absent, but the pulse rate may be moderately increased. The respiratory rate is usually faster than normal in spite of the difficulty in breathing. When the person is examined, the chest may appear more expanded than normal at the end of expiration. Loud wheezes and some bubbling and crackling sounds are usually audible throughout all parts of the lung.

The most important part of asthma treatment is adequate fluid intake. Regardless of the medication used, tripling the intake of liquids is beneficial. Steam inhalations are also helpful. Mild asthma responds well to inhalant sprays. Severe attacks require subcutaneous injections of 0.3 cc of a 1:1,000 solution of adrenaline, which can be repeated every five to ten minutes for several doses. The pulse rate rises, often to an uncomfortably high level, following adrenaline. If more than a few injections are given, or if the series is repeated after several hours, pulse and blood pressure should be recorded ten minutes after each injection.

Inhalation of nebulized medication has become popular in recent years. When nebulizers are used only occasionally and only for severe attacks, they can be dramatically effective. However, nebulizers should not be used more frequently than once or twice an hour and should rarely be used for more than one day. Many asthmatics carry a nebulizer or at least know which one is effective.

Since asthma further limits the amount of oxygen obtainable by the body, oxygen inhalation is usually helpful at high altitudes, but any mucus blocking the airways must be coughed up first. The best way to ensure that such obstructions are eliminated is to provide plenty of liquids and the most appropriate medication.

Prevention of asthmatic attacks is important. Individuals with known allergies should learn to avoid the allergens whenever possible.

Severe asthmatics should obtain detailed instructions and take with them the medications required for their care. Since persons who have long-standing severe asthma tend to have chronic obstructive pulmonary disease as well, they may be unwise to venture above 8,000 feet (2,400 m). Some physicians have the impression that persons with asthma tend to be more susceptible to high altitude pulmonary edema, but this predisposition has been neither proven or disproven.

Persons with asthma are advised to allow more time for acclimatization. Fortunately, above snowline the allergens causing asthma are rarely encountered, and mild asthmatics may have no difficulty with snow and ice climbing.

Pneumothorax

Occasionally lung tissue may rupture spontaneously, allowing air to leak into the chest cavity. Lacerations of the lung can also occur with penetrating or nonpenetrating injuries that fracture and displace ribs. The lung on the side of the air leak tends to retract due to its inherent elasticity and does not expand well during inspiration. As a result, pulmonary function is compromised. This condition is known as pneumothorax, meaning "air in the chest."

Rarely, the tear in the lung behaves like a valve, allowing air into the pleural space but not allowing it to leave, which causes the pressure within the space to build rapidly. The pressure collapses the lung and can shift the heart and its surrounding structures (the mediastinum) so that the opposite lung is compressed. If untreated, this disorder is usually lethal, particularly at higher elevations. This condition is labeled "tension pneumothorax" because the air is under increased pressure (fig. 10-3).

Pneumothorax should be suspected when unexplained shortness of breath appears suddenly in an otherwise healthy, active person. Sometimes the onset is associated with sudden pain. The diagnosis is confirmed when breath sounds can not be heard over the entire lung on the affected side. A tension pneumothorax should be suspected when shortness of breath is severe and the person is fighting for air. His lips and fingernails are usually purple. Sometimes the trachea just above the sternum is shifted to the side away from the pneumothorax; the point where the heart is felt may also be shifted in the same direction.

No treatment is needed unless a tension pneumothorax develops. Then the pressure must be relieved by inserting a needle or tube into the affected side of the chest, a simple procedure that may be life-saving but should be done only by a physician except in desperate circumstances. This procedure is discussed in greater detail in Chapter Eleven, "Chest Injuries," and in Appendix B, "Therapeutic Procedures."

Individuals with a spontaneous pneumothorax need to rest for a week or longer until the "leak" in the lung tissue has healed, as it usually does. In wilderness circumstances, the subject should be moved to a location where a physician's help can be obtained if a tension pneumothorax develops. Persons who have had one episode of spontaneous pneumothorax are more vulnerable to others. They may

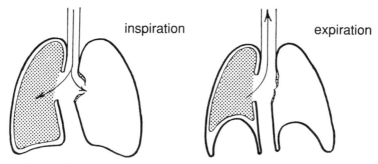

Figure 10-3. Pulmonary function with a tension pneumothorax. (Figures 10-3, 11-1, 11-4, 11-6, and 13-4 are adapted from *Surgery of the Chest*, 3rd ed., by Julian Johnson and Charles E. Kirby. Drawings by Edna Hill. Copyright 1964, Year Book Medical Publishers, Inc. Used by permission.)

consider surgery to try to eliminate the condition, and they certainly should learn, or have their colleagues learn, how to recognize and treat tension pneumothorax if it should develop.

THROMBOPHLEBITIS AND PULMONARY EMBOLISM

Blood clots in the leg veins (or rarely the arms) are not uncommon, particularly at high altitude. Thrombophlebitis, as this condition is called, was seldom recognized before 1950 but is now known to occur with some frequency. Complications also are common.

The major danger from thrombophlebitis lies in the tendency for the blood clots to break off and be carried through the heart into the lungs, a development known as pulmonary embolism. The clots (emboli) obstruct the pulmonary arteries, reducing pulmonary blood flow and the oxygenation of blood in the lungs. Extensive embolism or obstruction of a major pulmonary artery such as the artery to an entire lung is rapidly fatal.

An increased tendency of the blood to clot (increased coagulability) and slowing or even cessation of blood flow in the veins (stasis) favor the development of thrombophlebitis. Factors increasing the coagulability of blood are:

- Dehydration, which causes the blood to become thicker and more viscous
- An increase in the number of red blood cells due to high altitude, a normal mechanism of acclimatization that also increases the viscosity of blood
- Stress, from exertion and a hostile environment, which causes the blood to clot more readily

Factors predisposing to stasis are:

- Prolonged immobility, such as being stormbound for days in a small tent, immobile, and resting in cramped, awkward positions
- Low temperature, which produces constriction of the arteries in the extremi-

ties to conserve heat, thereby reducing the blood flow to the limbs and the volume of venous blood being returned to the heart

- Heavy packs, which increase stasis in the legs, or standing immobile for long periods of time, which is even more dangerous
- Tight clothing, which easily constricts and obstructs veins because they have thin walls and the pressure within them is low
- Trauma, such as a blow to the large leg or arm muscles, which increases the tendency for clotting

Oral contraceptive drugs also promote the development of thrombophlebitis and pulmonary embolism. Women taking such drugs should discontinue them three weeks before an outing if more than a few days will be spent above 10,000 feet (3,000 m).

Diagnosis of Thrombophlebitis

The most common symptom of thrombophlebitis is a deep, aching pain in the calf, inner side of the thigh, or back of the knee. The pain frequently comes on suddenly and is aggravated by walking. When the thrombosed vein is located in the calf, as it most frequently is, the overlying muscles are tender. Flexing the foot upward also causes pain in the calf. In the arm, thrombophlebitis causes aching and pain on motion of the large muscles.

Usually the affected leg is swollen, which can be detected by measuring the circumference of both legs at identical five-inch intervals from the ankle to the upper thigh. A difference in circumferences of one-half inch is common and of no significance; greater differences are cause for concern. The limb may be pale, is sometimes cyanotic, and may have diminished arterial pulsations. A slight fever is sometimes present and lasts an average of seven to ten days.

Rarely, clots form in the legs or pelvis without causing inflammation, a condition known as phlebothrombosis. In the absence of inflammation, these clots produce no symptoms. They also are more loosely attached to the vessel walls and more likely to be detached and carried to the lungs. Consequently, if a person is in pulmonary distress and other pulmonary disorders do not appear to be present, pulmonary embolism must be suspected even though signs of thrombophlebitis are absent.

Red, tender, slightly swollen streaks along the arms or legs can be indicative of thrombophlebitis, but embolism rarely results from involvement of these superficial veins. Such streaks are suggestive of infection.

Diagnosis of Pulmonary Embolism

Pulmonary embolism causes the sudden onset of pain in the chest. Cough, shortness of breath, and a rapid pulse usually accompany the pain. Later the pain becomes pleuritic and is aggravated by respiration, particularly deep breathing. White, frothy material is coughed up at first, but the sputum becomes bloody within a few hours. The respiratory and pulse rates are increased and a slight fever is frequently present. Signs of consolidation (increased or absent breath sounds and dullness to percussion) may appear over the involved area a day or so after onset.

If the embolus obstructs a large artery, the initial symptom may be the sudden onset of a sense of suffocation rather than pain. More severe shortness of breath, cyanosis, distension of neck veins, and signs of shock follow shortly. Pleuritic pain, cough, bloody sputum, and signs of consolidation usually develop a few hours later, although the pain of pleural involvement may be absent if the blood clot lodges in a central part of the lung.

A large pulmonary embolus will produce cardiovascular collapse and death within seconds. A smaller embolus causes respiratory difficulty, and the subject may die more slowly from hypoxia, particularly at high altitude.

Prevention

Prevention is important but difficult. Anyone confined to a tent by a storm should change position and exercise his feet and legs for a few minutes every hour. Constricting clothing should be removed. Hospitalized postoperative subjects often wear snug elastic stockings that come up to the knee, but these are of doubtful benefit and would be impractical in the wilderness. Short, tight stockings or gaiters may increase the risk of thrombosis. Extra fluids are essential at altitude, where dehydration promotes thrombophlebitis as well as hypothermia and other problems. Persons with varicose veins should either avoid high altitude, obtain instructions on how to deal with the problem, or have the condition surgically corrected.

Treatment

Aspirin decreases the tendency of the blood to clot, particularly at high altitude, and might be given when thrombophlebitis or pulmonary embolism is first suspected. In a hospital, stronger anticoagulant therapy is routinely given for thrombophlebitis with or without embolism, but the consequences of an overdose are dangerous without laboratory control. Moderate analgesics are usually adequate for pain.

Once thrombophlebitis develops, the individual should be immobilized. Walking or other movements may cause the clots to break off and embolize. The feet should be elevated slightly, and awkward positions should be avoided. A snug, but not tight, elastic bandage wrapped around the leg from toes to knees is thought by some to decrease the risk of embolism and is unlikely to worsen matters. Immobilization should be continued until the pain and tenderness disappear.

Because so much fluid is lost through breathing and insensible perspiration at altitude, dehydration is common and dangerous. Climbers, trekkers, and hikers, particularly those confined to camp by storms and those who already have thrombophlebitis, must force themselves to consume large quantities of fluids. Frostbite also predisposes to thrombophlebitis.

An expedition to a remote area is faced with a difficult decision when a member develops thrombophlebitis. Keeping the person quiet, his limb bandaged, and hydrating him carefully is desirable. On the other hand, staying for very long in a high altitude camp on snow or ice is difficult. Descent may be unavoidable. The dilemma is far greater once pulmonary embolism has occurred and life is threatened by subsequent emboli. Evacuation is essential, but the individual should be carried as much as possible. If walking is unavoidable, the affected limb should be carefully bandaged, particularly if embolism has occurred. Not to evacuate such persons to hospital care is too risky, but every precaution must be taken to ensure that minimum activity and stress result.

CHAPTER ELEVEN

CHEST INJURIES

C hest injuries are of particular importance because they interfere with the vital function of respiration. At high altitudes, where the oxygen content of air is low, even minor injuries to the chest may be life-threatening. In contrast to abdominal injuries, however, definite help can be given to individuals with chest injuries in wilderness situations.

Following any chest injury in which breathing is difficult and oxygenation marginal, propping the person in a sitting position is helpful. While lying down, the abdominal organs press on the diaphragm and squeeze the lungs into the upper part of the chest. Such encroachment is more likely to occur in obese people. In a sitting position these organs pull down on the diaphragm, giving the lungs more room for expansion and improving ventilation. Even rolling an obese person on his side helps, for the weight of his belly and abdominal organs rests on the ground, not against his lungs.

THE MECHANICS OF RESPIRATION

(The anatomy of the respiratory system is described in Chapter Ten, "Respiratory System Disorders.") During inspiration, muscles in the chest wall pull the ribs upward. Simultaneously the diaphragm contracts and pulls itself downward, which expands the chest and draws air into the lungs. In contrast, expiration is a passive recoil that requires no muscular action. Elastic tissue in the lung, which is stretched as the lung expands during inspiration, pulls the chest wall and diaphragm back into their original positions during expiration (fig. 11-1).

Each lung is enveloped by a thin membrane, the pleura; a continuation of this membrane lines the inner surface of the rib cage. The space between these two layers is called the pleural cavity. Normally the lungs fill the entire thorax so that the two layers of pleura are in intimate contact and no real space is present in the pleural "cavity." However, if the chest wall is perforated or a lung is punctured, air enters the pleural space through the defect. The elasticity of the lung causes it to collapse, and as the chest wall expands with each breath, air is pulled through the perforation into the pleural space instead of being pulled into the lung. This condition is known as pneumothorax (air in the thorax.) In the pleural space, air is not in contact with blood as it is in the alveoli. The resulting loss of oxygen transport can be fatal.

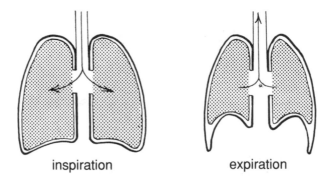

inspiration   expiration

Figure 11-1. Normal pulmonary function. (Adapted from *Surgery of the Chest*, 3rd ed.)

CLOSED CHEST INJURIES

Broken Rib

A forceful blow to the chest may break one or more ribs, but the ribs are so enmeshed by muscles that they rarely need to be splinted or realigned like other broken bones. Other than producing discomfort, most rib fractures are not serious injuries. (Rarely, one end of a broken rib is displaced inward and can puncture the lung and produce a pneumothorax.) However, the discomfort can be surprisingly disabling; movement of almost any part of the body causes pain at the fracture site. Pain also interferes with motion of the chest wall and movement of air within the underlying lung.

A broken rib should be suspected when a blow to the chest is followed by pain and tenderness at the point of impact, particularly when the pain is aggravated by deep breathing or movement. Rarely can a defect be palpated at the point of fracture because the ends of the rib are held in position by their surrounding muscles.

Adhesive strapping over the rib is not advisable, particularly at altitudes above 10,000 feet (3,000 m). Immobilization of the chest wall interferes even more with movement of the chest on that side, which allows secretions to collect in the immobile lung. Pneumonia often follows because the secretions are an ideal medium for bacterial growth. At lower elevations, if the pain can not be controlled with moderate analgesics, four or five strips of two- or three-inch adhesive tape can be applied to the chest to minimize movement of the injured area. The strips of tape should lie over and parallel with the fractured rib and should run from the midline in front past the vertebral column in back. Taping usually gives some relief from pain but should be removed as soon as the individual has been evacuated—two to three days at the most. Similar immobilization can also be provided by wrapping the chest with an elastic bandage, but since both sides of the chest are restrained, this technique is more dangerous.

A blow to the chest may damage organs adjacent to the thorax, such as the kidneys, liver, and spleen. Individuals who have suffered a blow to the lower chest must be carefully monitored for evidence of injury to these organs.

Pneumothorax

If a broken rib punctures the underlying lung, the tear in the pleura can rarely function as a one-way valve that allows air to enter the pleural space during inspiration, but closes and does not allow air to leave the space during expiration. As a result, the lung collapses and respiration can be severely impaired (fig. 11-2).

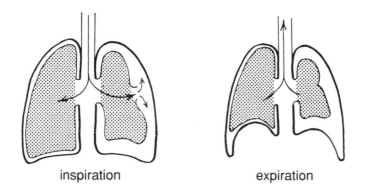

inspiration   expiration

Figure 11-2. Pulmonary function with a punctured lung and intact chest wall. (Adapted from *Surgery of the Chest*, 3rd ed.)

Typically a person with a pneumothorax has received a blow to the chest that is followed by respiratory distress. Pain and tenderness similar to that of an uncomplicated rib fracture are present; chest wall instability or flail (see below) is usually absent. When listening to the chest, preferably with a stethoscope, breath sounds are greatly diminished or absent over the entire chest on the side of the injury, a highly significant diagnostic finding. The pressure within the pleural space may push the heart to the opposite side, causing the point at which the heartbeat is felt to shift away from the injured side (fig. 11-3). The trachea in the lower part of the neck also may be pushed to the side opposite the pneumothorax, but these changes may be subtle and difficult to detect in wilderness conditions.

Occasionally pneumothorax occurs in a healthy person without any prior injury, an event called spontaneous pneumothorax. The individual typically complains of chest pain that has appeared suddenly and is associated with shortness of breath. These alarming symptoms in an older person and on the left side of the chest may suggest a heart attack. Although painful and frightening, spontaneous pneumothorax is rarely fatal. Some persons have repeated episodes and can rec-

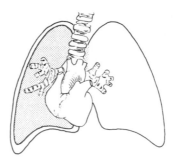

Figure 11-3. Collapse of the left lung and shift of heart and trachea to the right with left pneumothorax.

ognize the disorder when it occurs in a wilderness setting. Even though the condition ordinarily is not life-threatening, an individual with spontaneous pneumothorax should be evacuated. If shortness of breath is not severe, he may even be able to walk out.

Although oxygen partially alleviates symptoms of pneumothorax, the only definitive treatment is to remove the air trapped in the pleural cavity and allow the lung to expand. This procedure should be performed in a hospital, where the chance of infection is minimal. If, however, the person is so desperately short of breath and so cyanotic that he appears to be dying, tube thoracostomy may have to be performed in more primitive circumstances. Only a person who has practiced thoracostomy should attempt tube drainage of the chest. The possible dangers—almost certain major infection, puncture of the heart or a major blood vessel, missing the chest and puncturing the liver or spleen—outweigh the potential benefits in totally untrained hands. (See the technique for tube thoracostomy in Appendix B, "Therapeutic Procedures.")

Decompression of a pneumothorax produces immediate relief of respiratory distress. However, hazards still exist. The presence of a tube in the chest wall creates an opening through which bacteria can enter the pleural space. To reduce the risk of infection, the area around the tube must be kept clean and covered with sterile bandages. Penicillin may be administered every six hours if the probability of infection appears great.

Tube thoracostomy is not to be undertaken lightly and should be attempted only if the subject appears to be dying. **The person performing the procedure must have had prior experience with the technique under the guidance of a surgeon.** However, since the technique may be life-saving, particularly for traumatic pneumothorax at high altitude, it should be utilized if an experienced individual and adequate equipment are available.

Hemothorax

An injury to the chest may damage blood vessels in the chest wall or in the lung, causing bleeding into the pleural space. The hazards of hemothorax, as an accumulation of blood in the chest is called, are: collapse of the lung as blood fills the chest; the rare instances in which blood loss is sufficiently large to produce shock; the tendency of the clot to become infected; and constriction of the lung as the clot retracts weeks or months after the injury.

Blood accumulating in the chest after an injury should be removed; however, removal can be delayed until the individual is evacuated. The desperate respiratory distress that occurs with a tension pneumothorax is rare with a hemothorax, and the danger that the subject will bleed to death into his chest is small.

Hemothorax usually follows a severe, nonpenetrating injury to the chest and may produce signs and symptoms that simulate pneumothorax. However, tapping on the bare chest produces a dull, solid sound over the accumulating blood instead of the resonant or hollow sound heard over air-filled lungs or pleura. If the person can be placed in a sitting position, breath sounds may be absent over the lower part of the chest on the side of the injury and yet be present over the upper portion. (The breath sounds may be difficult to hear without a stethoscope.)

Bleeding into the chest cavity usually stops spontaneously within a few hours. If shock does appear, it should be treated. Nothing can be done to stop the bleeding without surgical intervention, and even that is impossible in hospitals that are not equipped for chest surgery. Evacuation should be carried out as soon as the blood pressure, pulse rate, respiratory rate, and general condition indicate the person can tolerate being moved.

If an individual is in such a remote area that he can not be evacuated for several days or weeks and bleeding is so severe that the lung can not expand properly, tube thoracostomy may be necessary to remove the blood from the chest.

Flail Chest

Fracture of a number of adjacent ribs in two or more places can produce a mobile, freely floating plate of chest wall that moves back and forth during respiration—a flail chest. When the chest expands, the negative pressure pulls the loosened segment of chest wall inward instead of pulling air into the lung; during expiration the loosened plate is forced outward (fig. 11-4). Inspiration and expi-

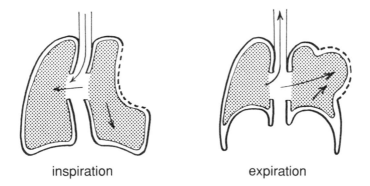

inspiration   expiration

Figure 11-4. Pulmonary function with a flail chest. (Adapted from *Surgery of the Chest*, 3rd ed.)

ration only move the chest wall instead of moving air into or out of the lungs, which results in severe respiratory distress, even if the damaged area is small. A large area of flail, particularly at high altitudes, may be fatal and requires immediate treatment.

The person typically has received a severe blow to the chest followed immediately by pain and difficulty with breathing. He is usually fighting for air and breathing very rapidly; his lips, skin, and nails may be cyanotic due to poor oxygenation. Careful examination of the chest discloses a mobile segment of chest wall that moves "paradoxically" with each respiration. When the rest of the chest expands on inspiration, the loosened segment of chest wall is pulled inward; when the chest contracts during expiration, the flail segment is pushed outward.

Flail chest must be differentiated from a simple broken rib that produces pain with breathing but does not interfere with the movement of air.

The treatment of flail chest centers upon immobilization of the loosened segment of chest wall and reestablishing normal respiratory function. In an emergency, the subject can simply be made to lie on the injured side (despite some initial pain) with a rolled-up piece of clothing beneath the loose segment of rib cage (fig. 11-5). The pressure effectively immobilizes the loosened portion of the chest wall and allows more adequate respiration. Such a simple measure may often prove life-saving.

Figure 11-5. Subject lying on a rolled-up garment to support a flail chest.

After fixation of the rib cage has been achieved with adhesive tape, immobilization of the loose chest wall fragment through external pressure on the broken rib segments by a sand bag or even a smooth rock properly padded, the person can lie on his back or be moved in a stretcher. The loosened segment of chest wall must not be allowed to move; any reasonable means of immobilization benefits respiratory function.

The lung underlying a flail chest is usually bruised and poorly aerated. Secretions accumulate in the damaged lung because drainage is impaired. To avoid pneumonia the subject must be encouraged or forced—despite the pain—to clear his lungs frequently by coughing.

The need for oxygen therapy can be determined by the degree of respiratory distress and the individual's general condition. If he has a severe flail and can not be moved immediately to a physician's care, penicillin should be given every six hours to reduce the danger of pneumonia. At altitudes over 10,000 feet (3,000 m), both antibiotic and oxygen therapy should be administered, even for relatively minor flail chest injuries that would not require such vigorous therapy at lower altitudes.

The advisability of emergency evacuation depends on the situation and the person's condition. Even with an extensive injury, the chest wall becomes relatively stable within about one week. However, during this period pneumonia and progressive hypoxia of life-threatening proportions can develop. If such complications appear, oxygen should be administered and the individual evacuated. He must be hospitalized where he can be placed on a mechanical ventilator if necessary.

PERFORATING CHEST INJURIES

A fall onto a pointed object such as an ice axe (particularly during an ice axe arrest) may actually punch a hole in the chest wall, producing one of the few medical emergencies in which minutes can determine success or failure. A hole in the thoracic wall allows air to be sucked through the wound into the pleural cavity, causing the lung to collapse. Subsequent respiratory efforts move air back and forth through the hole in the chest wall rather than through the trachea, and the person rapidly suffocates (fig. 11-6).

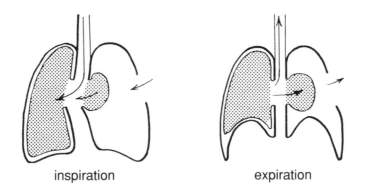

inspiration   expiration

Figure 11-6. Pulmonary function with a punctured chest wall. (Adapted from *Surgery of the Chest*, 3rd ed.)

The penetrating injury of the chest is almost always obvious, a so-called "sucking wound" through which air is sucked into the chest during inspiration. The subject begins fighting for air almost immediately and soon becomes cyanotic, loses consciousness, and goes into shock if untreated.

The hole in the chest must be tightly closed as quickly as possible. The best method of closing such a wound is with sterile, fine mesh; gauze impregnated with petroleum jelly; and an outer, thick, sterile dressing. If these materials are not available, the cleanest available substitutes must be utilized immediately. A clean handkerchief, or even a parka, can be stuffed over the opening. **The hole**

must be closed immediately or without exception the individual will die. A more ideal dressing may be applied later, but air must not be permitted to enter the chest while the coverings are being switched.

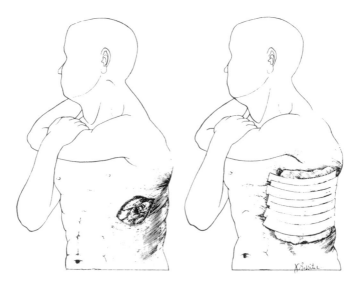

Figure 11-7. Open chest wound before and after bandaging.

Oxygen therapy should be instituted at the earliest opportunity and discontinued only when the subject's condition has definitely stabilized. Decompression of the chest with a chest tube may be necessary. Shock almost invariably accompanies a large penetrating wound of the chest and should be anticipated and treated. If the person is not allergic to penicillin, a penicillinase-resistant penicillin or a cephalosporin should be given every six hours until evacuation is completed.

All individuals with penetrating injuries of the chest must be evacuated at the earliest possible moment so that the hole in the chest wall can be permanently closed by surgery.

CHAPTER TWELVE

GASTROINTESTINAL DISORDERS

The gastrointestinal tract consists of the mouth and throat, esophagus, stomach, small and large intestines, liver, gallbladder, and pancreas. This system ingests food, converts it into forms that can be used by the body, and excretes the waste.

The esophagus aids in swallowing and propels the food into the stomach, where it is digested for thirty to ninety minutes by enzymes and hydrochloric acid. The food next passes into the small intestine (duodenum) where enzymes from the intestinal mucosa and the pancreas further prepare the partially digested food for absorption. Bile salts produced by the liver and stored in the gallbladder help emulsify fats so they can be absorbed. Absorption takes place in the middle and lower segments of the small intestine (jejunum and ileum). In the large intestine, water is extracted from the residual material. All of the blood from the small intestine first goes to the liver, where an array of complex biochemical reactions converts the absorbed nutrients to substances needed by other tissues and organs.

Diseases of many organs produce symptoms referable to the alimentary tract, particularly nausea and vomiting. Illnesses originating in the gastrointestinal tract produce similar symptoms and often cannot be distinguished without sophisticated diagnostic facilities. Furthermore, even when the nature of a disorder is known precisely, specific therapy may not be available. Therefore, the treatment for most gastrointestinal disorders that appear for the first time in a wilderness situation or in an underdeveloped country is limited to alleviating symptoms.

The signs of disease of the gastrointestinal system are nausea and vomiting, diarrhea, constipation, bleeding, jaundice, and pain. Pain that comes on suddenly is such an eminent problem that it is discussed separately in Chapter Thirteen, "Acute Abdominal Pain." Procedures for examining the abdomen are also described in that chapter.

NAUSEA AND VOMITING

The causes of vomiting are innumerable and include such widely differing conditions as motion sickness, head injuries, metabolic disorders, infections, pregnancy, ulcers, environmental heat, and appendicitis.

If the subject is stuporous or unconscious, a single bout of vomiting can be disastrous. The vomitus can be aspirated into the lungs, resulting in severe pneumonia that is difficult to treat. Respiratory obstruction can be lethal if the volume of aspirated material is large. At the first sign of vomiting, an unconscious patient must be rolled onto his side with his head lowered. He may be lifted by the waist twelve to eighteen inches if he has not been involved in an accident that could have produced a fractured spine. (If a blow to the head is responsible for the unconsciousness, he should be assumed to have a broken neck.) The head down position must be maintained until vomiting has ceased and the vomitus has been cleared from his mouth. **The subject must not be allowed to aspirate the vomited material.**

Protracted vomiting sometimes ruptures small blood vessels in the lining of the stomach and small amounts of blood appear in the vomitus. Chronic use of aspirin or excessive alcohol consumption can irritate the stomach and cause vomitus to be bloody. When ulcers of the stomach or duodenum cause vomiting, the vomitus may contain large quantities of blood.

Vomiting caused by minor disorders often stops without any treatment. After the first bout the individual usually feels better and is able to resume limited activity. If vomiting does not stop within a few hours, a serious underlying disease must be considered. Vomiting may be an important sign of brain injury, an acute abdominal disorder such as intestinal obstruction or appendicitis, drug overdose, or some other disease. If an individual has one of these disorders, control of vomiting with medications could delay diagnosis and definitive treatment.

When no underlying disease can be identified, vomiting can be treated symptomatically. If oral medications can be kept down, prochlorperazine (Compazine®) can be given. Therapy should continue until the subject has been asymptomatic for at least four hours. If oral drugs can not be retained, prochlorperazine rectal suppositories can be inserted every four to six hours until oral medications can be kept down. Treatment for more than twenty-four hours should be avoided. Drowsiness is a common side effect of all drugs used to treat vomiting; while taking prochlorperazine the subject must not take part in activities that could result in injury.

If vomiting is prolonged, the body becomes depleted of fluid and salt. On rare occasions, vomiting can not be stopped until the fluid and salt have been replaced; treating such intractable vomiting requires intravenous fluids. If fluids for intravenous therapy are not available, the person must be evacuated.

Following recovery, fluids should be replaced as quickly as possible to correct dehydration. The subject should eat bland foods, preferably liquids, for about twenty-four hours.

Motion Sickness

Symptoms of motion sickness can sometimes be reduced by lying still with the eyes open. Limiting the motion that causes the symptoms—by moving from the back to the front seat of a car, sitting over the wing of an airplane, or moving to the center of a ship—is often helpful.

Several over-the-counter drugs effectively control motion sickness. Dimenhydrinate (Dramamine®) is an old standby. Meclizine (Bonine® and Antivert®) or cyclizine (Marezine®) are more effective for some individuals.

Drug treatment is most effective if started one hour before the motion is encountered. The medication should be taken every four to six hours thereafter until the motion ceases, except for cyclizine, which needs to be taken only every twenty-four hours. Drowsiness is a common side effect of all of these agents; activities requiring alertness may not be advisable while taking them.

DIARRHEA

Diarrhea is the most notorious of traveler's illnesses. However, the most common cause is a change in food or water; most other causes are equally benign, although a few diseases characterized by diarrhea can be life-threatening.

Table 12-1 lists disorders that can usually be distinguished without laboratory facilities; each disorder has several causes. The two most common groups of disorders are traveler's diarrhea (noninvasive) and invasive bacterial diarrhea. These disorders are similar in many ways, but invasive bacterial infections are associated with chills and fever and the presence of pus, mucus, or blood in the stool, whereas traveler's diarrhea is not. Invasive bacterial infections should be treated with antimicrobial agents, but such drugs are less necessary for traveler's diarrhea, particularly when the cause is a viral infection. Antidiarrheal agents may be helpful with traveler's diarrhea but should be avoided with invasive infections because they can aggravate and prolong the illness.

The other disorders in table 12-1 have unique features that require special attention. They are listed according to the potential severity of the underlying disease and not the severity of the diarrhea. Any of the disorders may produce only mild symptoms, and none, except cholera, produce worse diarrhea than

---

TABLE 12-1.
Common Causes of Diarrhea

MILD	SEVERE
Acute	*Acute*
Traveler's diarrhea	Invasive bacterial infections
Staphylococcal enteritis	Cholera
Chronic	*Subacute*
Change of food or water	Typhoid fever
Disease of other organs	
Giardiasis	*Chronic*
Irritable colon syndrome*	Amebiasis
	Inflammatory bowel disease*

*Chronic disorders with preexisting symptoms

traveler's diarrhea, a self-limiting disorder that usually clears in a few days (although individuals with illnesses that last for months are being recognized with increasing frequency). Usually the only treatment needed for these disorders is fluid replacement. Amebiasis initially produces mild symptoms in most patients, but fatal complications can result from untreated infestations.

All organisms that cause diarrheal diseases are killed by bringing water to a boil, regardless of altitude, or by appropriate exposure to iodine. (See Chapter Five, "Immunizations, Sanitation, and Water Disinfection.") However, infectious bacteria may survive well in food stored in a refrigerator, at room temperature, and even at temperatures that are too hot to touch comfortably. Food and beverages are safe only if they have been brought to boiling or near boiling temperatures prior to consumption.

Traveler's Diarrhea

Most acute gastroinstestinal infections (gastroenteritis) occurring in visitors to other countries, particularly underdeveloped areas, are classified as traveler's diarrhea. About one-third of visitors from the United States, Canada, and Europe will develop diarrhea during their travels in underdeveloped countries. This group of disorders has many colorful names, such as Aztec two-step, Delhi belly, Montezuma's revenge, or simply *turista*. This disorder is not limited to travelers, however.

Enteropathogenic *Escherichia coli* are the most common cause of traveler's diarrhea. *E. coli are* bacteria normally found in everyone's large bowel. Individuals become resistant to toxins from the specific strains found in their environment, and for them these organisms do not cause disease. However, exposure to strains to which the individual has not developed resistance often produces illness.

Other noninvasive bacteria also cause traveler's diarrhea, and a high percentage of the severe diarrheal disorders acquired in the wilderness are of viral origin. Even *Giardia* have been associated with traveler's diarrhea.

Infection is usually spread by fecal contamination of water or food and is more common in countries with inadequate sewage disposal and water disinfection. However, travelers coming to the United States or Europe sometimes develop *turista*. The illness may be contracted anywhere.

Traveler's diarrhea can be prevented in several ways; avoiding infection is clearly best, but is not always easy. Undisinfected water is the major source of infection. Even in large, modern hotels, tap water may be contaminated and must be disinfected before being used even for brushing teeth. Many of the better (and more expensive) hotels provide vacuum bottles or pitchers of disinfected water for drinking. However, some of these hotels may still serve drinks containing ice prepared from undisinfected water. (Beer, bottled soft drinks, and bottled carbonated water are safe. Bottled noncarbonated water usually is safe, but not always.)

Previously peeled fruits and salads containing leafy vegetables are well-recognized sources of infection. Fruits with a protective rind that is not eaten are generally safe, but such fruits split open for display in markets are often splashed with undisinfected water so they will remain attractive. Melons sold by the pound are often injected with undisinfected water to increase their weight. All fruits and vegetables should be thoroughly washed in a strong solution of chlorine or iodine and peeled, if possible.

Contamination of food during preparation must be avoided. Modern concepts of sanitation, even such simple measures as hand washing after defecation, are totally alien to most natives of undeveloped countries. They must be monitored to ensure that they wash before preparing food. Stool cultures to detect carriers of infectious diseases are desirable for the native personnel in large parties, particularly those engaged in preparing meals, but are essentially impossible to obtain. Iodine disinfection of water used for food preparation as well as for drinking may be necessary. Unfortunately, such precautions are not universally effective and are difficult to sustain for a prolonged time.

The incubation period for traveler's diarrhea is usually twelve to forty-eight hours, and it usually lasts two to five days. The onset is characterized by rapidly developing generalized abdominal distress culminating in waves of cramps and diarrhea. During spasms of pain a person may draw his knees up against his abdomen for relief. However, the periods between spasms are relatively free of pain. Nausea is common and may be accompanied by vomiting; occasionally nausea and vomiting are the dominant features of the illness.

Mild generalized abdominal tenderness may be present, particularly in the lower abdomen, and the bowel sounds are usually much louder than normal. Chills and fever are mild or absent.

The diarrhea is frequently explosive at onset and is characterized by copious, watery, foul-smelling stools. The number of stools varies from three or four to as many as twenty—sometimes more. Mucus is occasionally present in the stool, particularly when stools are numerous; pus and blood are absent.

Antimicrobial agents can prevent traveler's diarrhea, but physicians are justifiably reluctant to recommend their routine use. All antibiotics have potentially significant side effects. They predispose individuals to the development of invasive bacterial infections and can induce drug resistance in bacteria, increasing the risk of infection by organisms that are antibiotic-resistant and more dangerous.

An over-the-counter drug, bismuth subsalicylate (Pepto-Bismol®), is approximately sixty-five percent effective in preventing traveler's diarrhea. The liquid form is so bulky that its use is impractical. Fortunately, the tablets appear to be effective (two tablets four times a day). This drug has no major toxicity and appears considerably safer for prophylactic use than antimicrobial agents. Aspirin, which also is a salicylate, should not be taken concomitantly with Pepto-Bismol®.

The essential element of treatment for vomiting and diarrhea is fluid and salt replacement. (The relief of other symptoms, although desirable, is of secondary importance.) These disorders often produce significant dehydration, although lethal dehydration is rare. The dehydration almost invariably encountered at high altitudes would definitely be aggravated by vomiting or diarrhea.

Urine volume and color are reliable indicators of dehydration; small volumes (less than 500 cc daily) of dark yellow or orange urine indicate substantial fluid depletion.

To replace fluids and salts, fruit juices, broths, and soups can be consumed. Rehydration with a sugar and salt solution may be more effective. (The sugar is a key ingredient because it promotes absorption of the salts.) Two formulas for replacement solutions are listed in table 12-2. Others can be found in standard references.

TABLE 12-2.
Oral Fluid Replacement Solutions

Sodium chloride	3.5 g/l	or	1/2 level teaspoon/l
Sodium bicarbonate	2.5 g/l	or	1/2 level teaspoon/l
Potassium chloride	1.5 g/l	or	1/4 level teaspoon/l
Glucose	20 g/l	or	6 level teaspoons/l
	or		
Sucrose (table sugar)	40 g/l	or	12 level teaspoons/l

U.S. Public Health Service Formula (Centers For Disease Control)

Glass #1	*Glass #2*
8 ounces fruit juice 1/2 teaspoon honey or corn syrup 1 pinch table salt	1/2 teaspoon baking soda (bicarbonate) 8 ounces water (disinfected)

Drink equal amounts from each glass, alternating between the two.

The components of oral replacement solutions can be packed in small units at home, can be purchased in prepackaged form, or can be made up in the field. The rather crude measurements listed (teaspoons) are sufficiently accurate for anyone with normally functioning heart and kidneys, which will retain what is needed and excrete the rest. Furthermore, diarrheal salt losses vary more than such measures. Disinfected water must be used to dissolve the salts and glucose. Persons with moderate diarrhea (five to ten watery stools per day) should drink one to three liters of solution in addition to their usual water intake every twenty-four hours. Persons with more severe diarrhea (ten or more watery stools per day) should drink enough solution to equal the volume of the estimated losses and an additional one-and-a-half to two liters per day.

Treatment of nausea and vomiting with prochlorperazine may be required for adequate amounts of oral fluids to be consumed. Bismuth subsalicylate (Pepto-

Bismol®), two tablets every six hours, may also be helpful.

Whether drugs that specifically control diarrhea should be used is controversial. Some evidence suggests these agents may prolong the illness even though the frequency of bowel movements is decreased. A compromise that appears reasonable is to administer medications only to control severe cramps or in circumstances where frequent bowel movements would be hazardous or substantially inconvenient and uncomfortable. Certainly the need to leave a tent five to ten times a night in an ice and snow environment would justify the use of a medication to lessen the frequency of bowel movements.

Paregoric (tincture of opium), codeine, and diphenoxylate (Lomotil®) are effective agents, but are potentially habituating and are available only by prescription. Loperamide (Imodium®) has similar actions and the suspension is available without a prescription. These drugs vary in their effectiveness for different individuals. The drug most effective for each particular individual should be administered; if the initial drug is not effective, one of the others may be tried.

An individual with severe diarrhea (more than ten stools a day) that has persisted for more than a few days, particularly if chills and fever are present and the stools contain blood, mucus, or pus, should seek a physician for diagnostic studies and treatment. If such care is unavailable, many authorities recommend treating such prolonged or severe traveler's diarrhea with an antidiarrheal agent such as loperamide (4 mg of Imodium® followed by 2 mg after each loose stool, not to exceed 16 mg a day) for two days, and an antibiotic such as trimethoprim-sulfamethoxazole (abbreviated TMP-SMX; trade names Bactrim DS® or Septra DS®) every twelve hours, doxycycline (Vibramycin®) every six hours, or ciprofloxacin (Cipro®) every twelve hours—all given for three to five days.

The amount of rest required varies widely. Few individuals are able to continue vigorous activities; most must restrict physical activity until symptoms improve or resolve.

Staphylococcal Enteritis

Staphylococcal enteritis is a type of acute gastroenteritis caused by a toxin produced by staphylococci. These bacteria are present on the hands of about half of the population, and contamination of food during preparation is common. Any food may harbor the organisms, but salads made with mayonnaise, sweets such as custards and cream pies, meat, and milk are most commonly contaminated. The staphylococcal toxin is produced when contaminated food is allowed to stand unrefrigerated for several hours, which allows the organisms to multiply and produce toxin. Subsequent reheating—even boiling—does not destroy the toxin or prevent illness. To prevent contamination and growth of the organism, food must be consumed or refrigerated immediately after it is prepared. (Food contamination with other organisms that have a very short incubation period can produce an identical disorder.)

The onset of cramps and diarrhea, with or without nausea and vomiting, occurs one to six hours—or an average of three hours—after contaminated food is ingested and is frequently abrupt. The diarrhea lasts until the gastrointestinal tract is emptied, rarely more than five to six hours. Most of the individuals who have eaten the contaminated food develop the disease, which establishes the diagnosis. Antibiotics are not effective; they do not neutralize the toxin. Antidiarrheal agents may help.

CHRONIC MILD DIARRHEA

Mild diarrhea consisting only of soft stools and one to four bowel movements a day has many different causes. A change in food, water, or surroundings is the most common. Excitement or anxiety frequently produces such symptoms. Diseases of other organs may be accompanied by mild diarrhea.

These disorders are classified as chronic because they may last for days or even weeks. However, the diarrhea is only bothersome, not incapacitating, and usually clears up without any therapy. Except for giardiasis, antimicrobial agents do not help and should be avoided. One capsule of loperamide (Imodium®) each morning may be helpful.

Individuals with persistent chronic diarrhea after return from an underdeveloped country should consult a physician. Occasionally persistent parasitic infestations that can become major illnesses if untreated cause such disorders.

Giardiasis

In recent years frantic alarms about the perils of giardiasis have aroused exaggerated concern about this infestation. Governmental agencies, particularly the U.S. Park Service and the National Forest Service, have filtered hundreds of gallons of water from wilderness streams, found one or two organisms (far less than enough to be infective), and erected garish signs proclaiming the water "hazardous."

Giardiasis is not a new problem. *Giardia* have always been present in wilderness streams and in the water supplies of most cities. They have not been detected because they are not isolated by routine bacterial cultures. This protozoal parasite is found all over the world. Many animals harbor and excrete the organism, resulting in contamination of wilderness streams, but the organism has been found in the municipal water supplies of a number of large U.S. cities and in cities as diverse as Leningrad and Katmandu.

In humans, the active parasites live in the upper intestinal tract, where they form numerous cysts that are passed in the stool. The cysts do not produce active disease but are resistant to disinfectants and other agents in their environment and do transmit the infestation. Fecal contamination of water is the most common route of transmittal. Less common, but significant, is direct passage from stool to the hands of a food preparer and to the food itself. Iodine in a concentration of eight parts per million effectively kills the cysts within ten minutes (twenty minutes if the water is cold—32°F to 40°F, or 0°C to 5°C). Chlorine treatment or bringing water to a boil also kills the cysts.

The symptoms of giardiasis vary widely. Clearly, most infested individuals have no symptoms at all. In one incident carefully studied by the Centers for Disease Control, disruption in a city's water disinfection system allowed the entire population to consume water heavily contaminated with *Giardia*. Only eleven percent of the exposed population developed symptomatic disease, although forty-six percent had organisms in their stools. In the same study, eight and one-half percent of the population of a neighboring city was found to have totally asymptomatic *Giardia* infestations.

Characteristic symptoms, when they occur, are mild to moderate abdominal discomfort, abdominal distention due to increased intestinal gas ("rotten egg burps"—belches that smell like hydrogen sulfide—are typical), and mild to moderate diarrhea. Stools are soft but not liquid, bulky, and foul-smelling; they do not contain blood, mucus, or pus. Two to four bowel movements a day are typical; cramps may occur. Mild to moderate symptoms of illness, including weakness, loss of appetite or even some nausea, and chilly sensations, may appear. Without treatment the infestation lasts seven to ten days. Apparently most people develop some type of immunity after that time, because symptoms and the organisms disappear and recurrent symptomatic infestations are rare.

Rare individuals, less than one percent of those with infestations, fail to rid themselves of the organisms and develop chronic infestations that often cause malabsorption, weight loss, ulcerlike stomach pain, and other chronic disturbances. Such prolonged infestations may result from mild immunologic deficiencies.

Occasionally giardiasis has been associated with the explosive onset of voluminous diarrhea typical of traveler's diarrhea.

Before attributing any disorder to *Giardia*, a definitive diagnosis is desirable. Until recently, a firm diagnosis has been possible only by identifying organisms in the stool, which is possible in approximately fifty percent of infested individuals. Recently an immunologic test for the detection of *Giardia* has become available, and preliminary evidence indicates that it is more accurate than searching for the organisms.

Travelers, including physicians, often overdiagnose giardiasis. However, if a laboratory is not available and typical symptoms persisting for six to seven days have not been relieved by measures effective for traveler's diarrhea, a therapeutic trial of one of the drugs listed below may be justified.

Two drugs (and perhaps a third) are equally effective. Metronidazole (Flagyl®) for five to ten days is the usual therapy in the United States; cures have been obtained with a single large dose of this drug. When alcohol is consumed while taking Flagyl®, severe vomiting results. Therefore, alcohol must be avoided during and for twenty-four hours after the consumption of Flagyl®.

Quinacrine (Atabrine®) for one week is probably more effective, but this drug has a bitter taste, commonly causes nausea and vomiting, and is not tolerated as well. Yellowing of the skin is a nonsignificant side effect of quinacrine; the benign discoloration should not be confused with jaundice. Both drugs have about an eighty percent cure rate. In the event of failure with one drug, the other can be tried.

Tinidazole is an agent similar to metronidazole (Flagyl®) that is sold under the trade name Tinebah® and can be purchased over the counter in many developing nations. It has often been taken by visitors to those countries for presumed giardiasis. The reported advantages of Tinebah® are its ease of administration—four tablets taken at the same time only once—and avoiding abstinence from alcohol. However, in view of the similarity of this agent to metronidazole, both advantages must be regarded with skepticism.

Irritable Colon Syndrome

Irritable colon syndrome, also known as "mucous colitis" or "spastic colon," is a common disturbance of large intestinal function that may result in either diarrhea or constipation. The syndrome is at least partially emotional in origin and is often related to stress. Most individuals with this disorder have a prior history of similar symptoms; its first occurrence during a wilderness outing would be unusual.

Most subjects have some pain, which may suggest some other disorder; distress is most common in the upper abdomen or the left lower quadrant and may be relieved by the passage of gas or feces.

Individuals with irritable colon syndrome often have other symptoms induced by nervous tension. Belching, loss of appetite, nausea, and occasionally vomiting are the more common gastrointestinal symptoms. Headache, sweating, flushing, shortness of breath, sighing respirations, and hyperventilation may be observed (see Chapter Ten, "Respiratory System Disorders").

The stools are usually thin and tapered (pencil-shaped) with diarrhea or constipation, and abundant mucus is usually present.

Treatment consists principally of recognizing the nature of the disorder and reassuring the patient. Drug therapy of any type is usually undesirable. Drugs such as paregoric or diphenoxylate are usually not effective and should not be used. The disorder disappears as soon as the stress is eliminated, although repeated episodes with subsequent stress are characteristic. A high-residue diet (food containing roughage) or bulk-forming agents such as Metamucil® may be helpful.

SEVERE DIARRHEAS

The acute and subacute severe diarrheas are all of bacterial origin and are most frequently transmitted by fecal contamination of drinking water. In areas where these diseases exist, all water must be carefully disinfected. Other precautions are described in the discussion of traveler's diarrhea earlier in this chapter.

Experienced physicians have difficulty distinguishing different invasive bacterial diarrheas in the wilderness. Nonphysicians in this situation can not expect to be able to make correct diagnoses. Individuals in any of the following categories who are considered to have an invasive gastrointestinal bacterial infection should contact a medical center with a bacteriologic laboratory as soon as possible:

1. Children under three years of age and adults over sixty-five, particularly those with other significant illnesses
2. Individuals who are pregnant
3. Anyone with severe diarrhea lasting more than forty-eight to seventy-two hours that is associated with any of the following: stools that contain blood or easily detected pus; pronounced abdominal tenderness; fever (morning temperature over 99°F or 37.2°C; evening temperature over 100°F or 37.8°C); dehydration (loss of more than five percent of usual body weight)

If timely evacuation is impossible, appropriate antimicrobial drugs should be administered. Under these circumstances, pregnant individuals present a special problem, since some of the drugs normally used may harm the developing child. Loperamide (Imodium®) is safe; TMP-SMX is relatively safe for the first eight months but should be avoided at term.

Precautions are necessary to avoid spread of the infection. A person with one of these diseases should be isolated as much as possible. Attendants should be limited to one or two individuals who are scrupulous about cleanliness.

The attendants should wear protective rubber or plastic gloves, if they are available, and must scrub their hands vigorously, preferably with an antibacterial soap such as pHisoHex® or Betadine®, after any contact with the subject. All feces and vomitus should be buried where contamination of water will not occur, preferably after being mixed with an antiseptic such as one percent Cresol®. All utensils and other instruments should be immersed in boiling water. Indispensable items, such as clothing or sleeping bags that can not be boiled, should be aired in bright sunlight for at least one or two days after the subject is recovering.

Invasive Bacterial Infections (Dysentery)

Invasive bacterial infections, or bacillary dysentery, are caused by a wide variety of bacteria, including *Salmonella, Shigella, Campylobacter, Yersinia, Aeromonas, Clostridium,* noncholera vibrios, and occasionally by other organisms. These organisms are found in temperate as well as tropical areas, but severe cases of bacillary dysentery occur most frequently in tropical or semitropical climates.

Salmonellae are particularly widespread. Virtually all domestic animals, including household pets—dogs, cats, birds, and turtles—and many wild animals harbor these bacteria. The number of asymptomatic human carriers has been estimated at two persons per thousand.

Infections are spread by contaminated water and food. Any item of food or drink can be contaminated; for salmonella, the greatest single source of human disease is poultry products—both meat and eggs—and raw meat of other types. Lack of hydrochloric acid in the stomach and alteration of the normal microbial flora in the intestinal tract by antibiotics increases susceptibility to infection by these organisms.

The incubation period varies from one to six days with an average of forty-eight hours (somewhat shorter for salmonella). The onset is often rather abrupt and is characterized by severe, intermittent abdominal cramps followed by diarrhea, which may be copious and soon progresses to watery, foul stools. The stools contain large amounts of mucus and pus and occasionally moderate amounts of blood, particularly four to five hours after the onset. Nausea is common but vomiting may not occur. Infection usually is associated with fever (100.5°F to 102°F, or 38°C to 39°C, or higher) and chilly feelings or frank, shaking chills. Abdominal tenderness may be pronounced, is most marked in the lower portion of the abdomen, and is frequently accompanied by spasm of the abdominal muscles. Abdominal pain may be sufficiently intense, localized, and associated with enough rebound tenderness to suggest an acute abdominal disorder requiring surgery. The subject is obviously ill and may be prostrate.

After six to eight hours the symptoms abate somewhat, but the disease may take seven to ten days to run its course. Considerable variation in the severity of symptoms is observed, even among persons infected at the same meal.

The most important aspect of treatment for invasive bacterial gastroenteritis is prompt correction of dehydration. Large amounts of fluids, such as those in table 12-2, should be administered. Intravenous fluids may be necessary for more severe cases. A bland diet may be given if it can be tolerated.

A hot-water bottle or other source of warmth placed on the abdomen may reduce some of the pain and tenderness. Drugs to stop the diarrhea should not be given because these drugs tend to produce intestinal paralysis, which prevents the subject from taking fluids orally. They also may make the fever and overall disability worse.

These infections should be treated with antibacterial agents. Ciprofloxacin (Cipro®) every twelve hours is the drug of choice; trimethoprim-sulfamethoxazole (TMP-SMX) every twelve hours is the second choice. (In Latin America, twenty-five percent of *Shigella* currently are resistant to TMP-SMX.) The usual duration of therapy is one week.

Antimicrobial therapy frequently produces marked improvement in twenty-four hours or less but must be continued for at least five days or longer if symptoms persist.

Individuals with these infections require rest; most should be in bed. People with bacillary dysentery frequently require seven to ten days to recover their strength after symptoms have disappeared.

Cholera

Cholera, once a scourge throughout the world, is almost nonexistent where modern sanitation and water purification methods are practiced. However, infections that claim many lives are common in some areas. A major outbreak that has claimed many lives is rampant in Peru, Ecuador, and Colombia as this is written. In many Southeast Asian countries, the early monsoons wash feces that has collected on the ground and in the streets into streams and rivers and regularly precipitate epidemics. When accurately diagnosed, cholera can be effectively treated, but such care is unavailable for the poor in many undeveloped countries.

Although cholera is transmitted primarily by contaminated water, the infection may also be contracted from food, particularly items that are not cooked. A vaccine has been developed but is only about fifty percent effective and lasts only about six months. The vaccine is not recommended by the CDC and other authorities, but vaccination is required by some countries for entry by individuals who have been visiting or living in an area where cholera is endemic.

Fortunately, the cholera vibrio can not survive for very long outside the human body. As a result, most infections occur near areas of significant population and thus in areas where hospitals are available. However, undiagnosed subjects with mild symptoms and carriers, although much rarer than carriers of the salmonella that causes typhoid fever, may spread the organisms a considerable distance from hospitals. The speed with which prostration appears in severe infections usually prevents evacuation and mandates treatment in the field.

The incubation period for cholera is one to three days, during which the subject may notice mild diarrhea, depression, and lassitude. The end of the incubation period is signaled by the explosive onset of voluminous, thin, watery diarrhea. The infection can become overwhelming with amazing speed, leaving the subject severely dehydrated and in shock from fluid loss in one to three hours.

The gastrointestinal tract is quickly emptied and the stools lose their fecal character and foul smell. The patient is constantly dribbling stools consisting almost entirely of water. Flecks of mucus that look like grains of rice floating in water have resulted in the name "rice water stools" for this material. The stools rarely contain blood.

Frequently, no warning of the need to defecate is felt, resulting in repeated, often uncontrollable bowel evacuations. Similarly, vomiting may occur without antecedent nausea, although vomiting is uncommon after the onset. As the subject becomes dehydrated, fever and a rapid pulse appear. The blood pressure frequently drops below normal and the weak pulse becomes difficult to feel. The features become gaunt, the eyes shrunken, and the skin shriveled and dry. Urinary output falls to less than 500 ml per day.

The treatment for cholera is fluid replacement. The entire volume of stool and vomitus must be replaced with oral or intravenous salt solutions. Stool volumes must be measured if replacement is to be accurate. Intravenous administration of fluids is often necessary during the early stages of the disease, particularly if vomiting is substantial, and may be life-saving if the subject is severely dehydrated and in shock. Two to four liters of saline or Ringer's lactate may be required in the first hour and as much as eight or more liters during the first day. After dehydration has been corrected and the subject is no longer in shock, he usually is able to take fluids orally. Either of the replacement solutions listed in table 12-2 is suitable.

Individuals with cholera are severely ill and obviously require bed rest. A canvas cot with a hole in the center through which the individual can defecate without having to move helps make him more comfortable and facilitates the collection and measuring of the stools during the first few days of the illness. Feces must be disposed of carefully to avoid contamination of water supplies and infecting others.

Tetracycline every six hours helps reduce the duration of diarrhea but is only an adjunct to therapy and can not substitute for fluid and electrolyte replacement. TMP-SMX and ciprofloxacin (Cipro®) are the second and third drugs of choice. Sedatives only make care of the subject more difficult and should be avoided.

Cholera is not very contagious and is spread principally by feces. Sanitary disposal of feces and vomitus must be strictly enforced, and all contaminated articles, including clothing, bedding, and utensils, must be cleaned.

The acute phase of the infection rarely lasts more than three to five days. The subject usually is able to eat a bland diet by the third day. However, several weeks are required for full recovery.

Typhoid Fever

Typhoid fever is a generalized as well as a gastrointestinal infection caused by *Salmonella typhi*. The organisms invade the wall of the small bowel and enter the blood stream.

Occasionally people who have recovered from typhoid fever continue to harbor the organisms in the gastrointestinal tract and excrete them in their stools, thus becoming carriers. The bacteria can survive for weeks or months under natural conditions. Uncooked foods, salads, raw milk, and contaminated water are the most important sources of infection.

The incubation period is seven to fourteen days. Symptoms during the first week consist of fever, headache, and abdominal pain. The onset is usually insidious. Often there is no change in bowel habits during the initial ten days of illness. Near the end of the first week, enlargement of the spleen may be detectable. A brief, somewhat diagnostic rash can be seen in seventy percent of light-skinned individuals about seven to ten days after the onset of symptoms. The rash consists of "rose spots," which are deeply red and usually few in number, measure two to four millimeters in diameter, often present in clusters, blanch on pressure, and occur most often on the lower chest and upper abdominal wall. During the second week of illness, fever becomes more continuous and many individuals are severely ill. The pulse rate is often slow in comparison to the severity of the fever, an important diagnostic feature. Cough and nose bleeds may occur. In the third week, extreme toxicity, irrationality or confusion, and greenish, pea-soup diarrhea may occur. The latter may presage the dire complications of perforation of the intestine or intestinal hemorrhage. For survivors, the fourth week often brings improvement in their status. However, typhoid fever is a long-lasting and debilitating infection.

For typhoid fever, supportive care and maintenance of fluid intake are important. Aspirin may cause severe sweating and may lower blood pressure; cautious use is acceptable only if sponging with tepid water does not control the high fever.

Ciprofloxacin (Cipro®) every twelve hours is the antimicrobial drug of choice for the treatment of typhoid fever. Chloramphenicol has been relegated to second choice for two reasons: typhoid bacteria from central Mexico and Vietnam are often resistant to chloramphenicol, and this drug may rarely cause a potentially lethal anemia after prolonged therapy. The usual duration of therapy is two weeks.

Prior to travel to an area where typhoid may be encountered, immunization for typhoid and paratyphoid fever should be obtained. Although immunization does not completely prevent infection, it does reduce the severity of the disease and reduces the incidence of complications. Oral typhoid vaccine is now available.

Amebiasis

Amebiasis is caused by the parasite *Endamoeba histolytica*. Although generally thought of as a tropical disease, amebiasis is by no means limited to the tropics.

These organisms invade the wall of the large intestine; the adults form cysts that are passed in feces and spread the infection. The cysts are most commonly ingested in contaminated water. Food that has been fertilized with human excreta, carelessness in food preparation, and insects—particularly flies—are other sources of infestation. Iodine in appropriate concentrations and boiling destroy the cysts effectively.

Amebiasis is usually a very mild disorder in its early stages and symptoms may be entirely absent. Mild diarrhea with soft stools and a moderately increased number of bowel movements is more common. Occasional individuals develop constipation rather than diarrhea. A few individuals have more severe symptoms, including numerous watery stools that contain mucus or even blood and abdominal cramps. However, a period of mild gastrointestinal dysfunction usually precedes the onset of the more severe stage.

Easy fatigability, a low fever, and vague pains in the muscles, back, or joints are frequently present. Nervousness, irritability, and dizziness occasionally develop. Typically, no abnormality can be found by physical examination, although slight tenderness in the right lower quadrant of the abdomen is sometimes present. The diagnosis is suggested by the chronicity and mildness of the diarrhea and a history of exposure to conditions in which infection is likely. Laboratory facilities are required to make a definitive diagnosis.

If amebiasis is suspected, metronidazole (Flagyl®) should be given three times a day for five to ten days. Occasionally metronidazole may not completely eradicate the infection.

All persons visiting an area in which amebiasis is prevalent should be examined for infestation upon their return. The amoebae may lie quietly within the large intestine for years and then spread to the liver, where they form abscesses from which they occasionally even invade the lung. This form of the disease has a high mortality rate.

CONSTIPATION AND RECTAL PROBLEMS

Healthy adults rarely need to be concerned about constipation. The concept that normal individuals should have a bowel movement every day is a myth. Bowel rhythm can vary widely. For some individuals three stools a day is normal; others have one stool every three days. A change in bowel habits for which no cause can be identified may be significant, but new foods or alteration in daily schedule can produce such changes.

The type of food consumed plays a large part in determining the character and frequency of stools. Foods that are almost completely absorbed, such as liquids or carbohydrates, can not be expected to produce a copious stool; the converse is true for foods with a large, unabsorbed residue such as bran or leafy vegetables. Reduced food intake due to illness or dieting leads to smaller stool volume.

Constipation is more accurately defined as the passage of hard, dry stools rather than a specified frequency of bowel movements. Reduced intake of fluids, disruption of normal schedules, and travel by public conveyance with infrequent rest stops all tend to cause constipation. An adequate fluid intake—two quarts a day—and the consumption of fruits and other foods that loosen the stools, and bran or high-fiber cereals that provide bulk, help to maintain normal bowel function.

In general, laxatives have very little prophylactic or therapeutic value. If, in an unusual situation, a laxative becomes necessary, the best and safest is Milk of Magnesia®, either one or two tablespoons or two to four tablets at bedtime.

Fecal Impaction

Under conditions in which the urge to defecate is resisted, such as weather or illness that confines individuals to their tents, the normal bowel reflexes may become insensitive and permit stool to accumulate in the rectum. Dehydration may cause the water in the stool to be reabsorbed with such avidity that a bulky, hard residue that can not be evacuated in a normal manner results.

The best way to determine whether impaction has occurred is to insert a lubricated and gloved index finger into the rectum. If a mass of hard stool is found, it must be extracted. The mass of stool should be broken up with the index finger and the fragments removed as gently as possible (fig. 12-1). Injury of the rectal and anal tissues must be avoided. Following manual removal of the impaction, the causes of the impaction should be corrected.

Although breaking up and extracting a fecal impaction is aesthetically unpleasant, no alternative exists. Enema fluids will not enter the solidified fecal mass;

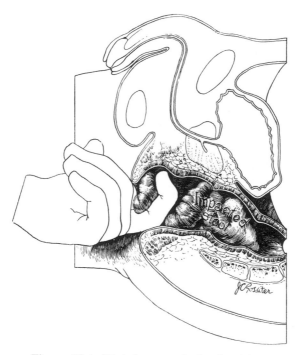

Figure 12-1. Digital removal of a fecal impaction.

laxatives have no effect on the dilated, flaccid rectal wall. Paradoxically, fecal impaction may be accompanied by the passage of a number of small, watery stools—the only material that can get past the impacted mass.

Anal Fissure

With constipation the stool may become so hard and bulky that its passage causes a small tear, or fissure, in the skin of the anus. Subsequent bowel movements are painful and may be associated with a small amount of bleeding.

Avoiding bulky, hard stools by consuming adequate fluids often allows the fissure to heal. A low-residue diet that is low in fiber and consists of foods that are almost totally absorbed, such as milk, soups, and carbohydrates, may avert bowel movements for several days and allow healing, but this diet is constipating. Straining at stool should be avoided indefinitely.

One tablespoon (15 cc) of mineral oil twice a day lubricates the stool and reduces the pain with bowel movements. (Mineral oil is not a laxative—only a lubricant.) If the pain persists between bowel movements, a bland anesthetic ointment such as dibucaine may be applied around the fissure. The ointment or a rectal suppository containing dibucaine may need to be inserted into the anal canal. The anal area should be cleaned gently after each bowel movement; aggressive wiping, particularly with coarse paper, scratching, and rubbing should be avoided. Persistent pain or bleeding should be brought to the attention of a physician as soon as possible.

Hemorrhoids

Hemorrhoids ("piles") are abnormally dilated veins that protrude from the anus. They are usually present before an individual begins an outing, but can be aggravated by the constipation that commonly develops with new foods and irregular schedules. Hemorrhoids usually are more annoying than disabling, but they can be a source of considerable itching and discomfort and can cause severe pain if they become prolapsed and thrombosed. Hemorrhoids bleed modestly following a hard or bulky bowel movement, but serious bleeding is rare. The blood is usually noted on the toilet paper or on the outside of the stool; blood mixed with the bowel movement suggests bleeding from within the colon.

Individuals with substantial hemorrhoids should have them assessed by a surgeon (proctologist) before a major wilderness outing. If hemorrhoids become bothersome in the field, measures to soften and lubricate the stool, most importantly a generous fluid intake and one tablespoon of mineral oil twice a day, may provide relief. Bearing down during bowel movements should be avoided. Sitting in warm water for fifteen to thirty minutes several times a day helps relieve symptoms but interferes with outdoor activities. Bulk formers such as Metamucil® may be helpful during an acute episode. An anesthetic ointment such as dibucaine or hemorrhoidal suppositories may help relieve symptoms. However, allergy to local anesthetic creams can result in a contact dermatitis of the anal skin. If symptoms worsen after use of dibucaine ointment, it should be replaced with one percent hydrocortisone ointment.

Thrombosed Hemorrhoid

The blood within a hemorrhoid occasionally clots, resulting in significant anal pain that may come on gradually or suddenly. A purple nodule that is firm and tender can be felt in the wall of the anus or can be seen protruding from its opening. Clots smaller than one-half inch (1.25 cm) in diameter are best allowed to resolve spontaneously. Clots larger than one inch (2.5 cm) may require surgical therapy. The severity of the pain should determine how clots between these two sizes should be treated.

An incision in the top of the thrombosed hemorrhoid and evacuation of the clot can provide relief of pain that frequently is dramatic. If the thrombosed hemorrhoid is large, many days of distress can be avoided. Before incision, the anus should be washed with soap and water. Acetaminophen and codeine can be given prior to incision; ice or snow pressed against the top of the nodule provides surprising anesthesia. The incision should be left open and pads should be left in the intergluteal cleft to reduce soiling by blood. Warm baths help relieve pain and anal muscle spasm.

Rectal Abscess

Abscesses in the tissues surrounding the rectum and anus usually follow long-standing anal problems, particularly infection associated with fissures or hemorrhoids, which should be corrected before a prolonged wilderness outing is undertaken. Abscesses in this location are not basically different from abscesses elsewhere in the body.

The cardinal symptom of a rectal abscess is throbbing pain in the region of the anus. Malaise, fever, and chills are common, and the patient may appear acutely ill. Examination usually reveals the characteristic signs of an abscess—a mass that is red, tender, and warm. The abscess may come to a point ("head") in the skin adjacent to the anus. A few rectal abscesses are located deeper beneath the skin and can only be felt during digital examination of the rectum.

Rectal abscesses should be treated just like abscesses anywhere else—with incision and drainage. If the abscess comes to a point in the skin beside the anus, an incision should be made in the center of the fluctuant area. If a deeper abscess is felt or the surrounding inflammation is extensive, the patient should be evacuated; drainage of such abscesses should be carried out by a surgeon. Serious complications can follow an abscess in this location that is not properly treated. If the patient has a fever, ampicillin or tetracycline should be administered every six hours during evacuation.

PEPTIC ULCER AND RELATED PROBLEMS

A peptic ulcer is a crater in the lining of the stomach or intestine produced by the digestive action of the enzymes and acids from the stomach (fig. 12-2). The cause of peptic ulcers is not well understood, but stress often appears to play a role. Many ulcers are associated with infection by *Helicobacter pylori*. Drugs such as aspirin, steroids, and the nonsteroidal anti-inflammatory agents may cause ulceration.

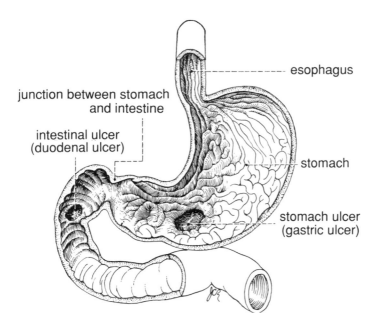

Figure 12-2. Gastric and duodenal ulcers.

An uncomplicated ulcer is not usually disabling, although the pain can be substantial. An ulcer is dangerous because it may hemorrhage or perforate. These are disabling, life-endangering complications that require immediate evacuation to a medical center. Perforation is discussed in Chapter Thirteen, "Acute Abdominal Pain."

The characteristic symptom of an ulcer is gnawing pain, usually located high in the upper portion of the abdomen near the midline. The pain is quite localized and the subject usually can indicate a precise point of origin with his fingertip. Typically, the pain comes on one to four hours after eating or between midnight and two o'clock in the morning. Bland food, milk, or antacids usually relieve the pain.

The pain is thought to be caused by the effects of stomach acid on the ulcer. Acid is a factor in all peptic ulcers. Food and antacids tend to neutralize the acid and thus relieve the pain. The characteristic times at which the pain occurs are the periods when there is no food in the stomach to counteract the acid. (No explanation for the absence of pain in the early morning, when the stomach is totally empty, has been found.)

Treatment

Ulcer therapy is primarily directed toward reducing the acidity of the stomach contents. Antacids have been used in the past and are still valuable. However, newer, more effective approaches include drugs that block the secretion of acid and other agents that create a barrier between the acid and the ulcerated area.

Antacids are best taken between meals; consumption within an hour of other anti-ulcer drugs should be avoided. Since overdosage with antacids is rarely a problem, more frequent doses may be administered if pain persists. Liquid antacids are more effective than tablets but are less portable. Many preparations are available, but some tablets are ineffective. The most effective tablet is Alkets®. Titralac® and Robalate® are also effective, but sometimes are not as readily available. Rolaids® or Tums® may be considered if none of the three preferred tablets is obtainable.

Antacid therapy has become less important since histamine H_2 receptor antagonists (H_2 blockers) have become available. These drugs are very effective for treating peptic ulcer disease. Famotidine (Pepcid®), ranitidine (Zantac®), and cimetidine (Tagamet®) are H_2 blockers currently being used; all are equally effective in appropriate dosage. Famotidine (Pepcid®) is given as a single dose at bedtime and may be simpler to administer if others must be taken more frequently.

Sucralfate (Carafate®) is another relatively new drug that is effective in the treatment of peptic ulcers. It forms a complex that adheres to the surface of the ulcer and protects it from the action of acid, digestive enzymes, and bile salts. Another agent, misoprostol (Cytotec®), a synthetic prostaglandin, inhibits gastric acid secretion and also has mucosal protective effects. It is currently used mostly to prevent gastric ulcers during the administration of nonsteroidal anti-inflammatory medications.

Aspirin in any form must be absolutely avoided; it increases the risk of bleeding fifteenfold. Smokers with ulcers should cease smoking entirely; less desirably, they should substantially decrease their nicotine usage. Alcohol and caffeine should be avoided. A mild tranquilizer may help highly stressed individuals.

Symptoms normally improve within a few days, but full healing takes six to eight weeks. Physical activity may continue during treatment, but strenuous exertion, particularly if stressful, is best avoided for at least a week after the institution of appropriate therapy. Persistent symptoms in spite of the institution of treatment merit the care of a physician.

Indigestion

Indigestion is a vague, poorly defined disorder that often is not associated with any demonstrable abnormality of the upper gastrointestinal system. The symptoms of indigestion may be confused with those of an ulcer. Since an ulcer poses a threat of severe complications but indigestion does not, the conditions should be distinguished.

The symptoms of an ulcer and indigestion usually differ in several respects. Instead of pain, indigestion more commonly produces a sense of fullness, excessive belching, or regurgitating small amounts of food or sour stomach contents, although a burning sensation (heartburn) may be present beneath the breastbone. Sour stomach contents may reach the back of the throat. Pain from indigestion may be felt in any portion of the abdomen; ulcer pain usually occurs in the central upper abdomen. Indigestion symptoms usually get worse with eating; ulcer symptoms are usually improved during and for an hour or so after food consumption. The symptoms of indigestion become less noticeable with time and the passage of food from the stomach, also the opposite of ulcer symptoms. Indigestion symptoms are intermittent; ulcer symptoms are more persistent. If indigestion becomes sufficiently severe, it can be treated with antacids or antispasmodics, such as chlordiazepoxide and clidinium (Librax®) or propantheline (Pro-Banthine®). Indigestion does not respond to H_2 blockers. Eating smaller meals may also be beneficial.

Heartburn responds promptly to the administration of a liquid antacid; H_2 blockers also provide relief, which is usually less prompt but longer-lasting. Combining both drugs often produces better symptom control than either alone. Individuals with this condition should not eat for several hours before going to bed, so that their stomachs will be empty, and should endeavor to sleep with the head and shoulders elevated so that gravity can help prevent stomach contents entering the esophagus.

GASTROINTESTINAL HEMORRHAGE

One of the most serious problems that can occur in the wilderness is massive hemorrhage from the stomach or intestines. Even with expert treatment, about ten percent of elderly patients hospitalized with this condition die. (Death rates in young adults are lower.) Since blood transfusions and other forms of intensive medical and surgical care are required to treat this life-threatening disorder, every effort must be made to get the individual to a hospital as quickly as possible.

If, in a remote area, helicopter transport can not be achieved promptly, the condition must be managed in the field. Attempting litter evacuation or walking out with assistance while active bleeding is occurring is unwise. Fortunately, a young person usually stops bleeding within twelve to twenty-four hours. Six to twelve hours after bleeding appears to have stopped, a choice between remaining in camp at rest for one to three days and attempting to reach a hospital must be made. A slow pulse, cessation of vomiting, and a normal brown color of the stools are indications that relatively little blood has been lost and that bleeding has stopped. However, rebleeding can occur at any time. Careful consideration must be given to the unique circumstances found in every situation.

The subject is usually very weak after a significant bleeding episode and requires assistance during evacuation. He should by no means attempt to continue vigorous activities, even if he feels well rested.

Except for occasional individuals who bleed slightly after prolonged retching, essentially all gastrointestinal bleeding in otherwise healthy young adults is due to peptic ulcer. Symptoms of an ulcer, although usually present prior to the hemorrhage, may be totally absent.

The signs and symptoms of serious gastrointestinal bleeding include:

• Faintness or weakness, which is more prominent when erect than when lying down

- Vomiting obvious blood
- Vomiting "coffee ground" material (blood that has been partially digested in the stomach)
- Rectal passage of obvious blood
- Passage of liquid or solid "tarry black" stools (blood that has been digested in the intestines. Iron, which is contained in vitamin and mineral preparations, and Pepto-Bismol® can cause stools to have a dark color.)
- Shock

No medications currently available control heavy bleeding from peptic ulcers. When the bleeding ceases, drugs may lessen the likelihood of rebleeding. The most effective drug for this purpose is omeprazole (Prilosec®) for twenty-four hours. Any of the H_2 blockers or sucralfate (Carafate®) may be helpful. Smoking must cease! Aspirin, alcohol, and caffeine must be avoided. The subject should rest as much as possible. If substantial blood has been lost and the subject becomes lightheaded when erect, he should be kept supine. If signs of shock, particularly low blood pressure, appear, appropriate treatment should be instituted.

DISEASES OF THE LIVER

Jaundice

Jaundice is produced by diseases of the liver. One of the numerous functions of the liver is to remove from the blood the pigment resulting from the normal destruction of old red blood cells. This pigment, bilirubin, is excreted into the intestine through the bile ducts and, following further changes in the intestinal tract, imparts the normal brown color to the stool.

In diseases that severely damage the liver bilirubin is not removed from the blood. It accumulates in the body and imparts a yellow or bronze color to the whites of the eyes and later the skin. If bilirubin is excreted into the intestine in small amounts or not at all, the stools become pale or "clay-colored." The pigment is partially excreted by the kidneys, imparting a brown color to the urine and causing the foam produced by shaking to have a yellow color instead of the normal white appearance.

When jaundice is suspected, the subject should be examined in daylight. Flashlights and other artificial lights usually produce a yellowish color that can simulate jaundice.

Hepatitis

Hepatitis, an inflammatory disorder of the liver caused by infection with viruses that selectively involve that organ, is the most important cause of painless jaundice likely to occur for the first time in wilderness conditions. (Jaundice associated with pain is discussed in Chapter Thirteen, "Acute Abdominal Pain.") An individual who has had previous attacks of jaundice should be evaluated by a physician and instructed in the treatment for his condition prior to undertaking an outing.) Untreated malaria and other conditions cause jaundice on rare occasions due to the excessive destruction of red blood cells. However, such disorders can usually be recognized from other findings.

Several distinct hepatitis viruses have now been recognized: hepatitis A, B, C, the delta agent (hepatitis D), and hepatitis E. Hepatitis A is an RNA virus that is spread principally by fecal contamination of water and food, particularly shellfish. Infections are common but almost never fatal; well over ninety percent of infected individuals have such minor symptoms that they do not realize they are ill. If jaundice does develop, it rarely lasts more than a month. (Such individuals are usually too sick to continue a wilderness outing.) Chronic liver disease does not follow hepatitis A infections. Diagnostic blood tests and a blood test to determine whether a person has had previous contact with the virus and is immune are available; a vaccine is not. Gamma globulin administered immediately before leaving for an underdeveloped country reduces the severity of or prevents infections.

Hepatitis B is caused by a DNA virus that is spread principally by body fluids through personal contact, particularly sexual contact. As with hepatitis A, most individuals do not realize they have an infection, but up to ten percent may be quite ill, a few die, and approximately five percent develop chronic liver disease. Approximately half of the individuals with chronic liver disease develop cirrhosis (scarring of the liver), an eventually lethal disorder. Hepatitis B is directly responsible for most cases of hepatocellular carcinoma (cancer developing in the liver), which is the most common malignant tumor worldwide, although it is uncommon in the United States. A safe and effective vaccine for hepatitis B is available; the vaccine costs about $120 for a course of three injections, which is far less than hospitalization for one day. Immunization may not be needed by everyone, but it is essential for medical workers or others who come in contact with blood and is desirable for travelers to underdeveloped countries.

The delta agent (hepatitis D) is an incomplete DNA virus that can produce infections only in association with hepatitis B. However, it may cause acute hepatitis B infections to become rapidly fatal and promote chronic infections to cirrhosis. Immunization against hepatitis B prevents infection by the delta agent.

Many of the infections previously termed non-A, non-B hepatitis are now known to be caused by hepatitis C, a viral agent that was identified in 1989 and accounts for roughly thirty percent of the cases of acute hepatitis and a higher percentage of chronic, long-standing infections in the United States. About fifty percent of hepatitis C infections result in chronic liver disease, leaving the individual with prolonged fatigue or weakness. Approximately twenty percent of patients with chronic hepatitis C develop cirrhosis, an ultimately lethal disorder. Ninety to ninety-five percent of hepatitis following blood transfusion has been caused by hepatitis C, although procedures for screening for this infection introduced in 1990 give hope for eliminating this problem.

Hepatitis C is an RNA virus that is transmitted through broken skin or mucous membranes. Intravenous drug use accounts for forty percent of the infections, sexual contact for ten percent, blood transfusion for five to ten percent, and exposure to blood by nurses, ambulance attendants, and similar medical professionals for five percent. The routes of inoculation for the remaining one-third of the infections are unidentified. Blood tests for this recently recognized virus are now available, but development of a vaccine is only beginning. The effectiveness of gamma globulin for preventing infection has not been determined.

Another form of non-A, non-B hepatitis—one of the more important forms worldwide—is caused by hepatitis E virus, which is rarely encountered in the United States. The virus was first identified in 1989 and as yet is poorly characterized. It has been linked to epidemics in Africa and Asia and to two outbreaks in Mexico. Infection usually results from ingestion of water contaminated with sewage and can be prevented by routine disinfection. Infection can also be spread by close personal contact. In some outbreaks the mortality during pregnancy has been as high as ten percent. The effectiveness of gamma globulin for preventing or ameliorating the infection is unknown. No diagnostic blood test is available, but the virus can be identified in stool samples. Development of a vaccine has hardly begun.

The onset of hepatitis may be abrupt or insidious and follows an incubation period ranging from three weeks to six months. The earliest symptoms are loss of appetite, general malaise, and easy fatigability. Later a low fever and nausea and vomiting appear. Many smokers have a peculiar loss of their taste for cigarettes. In individuals with more severe infections the symptoms increase in severity. Light-colored stools and dark urine may precede the appearance of jaundice by several days. Vague upper abdominal discomfort and tenderness may be present, particularly in the right upper quadrant, but severe pain is absent. After the appearance of jaundice, some individuals experience ill-defined joint or muscular pains. A highly variable skin rash may be present, and some individuals have generalized itching. When jaundice does develop it often lasts three to six weeks; the malaise, easy fatigability, and loss of appetite may persist for several more months.

No specific treatment for hepatitis is available. A study of previously healthy young adults in the U.S. Army indicated that restriction of exercise had no effect on the course of the disease for that rather select group of individuals. Most wilderness explorers fall into the same group of previously healthy, relatively young adults. However, most individuals do not feel capable of more than very mild exercise. A nourishing diet that is high in proteins and carbohydrates and supplemented with vitamins should be provided.

All drug therapy should be avoided if possible, including alcohol and drugs to promote sleep. Most drugs are metabolized by the liver. When that organ's function is impaired by hepatitis, such metabolism may be much slower than normal. If the drugs are not completely metabolized between doses, they can accumulate in the blood and may rapidly reach toxic concentrations.

Most individuals with hepatitis should be evacuated. Recovery usually takes so long that delaying evacuation until the person is well is impossible. In addition, complications that require a physician's care may develop.

CHAPTER THIRTEEN

ACUTE ABDOMINAL PAIN

An episode of acute abdominal pain can be frightening because its successful management might require surgery. However, most disorders producing pain in the abdomen do not require any specific therapy; most others can be effectively treated without operation.

In wilderness situations the decision of overwhelming importance is whether surgery (and therefore emergency evacuation) is necessary. If any doubt exists, the person must be evacuated, because true abdominal emergencies that are not promptly and properly treated carry a mortality rate approaching 100 percent. Disrupting a carefully planned expedition because a member has a bellyache requires mature judgment, but that decision could reflect wisdom just as surely as turning back within view of a summit when avalanche conditions are encountered.

During evacuation the person should be carried on a litter in the supine position with the head and knees moderately elevated. Ordinarily the individual should not eat or drink anything, although occasional sips of water may be acceptable for comfort. Continuous antibiotic therapy, analgesics, intravenous fluids, and nasogastric intubation should be used when available.

SIGNS AND SYMPTOMS

The key to proper treatment is an accurate diagnosis. This, in turn, requires a careful history and physical examination. Pertinent elements in the history include:

Pain

- Exact time of onset
- Nature of onset—gradual or sudden
- Location—above or below the umbilicus; right side, left side, or midline; change in location or radiation
- Nature of pain—sharp, stabbing, gnawing, cramping; constant or intermittent
- Progression of pain since onset
- Events relieving or aggravating pain—coughing, deep breathing, voiding, bowel movements, position of body

Other Symptoms

- Nausea and vomiting—time of onset in relation to onset of pain; vomiting blood
- Diarrhea or constipation—time of last bowel movement
- Chills or fever
- Blood in the urine
- Presence of a hernia—reducibility
- Other members of the party with a similar disorder

Past History

- History of having eaten food not eaten by other members of the group
- Previous episodes of similar pain—diagnosis and treatment at that time
- History of pain relieved by milk, food, or antacids
- History of indigestion or pain following ingestion of fried or fatty foods
- History of jaundice
- History of previous abdominal operations
- Time of last menstrual period—any abnormalities

PHYSICAL EXAMINATION

The physical examination should be performed in a quiet, secluded spot where the person can be warm and comfortable. He should be lying on his back with his hands at his sides and his entire abdomen from the nipple line to the crotch bared for examination.

The abdomen should be examined by observation, auscultation, and palpation. Spasms of pain, aggravation of pain by breathing, and the presence of scars from previous operations should be noted. The examiner should place his ear or a stethoscope against the abdomen and listen for increased or absent bowel sounds. Increased bowel sounds can frequently be heard several feet away. The absence of bowel sounds, which indicates intestinal paralysis (paralytic ileus), can be diagnosed only when no sounds are heard after listening for at least two or three minutes.

Palpation of the abdomen is a skill that requires years of practice and experience to perfect. However, even a beginner—with a little instruction—who takes his time and is gentle can obtain valuable diagnostic clues. The examiner's warm hands should be placed gently on the abdomen with the palms down. Gentle pressure should be exerted with the pads of the fingers. Jabbing with the fingertips produces pain and contraction of the abdominal muscles so that no information can be gained from the examination.

Areas of maximum tenderness must be accurately located. Spasm of the abdominal muscles over tender areas should be identified. Rebound tenderness, which is a sudden, sharp pain occurring when the pressure over a tender area is suddenly released, should be sought. Referred tenderness is pain in one portion of the abdomen elicited by pressure in another area. It is caused by the intestines shifting away from the site being depressed and irritating the diseased organ and

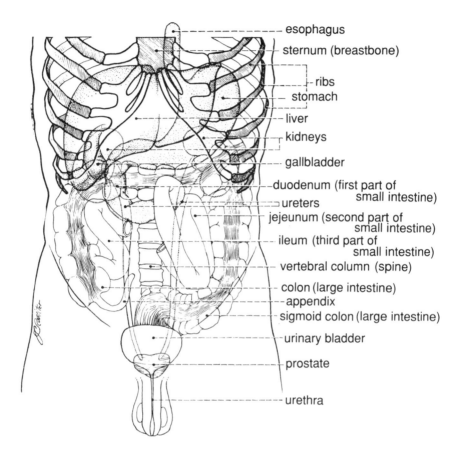

Figure 13-1. Organs of the abdominal cavity.

often identifies the site of inflammation. A typical example is pain on the right side of the abdomen produced by pressure on the left side in many individuals with acute appendicitis.

In general, pain associated with diarrhea or pain not associated with nausea and vomiting is not a sign of disease requiring operation. Pain that lasts for more than six hours or is so severe that it prevents the person from sleeping suggests a condition requiring surgery. Abdominal distension, paralytic ileus, rebound pain, precisely localized tenderness, and rigidity of the abdominal muscles are usually indicative of a serious intra-abdominal condition that is best treated by operation. Jaundice is typical of gallbladder or liver disease. A jaundiced individual usually should be evacuated regardless of whether surgery is needed, since persons who are jaundiced as the result of hepatitis usually require at least several weeks for full recovery.

REPORTING HISTORY AND PHYSICAL FINDINGS

Whenever possible, the decision to evacuate someone with abdominal pain from a remote area should be shared with an expert by radio or telephone, since evacuation would disrupt the outing and perhaps require considerable expense and manpower. To facilitate an appropriate decision, the examiner in the wilderness must give the history and the findings by physical examination to the consultant physician in a systematic and detailed manner. This can best be accomplished by following the outline for the history provided above. Recording all data before the discussion is held would be helpful. In addition, these questions should be anticipated:

- What is the temperature, pulse, and respiratory rate?
- Does the person look sick?
- Does the individual appear to be complaining for an ulterior or perhaps subconscious motive? Does he appear to overreact to pain?
- Is the abdomen rigid due to involuntary muscle spasm?
- Where is the pain most severe: (a) as the person lies unexamined? (b) with gentle probing? (c) after sudden release of the probing fingers (rebound pain)?
- Is a hernia or intra-abdominal mass present?

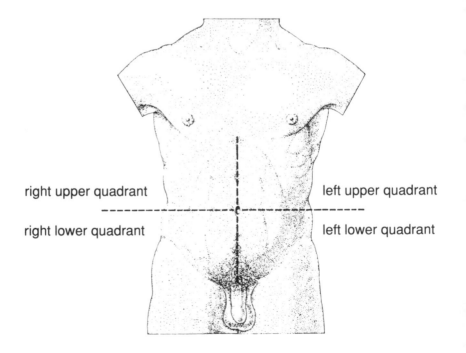

right upper quadrant | left upper quadrant

right lower quadrant | left lower quadrant

Figure 13-2. The four quadrants of the abdomen.

CONDITIONS THAT DO *NOT* REQUIRE EVACUATION

Gastroenteritis

The most common cause of abdominal pain in a remote location is acute gastroenteritis, which is discussed in Chapter Twelve, "Gastrointestinal Disorders." Gradually increasing, diffuse abdominal pain that culminates in waves of abdominal cramps and diarrhea is typical of acute gastroenteritis. During spasms of pain the knees are frequently drawn up to the abdomen for relief, but the periods between spasms are relatively free from pain. Generalized abdominal tenderness is often present and may be slightly greater in the lower abdomen. Bowel sounds are louder than normal. Nausea and vomiting are the most prominent symptoms; chills and fever may also be present.

Gastroenteritis must be distinguished principally from appendicitis. With appendicitis:

- No history of food contamination or others suffering from the same disease can be elicited.
- Pain is localized and steady, not cramping.
- Diarrhea is extremely rare.

The onset of appendicitis is usually gradual and the pain is relatively constant. Tenderness, if present, is localized in the right lower quadrant of the abdomen.

Mittelschmerz

Mittelschmerz, which is German for "middle pain," occurs in women midway between menstrual periods and is produced by minor bleeding that accompanies ovulation. Women with this disorder usually have had previous episodes of such pain and can frequently identify the condition.

The pain comes on gradually, may be severe, and usually is localized in either the right or left lower abdominal quadrants, depending upon which ovary is the source. Vomiting or diarrhea usually does not occur. The abdomen is usually soft, but tenderness may be elicited by deep palpation in one of the lower quadrants.

Mittelschmerz may be difficult to differentiate from appendicitis if the right ovary is involved. The gynecologic condition should be suspected if the pain occurs halfway between menstrual periods.

No specific treatment is necessary. The pain can usually be controlled with moderate analgesics and usually disappears within thirty-six to forty-eight hours. Symptoms persisting for a longer time should prompt reconsideration of the diagnosis.

Acute Salpingitis

Acute salpingitis is an infection of the fallopian tubes, the structures that conduct ova (eggs) from the ovaries to the uterus. The infection is caused by many organisms, particularly gonorrhea and chlamydia. The incidence of such infections is slightly increased in women with intrauterine contraceptive devices (IUDs).

The pain usually develops gradually but can become quite severe. Both fallopian tubes are usually involved to some extent, which causes pain in both the right and left lower quadrants of the abdomen. However, the pain commonly is much more severe on one side than the other. The pain may be accompanied by nausea and vomiting. Typically a high fever, 103°F (39.5°C) or higher, is present. Tenderness, muscle spasm, and rebound pain may be present in either or both of the lower abdominal quadrants.

Acute salpingitis may be very difficult to differentiate from appendicitis if the right tube is involved. The presence of a high fever is suggestive of salpingitis but can also occur with appendicitis, particularly if the appendix has ruptured. A history of sexual exposure followed by a vaginal discharge is suggestive of gonorrhea, but individuals with that infection can also develop appendicitis. Pain or tenderness in both sides of the lower abdomen is evidence of salpingitis.

If distinction from appendicitis is not possible, the person should be treated as if she had appendicitis. If a definite diagnosis of salpingitis is made, the woman does not have to be evacuated. Surgery is not required for acute salpingitis. However, treatment for the infection should be instituted. (See Chapter Eighteen, "Genitourinary Disorders.")

Kidney Stone

Occasionally minerals are precipitated from the urine and deposited in the kidney to form a stone. This stone may be swept into the bladder by the urinary stream, causing excruciating pain as it passes through the narrow duct (ureter) that connects the kidney with the bladder.

The symptoms produced by passage of a kidney stone usually appear suddenly and are characterized by sharp, stabbing flank pain, which may come and go in waves of increasing intensity. The pain usually begins in the back at the level of the lowest ribs, but frequently radiates around the side to the lower abdomen and into the groin or scrotum. The person typically writhes in pain and is unable to lie still.

Bright red blood is often found in the urine but may be present in only small amounts. (See Chapter Eighteen, "Genitourinary Disorders.") Pain on urination and increased frequency of urination are common. Nausea, vomiting, and cold sweats are usually present; chills and fever are occasionally present.

A kidney stone rarely requires emergency surgery. Despite the alarming bloody urine, there is no risk of life-threatening blood loss. The pain may last for twenty-four hours or more but usually subsides spontaneously in a shorter period of time as the stone is passed into the bladder.

A strong analgesic can be given intramuscularly every four hours to lessen the pain. (Complete pain relief may not be possible.) If the person is not vomiting, he should drink as much water as possible to help flush out the stone.

Following subsidence of the pain, the likelihood of a subsequent attack is slight, and the person can resume his usual activities as soon as he feels capable. However, if the stone is not passed and pain continues for forty-eight hours or more, the individual should be evacuated. Serious renal damage can result if the stone remains in the ureter and obstructs the flow of urine.

CONDITIONS THAT *DO* REQUIRE EVACUATION

Appendicitis

Appendicitis is the most common disorder producing acute abdominal pain that requires operation. Although much discussed, prophylactic appendectomy for individuals who are frequently in remote areas for prolonged periods is not advised.

The onset of appendicitis is characterized by vague abdominal discomfort that becomes progressively worse. Cramps are usually absent. The earliest symptoms are frequently located in the midabdomen. One to three hours later the pain shifts to the right lower quadrant. During this time the subject usually becomes nauseated and vomits several times. One or two bowel movements may occur, but diarrhea is uncommon. Rarely has the person had any previous similar attacks.

The area of maximum tenderness is in the right lower quadrant of the abdomen. Later, referred tenderness, rebound tenderness, and muscle spasm appear in the same area. Usually a low fever of about 101°F (38.5°C) is present, but chills are rare.

If the appendix ruptures, pain may abruptly disappear. A few hours later the pain usually returns but is more diffuse and is associated with signs of peritonitis. After a day or so the infection can remain localized to the area around the appendix, forming an abscess. With this complication the individual is ill and has a low fever. Occasionally he may have no other symptoms, but such persons should be evacuated promptly. The abscess may rupture a week or more later, producing an overwhelming, rapidly fatal peritonitis.

Antibiotic therapy should be started at once. If the individual is not vomiting, chloramphenicol should be given orally every six hours. If oral therapy is not possible, chloramphenicol can be given intravenously, or ampicillin and gentamicin can be given intramuscularly every six hours. If the subject is in severe pain, a strong analgesic can be given intramuscularly every four hours. However, such agents mask the physical findings characteristic of appendicitis and should not be administered within four hours of the time the individual is to be examined by a physician.

Appendicitis is best treated by immediate surgery. Therefore, the person should be evacuated as quickly as possible. Intravenous fluids may be required to avoid dehydration if the subject is vomiting and evacuation requires more than thirty-six hours. If gastric distension and paralytic ileus appear, nasogastric suction should be instituted. (See Appendix B, "Therapeutic Procedures.")

Some cases of appendicitis have been managed successfully with antibiotics alone, but such therapy should be undertaken only in a truly remote area from which evacuation is not feasible. Rarely, a person thought to have appendicitis gets well spontaneously, recovers his appetite, and can resume his customary physical activity. In most of these individuals the original diagnosis was probably erroneous. Only a physician with access to a laboratory can determine whether an infection was originally present and has merely become quiescent. Therefore, the subject should be evacuated in less remote circumstances or if there is any question about his condition.

Intestinal Obstruction

Intestinal obstruction is produced by a number of conditions that block the passage of food through the intestines. The symptoms are similar regardless of the cause of the obstruction, but vary according to the location of the obstruction in the gastrointestinal tract. Bands of fibrous tissue from previous abdominal surgery are a frequent cause of this disorder. Some individuals have a history of repeated episodes of obstruction.

The onset of symptoms is gradual and is characterized by waves of cramping pain that increase rapidly in severity. The person is frequently free of pain between spasms. Nausea and vomiting, which are usually present, occur early in obstructions located in the upper portion of the intestine. If the obstruction is lower in the small intestine or in the large intestine, vomiting may not occur for several hours or even longer after the onset of pain.

The subject appears quite ill and usually has a rapid pulse. Sometimes other signs of shock are present. The abdomen is distended, particularly with obstructions in the lower part of the intestinal tract. Scars from previous abdominal operations are frequently present. Bowel sounds are much louder than normal, occasionally being audible a considerable distance away. However, twelve to twenty-four hours after onset of the obstruction, the intestines become so distended by fluid and air that contractions cease and the bowel sounds disappear. Signs of peritonitis—diffuse abdominal pain and tenderness, and spasm of the abdominal muscles—are usually present at this stage.

The early stages of intestinal obstruction may simulate acute gastroenteritis. One or two bowel movements may occur early in the course of the disease, but persisting diarrhea is rarely present with obstruction.

Immediate evacuation is imperative since surgery is almost always necessary. Nasogastric suction should be instituted if possible. (See Appendix B, "Therapeutic Procedures.") Intravenous fluid therapy (and the replacement, with balanced salt solution, of all fluids lost through vomiting or gastric suction) is necessary if evacuation requires more than thirty-six hours. Antibiotic treatment for peritonitis also should be instituted. No fluids or medications should be given orally.

PERFORATED PEPTIC ULCER

Perforation is one of the complications that can occur with a peptic ulcer. (See Chapter Twelve, "Gastrointestinal Disorders.") The same processes that have digested the lining of the stomach or intestine to form the ulcer crater continue their action until the ulcer penetrates the wall of the organ. The resulting perforation permits stomach acids and other intestinal contents to enter the abdominal cavity. These substances cause an intense chemical irritation of the peritoneum and may initiate a severe infection.

The subject usually has a history of peptic ulcer symptoms—upper abdominal pain coming on two to six hours after eating and relieved by food, milk, and antacids. However, approximately twenty percent of individuals with a perforated ulcer do not have such prior symptoms.

(Parasitic infestation can also cause intestinal perforation, but such events are limited almost entirely to porters or other residents of underdeveloped countries who usually carry numerous intestinal parasites at all times. The signs and symptoms are similar to those of a perforated peptic ulcer, and the treatment is essentially the same. The person would not have a previous history suggestive of peptic ulcer, and most residents of such areas have lived with their parasites for so long they are not aware that symptoms produced by the infestation are abnormal.)

At the time of perforation the person suffers an abrupt, almost instantaneous onset of severe upper abdominal pain that is sharp and continuous and may spread over the entire abdomen. The pain is followed shortly by the vomiting of recently ingested food or of bile. The individual appears quite sick and gets progressively worse for the next twelve to twenty-four hours.

The abdomen is diffusely tender, but pain is more marked in the upper quadrants. Spasm of the abdominal muscles is prominent, particularly in the upper abdomen. Bowel sounds disappear shortly after the perforation, and distention of the abdomen soon follows due to intestinal paralysis.

A perforated ulcer is an acute emergency requiring immediate evacuation. Treatment for peritonitis should be administered during evacuation. Occasionally the perforation seals, and the individual begins to get better, but he still must be evacuated to a medical facility where definitive treatment for his ulcer can be instituted and the complications following his perforation attended.

Incarcerated Hernia

A hernia (or "rupture") is a protrusion of the intestine from its proper location within the abdominal cavity. The most common hernia is an inguinal hernia, which presents in the groin and may extend into the scrotum (fig. 13-3). Usually such hernias are easily reduced (pushed back into the abdomen) and have existed for months or even years. The hernia itself does not constitute an emergency, but the intestine may be trapped (incarcerated) in the extruded position, resulting in intestinal obstruction.

Most hernias occur in males; the bulge in the groin is usually obvious, particularly if the hernia extends into the scrotum. Occasionally women have hernias, which appear as smaller bulges in the groin. Although inconspicuous, they may cause complications just as in men.

The operative repair of a hernia is a relatively minor procedure that is carried out whenever a hernia is detected. Such repair should be carried out before any extended outing to a remote wilderness area. However, the mere detection for the first time of a hernia while on an excursion is not an indication for interrupting the outing because the probability of complications is small.

An individual with an incarcerated hernia usually has a history of a hernia that has always been easily reduced but that has become unreducible and painful. The resulting intestinal obstruction causes vomiting, abdominal distension, and cessation of bowel movements. An obvious mass that is swollen and tender is usually present in the groin or scrotum. The abdomen may be distended, and the individual may be vomiting.

The initial treatment should consist of trying to reduce the hernia. The subject should lie flat on his back, preferably with his head and chest lower than his

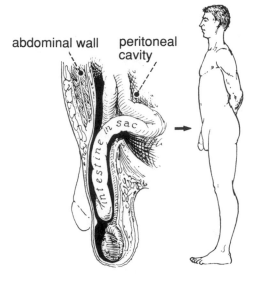

abdominal wall   peritoneal
                  cavity

Figure 13-3. Anatomy of an inguinal hernia.

abdomen so that gravity can help return the intestine into the abdominal cavity. If he is tense and straining, a strong analgesic should be given to produce relaxation and help reduce the hernia. Moderate, steady pressure on the hernia for ten minutes or longer may ultimately make the mass of intestine pop back into the abdominal cavity through the narrow neck of the sac and temporarily relieve the emergency.

If the hernia can not be reduced, the mass remains tender and inflamed, and the subject keeps vomiting and getting sicker, the bowel is probably becoming gangrenous. Immediate evacuation is mandatory. During evacuation the individual should be treated for intestinal obstruction. Intravenous fluids are required if evacuation takes more than thirty-six to forty-eight hours.

If the hernia is reduced within a few hours and the herniated mass goes back into the abdomen, there is little probability that the bowel is gangrenous. The subject should be observed for a day or two but can continue his ordinary activities. If pain relief does not occur, gangrene of the intestine that has been pushed back into the abdomen should be suspected, and the subject should be urgently evacuated. On short outings, anyone who has had an incarcerated hernia usually should be evacuated. Often he can walk out.

Acute Gallbladder Disease

The gallbladder is a saclike organ on the undersurface of the liver in which bile is stored until it is secreted into the small intestine. Sometimes the bile salts precipitate, forming gallstones, a common disorder in older age groups. Subsequent contractions of the gallbladder to expel bile are painful. This condition, known as chronic cholecystitis or chronic gallbladder disease, is characterized by recurrent episodes of colicky pain and tenderness in the right upper quadrant of the abdomen. Rarely, these attacks are associated with jaundice. Individuals with gallstones poorly tolerate fried or fatty foods, which cause belching, indigestion, and abdominal distress or pain.

Anyone with acute gallbladder disease usually has a history of chronic cholecystitis. However, with acute cholecystitis he typically suffers pain that is more severe than usual. The pain comes on suddenly and is located immediately below the ribs on the right. The pain may be intermittent or continuous and may radiate to the back or to the right shoulder blade. Vomiting is common; diarrhea is rare. The person appears obviously ill and is frequently jaundiced. The urine is often dark and the stools may be light gray or clay-colored, particularly two to three days after the onset.

Tenderness, rebound tenderness, and referred pain are all in the right upper quadrant. The temperature may be mildly elevated (99°F to 101°F, or 37.5°C to 38.5°C).

Treatment consists of rest with nothing being taken by mouth until vomiting stops. Then only clear liquids should be ingested. All fried or fatty foods, including milk, must be avoided. A strong analgesic given intramuscularly usually is required to control the pain. Meperidine is preferable. In an isolated area, ampicillin should be given intramuscularly every six hours as long as the pain continues.

The attack usually subsides spontaneously within one or two days. If the individual has had previous attacks, he may even be able to continue his customary activities after he has regained his strength. (If a person has had previous attacks of acute cholecystitis, he should seriously consider having his gallbladder removed—a cholecystectomy—before a prolonged expedition.) The safest course for anyone who has suffered an acute attack of cholecystitis is to be evacuated. Ordinarily the person can walk out. Although most individuals with acute gallbladder disease do not require emergency surgery, such treatment is needed by some. Moving any such individual to a hospital is by far the safest course. Occasionally, gallbladder colic is difficult to differentiate from appendicitis, pancreatitis, or a perforated ulcer.

Acute Pancreatitis

Acute pancreatitis is a severe inflammatory disorder of unknown cause involving the pancreas, an organ located in the upper portion of the abdomen behind the lower border of the stomach. Some individuals suffer recurrent attacks of this disorder, which is characterized by severe pain. The syndrome occurs most frequently in alcoholics, but nondrinkers suffer occasional episodes.

Pancreatitis typically develops after a heavy meal or the ingestion of large amounts of alcohol. Characteristic symptoms are acute pain, nausea, and vomiting; diarrhea is rare. The pain is located in the upper part of the abdomen in the midline or on the left side, but frequently radiates to the back and to the shoulder blades. The onset is relatively rapid, building up to peak intensity over a few minutes to a few hours, but is not as abrupt as the onset of symptoms of a perforated ulcer.

In severe cases the disease may progress in a few hours to prostration, cyanosis, and shock with a rapid pulse and low blood pressure. Fever from 100°F to 103°F (38°C to 39°C) may occur and persists as long as the disease is active.

Upper abdominal tenderness is typical, but rebound tenderness is not characteristic because the stomach is interposed between the pancreas and the abdominal wall.

Acute pancreatitis may be difficult to distinguish from acute inflammation of the gallbladder. Pancreatitis has a more rapid onset, has maximum pain and tenderness located in the midline or on the left side of the upper abdomen rather than the right, and may be associated with severe prostration and shock. Pancreatitis is also characterized by the frequent failure of strong analgesics to completely relieve the pain. However, many individuals with pancreatitis have gallstones and a history of gallbladder disease, including intolerance of fried or fatty foods.

Therapy for acute pancreatitis consists of rapid evacuation, efforts to relieve pain, inactivation of the gastrointestinal system, and general care of the individual. Although the treatment of acute pancreatitis does not necessitate surgery, it does require expert medical care in an intensive care unit. This disease causes an appreciable number of deaths, even with the best treatment. Furthermore, complications that require a physician's attention are relatively common. Therefore, evacuation is essential.

A strong analgesic (preferably meperidine) should be administered intramuscularly every three to four hours for pain. Nitroglycerin tablets sublingually every two to three hours occasionally provide some relief.

Nothing should be given by mouth, and nasogastric suction should be instituted if possible. (See Appendix B, "Therapeutic Procedures.") Food stimulates pancreatic activity and prolongs the pain. An antispasmodic given intramuscularly every four hours reduces stomach activity and diminishes the secretory activity of the pancreas. Intravenous fluids must be administered to provide daily fluid requirements as well as to replace with salt solution the losses due to vomiting or gastric suction. Shock should be treated in the same manner as shock from other causes.

Some persons have a milder, chronic form of pancreatitis and usually have a history of previous, moderately severe episodes. Characteristically they have a history of alcohol abuse. Most such episodes subside with less rigorous treatment, but such individuals should also be evacuated.

Peritonitis

A number of intra-abdominal catastrophes produce peritonitis—inflammation (with or without infection) of the membrane lining the abdominal cavity. The appearance of individuals with peritonitis is similar regardless of the underlying cause. The subjects lie very quietly, since motion is painful. They are pale, usually have a temperature over 101°F (38.5°C), and are obviously very sick. Their appetite is entirely gone, nausea is usually present, and they may be vomiting. Their abdomens are somewhat distended, sometimes severely, and are diffusely tender and firm to palpation. No bowel sounds can be heard and no flatus is passed. Signs and symptoms of the disease causing the infection are also present.

These subjects must be evacuated by stretcher as rapidly as possible. During evacuation they should be made comfortable with strong analgesics, given nothing by mouth, and kept supine, warm, and quiet. Gentamicin and clindamycin should be administered intramuscularly or intravenously every six to eight hours. Nasogastric suction should be instituted when possible. (See Appendix B, "Therapeutic Procedures.") Intravenous fluid administration is required if evacuation takes more than thirty-six hours. All fluids lost by vomiting or nasogastric suction should be replaced with a balanced salt solution.

ABDOMINAL PAIN

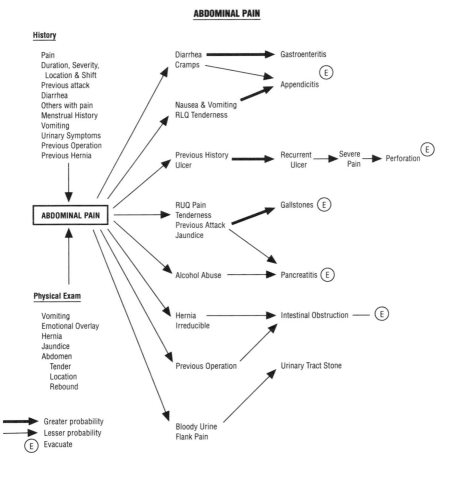

Figure 13-4. Algorithm for diagnosing acute abdominal pain.

CHAPTER FOURTEEN

ABDOMINAL INJURIES

The definitive treatment for a severe abdominal injury consists of surgery, which is out of the question in a wilderness setting. Therefore, management of severe abdominal trauma in such situations consists of recognizing the severity (or triviality) of an injury and deciding whether immediate evacuation is required. As with all injuries, a conservative approach should be adopted; if any question exists about the diagnosis, the worst should be assumed.

Under no circumstances should pseudoheroic attempts at surgical intervention be made. The results would be uniformly fatal without proper anesthesia, sterile operating conditions, or the proper instruments. Operative intervention under primitive conditions by untrained hands would be more deadly than most injuries. Even the most severe trauma can occasionally be successfully managed without surgery.

DIAGNOSIS

Before any decision can be made concerning the care for someone involved in an accident, an accurate diagnosis must be made. The first step is obtaining an account of the accident. Exact details of the mishap, including the site and direction of a blow to the abdomen, are helpful in diagnosing the abdominal injury. A blow to the left upper quadrant of the abdomen or lower part of the chest may rupture the spleen; a blow to the corresponding area on the right side would injure the liver. Trauma to either flank or the back may damage a kidney (figs. 14-1 and 14-2).

The abdomen must be carefully examined as described in Chapter Thirteen, "Acute Abdominal Pain." Close attention should also be given to blood pressure, pulse rate, respiratory rate, color of the skin and fingernails, and other signs of shock. The vital signs must be recorded hourly for at least the first twelve hours after injury. The urine should be examined for blood.

Attention must not be focused on the abdomen to the extent that other injuries are overlooked or neglected. At some time in the subject's care, preferably early, a complete examination must be performed.

If the individual is to be evacuated to a physician, a written account of the accident and all diagnostic findings, along with a detailed record of subsequent events, should accompany him. The exact time of the accident, all medications

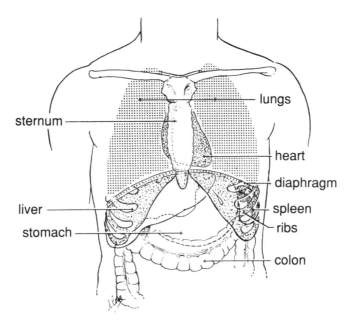

Figure 14-1. Location of the liver and spleen in relation to the lower ribs anteriorly.

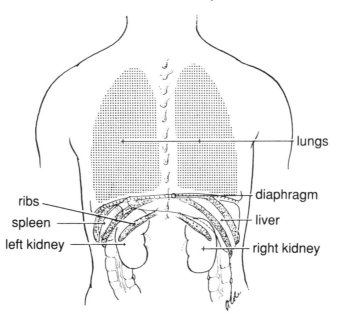

Figure 14-2. Location of the liver, spleen and kidneys in relation to the lower ribs posteriorly.

and the time they are administered, hourly measurements of pulse and respiratory rates, and observations about his general condition must be written down.

TREATMENT

Since the individual may require immediate evacuation to a surgical facility, he should be carried with all reasonable haste to a point from which he can be evacuated. The sooner this can be accomplished, the better such persons withstand the subsequent rigors of bleeding or peritonitis. Individuals with severe abdominal injuries usually require litter evacuation of some kind.

Abdominal trauma frequently produces rather severe pain, but the pain may not be proportional to the severity of the injury. Even minor abdominal trauma may be quite painful at first, although the discomfort usually subsides in the hours that follow. In general, the person should be kept comfortable with moderate or strong analgesics. Intravenous administration may be necessary if shock is present. If injected intramuscularly, these drugs may not be well absorbed, and an overdose could occur after the circulation is restored. The subject should not be given so much medication that he can not be easily aroused. If he can be evacuated promptly, analgesics should not be given, since such medications tend to mask some vital diagnostic signs. If evacuation is not necessary or must be delayed, more liberal use of analgesics, particularly strong analgesics, can be made.

Severe abdominal trauma may produce bleeding into the peritoneal cavity, rupture of abdominal organs, or both. Peritonitis inevitably results, although the inflammation following hemorrhage is due to irritation by the blood rather than infection. Gastric distension, absence of bowel sounds, nausea and vomiting, and other signs of peritonitis are usually present. (The diagnosis and treatment of peritonitis are described in greater detail in Chapter Thirteen, "Acute Abdominal Pain.")

Shock usually follows abdominal trauma, particularly trauma that causes intra-abdominal hemorrhage, and should be anticipated and treated.

NONPENETRATING INJURIES

Blunt or nonpenetrating injuries to the abdomen may produce:

- Contusion of the abdominal wall
- Internal bleeding due to a ruptured spleen, liver, or kidney
- Rupture of other internal organs such as the urinary bladder or, rarely, the intestines
- Combinations of the above

Contusion of the Abdominal Wall

A blow to the abdomen can cause a bruise that may be very painful. Although the area of impact may be quite tender, the abdomen around it is not so sensitive.

If the internal organs have been injured, tenderness is usually diffuse. In the first hour after injury, deciding whether a severe blow has produced merely a bruise or serious intra-abdominal damage may be quite difficult. Therefore, a delay of several hours may be necessary before the severity of the injury can be determined. A large black and blue area may blossom twenty-four to thirty-six hours after the injury as blood lost at the time of injury works its way out under the skin. This discoloration is of no significance, does not require treatment, and subsides spontaneously in time regardless of its extent.

After a tumbling fall, as may occur on boulders or on a steep ice slope, bruises often appear in areas that the person had not realized were injured. Frequently he feels far more sore and stiff a day or two after a fall than immediately after the injury. If there is no associated injury, the individual usually recovers after a few days of rest and mild to moderate analgesia every four to six hours.

Internal Bleeding

A blow to the abdomen may rupture the liver, spleen, kidney, or a combination of the three. Rupture is more likely if the blow falls immediately over the organ. The liver lies in the right upper quadrant; the spleen in the left upper quadrant. Both are tucked under the rib cage but can be injured by blows to the upper abdomen or to the lower part of the chest. The kidneys, which lie on either side of the backbone, may be damaged by a blow from the back. These organs are solid and may shatter when hit directly. Blood from an injured liver or spleen flows unimpeded into the abdominal cavity. The hemorrhage usually does not stop without surgical intervention. In contrast, the kidney is enveloped in a tough, fibrous sheath that contains the bleeding. Blood from a ruptured kidney appears in the urine.

Ruptured Kidney

A ruptured kidney is usually manifested by:

- History of a blow in the flank
- Pain, tenderness, and discoloration at the point of injury
- Blood in the urine

Bleeding from kidney injuries usually stops spontaneously; rarely is surgery necessary. The presence of large amounts of blood in the urine for more than six hours, a drop in blood pressure, or a consistently elevated pulse rate are indications that bleeding has assumed dangerous proportions. The individual should be treated for shock and evacuated as rapidly as possible. If bleeding from a damaged kidney stops, the subject must still wait ten to fourteen days before resuming vigorous activity since delayed bleeding sometimes occurs.

Ruptured Liver or Spleen

The subject characteristically has a history of a blow to the upper abdomen or lower chest. Pain, tenderness, and evidence of contusion are usually found in the area of impact, and one or more ribs may be broken. Shortly after the injury, intra-abdominal pain appears, first in the region of the injury and later more diffusely throughout the abdomen. The pain is usually aggravated by breathing deeply and may be associated with pain in the shoulder.

An individual with a ruptured liver or spleen usually appears to be in reasonably good condition at first. As hours go by, his condition deteriorates. The pulse becomes weak and rapid, and pallor, restlessness, and other signs of shock appear. With the spread of pain, the abdomen becomes tender, and rebound tenderness, distension, absence of bowel sounds, and other signs of peritonitis develop.

A person with an injury of the spleen may recover from the initial accident only to bleed massively when a clot breaks loose from the splenic surface several days or even a week later. Signs of intra-abdominal hemorrhage appear rapidly after such events.

Subjects with such injuries must be evacuated to the care of a surgeon as rapidly as possible. Hemorrhage rarely stops spontaneously; most individuals bleed to death if not surgically treated. The sooner an operation can be performed, the better are the chances of survival.

During evacuation shock must be anticipated—if it is not already present—and treatment should be started. Pulse, respiratory rate, and blood pressure should be recorded every hour to assist the surgeon who is to assume care of the subject.

Ruptured Intra-abdominal Organ

Severe blunt abdominal trauma may rupture one of the hollow intra-abdominal organs such as the intestines or the urinary bladder. The contents of the damaged organ are spilled into the abdominal cavity, producing peritonitis. Rupture of the urinary bladder usually occurs only if the bladder is full at the time of the injury and is usually associated with a fractured pelvis.

Following injury, the pain gradually becomes worse and spreads over the entire abdomen as peritonitis becomes generalized. Diffuse tenderness, abdominal distension, vomiting, and fever soon appear. If the bladder is ruptured, no more urine is voided except for a few drops that are mostly blood.

Treatment is the same as for peritonitis of any cause, as described in Chapter Thirteen, "Acute Abdominal Pain."

PENETRATING ABDOMINAL INJURIES

Perforating injuries of the abdomen are rare in the wilderness, but occasionally are caused by a fall on a sharp object or even a gunshot wound. These injuries are extremely serious and require operative treatment. Not only are the abdominal organs injured, but the abdominal cavity is contaminated from external sources, causing severe peritonitis.

The diagnosis is usually obvious, but a perforating abdominal wound may be overlooked following a shotgun injury in which the pellets have scattered widely. Attention must not be limited to the area of most obvious injury. The person should be stripped of all clothes and the entire abdomen and back carefully checked for pellet holes.

Evacuation should be carried out as quickly as possible. During evacuation the individual should be treated for peritonitis. Shock should be anticipated and treated.

A sterile dressing should be placed over the wound. In contrast to the usual care given soft-tissue injuries, the wound should not be washed, because such efforts only introduce more infection. Any loops of bowel protruding through the wound should be pushed back into the abdomen with the cleanest technique possible, and the wound should be covered with a dressing that is sufficiently snug to prevent the bowel from popping back out again. This dressing should not be changed once it is in place because further contamination of the wound would result and no benefit can be expected.

CHAPTER FIFTEEN

NEURAL DISORDERS

The nervous system has two major components: the central nervous system (CNS), which consists of the brain and spinal cord, and the peripheral nervous system, which comprises the numerous nerves that transmit impulses from and to the CNS. Almost everything that happens in the body—voluntary and involuntary movement, respiration, blood circulation, even endocrine function— is controlled or regulated by the nervous system. The diseases of this complex system are numerous and often disabling. However, most of these diseases come on too slowly to create problems on a wilderness outing, even on trips lasting several months.

SIGNS AND SYMPTOMS

The signs and symptoms produced by diseases of the nervous system consist of altered intellectual function, impaired control of movement (motor disturbances), sensory disturbances, loss of function of specific nerves, and a group of unrelated, less specific signs that includes headache, nausea and vomiting, and changes in pulse rate and blood pressure.

Altered Intellectual Function

Alterations of intellectual function usually produce personality changes first, most commonly increased irritability or silliness. Impairment of the individual's contact with his surroundings shows up later and is manifested initially by forgetfulness and confusion, but can progress to hallucinations, delirium, or complete loss of consciousness (coma).

Motor Disturbances

Motor disturbances, when early or mild, result in loss of coordination that causes stumbling or falling, or the inability to perform delicate or repetitive movements with the hands. More severe dysfunction causes weakness, convulsions, or total paralysis.

Sensory Disturbances

Sensory disturbances most commonly consist of paresthesias, tingling or prickly sensations like those felt when a limb "goes to sleep." Such sensations may not be indicative of nervous system disease. Acetazolamide, which is frequently administered to treat or prevent acute mountain sickness, commonly produces similar symptoms. Total anesthesia is rare. Anesthesia of an entire limb or a sharply circumscribed portion of a limb in a "stocking" pattern is due to "hysteria" rather than organic disease. The distribution of nerves does not allow this pattern of anesthesia to be produced by disorders that are not of emotional origin.

Individual Nerve Loss

Dysfunction of nerves that originate in the brain causes highly varied symptoms. Disturbed function of nerves to the eyes may cause blindness (occasionally limited to only a portion of the field of vision), paralysis of eye movements, or double vision. The pupils may fail to contract when exposed to light or may differ greatly in size. Vision may be blurred.

Disorders of nerves to the muscles of the face cause weakness or paralysis of facial movements and drooling on the affected side. Swallowing is impaired when the nerves to the muscles of the throat are affected, and fluids may be regurgitated through the nose or aspirated into the lungs. Disturbances of the nerves to the ear cause ringing or buzzing, vertigo, or hearing loss. Damage to other nerves may cause loss of smell, loss of taste, severe facial pain, weakness of the muscles of the neck, or impairment of respiration.

Damage to the nerves originating in the spinal cord causes paralysis or sensory disturbances, commonly anesthesia, in the portion of the body supplied by the injured nerves. Reflexes such as the knee jerk may be lost.

Other Signs and Symptoms

Blood clots, tumors, infections, or any disorder that increases the pressure within the skull can cause nausea and vomiting—the latter typically occurring without warning—a slower pulse rate, and a wider than normal separation of diastolic and systolic blood pressures. Headache associated with nervous system disease is often severe. Fever with central nervous system infections is often high; in other nervous system disorders the temperature is normal or only slightly elevated.

COMMON NERVOUS SYSTEM DISORDERS

The common nervous system disorders are usually not very serious and are frequently brief in duration.

Headache

Headache is a very common ailment suffered occasionally by all but a few fortunate individuals. Often a specific cause for a headache can not be identified, and the disorder is thought of as a disease in itself, although it is often a symptom of another illness. Headache after a rapid ascent to high altitude is common and is usually a symptom of acute mountain sickness.

The pain of a headache may be located in the back of the neck, behind the eyes, or all areas in between. Little significance can be attached to the location of the pain except when it is limited to one side of the head, which is typically a sign of a vascular headache (migraine).

A severe, persistent headache in an individual who usually does not suffer from headaches may be a sign of serious disease. Headache associated with confusion, forgetfulness, dizziness, nausea and vomiting, and—rarely—convulsions or loss of consciousness may be the result of an acute increase in blood pressure (hypertensive encephalopathy). This disorder usually occurs in persons with preexisting hypertension but requires prompt treatment. (See Chapter Nine, "Heart and Blood Vessel Disorders.") Headache associated with fever and a stiff neck are characteristic of meningitis. Following a head injury, increasing severity of a headache may be indicative of the development of a blood clot within the skull. (See Chapter Sixteen, "Head and Neck Injuries.")

Acetaminophen, ibuprofen, or aspirin every three to four hours relieves the pain of most headaches; acetaminophen or aspirin taken with codeine at the same frequency is adequate for most of the remainder. Individuals with frequent headaches should consult a physician. Some causes of recurrent headaches, such as brain tumors or high blood pressure, are quite serious, but usually come on so slowly they would cause problems in the wilderness only on a protracted expedition, although the sudden onset of symptoms of a brain tumor during ascent to high altitude has recently been reported.

Fainting (Syncope)

Fainting is a common disorder that usually is not a sign of organic disease. It typically follows emotional stress and sometimes occurs without an identifiable cause. When fainting is the result of disease, the disorder most often involves the heart and not the nervous system; therefore this condition is discussed in Chapter Nine, "Heart and Blood Vessel Disorders."

Convulsions

Convulsions may be a sign of disease of the nervous system but also occur with diseases that only affect the brain indirectly. Convulsions associated with renal failure are not uncommon. Many convulsions, particularly in young people, are solitary events for which no cause can be established and which never recur.

Epilepsy, a condition with which a person suffers repeated convulsions, can be controlled with medications. Convulsions rarely recur as long as the prescribed treatment is diligently followed. A person with epilepsy need not refrain from wilderness activities if his disorder is controlled and he is conscientious about taking his medications. His outing partners should be informed of his condition so they can learn the measures to take should a convulsion occur. However, the stigma once attached to epilepsy is completely unwarranted.

The onset of a convulsion is usually sudden and may be marked by a sound of some kind. The person characteristically loses consciousness and falls to the ground, his body twisting and writhing, his limbs twitching, jerking, or flailing about. The jaw may be involved and he may bite his tongue. He may salivate profusely and may defecate or void uncontrollably.

In any single convulsive episode all or none of these features may be present. Sometimes only slight twitching of the extremities is present. A person who is unconscious from a head injury may exhibit only a series of jerking movements that gradually increase in intensity and then subside. Limbs paralyzed by injury do not move.

Nothing can shorten or terminate the convulsive episode. The only helpful measure is to keep the subject from injuring himself. His arms and legs should be restrained only enough to prevent striking nearby objects as he flails about. Attempts to hold the extremities absolutely still may produce muscular or tendinous injuries. Clothing around his neck should be loosened to prevent strangulation.

The convulsion usually lasts only one or two minutes but can persist for five minutes or even longer. A period of unconsciousness almost always follows and can last from a few minutes to several hours. The coma may be so deep the individual is completely unresponsive, even to painful stimuli, and requires the same care as any comatose person, particularly maintenance of an open airway. He should be permitted to awaken without stimulation and allowed to rest until strength has returned and he feels that he has fully recovered. He must not be left alone for at least twelve hours, the time in which recurrences are most likely.

Anyone suffering an unexplained convulsion should be examined by a physician without delay so that any underlying disease can be diagnosed and treated.

MENINGITIS AND ENCEPHALITIS

Meningitis is an infection—usually bacterial—of the membranes surrounding the brain and spinal cord. Encephalitis is an infection of the brain itself, usually viral. These diseases produce similar signs and symptoms, are treated the same in the wilderness, and are discussed as a single category. (Rabies, a form of encephalitis, is discussed in Chapter Twenty-four, "Animal Bites and Stings.")

These diseases are spread by human contact or by insects, particularly mosquitoes. Meningitis can result from the direct spread by bacteria from a chronic infection of areas such as the sinuses, ears, or mastoids, or from an open fracture of the skull. A number of organisms can cause meningitis or encephalitis, and each organism varies in the effects it produces. The signs, symptoms, and severity of this group of infections cover a wide spectrum.

Headache, usually severe, is the most common initial symptom. Fever is usually present and may be high. Nausea and vomiting sometimes occur. Paralysis is rare and usually involves only one or two nerves, those originating in the brain more commonly than those from the spinal cord. Confusion, delirium, or coma may ensue and are fairly common with encephalitis.

The most specific diagnostic signs of central nervous system infections result from involvement of the fibrous membranes that cover the brain, which are severely inflamed with meningitis and to some extent with encephalitis. Movement of these membranes by bending the neck or back causes pain. In order to prevent such movement, the muscles surrounding the vertebral column go into spasm. A subject with one of these disorders is unable to touch his chin to his chest, although normally that maneuver is very easy. If he is placed on his back and his leg is lifted with the knees bent, straightening the leg causes pain in the back. This maneuver pulls on nerves in the leg, which produces movement of the spinal cord and its coverings, resulting in pain.

The treatment for meningitis and encephalitis consists primarily of control of the infection. Large amounts of antibiotics are needed and should be given intravenously if preparations suitable for administration by that route are available. High blood concentrations of the antibiotic are required for therapeutic quantities to get into the brain and cerebrospinal fluid, where the infection is located. Penicillin or ampicillin is the drug of choice for individuals who are not allergic to penicillin. Eight to twelve grams per day, depending on the person's size, should be given in six equally divided doses. If the individual is allergic to penicillin, chloramphenicol should be substituted. Four to six grams per day of this drug should be administered in four equal doses.

Fever can be very high with these infections, and should be lowered if it goes above 104°F (40°C) orally. Acetaminophen or aspirin can be given every four hours; cooling (by covering the arms and legs with wet cloths or clothing and fanning) may be required.

The headache that accompanies these disorders is frequently severe but can usually be controlled with acetaminophen or aspirin and codeine every four hours. Medications for sleep or medications for pain stronger than codeine should not be given because they depress brain function.

Fluid balance must be maintained; intravenous fluids may be necessary. Coma requires the same care as unconsciousness from any cause. Evacuation to a lower altitude or oxygen administration is desirable. The subject should be isolated with only one or two attendants to prevent spread of the disease. Evacuation to a hospital is always desirable and often essential.

STROKE

"Stroke" is a term for a group of disorders that are also called "cerebral vascular accidents" because rupture or obstruction of arteries in the brain destroys the tissue they supply. The most common of these disorders are hemorrhage, which can obliterate significant portions of the brain, and clotting within an artery, which causes the death (necrosis or infarction) of tissue supplied by that blood vessel.

Most strokes result from arteriosclerosis (hardening of the arteries), are associated with high blood pressure, and occur in older people. However, strokes can occur in young adults with severe, untreated hypertension. The dehydration and increased numbers of red blood cells typical of high altitudes increase blood viscosity and the risk of stroke. The individuals most likely to have strokes in the wilderness are members of support teams, such as the porters who play such a vital role in expeditionary mountaineering. Many of these individuals have never had any professional medical care, not even a routine physical examination, and do not know whether they have high blood pressure. They should be screened for hypertension as well as other diseases, particularly infectious diseases such as tuberculosis, and affected individuals should be excluded from the expedition, although the political situation in many areas does not permit such discrimination. (Participants in such expeditions should have been examined by a physician beforehand, and hypertension or other disorders predisposing them to strokes should have been detected and treated.)

Although many persons survive strokes, frequently with surprisingly little or no disability, the prognosis is still serious, particularly at high altitudes, where cold and reduced atmospheric oxygen add to the stress.

The onset is quite variable. With milder strokes, headache is commonly present. Other symptoms, which may be transient, include weakness of an arm or leg or one-half of the body; vague, unusual sensations such as tingling, "pins and needles" sensations, or numbness; visual disturbances such as blurred vision or partial blindness (which may not be noticed by the subject); and difficulties with speech, both speaking and understanding the speech of others. Personality changes such as combativeness, indecisiveness, or irritability may occur.

More severe strokes may be preceded by a headache, but unconsciousness follows fairly quickly and rapidly progresses to a deep coma in which no response to any stimuli can be elicited. (These events may take place almost instantaneously.) Breathing is noisy and may be very irregular (Cheyne-Stokes respirations). Paralysis is usually present, most commonly affects one side of the body, and may include the face as well as the extremities. However, the paralysis may be difficult to evaluate if the individual is comatose.

Regardless of the severity of symptoms, anyone with a stroke should be evacuated to a lower altitude without delay. Oxygen should be administered at altitudes above 8,000 feet (2,400 m). An open airway must be maintained if the individual is unconscious. Elevated blood pressure should be treated if medications are available. After a lower elevation is reached, a conscious individual with hypertension should rest for several days. A physician's care is essential. If the subject has only transient symptoms, more disabling damage can often be prevented. For individuals with more severe disease, such recovery as will occur requires months.

CHAPTER SIXTEEN

HEAD AND NECK INJURIES

BRAIN INJURIES

B rain injuries are among the most common causes of death in wilderness accidents. Usually the only care possible for persons with such injuries outside of a hospital is maintenance of an open airway. (Injuries to other parts of the body also must be treated.)

Unconsciousness following a blow to the head indicates that the brain has been injured. The severity of the injury correlates roughly with the duration and depth of coma. A person who responds in some fashion when called by name, or responds to pinching or similar painful stimuli, usually has not suffered serious brain damage and often regains consciousness in a short period of time. Someone who is completely flaccid and has dilated pupils, a slow pulse, and irregular respirations has a more severe injury. Widely dilated pupils that do not contract when exposed to light usually indicate brain damage that few survive. Bleeding from within the ears is a sign of fracture of the base of the skull, which is often associated with lethal injury to the brain.

Occasionally a person who has received a blow to the head may regain consciousness only to lapse into coma later as the result of continued bleeding within the skull (see Subdural Hematoma, below). Considerable perspicacity is required to recognize the subtle changes of this disorder at a time when effective treatment can be instituted.

Treatment

No specific treatment can be given for a brain injury in the field. The person must be evacuated to the care of a neurosurgeon. However, an open airway must be maintained during evacuation if the subject is unconscious. The only reason for evacuating an unconscious individual whose airway can not be kept open is burial!

Evacuating a comatose subject is so difficult that waiting until he has regained consciousness is highly desirable. In a particularly exposed and hazardous situation, such as on a sheer rock wall, a delay of several hours is fully justified. However, if the subject is not awake at the end of this time or shows signs of deepening coma, he can not be expected to regain consciousness without medical treatment. Even if he does regain consciousness later, recovery is usually so slow that he can not assist in his rescue (although he would be able to keep his airway open). The absolute necessity for maintaining an airway during evacuation, and the difficulty in doing so during descent from such a position, may require that the person be left on the wall with someone to care for him while the rest of the party goes for help.

Approximately fifteen percent of all severe head injuries are associated with a broken neck. All individuals who are unconscious as the result of a traumatic head injury must be immobilized as if they were known to have a cervical fracture.

Injuries to other areas of the body must be found and treated. Diligence is required when the person is unconscious and not able to point out painful areas. Many serious injuries are neglected for long periods because the individual is lying on his back and no one examines that area. Any lucid interval must be utilized to ensure that no injuries have been missed. Shock rarely results from brain injury alone, and the presence of shock should prompt a search for other injuries, particularly damage to the abdominal organs and fractures of the legs or pelvis.

Oxygen should be administered to anyone with a brain injury, regardless of altitude, if it is available. Such injuries depress respiratory function at a time when an adequate supply of oxygen for the brain is essential.

During evacuation, the person should be transported in the supine position, ideally with his head slightly elevated to promote drainage of blood from the brain and help reduce swelling and congestion. However, if he is vomiting, his head must be lower than the rest of his body to prevent aspiration. The presence of severe facial fractures greatly magnifies the difficulty of maintaining an open airway. If a tracheostomy can not be performed, considerable ingenuity may be needed to keep the person breathing.

Pulse, respiration, and blood pressure should be recorded at hourly intervals for the first twelve hours after injury, and every four hours afterward, until evacuation is complete. Such records are of vital importance for an individual with a brain injury because they often reflect his status more accurately than any other data, even sophisticated electronic monitoring or laboratory results.

If the subject is not hospitalized, either because he regains consciousness promptly and the injury does not appear to be of sufficient severity, or other circumstances prevent hospitalization, he should be monitored for at least a week after his injury. A blood clot within the skull may produce no signs or symptoms at the time of the accident, but can enlarge and prove lethal a few days or weeks later if not promptly recognized and treated.

SUBDURAL HEMATOMA

Among the brain's unique features is its snugly fitting envelope of bone, the skull. Although the skull is essential for protecting the very soft brain from injury, its presence occasionally is a disadvantage. Bleeding or swelling, which accompany injuries to any tissue, compress the brain within this rigid covering and frequently produce damage and dysfunction far out of proportion to the original injury. A hemorrhage that would be of no significance at another site can often cause death when confined within the skull. Swelling (edema) without hemorrhage or physical injury is a potentially lethal high altitude disorder. (See Chapter Twenty-one, "Medical Problems of High Altitude.")

Occasionally a blow to the head, although not severely injuring the brain at the time, tears some of the blood vessels around the brain. Blood from the torn vessels pours out into the narrow space between the brain and the skull and produces a clot that compresses the brain—a subdural hematoma (fig. 16-1). Death is usually the final outcome if the clot is not evacuated, or is evacuated too late.

The speed with which this clot develops depends on the number and size of the blood vessels that have been damaged. Following severe injuries bleeding may become apparent within a few hours, but signs of injury commonly do not appear for two or three weeks, occasionally even longer. Even though the bleeding stops, the clot can continue to enlarge because osmotic pressure created by proteins released from destroyed red blood cells pulls in water. The prognosis correlates fairly well with the speed with which the hematoma becomes evident. A person with a subdural hematoma that develops within twenty-four to forty-eight hours has a poor prognosis. One that develops two to three weeks after injury is associated with a much more favorable prognosis—if detected and removed promptly.

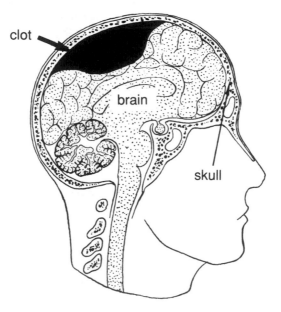

Figure 16-1. Subdural hematoma.

An epidural hematoma is a similar disorder that typically follows a fracture of the skull. The clot is located between the bone and its covering fibrous membrane, the dura, but the effect on the brain is the same. The damaged blood vessel producing an epidural hematoma is usually a medium-size artery rather than the veins that produce a subdural hematoma. As a result, signs of an epidural hematoma usually come on faster and are more severe.

Diagnosis

The typical individual who develops a subdural hematoma suffers a blow to the head that leaves him unconscious for thirty to sixty minutes. Subsequently he regains consciousness and appears normal. Some time afterward he begins to exhibit signs and symptoms of brain dysfunction and, after a variable period of time, lapses into unconsciousness again.

When coma occurs the second time, the subject is in critical condition and must be evacuated immediately if he is to have any chance for survival. A much more favorable outcome is usually possible, and evacuation is certainly much easier, if signs of the developing clot can be recognized before unconsciousness ensues.

Although few subdural hematomas follow injuries that produce unconsciousness of less than twenty minutes' duration, hematomas occasionally follow less severe injuries and may rarely develop after a blow that does not produce unconsciousness at all. Anyone who has incurred a significant blow to the head must be closely watched. However, the period of twenty minutes is a valuable reference point for evaluating the seriousness of a head injury; anyone unconscious for a longer time must be considered to have a significant risk of developing a subdural hematoma.

The intellect is the highest function of the brain and is frequently the first to be impaired in central nervous system disorders. Changes in personality, such as silliness or irritability, are often the first to appear; confusion and irrational speech or behavior show up later. Anyone rendered unconscious by trauma may be mildly confused or irrational for a few hours after regaining consciousness. However, such signs are suggestive of a more serious disorder if they persist for more than twenty-four hours or if they begin to get worse instead of improving.

Headaches may follow almost insignificant injuries. However, headache associated with nausea, with or without vomiting, usually indicates significant, although not necessarily severe, brain injury. Stumbling, loss of coordination, loss of ability to stand with the eyes closed, and weakness are signs of more severe cerebral damage. Inequality of the pupils (that did not previously exist) is a definite and important sign of brain injury and should be specifically sought.

None of these signs is diagnostic of a subdural hematoma; most can be produced by diseases of other organs. However, deterioration in a person's condition, an increase in the severity of signs and symptoms of brain injury, or the concurrence of several such signs following a head injury should prompt immediate evacuation. Paralysis, loss of sensation, disturbances of vision or hearing, and loss of consciousness are signs that develop later in the course of the disorder. Evacuation should not be delayed until these late signs have appeared.

Treatment

Treatment for a subdural hematoma consists of its surgical removal, which can not be performed safely outside of a hospital. The only recourse is evacuation of the subject to the care of a neurosurgeon. The more quickly evacuation is accomplished, the better are the person's chances for complete recovery.

A rapidly developing subdural hematoma in a remote area is of such grave significance, and evacuating an unconscious subject is so difficult, that the occurrence of a head injury on a weekend outing or similar short trip calls for immediate termination of the outing while the individual is still able to walk to a location where medical care is available. On a more extended expedition, the person should at least be returned to a point from which he can be evacuated if he becomes incapacitated.

SKULL FRACTURE

Skull fractures are often surprisingly difficult to diagnose. Nonfatal fractures may occur with relatively little brain injury and no detectable deformity. (In contrast, fatal brain injuries fairly commonly do not fracture the skull.) A few fractures result in a small portion of the skull being depressed into the brain. Larger depressed fractures or fractures accompanied by any obvious deformity are usually lethal.

With a skull fracture, the typical signs of a fracture in any other bone—pain, tenderness, swelling, and discoloration—are often masked (or mimicked) by contusions or lacerations of the scalp that produce swelling and bleeding. Occasionally, signs typical of a fracture are present on the opposite side of the head from the point of impact. In this location, pain, tenderness, swelling, and discoloration are indicative of a fracture. This injury, the so-called *"contre-coup"* fracture, is produced by the coincidence of the forces created by the impact at a point on the opposite side of the skull. Paradoxically, the skull may not be fractured at the point where the blow actually landed.

Fractures of the base of the skull frequently produce bleeding from the ears or nose. (The blood comes from within the ears or nose, not from lacerations of the surrounding skin.) Similarly, the clear, straw-colored fluid that surrounds the brain, cerebrospinal fluid, may leak from defects in the bones of the ear or nose after a basilar skull fracture. However, so much force is required to produce a fracture of the base of the skull that the associated brain injury often proves fatal immediately or within two or three days.

If fractures of the skull involve the bony orbit of the eye, the eye on the injured side typically drops back into its socket and appears sunken when compared with the opposite eye.

Until x-ray examination can determine whether a fracture is present, the safest course is to assume that any head injury that has resulted in more than transient unconsciousness has also fractured the skull. Under expedition circumstances, a headache persisting for more than two or three days, the appearance of other signs of fracture or brain injury, or blood or cerebrospinal fluid leaking from the nose or ears should prompt immediate evacuation to an area where x-ray studies can be made and definitive treatment instituted.

No specific treatment for a skull fracture can be given outside of a hospital. The subject should be evacuated promptly. Special precautions to prevent further injuries to the head may be needed. Injuries to other areas of the body must receive attention. If blood or cerebrospinal fluid is leaking from the nose or ears, penicillin should be given every six hours to reduce the possibility of infection spreading from these areas to the brain.

SCALP INJURIES

Scalp injuries differ from other skin injuries in two important respects: the scalp contains numerous blood vessels that bleed profusely from minor injuries, and infection in a scalp wound can spread to the brain. Fortunately, the scalp is more resistant to infection than most other soft tissues.

The treatment for scalp injuries is similar to the care for soft-tissue injuries anywhere else. Bleeding can be controlled by pressing down firmly with the fingertips or with gauze pads on both sides of the injury. Special care must be taken to flush all foreign material out of the wound.

A foreign body embedded in the skull or brain should not be disturbed. The wound should be bandaged with the object in place. Thick dressings must be applied to prevent dislocation of the object during transport, and the individual must be evacuated immediately. If evacuation requires more than a day, he should be given penicillin or a penicillinase-resistant penicillin, intravenously if possible, in twice the usual dose every six hours.

If the underlying bone is visible while a scalp wound is being cleaned, it should be examined (but not probed) for a fracture. If a fracture is found or suspected, similar antibiotic therapy should be given and the person should be evacuated.

FACIAL INJURIES

Soft-tissue Injuries

The tissues of the face have a greater blood supply than most other areas, tend to heal faster, and have greater resistance to infection. Tags of skin around facial wounds should not be trimmed away unless they are so badly damaged that survival is obviously impossible. Many such skin fragments can be saved and may reduce the need for skin grafting at a later date. Scarring may also be reduced by preserving these fragments.

Fractures

Facial fractures are uncomfortable but do not require splinting and seldom interfere with locomotion. Delayed treatment is often the preferred method of caring for hospitalized individuals with such injuries. Therefore, treating facial fractures is rarely an urgent problem. However, such fractures can make the maintenance of an open airway difficult, particularly for unconscious individuals. A fractured jaw may permit the tongue to drop back into the throat, completely obstructing the passage of air. Extensive fractures of the nose and adjacent bones can allow the nasal air passages to collapse.

Brain injuries, skull fractures, and fractures of the neck frequently accompany facial fractures and must be recognized and treated.

Fractures should be suspected after any forceful blow to the face that produces pain, tenderness, swelling, and discoloration. Such fractures rarely cause any obvious deformity, except for some fractures of the nose or jaw. Some discontinuity of the bones can occasionally be felt. A broken nose frequently bleeds rather profusely. Double vision is a sign of fractures of the bones about the eye.

Except for fractures of the lower jaw, facial fractures do not require splinting. A broken jaw can be splinted with a bandage that passes under the chin and over the top of the head, binding the lower jaw to the upper. However, individuals splinted in this manner may have difficulty breathing, particularly if they are stuporous or comatose. Fractures of the jaw should not be splinted if the person needs to breathe through his mouth.

The maintenance of an open airway in a person with facial fractures may require diligence and perseverance. A finger must be swept through the mouth of an unconscious individual with a broken upper or lower jaw to remove tooth or bone fragments and prevent them from entering the airway. If a tracheostomy can not be performed and an oral airway is not available or not tolerated, the subject may have to be transported in a face-down position, particularly if severe bleeding or swelling is present. Obviously, his face must be kept free of pillows, sleeping bags, and the stretcher while he is in this position.

Nose Bleeds

Nose bleeds are very common following minor injuries to the nose; fractures of the nasal bones are usually accompanied by rather severe bleeding. Nose bleeds without any antecedent trauma are even more common and may be severe. Anyone with repeated or severe nose bleeds should consult a physician since such incidents may be signs of a serious disorder.

An individual with a nose bleed should be in an upright position, seated or standing, and leaning forward. Leaning backward or lying down permits blood to drain back into the throat, where it is swallowed, which usually produces nausea and vomiting.

Many different maneuvers for stopping nose bleeds have been devised. Almost all are equally ineffective. However, most nose bleeds stop spontaneously, and no specific treatment is needed. Pinching the nostrils together along their full length is probably as effective as any other maneuver.

If bleeding persists, a cotton pledget can be moistened with phenylephrine nose drops or spray and formed into an elongated roll. After both nostrils have been blown clear of clots and mucus, the cotton roll should be inserted in the side that is bleeding. The nose should be held closed with gentle pressure for three to five minutes. After the pressure has been released, another two or three minutes should be allowed to pass, and then the cotton roll can be gently removed. If bleeding persists, this procedure can be repeated as often as necessary until the bleeding is controlled. This technique is usually effective eventually, even with nasal fractures.

EYE INJURIES

Eye injuries must always receive immediate and careful attention. Apparently trivial injuries can cause total loss of vision if neglected. Eyelid injuries can be almost as devastating as injuries of the globe.

Injuries to the Globe

Eye injuries are usually obvious, particularly for the person who has one, but may be overlooked if he is unconscious. Such injuries must always be suspected in the presence of head or facial injuries, or injuries of the opposite eye.

Penetrating or lacerating injuries of the eye produce visible damage. Contusions can cause hemorrhage within the eye and loss of vision with no externally visible sign of injury. Injuries of the nerves and muscles of the eye, or of the surrounding bone, can produce double vision or loss of vision. Because the eye is located within a socket of bone that protects it, those injuries that do occur are often associated with damage to the adjacent bone and soft tissues.

The treatment outside of a hospital for all visible or suspected eye injuries (including sudden, unexplained loss of vision) consists of bandaging the eye and evacuating the individual to an ophthalmologist. Removing foreign bodies or any other manipulations almost inevitably produce greater damage and should not be attempted. Delays of ten to fourteen days in treating such injuries usually make no difference in the final results.

All dirt and debris should be washed away as gently as possible with lukewarm, disinfected water or saline. No attempts should be made to remove blood clots attached to the eye, because distinguishing between blood clots and retina that has been extruded through a wound is usually impossible. Eyelid injuries must also receive careful attention.

During evacuation the eye must be covered. The uninjured eye should be covered by an opaque shield containing a small hole in the center. This type of shield permits the wearer to see only straight ahead and minimizes eye movements, thereby tending to splint the injured eye.

Penicillin should be given orally every six hours to persons with penetrating injuries if evacuation requires more than one day. Moderate or strong analgesics may be given every four hours for pain; medications for sleep or tranquilizers may be required, because such injuries arouse much anxiety. The subject must not be permitted to touch his injured eye or finger its bandage.

Eyelid Injuries

Vision can be destroyed by injuries to the eyelid as well as by injuries to the eye itself. If the eye is not continuously moistened by the tears the lid spreads over its surface, it rapidly dries, which kills the cells lining the cornea and can lead to scarring and blindness.

A torn or lacerated eyelid, after being washed free of all dirt and foreign material, should be returned as closely as possible to its original position. The eye must be completely covered. A snugly fitting bandage should be applied to hold the fragments in place. The opposite eye should also be snugly bandaged to prevent blinking or other movements that would disturb the alignment of the injured lid.

Rarely, the entire lid may be ripped away. If the lower lid is lost, the upper lid can be pulled down with adhesive tape to cover the entire eye. If the upper lid or both eyelids are lost, the exposed eye should be covered with a thick layer of ophthalmic ointment. A sterile dressing of soft material should be placed over the eye and held in place with a snug bandage.

Individuals with such severe eyelid injuries should be evacuated as quickly as possible. Antibiotics are not necessary and should not be given unless the injury is unusually contaminated. The tears contain antibacterial substances that eliminate most bacteria.

Minor lacerations, scratches, or abrasions that do not perforate the eyelid are not serious injuries and should be treated in the same manner as similar skin injuries anyplace else.

Foreign Bodies

Foreign bodies in the eye are very common, are usually easily removed, and are rarely followed by significant complications. Such objects most commonly adhere to the inner surface of an eyelid and can be removed by pulling one eyelid over the lashes of the other. If necessary, the eyelid can be folded outward over a match stem or similar object, and the foreign material can be brushed away with the edge of a clean handkerchief or a wisp of sterile cotton (fig. 16-2). Occasionally the foreign material produces mild conjunctivitis, which should be treated as described in Chapter Seventeen "Eye, Ear, Nose, and Throat Disorders."

A foreign body may become embedded in the superficial layer of the eye itself. An ophthalmologist should remove the offending object, but in circumstances

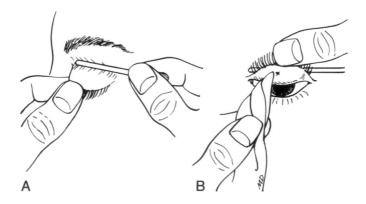

Figure 16-2. Technique for everting an eyelid and removing a foreign body.

where a physician is not available, attempts can be made to brush it away with a sterile cotton swab or the corner of a clean, folded handkerchief. If the object can not be brushed away, it can occasionally be removed with the tip of a needle. Obviously, great care must be exercised. If these measures are not successful, the eye should be bandaged and medical assistance obtained. The subject should be treated for conjunctivitis even though evidence of infection is not present.

Foreign objects that appear to actually penetrate the eye should never be removed or manipulated by anyone other than an ophthalmologist.

EAR INJURIES

Ear injuries are uncommon. Most are simple skin injuries, and should be treated in the same way as similar injuries located anyplace else. More severe injuries are often associated with severe head or brain injuries.

One cause of ear injuries is cleaning the external canal with long, narrow objects such as match stems. The admonition "never put anything in your ear smaller than your elbow" is wise, particularly in a remote area. If an accumulation of wax, a foreign body, or a small insect causes problems, it should be removed by irrigating the ear with lukewarm water, preferably with a soft rubber bulb designed specifically for this purpose.

Occasionally a traumatic injury causes a blood clot beneath the skin of the external portion of the ear. If the clot is large enough to cover one-third or more of the ear, it can cause a permanent "cauliflower ear" if allowed to persist. Such clots should be drained to avoid this type of scarring. The skin should be cleaned and swabbed with an antiseptic. Then one or more one-eighth-inch (3 mm) incisions should be made and the blood expressed with gentle pressure. Removal of all of the blood is not necessary and would probably aggravate the underlying injury.

Barotrauma

The middle ear and the paranasal sinuses are lined by thin mucous membranes and filled with air. These chambers have narrow openings to the nose or throat through which air moves to equalize the pressure within the chamber with atmospheric pressure. The opening into the middle ear, the eustachian tube, is much longer than the openings into the sinuses, and barotrauma is more common in the ear (fig. 16-3).

As atmospheric pressure decreases during an ascent to higher altitudes, air usually leaves these chambers without difficulty. However, increasing atmospheric pressure during a descent to lower elevations tends to close the chamber openings. Active measures such as swallowing or yawning may be required to open the eustachian tube. A light "pop" is often heard as the pressure is suddenly equalized. However, when the difference in pressure between the middle ear and the atmosphere is 90 mm Hg or more, the eustachian tube can no longer be opened by swallowing. In air, this pressure differential requires a change in altitude of about 3,750 feet (1,150 m) near sea level and can develop only when descent is rapid, as occurs in aircraft or rarely in automobiles on steep mountain

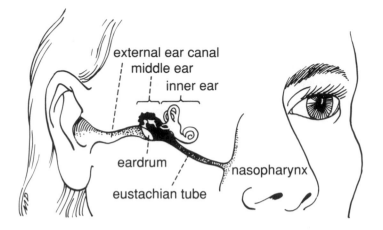

Figure 16-3. Anatomy of the ear and eustachian tube. (Adapted from *Dorland's Illustrated Medical Dictionary,* 26th ed., by W.B. Saunders.)

roads. However, under water and near the surface, such pressure differences can develop with a descent of only a few feet. Colds or nasal allergies cause swelling of the mucosa around the eustachian tube or the ducts into the nasal sinuses, which can partially obstruct the openings and hinder pressure equalization.

If the pressure within the chambers is not equalized with the atmosphere, a sense of fullness or pain develops. Hearing is diminished if the middle ear is involved. As the pressure differential increases, the ears and sinuses become more and more painful. Involvement of the middle ear also can cause sensations of noise, lightheadedness, and hearing loss.

As soon as an individual becomes aware of symptoms in his nose or ears, he should begin trying to equalize the pressure. Scuba divers, for whom barotrauma is a constant threat, commonly pinch their noses and forcibly exhale against the obstruction to open the eustachian tubes. Subjects with colds or hay fever should be aware of their increased risk of barotrauma and should not dive, or at least should be prepared with decongestants to reduce mucosal swelling. A phenylephrine spray or similar preparation is usually adequate; oxymetazoline also is adequate and is longer-lasting. The spray must be applied a second time after an interval of several minutes so it can enter the deeper recesses of the nose. A systemic decongestant can also be taken in advance of the descent. (Decongestants are often combined with antihistamines. Such combinations should not be taken if drowsiness is likely to create problems.)

If precautions are not successful or are neglected, or if the individual is unconscious, an aerotitis media or aerosinusitis may develop. The reduced pressure (negative pressure) within the chambers causes hemorrhage into the mucosa, which is usually quite painful. However, it rarely cause any other problems, and the pain usually disappears within twenty-four hours. The person should be given a systemic decongestant to promote drainage. Acetaminophen or aspirin, with codeine if needed, may be given to help relieve the pain.

NECK INJURIES

Injuries to the neck can damage vital structures. Massive hemorrhage usually follows injury of the large blood vessels. Hoarseness, coughing up blood, or diffuse swelling that feels spongy or "crackles" (crepitant) indicates injury to the air passages. Persons with such injuries must be evacuated without delay. Swelling associated with the injury may lead to airway obstruction, so preparations should be made for a tracheostomy. If the bandage over the wound encircles the neck (which is undesirable but is often the only way to keep the bandage in place), it must be loose enough to accommodate subsequent swelling that could result in obstruction of blood flow.

CHAPTER SEVENTEEN

EYE, EAR, NOSE, AND THROAT DISORDERS

D iseases of the eyes, ears, nose, and throat are the most common of all disorders if the common cold is included, are inconvenient rather than disabling, and except for allergies are of relatively short duration. However, all diseases of these organs, even colds, carry some threat of severe complications and must be respected and treated carefully, particularly in the wilderness. Because loss of vision is so devastating, the eyes must be protected and any disorders must be treated with particular care.

DISORDERS OF THE EYE

Conjunctivitis

Conjunctivitis is an inflammatory disorder of the delicate membrane that covers the visible white portion of the eye surface (the sclera) and the inner surface of the eyelids. Inflammation is most frequently caused by irritation from a foreign body, smog, or smoke, but is sometimes the result of a bacterial or viral infection. "Pink eye," a common type of conjunctivitis that can reach epidemic proportions among school children, is produced by the bacteria that were the most common cause of pneumonia in preantibiotic days. Trachoma, a form of chlamydial conjunctivitis, is the most common cause of blindness in those areas of the world where it occurs frequently, particularly Southeast Asia.

A person with conjunctivitis feels as if he has something in his eye, even after the foreign body has been removed. Movement of the eye aggravates the irritation. The eye appears red and the blood vessels on its surface are engorged. The flow of tears is increased. Exudate may be crusted on the margins of the eyelids and the eyelashes and may seal the lids together during sleep.

If the conjunctivitis results from smoke or a similar irritant, steroid-free eye drops that contain an antihistamine and a decongestant (such as Vasocon-A®, Optihist®, or Vernacel®) can provide symptomatic relief and reduce swelling of the eyelids and excessive tearing.

If exudate indicates an infection is present, an antibiotic ophthalmic ointment or solution (eye drops) should be placed beneath the lower lid every four hours until symptoms have disappeared. Antibiotic preparations should not be used except when clearly indicated. Allergy is fairly common, and the allergic reaction can be worse than the original condition.

If symptoms persist for more than three days and the conjunctivitis appears to be severe, tetracycline should be administered orally every six hours. Dark glasses or blinders with only a pinhole to see through help reduce the discomfort. Since many forms of conjunctivitis are infective, contact between the subject and other members of the party should be limited.

Subconjunctival Hemorrhage

Occasionally, exertion or coughing (sometimes no identifiable event) causes hemorrhages that range in size from a few millimeters to almost the entire visible part of the eye in the sclera. Although alarming, these hemorrhages are of no real significance, are not related to high altitude retinal hemorrhages, and require no treatment. They disappear in ten to fifteen days, depending upon the size of the hemorrhage. Hot compresses applied to the eye may speed resolution a little, but are not at all necessary.

Eyeglasses and Contact Lenses

All eyeglasses worn in the wilderness, whether needed to correct visual defects or for protection from sunlight, should be made of shatter-resistant (tempered) glass. A second pair should be carried in a secure place where they can not be broken or lost. However, in an emergency, cardboard with a central pinhole provides effective sunlight protection and also affords surprisingly good correction for individuals with refractive errors.

Wearers of contact lenses frequently have greater problems with the lenses at higher altitudes, particularly at the elevations encountered in Himalayan mountaineering. Five members of the 1975 British Everest Expedition tried using contact lenses during an attempt on the southwest face. Two had little trouble with eyeglasses and reverted to them early in the expedition. The other three had problems with glasses misting up and were eager to try contact lenses. However, above 26,000 feet (7,900 m), all three reverted to glasses due to a variety of problems, including slipping and loss of the lenses. The minimum surface oxygen tension for normal corneal function is about 15 mm Hg. At extreme altitudes, where the oxygen level is low, contact lenses may further decrease the surface oxygen tension, which may be the reason they are not as well tolerated at such elevations.

DISORDERS OF THE NOSE

The Common Cold

A variety of viruses cause upper respiratory infections (colds). Some generalized viral infections, particularly measles, often mimic a cold during their initial stages. The viruses are spread by personal contact. Chilling may play a role in contracting the disease by increasing susceptibility to infection, but in the absence of the causative viruses, cold exposure alone can not produce infection.

Secondary bacterial infections and allergy to the virus or bacteria cause many of the symptoms of a cold. A sense of dryness, scratchiness, or tickling in the throat or back of the nose usually appears first and is followed in a few hours by nasal stuffiness, sneezing, and a thin, watery nasal discharge. After forty-eight hours, when the disease is fully developed, the eyes are often red and watery, the voice husky, and the nose obstructed. An abundant nasal discharge is present, and taste and smell are diminished. A cough is commonly present and typically is dry at first; later, a moderate amount of mucoid material may be coughed up. The individual characteristically is uncomfortable but not seriously ill. Fever is usually absent but may be as high as 102°F (39°C). The throat may be sore, but exudates are not present (see Streptococcal Pharyngitis below), and the lymph nodes around the neck and jaw usually are not enlarged.

No effective treatment for a cold has been developed, although some measures to alleviate the symptoms are available. The disease usually lasts seven to ten days. Strenuous activity during the first few days, when symptoms are most severe, should probably be avoided, particularly at higher altitudes, in order to reduce the probability of complications such as sinusitis or bronchopneumonia. Moderate exercise at low altitudes and limited work at higher altitudes for the additional three to six days required for complete recovery are usually well tolerated.

A decongestant nasal spray may be used to reduce nasal congestion and obstruction. However, symptoms may be worse after the decongestant wears off than they were beforehand, particularly after short-acting decongestants such as phenylephrine. Decongestant sprays should probably be reserved for the times when they are needed most, such as at night to permit restful sleep. When first administered, a decongestant usually relieves obstruction by reducing the swelling of the mucous membrane over the more prominent portions of the nasal passages. A second spray five to ten minutes later may be necessary to reach the recesses of the nasal cavity. Swelling in these areas should be relieved to promote drainage and reduce the risk of sinusitis or a severe bacterial infection. A systemic decongestant or a combined decongestant and antihistamine may be beneficial when taken orally.

Antibiotics have no significant effect on the viruses that cause colds and should not be administered for most individuals. The rare serious complications of colds may require antibiotic therapy, but such therapy should not be given until the conditions actually develop. Prophylactic antibiotic therapy should be avoided, even at high altitudes, because the bacteria producing any subsequent infection would be resistant to the antibiotics. However, the uncommon individuals who almost invariably develop a bacterial bronchitis or bronchopneumonia following a cold should be considered exceptions to this rule.

Sinusitis

Sinusitis is an infection of one of the sinuses, air-filled spaces within the bones of the face that are lined by a thin mucous membrane similar to that of the nose and are connected with the nose by narrow canals (fig. 17-1). The sinuses serve

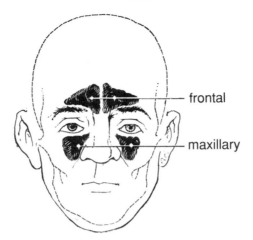

Figure 17-1. Location of the frontal and maxillary sinuses.

to make the skull lighter in weight than it would be if these areas were occupied by solid bone.

Sinusitis most commonly results from obstruction of the canals that drain the sinuses, usually produced by swelling of the mucous membrane around the openings due to a cold or allergy. Mucus collects within the sinuses, becomes infected, and the infection spreads to the surrounding tissues.

Sinusitis, although accompanied by a headache, is rarely disabling by itself. Complications do occur, and spread of the infection to the bones of the skull or to the brain itself can result in chronic osteomyelitis, meningitis, or a brain abscess. However, these potentially lethal complications usually follow prolonged chronic sinusitis, which should be eradicated before an extended wilderness outing.

Acute sinusitis usually accompanies or follows a cold or hay fever. The most prominent symptom is headache, which may be located in the front of the head, "behind the eyes," or occasionally in the back of the head. A purulent discharge frequently drains into the nose and back into the throat, where it may be swallowed—so-called "postnasal drip."

Fever rarely gets higher than 102°F (39°C) and may be entirely absent. Tenderness may be present over the involved sinus. Infection in the maxillary sinuses may produce pain or tenderness in the teeth of the upper jaw. If a small flashlight or penlight is placed in the subject's mouth and his lips closed over it, fluid in the maxillary sinuses can be detected by the failure of the sinus to be illuminated. (This examination must be carried out in darkness and a normal individual should be examined at the same time for comparison. If both sinuses are involved, as often happens, an inexperienced examiner would be unable to recognize any abnormality.) The frontal sinuses can be illuminated by pressing the flashlight into the upper inner corners of the eye sockets, just below the eyebrows.

The treatment for sinusitis consists of drainage and antibiotic therapy. A decongestant nasal spray should be administered at regular intervals to reduce the swelling of the nasal mucosa and permit drainage through the canals that enter the sinuses. Spraying should be repeated ten minutes after the first application to make sure the spray reaches the recesses where the openings of these canals are located. A systemic decongestant should also be administered. In a remote area, penicillin or tetracycline should be given orally every six hours. Treatment should be continued until all signs of sinusitis have been absent for two days.

Acute sinusitis usually clears up within a few days. Symptoms persisting for more than seven to ten days may be indicative of a complication and should prompt serious consideration of evacuation. Swelling around the eyes or nose is a definite sign of spread of the infection, and an indication that immediate evacuation is needed.

Nose Bleed

Nose bleed is commonly a result of trauma, but many nose bleeds do not follow an injury. Regardless of the cause, the treatment is similar. Care for this problem is discussed in Chapter Sixteen, "Head and Neck Injuries."

SORE THROAT

Sore throat is a common symptom that is produced by a number of different conditions.

Drying

Prolonged mouth breathing, particularly in hot, dry climates or at high altitudes where air has a very low relative humidity when warmed to body temperature, causes drying of the mouth and throat, resulting in a sore throat. An irritating, dry, hacking cough is usually present also. This condition can be identified by recognizing the existence of conditions causing drying of the throat and excluding the presence of other diseases characterized by sore throat. Drying of the throat is not accompanied by chills or fever, or by enlargement of the lymph nodes of the neck or under the jaw. The throat may be mildly inflamed, but exudates are not present.

Treatment of any kind is usually disappointing. Lozenges containing anesthetics or antibiotics are available. However, hard candy or rock sugar melted in the mouth (not chewed) is probably just as effective, is much less expensive and easier to obtain, and does not carry the dangers associated with indiscriminate antibiotic use. Lozenges should be taken only about every four hours, but candy can be consumed freely. Additionally, candy has nutritional value, which is important at high altitudes, where loss of appetite makes the ingestion of any food a problem.

Viral Pharyngitis

In conditions that do not produce drying, viral infections are the most common cause of sore throats. Viral pharyngitis (viral sore throat) most commonly accompanies a cold but frequently is not associated with another disorder. The person usually does not feel or appear seriously ill, although a few individuals feel much worse than most others. Fever may be present but is rarely higher than 101°F (38.5°C). The throat is inflamed, but exudates are not present and enlargement of lymph nodes is rare.

Before accepting a diagnosis of viral pharyngitis, the presence of streptococcal pharyngitis must be ruled out.

Viral sore throat usually clears up in three to six days without therapy. Lozenges may provide some relief, but hard candies melted in the mouth are equally effective. Antibiotics are of no benefit and should be avoided unless streptococcal infection is seriously suspected. However, it may be impossible to distinguish between these two infections without laboratory facilities.

Streptococcal Pharyngitis

Streptococcal pharyngitis, or "strep throat," is encountered less frequently than other causes of sore throat but can be treated much more satisfactorily. This infection is caused by bacteria known as streptococci and is potentially dangerous because it can lead to rheumatic fever—which may damage the heart valves—or glomerulonephritis, a kidney disease.

Anyone with streptococcal pharyngitis typically feels and appears ill. Fever is usually present and may reach 103°F (39.5°C) or higher. Chills often occur. The throat appears beefy red, and exudates, which are similar to the pus found in boils or infected wounds, can be seen as white or pale yellow points or patches scattered over the throat, particularly on the tonsils. The lymph nodes in the neck and under the jaw usually are enlarged and tender.

Fever, exudates, enlarged lymph nodes, and general malaise serve to differentiate "strep throat" from other forms of pharyngitis. However, malaise may not be marked, lymph node enlargement may not be prominent, and fever may not be very high. Therefore, any sore throat should be regarded with suspicion. In a remote area, if the possibility of streptococcal infection appears significant, antibiotic therapy should be instituted.

Treatment for streptococcal pharyngitis consists of the oral administration of penicillin every six hours for ten days. Symptoms and signs of the disease usually disappear completely within twenty-four to forty-eight hours. Nonetheless, therapy must be continued for ten days to ensure complete eradication of the infection and the prevention of complications, particularly rheumatic fever. Individuals allergic to penicillin should be treated with erythromycin.

DISORDERS OF THE MOUTH

Toothache

Toothache is almost invariably due to an infection. The infection initially produces a cavity in a tooth, but later it can spread to the surrounding bone and soft tissue to produce an abscess. Adequate dental care should almost completely prevent abscesses, but such infections are fairly common among natives of underdeveloped countries for whom dental care is not available.

Usually a cavity is obvious. The tooth may have broken off so that only a jagged stump remains. Swelling in the gum and jaw indicates that the tooth has become abscessed; one whole side of the face may be swollen. Fever and occasionally chills accompany an abscess.

A small wad of cotton soaked in oil of cloves and inserted in the cavity usually reduces the pain if no abscess is present. Mild or moderate analgesics every four hours also help to relieve discomfort.

The presence of an abscess is an indication that the tooth should be pulled. However, extraction should be attempted only in remote situations and only when dental forceps are available. Large quantities of an antibiotic such as penicillin or ampicillin should be administered intramuscularly thirty minutes prior to the extraction to help destroy the bacteria invariably released into the blood stream during an extraction. (Chills and fever are common in the twenty-four hours after the tooth is pulled.)

If the person is to be evacuated to a dentist for the extraction, he should be given penicillin or ampicillin every six hours until evacuation is completed. An analgesic may or may not be needed. Sometimes extraction of an abscessed tooth is surprisingly painless.

Canker Sores

Canker sores are small, painful ulcers that appear in the mouth without apparent cause. They first appear as small blisters that soon rupture, leaving small, white ulcers surrounded by an area of inflammation. Such sores may be caused by *Herpes simplex* infection.

No therapy is effective for curing these ulcers, but they disappear in a few days without treatment. A mouthwash consisting of a teaspoon (4 cc) of sodium bicarbonate (baking soda) in a glass of water is soothing; a mouthwash of half water and half three percent hydrogen peroxide solution helps prevent secondary infection.

Herpes

Oral herpes (also known as "cold sores" or "fever blisters") is a viral infection *(Herpes simplex)* that produces small, painful blisters on the lips and skin around the mouth. The viruses persist in the tissues, so blisters recur in the same location. Herpes sores commonly result from sunburn of the lips or face, may accompany severe infections such as pneumonia or meningitis, but most commonly can not be associated with any disorder.

An initial small, painful swelling rapidly develops into one or more small blisters containing a clear fluid and surrounded by a thin margin of inflamed skin. The blisters may rupture, particularly if they are traumatized, resulting in bleeding and crusting. Fever or other symptoms are rarely experienced.

The application of a local anesthetic may provide some symptomatic relief, but no specific treatment is available. The blisters usually heal in five to ten days, and although uncomfortable and perhaps unsightly, they usually cause no significant disability. Avoiding sunburn of the lips helps prevent herpes sores.

Ear Infections

Ear infections frequently occur in infants and young children but are uncommon in older persons. The eustachian tube, which drains the middle ear, is easily blocked by swelling of the mucous membrane or enlargement of the adenoids in young people. However, this tube is larger in adults and these disorders rarely produce obstruction. In the absence of eustachian obstruction, ear infections are uncommon.

A cold, sinusitis, or hay fever usually precedes the ear infection. The principal symptom is pain in the ear. Fever or malaise may be present. Infrequently a purulent discharge from the ear can be found.

Therapy consists of the oral administration of penicillin every six hours until all signs of infection have been absent for two days. A systemic decongestant should also be given to help reduce swelling around the opening of the eustachian tube. A hot-water bottle and mild to moderate analgesics every three to four hours help reduce the pain. A warm (not hot), bland oil such as olive oil inserted into the ear also helps relieve the pain.

CHAPTER EIGHTEEN

GENITOURINARY DISORDERS

The urinary tract is made up of the kidneys, ureters, urinary bladder, and urethra. The genital system includes the ovaries, fallopian tubes, uterus, vagina, and external genitalia in females; the testes, epididymides, vasa deferentia, seminal vesicles, prostate gland, and external genitalia in males (fig. 18-1).

The kidneys filter blood and excrete unneeded substances and water. Urine is transported by the ureters from the kidneys to the urinary bladder, where it is held until voided through the urethra.

Normally hydrated adult males of average size with normal renal function form approximately 1 cc of urine per minute. About 60 cc is formed per hour; 1,500

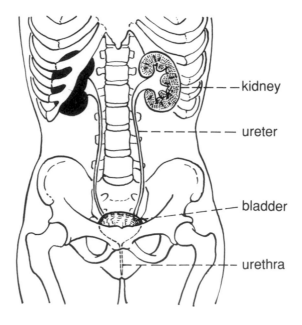

Figure 18-1. Anatomy of the urinary tract.

cc is excreted per day. Persons with smaller or larger bodies produce somewhat smaller or larger urine volumes, although urinary output does not vary directly with size. Dehydration reduces urine volume; overhydration increases urinary output.

ACUTE URINARY TRACT DISORDERS

The most common symptoms or signs of acute urinary tract disease are:

- Pain in the back or flank
- Burning with urination
- Blood in the urine
- Changes in urine volume

Pain is usually indicative of kidney disease and is characteristically located to one side of the vertebral column at the point where it is joined by the lowest ribs. However, the pain frequently radiates to the sides just above the pelvis and around to the groin.

A burning sensation with voiding is unmistakable, is often described as the sensation of passing gravel, and usually results from inflammatory diseases of the urinary bladder, prostate, or urethra.

Bleeding can be obvious or may produce only cloudy or "smoky" urine. If the urine is allowed to stand so the cells can settle out, a red sludge often can be seen at the bottom of the container, confirming the presence of blood. Surprisingly small amounts of blood can be detected in this way.

Changes in urinary volume, except for very large deviations, usually go unnoticed unless the urinary output is measured. In the wilderness dehydration is by far the most common cause for a change in urinary output. However, some renal diseases can result in total or near total cessation of kidney function. Uncommonly, a larger volume of very dilute urine is excreted.

Cystitis

Cystitis is inflammation of the urinary bladder that occurs with or without infection. This disorder is rare in young males but is common in females. When cystitis is associated with pyelonephritis, symptoms of the latter predominate.

The principal symptom of cystitis is burning or pain during voiding. The pain may increase somewhat as the bladder is emptied but disappears gradually after flow has stopped. The frequency of voiding may be increased because the irritated bladder feels full with a smaller urine volume. Fever or other symptoms are rare. Slight bleeding sometimes occurs; rarely bleeding may be severe enough to make the urine obviously bloody.

Usually no treatment is needed for cystitis and the symptoms disappear in two or three days. If symptoms are severe, persist for a longer time, or are associated with fever, ampicillin, trimethoprim-sulfamethoxazole, a cephalosporin, or ciprofloxacin may be administered. These drugs are excreted by the kidneys and reach high concentrations in the urine. They should be given orally four times a day for at least one week, or until the person has been completely free of symptoms for two days, if that takes longer. Large quantities of fluids must be consumed also.

Pyelonephritis

Pyelonephritis, an infection of one or sometimes both kidneys, is characterized by the rather sudden onset of high fever, often with chills, and flank pain over the kidney. The subject often feels and appears ill. Back pain of moderate severity is usually present. Pressing or gentle pounding with the fist just below the lower rib on either side of the vertebral column reveals tenderness. Symptoms of cystitis are often present, and slight to moderate bleeding may occur.

The individual should drink large quantities of fluids, at least twice the usual daily requirement. Fluid intake and urinary output should be recorded. Evacuation from altitudes above 14,000 feet (4,300 m) is desirable.

Antibacterial therapy is important. Trimethoprim-sulfamethoxazole, ampicillin, a cephalosporin, or ciprofloxacin should be given orally every six hours and should be continued for five days after all signs of disease have disappeared, or for a minimum of ten days. Individuals with repeated episodes of pyelonephritis should consult a physician; irreversible kidney disease can result. An underlying disorder, such as kidney stones, may be present.

Acute Renal Failure

Renal failure, a drastic reduction or total cessation of kidney function, occasionally follows a severe injury, particularly if the person is in shock for several hours or longer. (Certain poisons, drug reactions, and other disorders can also cause acute renal failure.) If the person can be kept alive through the period of reduced renal function, which may last from a few days to several months, complete recovery is usually possible.

The principal manifestation of renal failure is reduced urinary output. Dehydration may also cause a low urinary output, but when a dehydrated subject is given fluid, the urinary volume increases. An individual with acute renal failure can not increase his urinary output, no matter how much fluid he is given. With dehydration the urine is concentrated and has a deep yellow or orange color; with acute renal failure the small amount of urine produced is typically dilute. Any adequately hydrated subject with a urinary output of less than 400 cc per day of dilute urine following a severe injury should be considered to be in renal failure.

Weakness, loss of appetite, nausea, vomiting, diarrhea, muscle twitching, confusion, convulsions, and eventually coma appear sometime after the onset of renal failure, usually from three to ten days after injury. Usually few symptoms related to diminished renal function are present for the first two or three days. However, weakness becomes apparent on about the third day, and the other symptoms soon follow.

Urinary retention due to spasm of the bladder muscles, and rupture of the urinary bladder, simulate renal failure because urinary output ceases. However, urinary retention is usually accompanied by a strong urge to urinate as well as by pain in the bladder or lower abdomen. (If urethral catheterization discloses the bladder to be empty, urinary retention can be ruled out.) Following bladder rupture, evidence of an abdominal or pelvic injury, including abdominal pain and tenderness, is usually obvious. (See Chapter Fourteen, "Abdominal Injuries.") However, acute renal failure can also be associated with an injury in which the bladder is ruptured.

Evacuation is urgent. Only a well-equipped medical center has the facilities to keep someone with acute renal failure alive for more than a few days. Some form of dialysis (artificial kidney) is essential.

During evacuation, fluid intake must be carefully controlled to prevent overloading with water. To establish the diagnosis of acute renal failure the person's previous state of hydration must be determined. If he appears to have been dehydrated, enough fluids must be given to correct that situation. If renal output does not return, subsequent fluids must be administered very carefully. Each day's fluid intake should be limited to one quart plus a quantity roughly equal to the urine volume. Unusual fluid losses caused by vomiting, sweating, or high elevation must also be replaced. (See Fluid Balance in Chapter Two, "Basic Medical Care and Evacuation.")

If nausea and vomiting, which are usually present after the third day, prevent taking fluids orally, intravenous fluids must be administered. The quart of water plus an amount equal to the previous day's urinary output and any unusual losses through the lungs should be replaced with a five or ten percent glucose solution. Fluids lost through vomiting and excessive sweating should be replaced with a balanced salt solution. To ensure that the volume replaced matches the amounts that have been lost, urine volume, losses from other sources, and oral or intravenous intake must be measured and recorded.

While he can, the subject should be encouraged to eat sweets such as hard candy or glucose tablets. However, citrus fruits and fruit juices must be avoided; they contain potassium, which can be toxic for a subject with reduced renal function.

Medications should be avoided because most drugs are excreted by the kidneys. In the absence of renal excretion, their concentration can rapidly build to toxic levels.

Acute Glomerulonephritis

Glomerulonephritis is a common disease of the renal glomeruli, the portion of the kidneys in which the blood is filtered. Chronic dialysis or kidney transplants are required for chronic glomerulonephritis more often than for any other disorder. However, chronic glomerulonephritis would rarely have such a rapid onset that it could cause problems on even an extended wilderness outing. Acute glomerulonephritis can appear much more rapidly.

Acute glomerulonephritis usually follows a "strep throat" or some other streptococcal infection by a few days or a few weeks and can be largely prevented by treating the initial streptococcal infection with penicillin. (A few individuals do not have identifiable preceding infections.)

Swelling or puffiness of the face, which is most striking upon arising in the morning, blood in the urine, and headache are the most common signs. A low fever and loss of appetite, nausea, and vomiting may be present. More severe disease is characterized by edema, particularly of the feet and ankles, and acute renal failure. The blood pressure commonly is elevated.

The urine may appear bloody, but more frequently blood can be detected only after the red blood cells have been permitted to settle to the bottom of a container. Protein is almost always present in the urine (proteinuria), and boiling causes the protein to precipitate as a thick, flocculent coagulum that resembles egg albumen. Proteinuria is the key feature for the diagnosis of glomerulonephritis. If present, the individual probably has this disorder; if absent, he does not.

The person should rest, and salt, which tends to promote edema and high blood pressure, should be restricted. Penicillin should be given four times a day for ten days in case a lingering streptococcal infection is present. Evacuation is desirable, but in a truly remote area may not be mandatory if a urinary output of more than 500 cc per day can be maintained. If the subject's urine volume falls below 400 cc, he should be considered to have acute renal failure (which can result from glomerulonephritis), his fluid intake and output must be monitored, and he should be evacuated to a hospital.

OTHER URINARY TRACT DISORDERS

Kidney Stones

Since the characteristic symptom of kidney stones is severe pain, this disorder is discussed in Chapter Thirteen, "Acute Abdominal Pain." Bloody urine and burning with voiding can also accompany the passage of a stone.

Hematuria

Hematuria, which means bloody urine, may be associated with traumatic injuries, tuberculosis, or tumors of the urinary tract, as well as the disorders discussed above. Traumatic urinary disorders are discussed in Chapter Fourteen, "Abdominal Injuries." Adequate treatment for tuberculosis or tumors is impossible in the wilderness.

Visibly bloody urine, particularly in the absence of any signs of a specific disorder, should prompt immediate medical consultation to determine the cause and institute appropriate therapy. Obvious hematuria is frequently a sign of a serious disorder. (The loss of blood itself is almost never of sufficient volume to be disabling.)

Hemoglobinuria

Severe injuries, burns, severe infections, and other disorders can destroy red blood cells and release hemoglobin into the blood. This pigment is excreted by the kidneys and imparts to the urine a faint pink to deep red color that resembles bloody urine.

Hemoglobinuria must be distinguished from hematuria, which is caused by entirely different conditions. If urine that contains hemoglobin is permitted to stand, no blood settles to the bottom of the container. Acute renal failure some-times follows disorders producing hemoglobinuria if the individual becomes de-hydrated or goes into shock. A fluid intake high enough to significantly increase urinary output helps prevent this complication.

Occasionally, strenuous exercise alone results in hemoglobinuria or myoglobinuria. (Myoglobin is a protein similar to hemoglobin that originates in muscle and can also be released by crushing injuries.) Such disorders can also cause acute renal failure but usually disappear with rest. The subject must main-tain a generous fluid intake to reduce the chances of renal failure.

The pigment from some foods or dyes, particularly beets, occasionally imparts a reddish color to the urine. However, the individual can usually remember the ingestion of these substances, and the pigment disappears from the urine within a few hours or days. Hemoglobinuria that is not associated with renal failure requires no therapy other than a high fluid intake.

FEMALE GENITAL PROBLEMS

Although gynecologic problems are common and widely variable, few appear so rapidly they could create problems on a wilderness outing. An examination by a physician beforehand should disclose any potential disorders and permit their correction before the outing is under way.

Dysmenorrhea

Dysmenorrhea means painful menstruation. Pain is caused by many different abnormalities, including a wrongly positioned uterus and the passage of blood clots. Most women with dysmenorrhea have had it most of their postpubertal lives, and encountering it for the first time on a wilderness outing would be most unusual. Exercise often relieves dysmenorrhea.

The pain typically is cramping, may be disabling (although it usually is less severe), and usually is worse the first day or two of the menstrual period. Mild or moderate analgesics help mask the pain. Prostaglandin antagonists such as ibuprofen are usually more effective.

Diminished physical activity may be of some benefit. Women bothered with this problem—and they are numerous—have usually learned to deal with it long before it creates problems in a wilderness situation.

Abnormal Bleeding

Abnormal uterine bleeding can take the form of excessive bleeding with men-strual periods, bleeding between periods, or both. Although numerous disorders can produce such bleeding, commonly no cause can be identified. No specific treatment can be given in a wilderness situation. The bleeding is rarely severe enough to create blood loss problems. If a hemorrhage of massive proportions does occur, packing the vagina with tampons, gauze, or anything available may help slow the bleeding during evacuation, although complete control of bleeding by such means probably can not be obtained. Such problems must be exceedingly rare. Exercise seems to help control abnormal bleeding for many women.

Pregnancy

Pregnancy, at least in its early stages, does not necessarily require curtailment of a woman's customary activities, but some precautions should be observed during wilderness activities. Fifteen to twenty percent of all pregnancies terminate in spontaneous abortions; most occur during the first three months of pregnancy. Occasionally such abortions are associated with severe bleeding that can not be controlled without hospital facilities. A woman in this stage of pregnancy should probably not enter an area so remote that evacuation within twelve to twenty-four hours could not be readily accomplished.

During the last three months of pregnancy, the enlarged uterus and the baby it contains often cause problems with balance. Activities that require balance are more difficult. A fall could injure the mother, baby, or both, even though such falls would not injure a woman who was not pregnant. Premature labor, whether caused by a fall or occurring spontaneously, could result in the birth, in less than optimal circumstances, of a small, immature baby who could not survive without the facilities available in a hospital.

Occasionally pregnancy creates or aggravates other medical problems, such as diabetes, hypertension, or cardiac disease. The mother should consult her physician for any special care such problems would require on a wilderness outing.

Contraceptives

One aspect of pregnancy—its prevention—does have direct implications for high altitude activities. Oral contraceptives appear to cause an increased incidence of venous thromboses and pulmonary embolism. High altitudes also predispose to the development of these disorders. (See Chapter Ten, "Respiratory System Disorders.") Women taking part in outings that require a prolonged stay at altitudes above 10,000 to 12,000 feet (3,000 to 3,700 m) should discontinue oral contraceptives several weeks in advance. If some other form of contraception is needed and an intrauterine contraceptive device (IUD) is selected, it should be inserted several months in advance to be sure it is well tolerated. These devices occasionally cause problems such as perforation, bleeding, or infection that could be difficult or impossible to control in the wilderness, but most of these complications show up during the first few months the devices are used.

MALE GENITAL PROBLEMS

Few male genital problems appear with sufficient speed or at a young enough age to cause problems in wilderness situations. Two exceptions are acute epididymitis and torsion of the testes, two entirely different disorders that have similar features and may be difficult to distinguish, even for a physician.

Epididymitis and Testicular Torsion

Epididymitis is an inflammatory disorder of the epididymis, an organ adjacent to the testis in which sperm collect before passing through the vas deferens to the seminal vesicle. Epididymitis sometimes is the result of gonorrheal infection, but cultures are rarely taken from the inflamed tissues. Most epididymitis probably has no relation to venereal infection; many cases may not result from infection at all.

Torsion refers to twisting of the testis within the scrotum. The spermatic cord, which contains the vas deferens and the arteries and veins supplying the testis, also is twisted, and the blood vessels, particularly the veins, are occluded. If the occlusion is not relieved, which usually requires surgery, the testis is deprived of its blood supply and "dies" within a few hours.

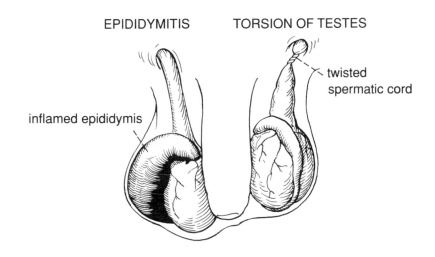

EPIDIDYMITIS   TORSION OF TESTES

twisted spermatic cord

inflamed epididymis

Figure 18-2. Testicular disorders.

Both of these disorders are quite painful. The scrotum is often distended and may be inflamed, particularly with epididymitis. The testis is usually swollen and quite tender. The pain of testicular torsion may appear rapidly; epididymitis usually develops more slowly. An enlarged, firm, nodular epididymis may be felt with epididymitis. Elevation of the scrotum and the application of cold packs are frequently helpful with epididymitis; elevation of the scrotum usually does not help relieve the pain of testicular torsion. With testicular torsion, the testis may be higher in the scrotum than the opposite testis because the cord is shortened by twisting.

The individual should rest as much as possible. (Many physicians keep patients with epididymitis confined to bed.) Both disorders are too painful for vigorous activity. Tetracycline, a cephalosporin, trimethaprim-sulfamethoxazole, or ciprofloxacin should be administered with either disorder. If the individual has a history of gonorrhea or exposure to gonorrhea within the previous two months, he should be treated as if he had gonorrhea. Subjects with testicular torsion who can not be evacuated right away need antibiotics to prevent the establishment of an infection in the dead tissue of the testis.

Almost everyone with either of these disorders must be evacuated. Individuals with testicular torsion require surgery, even if it can not be carried out quickly enough to save the testis. Individuals with epididymitis require rest and antibiotics. Two to three weeks may be required for complete healing. Resumption of activity before all symptoms have completely cleared frequently reactivates the disease. However, epididymitis has little tendency to spread to other tissues and probably could be adequately treated in base camp in truly remote circumstances.

Sexually Transmitted Infections

The venereal diseases are a group of infectious diseases spread by sexual contact; syphilis and gonorrhea are the most common. Herpes viral infections have been around for many years. Hepatitis B is spread mostly by sexual contact in developed nations but is not considered a venereal disease and is discussed in Chapter Twelve, "Gastrointestinal Disorders." Human immunodeficiency virus (HIV) also is spread by sexual contact. That infection and the acquired immune deficiency syndrome (AIDS) it produces are discussed in Chapter Nineteen, "Infections."

All venereal diseases are spread by intimate personal contact. Infection from toilet seats or similar sources essentially does not occur because the organisms can not survive outside the body.

At the present time the only dependable way to prevent such infections is to avoid sexual contact with infected individuals. Condoms do not completely prevent infection. Prophylactic antibiotic therapy has many disadvantages in addition to the significant risk of allergic reactions to the drugs.

Syphilis

Syphilis is produced by the spirochete *Treponema pallidum*. This infection has an interesting history. It apparently originated in the western hemisphere, was transported to Europe by members of Columbus's crew, and in an amazingly short time spread all over the world. The great variation in its clinical features, its long duration, and its ability to involve any of the body's organs and mimic many other diseases has been particularly fascinating. The discovery of penicillin therapy was a dramatic triumph.

Syphilitic infections have three stages. The primary stage is that of the chancre, a one-quarter- to one-half-inch (6 to 13 mm), painless ulcer that appears at the site of inoculation. Most chancres appear on the genitalia, but they are occasionally found on the mouth or lips, or the skin of other parts of the body. In women, chancres may be located within the vagina or on the uterine cervix, where they are not easily seen. Sometimes primary chancres never appear, or they go unnoticed, particularly when hidden in a location such as the vagina.

The secondary stage of syphilis is characterized by the appearance of a skin rash about six weeks after the primary lesion. However, many individuals do not manifest this stage of the disease. The appearance of this rash is highly variable, although it does not produce blisters, and it usually has a wide distribution, including the palms and soles and the mucous membranes of the mouth. The rash does not itch. It usually lasts from a few days to a few weeks.

In its tertiary stage, syphilis can produce fatal cardiac disease or disabling brain disease. However, tertiary syphilis takes years to develop and can be prevented by appropriate therapy.

A precise diagnosis of syphilis requires laboratory facilities not widely available in underdeveloped countries. Treatment in the wilderness should be based on a history of sexual contact and the presence of a primary chancre or the secondary skin rash. The infection is most contagious during the primary and secondary stages.

The preferred treatment for all stages of syphilis is penicillin. A single intramuscular injection of 2.4 million units of Benzathine penicillin G in each buttock should be administered for primary or secondary disease. Alternatively, single daily intramuscular injections of 600,000 units of procaine penicillin G may be given for eight days. Individuals allergic to penicillin can be treated with 0.5 gm of erythromycin or tetracycline four times a day for fifteen days. Follow-up care should be obtained from a physician after a wilderness outing to ensure the infection has been totally eradicated.

Gonorrhea

Gonorrhea is a common, widespread infection that in males is usually limited to the lower genital tract, principally the urethra. Infection at this site is associated with a purulent discharge, but the diagnostic feature is pain, which is often severe, with voiding. Residual infection may persist, particularly in the prostate, or the infection may spread to other parts of the body.

In females, gonorrhea is a much more insidious infection. Seventy-five percent of infected women have no initial symptoms at all. The infection must be diagnosed by bacterial cultures from the vagina or uterine cervix. Treatment must be based on a history of sexual contact with an infected individual when laboratory facilities for a definitive diagnosis are not available.

Gonorrhea is also a much more threatening disorder in females. Spread of the infection to other organs is much more common. Extension to the fallopian tubes produces painful infections with symptoms similar to those of appendicitis. (See Acute Salpingitis in Chapter Thirteen, "Acute Abdominal Pain.") Permanent sterility usually results. Spread to one or more joints can produce a destructive arthritis; involvement of the heart can cause disabling cardiac disease. Infections also occur in other tissues.

Unfortunately, strains of gonorrhea resistant to penicillin have emerged in recent years and are now found worldwide. In wilderness situations all gonorrhea should be assumed to be penicillin-resistant and treated with a single injection of ceftriaxone.

The treatment for susceptible strains is penicillin. Procaine penicillin G, 4.8 million units (3.0 gm), should be injected intramuscularly. Ideally, 1.0 gm of probenecid should be taken orally at the same time. Ampicillin, 3.5 gm orally, can be substituted for the penicillin. Subsequently, tetracycline should be given orally for seven days. For individuals allergic to penicillin, tetracycline for at least seven days can be substituted. A physician should be consulted after the wilderness outing to ensure no residual infection persists.

Genital Herpes

In spite of the attention it has attracted, genital herpes infection is little different from herpes occurring on the lips and known as "fever blisters." Although the genital infection is transmitted by sexual contact, it has the same tendency to recur in the same location that oral herpes does. Because the tissues are somewhat more sensitive, infections on the genitalia may be more uncomfortable than those around the mouth. No curative treatment has yet been developed; acyclovir (Zovirax®) does shorten the symptomatic period and the duration of virus shedding.

Other Considerations

Anyone with a suspected or known sexually transmitted infection should consult a physician for treatment. An untreated infection can be disastrous. The ease with which syphilis and gonorrhea can be treated has created a lack of concern for all such infections. To encourage individuals to obtain the therapy they need, many states have laws that permit physicians to treat minors without reporting the infection to parents or guardians.

CHAPTER NINETEEN

INFECTIONS

Infections occur whenever microorganisms invade body tissues and multiply or develop within them. Humans normally have many living organisms in such sites as the skin, throat, and intestines. Most of these organisms are harmless and rarely cause disease. However, when the body's defenses against infection are deficient, when organisms that are not harmless are present, or when an injury allows organisms to enter tissues in which they are not normally present, infection may result.

Many infections, such as influenza or traveler's diarrhea, are transmitted from one person to another, directly or indirectly, and are labeled "contagious." Others, such as urinary tract infections or appendicitis, though infectious, are not contagious. Many of the infections of concern to wilderness enthusiasts are transmitted by vectors such as mosquitoes (malaria and yellow fever) and ticks (Rocky Mountain spotted fever and Lyme disease). Few infections likely to occur in the wilderness are so contagious that isolation precautions need to be taken.

A boil or abscess in the skin typifies the pain, swelling, redness, and heat produced by the inflammation accompanying localized infections. If infections remain localized to a small area such as the superficial layers of the skin, fever and other systemic symptoms are usually absent. If a localized infection extends deeply, it may disseminate throughout the body if the organisms gain access to the bloodstream. Such infections typically produce chills, fever, and malaise and may be accompanied by headache, nausea, vomiting, or back pain.

When fever is accompanied by localized signs of disease, identification of its cause is not difficult. For example, burning pain on urination, frequent passage of small amounts of urine, and discomfort over the bladder or kidneys indicate that a urinary infection is probably the cause of any associated chills and fever. Similarly, if pleuritic chest pain is accompanied by a cough productive of thick, yellow sputum, the diagnosis is pneumonia. The infections discussed in this chapter are those that involve the skin and selected other generalized infections. Infections of specific organs are discussed in the chapters dealing with those organs or systems.

ANTIBIOTICS

Although a large number of antibiotics have been developed for the treatment of infectious diseases, organisms vary greatly in their sensitivity to individual drugs. An antibiotic that is effective against the specific causative organism must be used for each infection. Boils and similar skin infections, for example, are commonly caused by staphylococci that may be sensitive to the penicillin group of antibiotics. Typhoid fever and bacillary dysentery are caused by bacteria that may not be sensitive to penicillin but are susceptible to sulfa drugs and ciprofloxacin. Identifying the organism causing an infection so that the most appropriate antibiotic can be administered is highly desirable, but is not possible in the wilderness or even in remote towns and villages.

In order to eradicate an infection, antibiotics must be given in quantities large enough to produce blood and tissue concentrations that kill or inhibit the growth of the causative organisms. Dosage recommendations must be carefully followed. If nausea or vomiting prevent oral administration, or the antibiotic is not effective when given by that route, it must be administered by intramuscular injection. Intravenous administration outside a hospital can be hazardous but may be necessary when high blood concentrations of antibiotics are required, as in meningitis.

Once therapy with an antibiotic has been started, it should be continued until all organisms have been killed and until all signs and symptoms of the infection have been absent for several days. Treatment usually lasts from five to twenty days, depending on the infection. Shorter courses of therapy may result in relapse.

Antibiotics should not be given prophylactically to prevent infections except under special circumstances. For example, most individuals with colds or minor wounds should not be given penicillin to prevent pneumonia or a wound infection. Available evidence indicates that administration of antibiotics in this manner not only does not prevent subsequent infection, it may allow resistant organisms to multiply and produce an infection that is difficult to treat.

The most frequently used antibiotics are the penicillins. Penicillin V (Pen Vee K®) and others) is well absorbed from the intestines and is the usual form given orally. If intramuscular injection of penicillin is necessary, procaine penicillin G is used. The intravenous preparation of penicillin G is aqueous or crystalline penicillin G. Cloxacillin is given for staphylococcal infections. Ampicillin is usually effective against organisms that produce urinary tract infections. Trimethoprim-sulfamethoxazole (TMP-SMX, Bactrim®, Septra®), a combination of two agents, one of which is a sulfonamide, is useful for treating a wide variety of infections, particularly typhoid fever and bacillary dysentery. Ciprofloxacin is one of a newer class of antibiotics, the quinolones, which have a special application in bacillary dysentery, urinary tract infections, and traveler's diarrhea. Because it affects growing bones, ciprofloxacin should not be given to children.

Some individuals are allergic to the penicillins and may have severe, even fatal, reactions to either oral or intramuscular penicillin. (See Anaphylactic Shock in Chapter Twenty, "Allergies.") Before anyone receives any of the penicillins, he must be carefully questioned about previous allergic reactions. If he has a history suggestive of penicillin allergy, another totally different antibiotic effective against the infecting organism should be substituted. Allergies to other antibiotics and to sulfa drugs also occur.

BACTERIAL INFECTIONS

Infections of the respiratory tract and skin are the most common bacterial infections. Most of these disorders are relatively innocuous if treated properly. If mistreated, the result can be disastrous, widespread infection.

Abscesses

Abscesses, boils, carbuncles, and pimples are localized skin infections that differ only in size. They frequently occur at sites of injury and around hair follicles, particularly in the armpits and groins. They are almost always caused by staphylococci, which frequently are resistant to penicillin. Staphylococci release enzymes that cause clotting and obstruction of the blood vessels and lymphatics surrounding the site of the infection. The vascular obstruction blocks the spread of the bacteria and the infections usually remain localized, but the vascular obstruction also shuts out white blood cells, antibiotics, antibodies, and other protective substances. Other enzymes released by these bacteria destroy the tissues in the area of infection, producing a cavity that is filled with the mixture of bacteria, white blood cells, and liquefied tissue commonly known as "pus."

The treatment for such disorders consists primarily of drainage and is similar to the treatment for infected wounds. Pimples and small abscesses do not need to be surgically opened. They should be covered until they rupture spontaneously. Squeezing pimples forces the bacteria into the surrounding tissues and tends to spread the infection. A particularly dangerous area for such infections is the face around the nose and below the eyes. Squeezing a pimple in this region may force bacteria into veins and lymphatics of the head, which carry them directly to the brain.

Larger abscesses may have to be incised in order to drain. After the surrounding and overlying skin has been cleaned with a preparation such as povidone-iodine (Betadine®), alcohol, or clean water and soap, a small incision is made with a sterile scalpel or razor blade. A local anesthetic may be necessary. When the abscess has drained, it should be gently probed with sterile forceps to make certain no pockets of infection remain. Then the skin should be cleansed again and a small piece of sterile gauze inserted into the opening so it can not seal off. Finally, the entire area should be covered with sterile dressings.

Antibiotics are unnecessary for a small, uncomplicated abscess. If the abscess is larger than one inch (2.5 cm) in diameter, or if fever, chills, or other symptoms are present, cloxacillin, a cephalosporin such as cephradine (Anspor®, Velosef®), or TMP-SMX should be given every six hours until all evidence of infection has been absent for two days. If prompt improvement does not take place, the subject must be evacuated immediately.

Similar antibiotic therapy should be instituted, even without signs of blood stream or secondary infection, if the subject has multiple abscesses or if the person is a diabetic, since such persons are more susceptible to severe infections.

Cellulitis

Cellulitis is a bacterial infection of the skin and underlying tissues that is produced by organisms that do not cause obstruction of blood vessels. Such infections do not tend to remain localized and the bacteria can spread to other areas more easily. The site of the infection is usually red, swollen, hot, and tender and is usually not sharply demarcated. Fever is usually present.

Since the blood vessels remain open, these infections can be successfully treated without drainage. Cloxacillin, a cephalosporin, or cotrimoxazole should be administered every six hours until all signs of infection have been absent for two days. The individual should rest quietly until the infection has cleared. Due to its propensity to spread, cellulitis is a more dangerous infection than an abscess and its potential for complications must be respected.

Bacteremia

Bacteremia is defined as the presence of bacteria in the blood stream. The organisms may multiply in the blood and produce infections throughout the body. Bacteremia is usually preceded by a localized infection such as an infected wound, a urinary tract infection, or an abscess.

Bacterial blood stream invasion produces chills, high fever, sweating, and prostration. Specific signs may indicate spread of the infection to other parts of the body. Severe headache, a stiff neck, and nausea and vomiting typify involvement of the brain or its covering (meningitis). Cough, shortness of breath, and pain with breathing suggest pneumonia.

Prompt administration of antibiotics may be life-saving. Five hundred milligrams of cefazolin (Kefzol®) administered intramuscularly every eight hours and gentamicin (1.0 mg/kg body weight) intramuscularly every eight hours is a generally effective regimen, but only if no meningitis is present. If only aqueous penicillin G is available, 20 million units a day should be given intravenously. Individuals who do not respond to treatment within three to four days should be evacuated, since complications may occur in spite of antibiotic therapy.

A person with bacteremia should be provided with rest, warmth, a soft or liquid diet, and adequate fluids. Medications for pain and sleep are often helpful; aspirin or acetaminophen may be given to reduce fever. A temperature record must be kept and should include the times any drugs are administered.

Rocky Mountain Spotted Fever

Rocky Mountain spotted fever is caused by a bacterium, *Rickettsia rickettsii,* transmitted to humans by the bite of a wood or dog tick. Three to fourteen days after the bite, mild chilliness, loss of appetite, and a general run-down feeling usually appear. These mild symptoms are followed by chills, fever, headache, pain in the bones and muscles, sensitivity of the eyes to light, and confusion. Between two and six days after the onset of symptoms, a red rash appears on the wrists and ankles and spreads over the entire body. The rash may be present on the palms of the hands and the soles of the feet and consists of small, red spots. These spots are actually hemorrhages into the skin; in severe cases large, blotchy, red areas may appear all over the body. The fever lasts about two weeks. The person appears seriously ill without an obvious cause. Untreated infections have a mortality rate of twenty to thirty percent; treatment reduces the rate to three to ten percent.

Diagnosis is aided by a history of a tick bite in an endemic area. The most important endemic area is the middle Atlantic coastal states; fewer cases are seen west of the Mississippi, but the disease can occur in any of the forty-eight contiguous states (fig. 19-1).

Figure 19-1. Rocky Mountain spotted fever cases in the U.S., 1989–1990.

Tetracycline or chloramphenicol should be given every six hours until the temperature has been normal for two to three days. General measures such as bed rest, fluid replacement, aspirin every four hours if needed for high fever, and a medication for sleep are also important.

Rocky Mountain spotted fever can be prevented by careful daily inspection for ticks when in an endemic area. The ticks should be touched with a gasoline- or kerosene-soaked cotton pledget to make them detach and carefully extracted with tweezers so they are not crushed. The wound should be cleansed carefully. Individuals moving about in brush in an endemic area should keep their shirt sleeves rolled down with the cuffs buttoned. Shirt collars should be buttoned, heads should be covered, and long trousers should be closed by gaiters or tucked into boot tops. No reliable vaccine is available.

Relapsing Fever (Tick Fever)

Tick fever occurs in western and west-central states. (A recent small epidemic occurred on the south rim of the Grand Canyon.) Relapsing fever is a blood stream infection by a spiral bacterium transmitted to humans by a tick bite or, in some areas, by a louse. The ticks live on rodents and small animals such as chipmunks, squirrels, and rabbits. About two to fifteen days after the bite, chills, fever, headache, muscle aches and pains, joint pains, a cough, and often nausea and vomiting appear. A red rash may appear on the body and limbs. Bleeding from the nose, lungs, or gastrointestinal tract may occur but usually is not severe. The initial attack lasts two to eight days and may be followed by a remission lasting three to ten days. During remission, fever is absent and the individual may feel well. A relapse, during which the fever and all previous symptoms return, usually occurs seven to ten days later in untreated individuals. Hospitalization for identification of the organism in the blood is desirable. Tetracycline or chloramphenicol should be given every six hours for five to ten days.

Plague

Plague is a serious infection caused by *Pasteurella pestis,* an organism transmitted to humans by contact with rodents or rabbits or by flea bites. The organism is not widespread and is found chiefly in the western United States and rural areas of South America, Africa, and Asia, particularly Vietnam. After multiplying in the skin following a bite, the organisms spread to the regional lymph nodes and produce large swellings called buboes, which are responsible for the name "bubonic plague." Fortunately, involvement of the lungs is rare; when it does occur, the infection is termed "pneumonic" rather than "bubonic" and becomes transmissible by droplets in the air. The illness is characterized by high fever, chills, prostration, and shock. It may be rapidly fatal, particularly in the pneumonic form. Treatment with streptomycin and tetracycline should be administered by a physician whenever the infection is even suspected.

Tularemia

Tularemia is another infection transmitted to humans from wild rodents such as rabbits and muskrats. A red lump develops at the site of inoculation, then enlarges and ulcerates, draining pus.

Fever, chills, headache, and nausea begin suddenly when the organisms spread to the blood stream. Streptomycin and tetracycline should be given by a physician.

Lyme Disease

Lyme disease is a recently described combination of signs and symptoms related to infection by *Borrelia burgdorferi,* an organism transmitted to humans from deer and mice by the tick *Ixodes.* Lyme disease has been found throughout the United States and in parts of Europe (fig. 19-2). Because the tick is so small, the bite frequently goes unnoticed. The first and most characteristic symptom is a flat, red, expanding skin rash that can become quite large, and sometimes clears

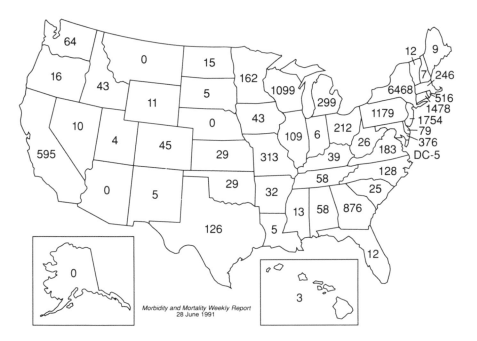

Figure 19-2. Lyme disease cases in the U.S., 1989–1990.

in its central area as it expands. Fever, malaise, and muscle aches resembling the flu may accompany the rash, which spontaneously fades in two to four weeks. In this stage, treatment with doxycycline, amoxicillin, or erythromycin is effective. Days to months after the original illness, headaches, fatigue, a stiff neck, and pain and swelling in joints and muscles occur. Even later, in the third stage, serious nervous system, joint, and skin complications may occur. The diagnosis of Lyme disease in the second or third stages is based on blood tests for antibodies to the organism. Treatment, particularly in the later stages when different drugs are used for longer times, is best undertaken by a physician.

VIRAL INFECTIONS

Influenza

Influenza, a viral infection caused by influenza viruses A or B, is an acute, self-limited disease of five to six days' duration. Although the infection is limited to the respiratory tract, symptoms may suggest a generalized disease. Influenza is spread by sneezing, coughing, or close contact with an infected person. Epidemics are common, particularly in winter months. The incubation period is one or two days. The onset is heralded by chilliness, fever, weakness, lassitude, headache, loss of appetite, and characteristic aching muscle pains. A dry, hacking cough is prominent and may be severe. Other respiratory tract symptoms are sometimes present but are usually not prominent. Fever usually lasts two to three days and occasionally reaches 104°F (40°C).

The signs and symptoms of upper respiratory tract involvement usually differentiate influenza from other systemic infections; the fever, muscle aches, and cough distinguish it from a common cold. A history of contact with other persons with influenza is helpful in making a diagnosis. Gastrointestinal symptoms are usually absent, but diarrhea may occur.

No specific treatment is available. Symptoms are partially relieved by rest, warmth, a light diet with abundant liquids, and medications such as aspirin every four hours to relieve discomfort. Medication to promote sleep may be helpful.

Antibiotics have no value for the routine treatment of influenza. However, if fever that returns after several days and a cough productive of purulent sputum indicate that pneumococcal or secondary staphylococcal pneumonia has developed, it should be treated with nafcillin every six hours by intramuscular injection until all signs of infection have been gone for two to three days.

Infectious Mononucleosis

Infectious mononucleosis is a common viral infection of young adults that appears to be spread through close personal contact. It is rarely severe, although sometimes it is incapacitating, and fatal complications may occur.

The most common symptom of infectious mononucleosis is a persistent, severe sore throat. Other complaints are not specific: fever, a feeling of tiredness, loss of energy, and easy fatigability. Lymph nodes in various portions of the body are usually enlarged, especially those in the sides and back of the neck.

The triad of sore throat, lymph node enlargement, and fever is characteristic, but this infection is notorious for its great variability. A skin rash, headache, weakness, loss of appetite, and generalized aching may also be present. Jaundice sometimes occurs (six percent of patients) and indicates the liver is involved.

No specific treatment is available; antibiotics are of no benefit. Rest is important, and the individual's activity should be limited while any symptoms of disease persist. Since minor abdominal trauma could easily rupture the spleen, which is enlarged and unusually fragile, climbing with a waist loop and other activities in which such injury is likely should be avoided. Recovery in most cases takes two to four weeks. If jaundice is present the individual should be evacuated.

Colorado Tick Fever

Colorado tick fever is a viral disease transmitted by the wood tick. It occurs in all western states and is far more common than Rocky Mountain spotted fever. Infections usually occur in spring and early summer, when ticks are active. Four to six days after exposure, chills and fever appear, along with headache and generalized aching. The eyes may be unusually sensitive to light. The initial attack lasts about two days, at which time the fever and other symptoms disappear, only to recur two to five days later. The outlook for complete recovery is good, even though no specific treatment is available. Bed rest, fluids, and aspirin are helpful. A physician should evaluate the individual to be sure that Rocky Mountain spotted fever, a more serious disorder that requires antibiotic treatment, is not present.

Yellow Fever

Yellow fever is an infection of humans and monkeys caused by a virus transmitted by the *Aedes aegypti* mosquito. It is chiefly found in South America and in Africa below the Sahara. Following an incubation period of three to six days, the illness begins with chills, fever, headache, and backache. The heart rate may be slow in relation to the severity of the fever. After three days the fever often falls temporarily, at which time the individual is flushed, nauseated, often vomiting, and may appear seriously ill. The eyes may be bloodshot and the tongue appears red. Bleeding from the gums and under the skin may occur; vomiting "coffee ground" material or black stools indicates bleeding is occurring in the stomach or intestines. Slight jaundice may be present. Mild cases may resemble influenza or malaria, but jaundice does not occur with influenza and only rarely with malaria. When present, it is an important sign of yellow fever and is responsible for this infection's name.

The treatment for yellow fever consists of bed rest and a liquid or soft diet high in carbohydrates. Fluid and salt replacement may be necessary for vomiting, diarrhea, or high fever. Aspirin every four hours for discomfort and bedtime medications for sleep are helpful. No specific treatment is available. If travel into a yellow fever area is planned, vaccination should be obtained. (See Chapter Five, "Immunizations, Sanitation, and Water Disinfection.")

PARASITIC INFESTATIONS

Malaria

Malaria is caused by protozoa of the genus *Plasmodium* and is transmitted by the bite of infected mosquitoes. When considered on a worldwide basis, malaria is one of the most common diseases. More than a million people die of malaria every year!

Malarial parasites are ingested along with the blood of an infected person or animal at the time that a female *Anopheles* mosquito bites. The parasites undergo fertilization and reproduce in the mosquito's gut and are transmitted to humans when the mosquito injects saliva into the skin during a subsequent bite. In the human, parasites invade red blood cells, multiply, and release daughter parasites, destroying the red blood cells in the process. The daughter parasites invade other red blood cells and the process is repeated. The periodic release of parasites produces recurrent episodes of fever; the destruction of red blood cells can eventually result in anemia.

The initial symptoms of malaria are muscular soreness and a low fever, which appear about six to ten days after a bite by an infected mosquito. Four to eight days later, the typical chills and fever appear. The chills are characterized by shivering, chattering teeth, blue and cold skin, and a feeling of chilliness that is not relieved by heating pads or blankets. An hour later the febrile stage begins with a flushed face, a feeling of intense heat, headache, often delirium, and temperature as high as 107°F (41.5°C). This stage lasts about two hours and is followed by drenching sweats and a fall in temperature. Headache, backache, and muscular aches may be very severe.

The repeated occurrence of febrile episodes at regular intervals, such as every day, every other day, or every three days—occasionally at irregular intervals—is characteristic of malaria. In severe cases vomiting, diarrhea, severe anemia, dark urine containing elements of destroyed red blood cells, shock, and coma may occur. Enlargement of the liver or spleen may be present.

Treatment consists of general supportive measures and specific drug therapy. Rest in bed and maintenance of body warmth during the chill is highly desirable. Since water losses by sweating may be severe, a large fluid intake should be encouraged. Fluids and salt lost by vomiting or diarrhea also must be replaced. A careful record of temperature and pulse should be kept. If possible, blood smears should be made during the chill for later identification of the parasites. During an acute episode of malaria, the subsequent period of therapy, and for two weeks following recovery, strenuous exercise should be avoided to prevent rupture of the spleen.

Specific treatment for malaria should be given by a physician. The most effective general regimen consists of chloroquine and primaquine. One gram of chloroquine phosphate should be given initially and should be followed by one-half gram in six hours and one-half gram on the second and third days. Fifteen milligrams of primaquine should be given every day for fourteen days.

Plasmodium falciparum malaria is the most dangerous form of malaria for two reasons: it produces the most severe infestations, and strains resistant to chloroquine have been found in most areas of the world, particularly South America, southeast Asia, and Africa. Expeditions into such areas should carry mefloquine, quinine, pyrimethamine, tetracycline, clindamycin, and sulfonamides to treat chloroquine-resistant falciparum malaria. Instruction by a physician should be obtained before using these drugs.

Before leaving for a region in which malaria is present, a travelers' clinic or the Centers for Disease Control (CDC) should be consulted to determine whether chloroquine-resistant falciparum malaria has been found in that area. Chloroquine prophylaxis effectively prevents malaria caused by strains that are not resistant. One-half gram of chloroquine phosphate should be taken on the same day of each week, beginning two weeks before entering an endemic area and continuing for five weeks after leaving. Any illness occurring within five weeks after leaving a malarial area should be reported to a physician. However, it may be easier to avoid malarial areas than to take chloroquine for five weeks, as this drug does occasionally cause itching and gastrointestinal complaints.

If travel is anticipated into areas where chloroquine-resistant malaria is present, mefloquine should be taken as a single 250-mg tablet once weekly beginning one week before travel and continuing for four weeks after return.

In cities and towns frequently visited by tourists, malaria is uncommon, and malaria-carrying mosquitoes are rarely found at elevations above 3,000 feet (900 m). In malarial areas, contact with mosquitoes should be minimized with screens or mosquito netting, protective clothing, and insect repellents. The best available repellent is N,N-diethyl-*m*-toluamide (DEET). It remains effective for up to eighteen hours, a considerable advantage over the odor repellents, which are effective for only two to four hours.

Babesiosis

Babesiosis is a malarialike parasitic disease occurring primarily along the northeast coast of the United States and in Mexico, Yugoslavia, and Ireland. The organism is transmitted from mice and voles to humans by *Ixodes* tick bites. The illness is characterized by fever, chills, sweats, headache, and muscle aches. Because red blood cells are destroyed by the parasite, anemia may result. The disease is usually self-limited, and most individuals recover uneventfully. In a few individuals, particularly those whose spleen has been removed, the disease is severe, rarely even fatal. Although there is no treatment of proven benefit, quinine and clindamycin have been used successfully in a few individuals.

Schistosomiasis (Bilharziasis)

Schistosomiasis is a parasitic infection caused by three different species of the genus *Schistosoma*. Schistosomiasis affects more than 200 million people worldwide, but most infested people have no symptoms or clinical evidence of disease. Depending upon the particular species, infestation can cause complications in the liver, bowel, or urinary tract. The life cycles of all species are similar. After the eggs leave the human host in stool or urine, they hatch into tiny miracidia that penetrate any of several species of freshwater snails. (The absence of an appropriate snail host in the waters of the United States probably accounts for the absence of disease in this country.) Within the snail the miracidia mature into free-living cercariae. When released from the snail into water, the cercariae are able to infest humans by penetrating through intact skin, a step that requires about thirty minutes. After two days the organisms spread through the blood stream to the lungs and liver. A month later the worms mature and migrate through veins to their final dwelling place in the intestines or urinary bladder. Adult worms live five to ten years.

The clinical manifestations of schistosomiasis occur in stages and are produced by the effects of the organism. Skin penetration by the cercariae usually is not associated with any reaction, but repeated exposure may lead to a red rash that is called swimmer's itch or schistosome dermatitis in the countries where such infestations occur.

Sometimes, with particularly heavy infestations, fever, chills, headache, and a cough occur when adult worms form and eggs are first produced. Such episodes are known as Katayama fever, or acute schistosomiasis. The liver, spleen, and lymph nodes are enlarged, and eosinophilia is present.

The chronic effects of infestation are produced when the body responds to the eggs. *S. mansoni* and *japonicum* adults live in the intestines and release their eggs into blood that goes to the liver. Scarring occurs around the eggs, producing obstruction to liver blood flow. First the liver and then the spleen become enlarged. In late stages, catastrophic gastrointestinal bleeding and liver failure may occur.

Different complications are associated with infestation by *S. haematobium* because the adults live in the veins around the urinary bladder instead of in the intestines. Scarring from the eggs of these organisms produces obstruction of the bladder and ureters. Blood in the urine and painful urination are the usual symptoms. Eventually, the chronic irritation associated with the infestation can lead to malignant changes. Squamous cell carcinoma of the urinary bladder is uncommon in most of the world but is one of the most common malignancies in areas in which schistosomiasis is endemic.

The three main *Schistosoma* species are found in freshwater lakes and rivers worldwide. Infections caused by *S. mansoni* are found throughout tropical and subtropical Africa, Arabia, South America (Brazil, Venezuela, and Surinam) and the Caribbean. *S. japonicum* occurs in Southeast Asia and the Philippines. *S. haematobium* occurs in Africa and the Middle East.

The diagnosis of schistosomiasis is made by finding the characteristic eggs in the stool or urine of individuals with any of the clinical manifestations of infection, such as dermatitis, Katayama fever, or liver disease. A serologic test is available through the CDC.

Safe and effective oral drugs have recently been introduced for the treatment of schistosomiasis. The most broadly effective is priziquantel (Biltricide®), which is given as a single dose of 40 mg/kg body weight for *S. mansoni* or *S. haematobium* and as 20 mg/kg body weight three times in one day for *S. japonicum*. Treatment should be undertaken only by a physician.

Avoiding infestation is far more desirable. The drugs kill the organisms but do not eliminate them from the body, and the dead organisms cause inflammatory reactions similar to—although considerably less severe than—those produced by the living eggs. Infestation can be avoided only by staying completely out of stagnant water (lakes or ponds) or slowly moving water (slowly flowing streams or rivers) in areas where the parasites are found. That means no swimming, no bathing, and not even wading. No other effective preventive measure exists. The snails that form an essential part of the schistosome life cycle do not live in rapidly moving water, so the schistosomes are not found there. However, the water does not have to be completely still; significant infestations have occurred among rafters on slowly moving streams that did not occur on the same rivers during flood season, when the water was flowing much faster.

Onchocerciasis

Onchocerciasis, or river blindness, is one of the most common causes of blindness in developing countries. It is caused by a filarial parasite transmitted to humans by the bite of black flies found near rivers in the higher elevations of tropical Africa, Central America, and South America. Adult worms live in hard, painless nodules under the skin and release microfilaria that cause intense itching in the skin and irritation of the eye. The diagnosis is made by examining skin biopsies or examining the eye for the organism. Effective treatment is now available with ivermectin.

Chagas' Disease

Chagas' disease, or American trypanosomiasis, is found from southern South America to northern Mexico. The causative organism, *Trypanosoma cruzi,* is transmitted from infected animals to humans by the bite of several kinds of reduviid bugs that inhabit the walls and ceilings of poorly constructed houses. After a bite, usually at night, redness and swelling occur locally and are followed by fever, headache, generalized lymph node swelling, and enlargement of the liver and spleen. Ten to thirty years later, signs of irreversible damage to the heart, esophagus, or colon appear. No clearly effective form of treatment in the late stages of the disease is available; nifurtimox may be useful early.

Trichinosis

Trichinosis is a parasitic disease caused by eating improperly cooked pork containing larvae of the roundworm *Trichinella spiralis.* After the larvae are ingested they attach themselves to the wall of the small bowel, mature, and produce eggs. When the eggs hatch, larvae are released; they spread throughout the body via the circulation and localize in muscles.

If infestation is heavy, penetration of the intestinal wall by the larvae one to four days after ingestion produces nausea, vomiting, abdominal cramps, and diarrhea that resemble food poisoning. The migration of the larvae to the muscles seven days after ingestion produces fever, chills, muscular weakness, a skin rash, and swelling of the face and tissues around the eyes. Headache may be severe.

The diagnosis is based upon the onset of characteristic symptoms following the ingestion of uncooked or improperly cooked pork or improperly prepared pork products such as salami. A skin test is also available. No specific treatment for trichinosis has been of proven value except for thiabendazole, which should be given by a physician. Symptomatic treatment consists of rest, aspirin and codeine, and sedatives to promote restful sleep. Prednisone may be beneficial in the early stages of the disease. Prevention is essential: all pork must be thoroughly cooked. In addition, freezing at 0°F (−18°C) for twenty-four hours or 5°F (−15°C) for twenty days usually kills all trichinae.

Acquired Immune Deficiency Syndrome (AIDS)

Acquired immune deficiency syndrome is not a single disease but a susceptibility to unusual infections and malignant tumors caused by a defect in the immune system. The disease results from infection with the human immunodeficiency virus (HIV), which destroys normal lymphocytes. The period of time between infection by HIV and the development of AIDS can be many years. During this latent phase the infected person has no symptoms but is capable of transmitting the infection. There are only two ways HIV can be transmitted: by sexual contact and by blood. Men transmit the virus to female partners and vice versa. Men transmit it to other men. Infected mothers transmit the infection to their babies through the blood stream. Transfusions of blood or blood products, injections with needles or syringes contaminated with blood, and splashing contaminated blood into open wounds are other ways blood can transmit the virus. Kissing, sharing utensils, using the same toilets, drinking from the same containers, touching, and other nonintimate contacts do not transmit the virus and are safe. No reason exists for excluding persons who are infected with HIV but do not have AIDS from wilderness outings. Before traveling to a foreign country, however, such individuals should determine whether a negative test for HIV is required for entry or to obtain a visa.

Blood transfusions are extremely risky in any country that does not effectively screen blood for HIV. A travelers' clinic or the CDC can supply up-to-date information. Similarly, injections from used syringes or needles are dangerous. The safest ways to avoid sexual transmission of infection are abstinence or monogamous sexual relations with a person known to be uninfected. Condoms reduce infections but do not eliminate all risk (fig. 19-3).

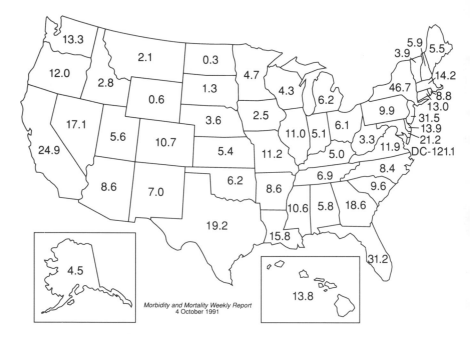

Figure 19-3. Acquired immune deficiency syndrome (AIDS) cases per 100,000 population in the U.S., 1990.

CHAPTER TWENTY

ALLERGIES

When foreign substances enter the body, the immune system responds by forming "antibodies," which combine with the foreign materials to facilitate their elimination. When the foreign substances (antigens) are bacteria or viruses, antibodies play a large role in preventing or eradicating infection. Other foreign antigens also elicit an antibody response.

Once a person has contacted an antigen, antibodies persist in his blood for years or even his lifetime. These persistent antibodies provide permanent immunity following infections such as measles or mumps. Vaccines are composed of dead or weakened organisms that elicit an antibody response without producing a full-blown infection, resulting in immunity. However, many vaccines do not elicit an antibody response as effective as that following an actual infection and must be repeated every few years.

Antibodies are proteins known as immunoglobulins. Various types of immunoglobulins are classified as G, M, A, E, and D and are usually abbreviated IgG, IgM, and so on. Occasionally a person reacts to an antigen by forming an excessive amount of antibody, particularly IgE, the principal antibody responsible for allergic reactions. Contact with that antigen—or allergen, as antigens that produce allergic reactions are called—results in a strong IgE response that releases histamine and related substances to produce the allergic reaction.

The periodic injection of gradually increasing amounts of an allergen can sometimes overwhelm the antibody response. This process, known as desensitization, eliminates or greatly reduces the allergic reaction. If desensitization is stopped, the original allergic condition usually returns. Nonetheless, desensitization can be useful in helping to control allergic reactions such as hypersensitivity to insect stings.

The substances to which an individual may become allergic are unlimited. Foods, pollens, animal dander, and dust are the most frequent offenders. Reactions to therapeutic agents are also common. Insect stings and penicillin are notorious for causing anaphylactic reactions, an uncommon type of allergic reaction that is explosive in onset and often lethal if not effectively treated.

HAY FEVER

Hay fever, or acute nasal allergy, is usually caused by pollens, dust, or other allergens in the air. Hay fever is rare in an ice and snow world but is a common problem—occasionally a severe problem—at lower altitudes. The nasal membranes are red and swollen, causing nasal stuffiness and nasal discharge. Frequent sneezing is common. The eyes are often red; excessive tearing is common.

An individual with recurrent hay fever so severe that it hinders his routine activities should consider desensitization. He should work out with his physician or allergist the medications that are most effective for him personally. Effective treatment for hay fever usually combines an antihistamine with a decongestant. However, some drugs and drug combinations are more effective for certain individuals than others. The combination of triprolidine—an antihistamine—with pseudoephedrine—a decongestant—(Actifed®, Histafed®, and others) is widely used to help control nasal allergies and the stuffiness of colds. This preparation has recently become available without a physician's prescription. A four percent solution of cromalyn sodium sprayed into the nose has been found effective for preventing the nasal symptoms of hay fever but has little effect on eye symptoms.

HIVES

Hives are often caused by food allergies—chocolate, seafood, and fresh fruit are the most common offenders—but can occur as an allergic reaction to almost any substance, including dusts and pollen, insect bites and stings, or drugs, occasionally even to drugs as commonly used as aspirin. Hives appear quickly following contact with the allergen, are often widely scattered, and consist of red or white raised wheals (bumps) that itch intensely. Hives may rapidly appear and disappear several times from a single allergen exposure. Repeated exposures to the same allergen usually reproduce the attacks indefinitely. However, the condition is more miserable than serious.

The treatment for recurrent episodes of hives consists of antihistamines. Those used for motion sickness are usually effective. Cornstarch packs or baths, or bland lotions, may help reduce itching. Spontaneous recovery occurs without treatment if further exposure to the allergen is avoided.

CONTACT DERMATITIS

A rash, typically composed of multiple small blisters on a red background, occasionally develops after contact with jewelry, the case of a wrist watch, or a similar material. Often the cause can not be determined, and the rash may not be located at the point of contact. The rash is usually more annoying than disabling, but may itch or burn. Severe cases should be treated in the same manner as poison ivy dermatitis.

Poison Ivy, Oak, and Sumac

Poison ivy, poison oak, and poison sumac produce an acute contact dermatitis due to the urushiols that are components of the sap of these three plants. Poison ivy and poison oak are closely related plants found throughout the United States that grow as shrubs or vines. Their leaves grow in clusters of three, a distinctive pattern that allows them to be easily recognized. Poison ivy leaves tend to have smooth edges, and poison oak leaves tend to be more lobulated or serrated; but the patterns overlap, and distinguishing between the two is not important. Poison sumac does not have this identifying feature, but this plant grows only in marshy areas east of the Mississippi and is encountered much less frequently (fig. 20-1).

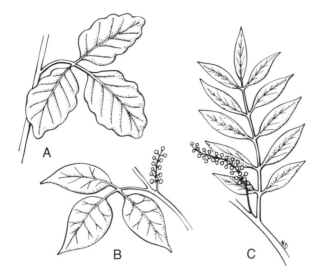

Figure 20-1. Typical appearance of the leaves of poison oak (A), poison ivy (B), and poison sumac (C).

The rash typically develops at the point of contact but may appear at sites that are far removed. The rash usually appears on the hands and face a few days after contact, but as long as a week may pass before it appears at other locations. The rash usually disappears in the same order it appeared after four to seven days.

Red streaks or patches that itch appear first and are followed in twelve to twenty-four hours by blisters that typically are arranged in lines. Later the blisters may break, resulting in oozing and crusting of the surface. Swelling of the underlying tissues, burning, and itching are usually present. Scratching should be avoided because it can introduce infection or cause scarring, but scratching does not spread the rash. The blisters are filled with serum, not the urushiol that causes the dermatitis.

Treatment depends upon the extent of the rash. If the area is small, no therapy at all may be needed. Calamine lotion may relieve itching. For more extensive eruptions, itching may be relieved by cool, salt-water compresses (two teaspoons [8 cc or 8 gm] of salt per quart of water) applied for ten minutes four times a day. A steroid ointment such as 0.25 percent hydrocortisone (now available over the counter) can be applied in limited amounts after the compresses.

Individuals with extensive, disabling poison ivy dermatitis require systemic steroid therapy. In urban surroundings such individuals have been defined as those sick enough to seek a physician's care. The physician should prescribe the medication.

Desensitization for poison ivy has been tried, but the side effects are as bad as the rash. No desensitizing agent has been approved by the Food and Drug Administration (FDA). Many over-the-counter preparations for poison ivy contain antihistamines, analgesics, or even antibiotics, which can produce a secondary allergic reaction that may be worse than the original problem.

ANAPHYLACTIC SHOCK

Anaphylactic shock is an acute, massive, allergic reaction that involves essentially the entire body. Fortunately, such reactions are uncommon, for death can occur within five to ten minutes if treatment is not administered immediately. (Deaths due to anaphylactic reactions undoubtedly still go unrecognized, are attributed to heart attacks or some similar disorder, and may be significantly more common than appreciated.)

Insect stings are one of the more common causes of anaphylactic shock. In the United States, deaths due to allergic reactions to insect stings far outnumber those caused by all other venomous animals, including poisonous snakes, spiders, and scorpions. (See Chapter Twenty-four, "Animal Bites and Stings.")

Drugs are another prominent cause of anaphylactic shock. The most common offenders are penicillin and foreign serum such as horse serum. The danger of anaphylactic shock demands that these medications be given to patients who may be allergic to them only if absolutely essential (such as a severely envenomated snake bite victim), and even then only in a hospital where the allergic reaction can be controlled. Anaphylactic reactions are most common after drugs have been injected but have been caused by orally administered medications. Very rarely, anaphylactic reactions have been caused by food to which an individual was allergic.

Diagnosis

The symptoms of anaphylactic shock usually appear five to fifteen minutes after exposure to the allergen. Occasionally an hour may pass before symptoms appear, and very rarely twenty-four hours can elapse, particularly after oral ingestion of the offending substance.

Organ systems involved by the reaction include:

- Respiratory: laryngeal edema; bronchospasm; rhinitis.
- Skin: hives; angioedema.
- Gastrointestinal: nausea; vomiting; cramps; diarrhea.
- Eyes: conjunctivitis.
- Cardiovascular: arrhythmia; shock.

The dominant feature of anaphylactic shock is severe respiratory distress that appears and progresses rapidly. Swelling of the tissues of the upper air passages, particularly the larynx (laryngeal edema), where the airway is already narrowed by the vocal cords, narrows the air passages and can produce lethal respiratory obstruction. Narrowing of the bronchi within the lungs—bronchospasm—produces respiratory difficulty that is similar to asthma but is much more severe. The cause—spasm of the muscles in the walls of small bronchi that results in severe constriction—is also similar. With anaphylaxis, the onset is more abrupt and usually develops within minutes. Sometimes a sense of pressure beneath the sternum is noted.

The skin is the next most common organ involved by anaphylaxis. Hives may be present and are widely distributed. Angioedema, or localized swelling, may occur on an extremity or around the eyes or mouth.

Nausea, vomiting, abdominal pain, and diarrhea may reflect involvement of the gastrointestinal system. Involvement of the eyes and nose causes changes that resemble a sudden, severe attack of hay fever. The eyes are swollen and red (conjunctivitis), and the flow of tears is greatly increased. The nose is plugged by a red, swollen mucosa and mucoid discharge. Rarely, involvement of the cardiovascular system can result in shock or a cardiac arrhythmia, which can be fatal.

Treatment

Anaphylactic shock is a true medical emergency for which minutes may make a difference between therapeutic success and failure. Treatment must be instituted without delay and consists of the injection of 0.3 cc of a 1:1,000 aqueous solution of epinephrine (adrenaline). The route of administration is determined by the subject's condition. If the reaction is caught early, when only moderate respiratory distress is present, the adrenaline should be injected subcutaneously. If the subject is in severe respiratory difficulty, the epinephrine should be injected intramuscularly, where it is absorbed more rapidly.

Epinephrine in 1:1,000 dilution is available in several forms in the United States. EpiPen® is a preloaded syringe that can be injected almost instantaneously with only one hand. After the cover is stripped away, the needle can be jabbed into the thigh or any other convenient location, through clothing if necessary. Although the ability to make an injection with one hand is useful for a few individuals, such as rock climbers, such speed is rarely needed, particularly after the first injection. Although the syringe contains 2.0 cc of solution, only a single 0.3-cc dose can be delivered. Ana-Kit® contains a syringe loaded with 1.0 cc of epinephrine that can deliver two 0.3-cc injections, but not as rapidly as the EpiPen®. Epinephrine is made by several pharmaceutical manufacturers; it is available from Wyeth-Ayerst in Tubex®, a preloaded syringe that contains 1.0 cc of solution, essentially all of which can be used. Specific directions accompany all of these devices, but an allergic individual should develop his own strategy for using one with the physician who writes the prescription for its purchase.

Some inhalers for asthmatics contain epinephrine. Such preparations are not recommended for anaphylactic shock because the response to them is inconsistent. Although they are cheaper than the injectable preparations and undoubtedly better than nothing, they are not totally reliable for the treatment of severe ana-phylactic reactions—the type that most needs reliable therapy.

Injections of epinephrine should be repeated every twelve to fifteen minutes if needed. In fact, subjects must be closely watched because many individuals relapse in fifteen to twenty minutes as the epinephrine wears off.

Respiratory obstruction due to laryngeal edema usually responds to epineph-rine but may require tracheostomy.

Other steps can help an individual with anaphylaxis, but none can substitute for epinephrine. If the allergen has been injected, placing tourniquets above the injection site and injecting epinephrine around the site helps slow absorption. Oxygen should be administered during the period of respiratory difficulty regard-less of the altitude. Other forms of treatment for shock should be instituted; appropriate care should be given if the individual is unconscious. Antihistamines may help control the itching of hives and other symptoms, but should be admin-istered only after anaphylaxis has been controlled.

Prevention of anaphylactic shock by avoiding the allergen or by desensitiza-tion is far safer than treatment. Desensitization for insect sting allergy with purified venoms is effective for many individuals. However, even after desen-sitization, individuals subject to anaphylactic shock from insect stings or similar uncontrollable allergens should always carry epinephrine. Effective desensitiza-tion for allergies to drugs such as penicillin is not practical.

SECTION THREE
ENVIRONMENTAL INJURIES

CHAPTER TWENTY-ONE

MEDICAL PROBLEMS
OF HIGH ALTITUDE

M edical problems associated with high altitude include a number of uncomfortable symptoms and some life-threatening conditions. All are primarily the result of a decreased oxygen concentration in the blood caused by the lower atmospheric pressure at high altitude. This chapter does not deal with the effects of sudden oxygen deprivation, as can occur in aircraft or balloons, but with the effects of more gradual ascents over hours, days, and weeks.

Three general principles apply to all altitude problems. First, individual susceptibility to the effects of high altitude varies enormously, and a schedule of ascent that suits most members of a group may be far too rapid for others. These differences are inherent and have nothing to do with the individual's state of training or with his determination or courage.

Second, the development of serious altitude illness can be avoided by very simple precautions. Individuals who get more than slightly sick have only themselves to blame.

Third, though the effects of altitude may mimic those produced by hypothermia, dehydration, carbon monoxide poisoning, or hypoglycemia, all of which can befall climbers in the arctic environment of high elevations, anyone ill at high altitude should be assumed to have a disorder caused or made worse by the altitude that can be cured or improved by immediate descent. At the very least, this assumption will facilitate later evacuation.

PHYSIOLOGY

Oxygen diffuses from the alveoli (air sacs) of the lung into the blood because the amount of oxygen (pressure or partial pressure) in the alveoli is greater than that in the blood. At high altitudes, the composition of the atmosphere is the same as at sea level, about twenty percent oxygen, but the pressure of oxygen (the number of molecules in a specific volume of air) is reduced proportionately with the atmospheric pressure. At 18,000 feet (5,500 m) the atmospheric pressure and the pressure of oxygen in the air is only half that at sea level, and at the top of Mount Everest (29,092 feet, or 8,828 m) it is a third. Because the atmosphere is flattened at the poles by the centrifugal effect of the earth's rotation, the atmosphere above a climber is thinner (and the atmospheric or barometric pressure is

TABLE 21-1.
Conversions Between Feet and Meters

Feet	Meters	Feet	Meters	Meters	Feet
1	0.30	14,000	4,267.21	1	3.28
10	3.05	15,000	4,572.01	10	32.81
100	30.48	16,000	4,876.81	100	328.08
1,000	304.80	17,000	5,181.61	1,000	3,280.83
2,000	609.60	18,000	5,486.41	2,000	6,561.67
3,000	914.40	19,000	5,791.21	3,000	9,842.50
4,000	1,219.20	20,000	6,096.01	4,000	13,123.33
5,000	1,524.00	21,000	6,400.81	5,000	16,404.17
6,000	1,828.80	22,000	6,705.61	6,000	19,685.00
7,000	2,133.60	23,000	7,010.41	7,000	22,965.83
8,000	2,438.40	24,000	7,315.21	8,000	26,246.67
9,000	2,743.21	25,000	7,620.02	9,000	29,527.50
10,000	3,048.01	26,000	7,924.82		
11,000	3,352.81	27,000	8,229.62		
12,000	3,657.61	28,000	8,534.42		
13,000	3,962.41	29,000	8,839.22		

lower) at 19,000 feet (5,790 m) on Mount McKinley (latitude 63°N) than above a climber at 19,000 feet on Kilimanjaro (latitude 3°S).

The human body operates most efficiently when the pressure of oxygen in arterial blood is 80 to 90 mm Hg, which provides the red blood cells with almost all the oxygen they can carry. (Ninety-five percent of the hemoglobin is saturated with oxygen.) At high altitudes the lower pressure of oxygen in the atmosphere results in a lower oxygen pressure in the blood. Without compensatory changes, at 18,000 feet (5,500 m) the blood oxygen pressure would be only 40 to 45 mm and the hemoglobin saturation only about seventy percent. With ascent, lack of oxygen stimulates an increase in the rate and depth of breathing. A consequence is that more carbon dioxide is lost (see table 21-2) and the blood becomes alkaline for the couple of days required for the kidneys to respond by getting rid of bicarbonate in the urine. The extra ventilation increases the blood oxygen pressure, but not to sea level values, and all the tissues of the body must function at a lower oxygen pressure. Oxygen consumption by the body at high altitude, however, remains essentially the same as at sea level for the same amount of physical work.

TABLE 21-2.
Gas Pressures at Various Altitudes (mm Hg)*

Meters	Feet	BarP	PiO_2	PaO_2	$PaCO_2$	SaO_2(%)
0	0	760	149	94	41	97
1,500	5,000	630	122	75-81	39	92
2,286	7,500	570		69–74	31–33	92–93
4,600	15,000	425	76	48–53	25	86
5,500	18,000	379	69	40	29	71
6,100	20,000	352	63	37–45	20	76
7,620	25,000	291		32–39	13	68
8,848	29,029	253	42	26–33	9.5–13.8	58

Abbreviations: BarP = barometric pressure; PiO_2 = pressure of inspired oxygen; PaO_2 = arterial oxygen pressure; $PaCO_2$ = arterial carbon dioxide pressure; SaO_2(%) = arterial hemoglobin oxygen saturation.

*Adapted from Hecht, H. H., 1971: A sea level view of altitude problems. *Amer. J. Med.*;50:703, and from Hackett, P. H., Roach, R. C., and Sutton, J. R.,1989: High Altitude Medicine, in Auerbach, P. S. and Geehr, E. C., eds.: *Management of Wilderness and Environmental Emergencies,* Second Edition. CV Mosby, St. Louis

ALTITUDE LEVELS

The altitudes encountered in mountaineering can be divided conveniently into the following three levels that have physiologic significance:

8,000 to 14,000 Feet (2,400 to 4,300 Meters)

This altitude range is encountered by tourists and climbers in the continental United States. However, very few cities frequented by tourists anywhere in the world are at elevations higher than 14,000 feet (4,300 m). Because a large number of individuals visit locations within this range of altitudes, most cases of altitude illness occur at these elevations. Though newcomers ascending above 5,000 feet (1,500 m) notice a decrease in athletic performance, 8,000 feet (2,400 m) is a rough threshold above which altitude illness occurs. While acute mountain sickness may occur in some unusually susceptible individuals below 8,000 feet (2,400 m), high altitude pulmonary edema is very rare below this altitude.

14,000 to 18,000 Feet (4,300 to 5,500 Meters)

In this range of elevations are located most high altitude base camps. Though such elevations are usually encountered only by experienced, well-conditioned climbers, trekkers in the Andes and Himalaya may also be at risk. Rapid ascent to such altitudes without prior acclimatization is dangerous and can cause all of the different types of altitude illness.

18,000 to 29,000 Feet (5,500 to 8,800 Meters)

At this range of altitudes most climbers are acclimatized, those who are susceptible to altitude illness usually have been weeded out, and altitude problems consist largely of altitude deterioration. A prolonged stay above 18,000 feet (5,500 m) usually results in loss of physical conditioning rather than increasing fitness and acclimatization.

DECREASED PHYSICAL PERFORMANCE AT HIGH ALTITUDE

At high altitude the maximal amount of work or exercise that can be performed is lower than at sea level, even for well-conditioned and acclimatized athletes or climbers. The decreased performance is directly related to altitude and is demonstrated by reduced climbing rates (fig. 21-1). Physical performance is lowest upon arrival at high altitude but can be progressively improved. Several changes are responsible for the diminished capacity for physical work at high elevations.

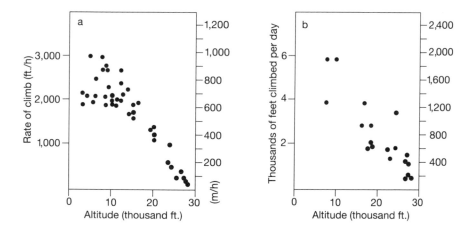

Figure 21-1. Rate of ascent and daily altitude gain at various altitudes.

Lower work and climbing rates should be expected at high altitude. Studies of the ability of Sherpas to carry varying loads at different speeds at 12,000 feet (3,700 m) suggest that only thirty to forty percent of maximal sea-level work capacity should be undertaken routinely at that altitude: 55- to 77-pound loads at about 2 mph (25- to 35-kg loads at 3.0 to 3.5 km/hr). At higher work rates, the subjects became exhausted after short work periods. Even these low rates must be further reduced at higher altitudes.

Decreased Cardiac Output

After several days at high altitude, the volume of blood pumped per minute by the heart (cardiac output) at any level of exercise is lower than during comparable exercise at sea level. In addition, the maximum heart rate that can be attained during heavy exercise is lower at high altitude (fig. 21-2).

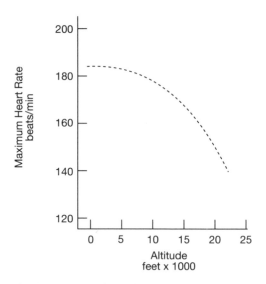

Figure 21-2. Decline of maximum heart rate with altitude.

Decreased Oxygen Saturation

During maximal exercise at sea level, arterial oxygen saturation remains normal, and exercise is not limited by the capacity of the lungs to transfer oxygen from air to blood. During exercise at high altitude, the lower oxygen pressure results in incomplete loading of red blood cells (or hemoglobin) with oxygen. For this reason, blood oxygen saturation falls during exercise at high altitude (fig. 21-3). The decrease is proportional to the exercise level and the altitude. This phenomenon may account for the frequent rest stops climbers make at extreme altitudes. Exercise decreases oxygen saturation, and resting allows the saturation to rise again.

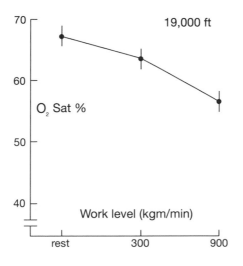

Figure 21-3. Blood oxygen content (saturation) under varying working conditions at 19,000-foot altitude.

Increased Work of Breathing

During heavy exercise at sea level, the work of moving air in and out of the lungs by the muscles of the chest wall and diaphragm consumes only a small part (about five percent) of the oxygen used by the body. During heavy exercise, when the body is consuming 3,000 ml of oxygen per minute, only about 150 ml per minute is needed for the work of breathing. At high altitude, the volume of air moved in and out of the lungs during exercise is greatly increased, which boosts the work of breathing. (The lower air density at high altitude reduces the work of breathing somewhat, but the net effect during heavy effort is an increase.) On the summit of Everest the oxygen cost of breathing requires so much of the total oxygen intake that little is left for vital organ function or for climbing. Habler and Messner described this problem vividly in their account of the ascent of the last 480 meters to the summit of Everest: "We can no longer keep on our feet to rest . . . every 10–15 steps we collapse into the snow to rest, then crawl on again."

Very high breathing rates at very high altitudes may result in fatigue of the respiratory muscles, reduced respiratory effort, decreased ventilation, and decreased arterial oxygen saturation.

Immediate Decrease in Blood Volume

Rapid ascent to high altitude is accompanied by a prompt decrease in blood (or plasma) volume because fluid moves out of the blood vessels into the tissues and cells. This decrease may persist for several weeks. The magnitude of the drop is five to ten percent of the sea-level blood volume, or the equivalent of one to two pints of blood. Inadequate fluid intake at high altitude may further decrease blood volume. Maximal work capacity is significantly impaired by a blood volume reduction of this magnitude.

Sleep Hypoxia

A decrease in arterial oxygen during sleep is now recognized as an important cause of high altitude discomfort and illness. During sleep at sea level, a slight drop in arterial hemoglobin oxygen saturation is produced by a slightly decreased rate and depth of breathing. During sleep at high altitude, decreased ventilation of the lungs is more marked, and much wider fluctuations (periodic breathing) occur. At high altitude, the brain centers that control respiration become less sensitive, particularly during sleep. Respiration often decreases or stops (apnea) until the blood carbon dioxide has risen so high and the oxygen fallen so low that breathing starts again. Typically, the depth of respirations progressively increases until the blood gases have become more normal, at which point respirations tail off again.

Sleep hypoxia may account, in part, for the inability of many individuals to sleep well at high altitude. It may also explain why headache and other symptoms of acute mountain sickness are more severe in the morning hours and why high altitude pulmonary edema often becomes more severe during the night. Part of the beneficial effect of acetazolamide for acute mountain sickness probably results from amelioration of sleep hypoxia.

At sea level the arterial hemoglobin is ninety-four to ninety-six percent saturated with oxygen, and the saturation falls only slightly during sleep. At 14,000 feet (4,300 m) the hemoglobin oxygen saturation is about eighty-six percent, but during sleep it may fall to seventy-five percent with occasional drops to sixty percent. Acetazolamide may not change the waking saturation but limits the decline during sleep to about eighty-two percent and eliminates the severe drops. Drugs such as barbiturates and tranquilizers that promote sleep intensify sleep hypoxia and should be avoided at high altitudes.

Individuals who have difficulty sleeping or experience other altitude-related discomforts during the first few days at high elevations may try taking acetazolamide. This drug should be taken twice daily beginning on the day before ascent and continuing for three to five days after arrival at high altitude. If no discomfort is expected at altitude, acetazolamide should not be used.

Sleep hypoxia probably decreases physical working capacity during the day, which provides a physiologic explanation for the wisdom behind the mountaineer's dictum "sleep low and climb high." Climbers also have noted better physical performance when low-flow oxygen has been used during sleep.

PHYSIOLOGY OF ACCLIMATIZATION

Human survival and effective function at 18,000 feet (5,500 m) and the ability to tolerate, without supplemental oxygen, 29,000 feet (8,800 m)—an altitude at which an unacclimatized person would rapidly lose consciousness and die—vividly demonstrates the ability of people to adapt or acclimatize to high altitudes. The most significant processes in acclimatization are an increase in respiratory volume, an increase in pulmonary artery pressure, an increase in cardiac output, an increase in the number of red blood cells, an increase in the oxygen-delivery capability of red blood cells, and changes in body tissues to promote normal function at low oxygen pressures.

Increased Respiratory Volume (Ventilation)

An increase in the depth and to a lesser extent the rate of respiration usually begins at about 3,000 feet (900 m) and may not reach a constant value for several days after arrival at a high altitude. As a result of this change, more oxygen is delivered to the alveoli of the lung to be absorbed into the blood. The increase in ventilation is most obvious during exercise. Those who have just arrived at high altitude may experience unusual shortness of breath during only moderate exertion.

Increased Pulmonary Artery Pressure

In response to a reduced concentration of oxygen in the alveoli from any cause, including the hypoxia of high altitude, pressure in the pulmonary arteries is elevated. The capillaries in all portions of the lung, many of which are closed during quiet respiration at sea level, are "forced" open and are perfused with blood, "maximizing" the capacity of the pulmonary circulation to absorb oxygen.

Increased Cardiac Output

During the first few days at high altitude, the volume of blood pumped by the heart at rest or at any exercise level is higher than at sea level, which increases the amount of oxygen delivered to the tissues. However, after seven to ten days the cardiac output for any level of exercise is less than at sea level, and more time is required for any specific amount of work, whether running a mile or carrying a specified load a designated distance.

Increased Number of Red Blood Cells

Shortly after arrival at high altitude a slight increase in the concentration of red cells in the blood results from loss of water from the blood into the tissues. Later, production of red blood cells by the bone marrow increases, and the blood actually contains more red cells than at sea level.

The increased number of red cells should permit the blood to carry more oxygen, but it is likely that this benefit is more than offset by a dramatic increase in blood viscosity and the threat of thrombosis as the proportion of red cells (hematocrit) rises above sixty percent. Dilution of the blood of four acclimatized climbers at the Everest base camp at 17,700 feet (5,400 m) in 1981 with an albumin solution, which reduced the concentration of red blood cells from 58.3 percent to 50.5 percent of the blood volume, resulted in no changes in exercise tolerance or maximal oxygen uptake.

Increased Oxygen Delivery Capacity

Red blood cells contain the enzyme 2,3 diphosphoglycerate (DPG), which facilitates the release of oxygen from hemoglobin to the tissues. The concentration of DPG in the blood increases during ascent to high altitudes. This increase may allow oxygen to be released to the tissues more easily, at least at altitudes below 20,000 feet (6,100 m). At higher elevations, the extreme alkalinity of the blood caused by breathing off carbon dioxide may help the blood take on oxygen in the lungs.

Changes in Body Tissues

Prolonged residence at high altitude is accompanied by changes that permit normal function by the oxygen consuming tissues, particularly muscle, at very low oxygen pressures. These changes include an increase in the number of capillaries within the muscle, an increase in the intramuscular oxygen carrying protein myoglobin, an increase in the concentration of intracellular oxidative enzymes, and an increase in the number of mitochondria, the intracellular structures within which oxidative enzymes are located.

Other Considerations

The time required for the different adaptive processes varies. The respiratory and biochemical changes are complete in six to eight days. In contrast, the increase in the number of red blood cells requires six weeks to reach ninety percent of maximum. In general, about eighty percent of adaptation is complete by ten days, and ninety-five percent is complete at six weeks. Climbing at high altitude probably increases the strength and size of muscles used in respiration over a six-week period. Longer periods of acclimatization result in only minor increases in altitude tolerance but may improve muscular strength and endurance. In the 1968 Olympic Games, held in Mexico City at an altitude of 7,300 feet (3,335 m), four of the five endurance track events (over two minutes' duration)—the 1,500-meter and 10,000-meter races, the 3,000-meter steeplechase, and the marathon—were won by men who lived at high altitudes.

ACHIEVING ACCLIMATIZATION

Individuals vary widely in their ability to acclimatize, not only in the degree of acclimatization they can achieve, but in the time required. The following are three examples of the way acclimatization could be achieved.

Intermediate Staging

Prior to climbing and sleeping at altitudes of 10,000 to 14,000 feet (3,000 to 4,300 m), gradually increasing exercise could be carried out at an intermediate altitude of 6,000 to 8,000 feet (1,800 to 2,400 m) for three to four days. Such staging would provide sufficient acclimatization to prevent most altitude problems at higher elevations. Prior to going to 15,000 to 18,000 feet (4,600 to 5,500

m) a second stage of two to three days at 12,000 to 13,000 feet (3,700 to 4,000 m) would be helpful. For example, to climb the volcanoes in Mexico (17,600 to 18,700 feet, or 5,365 to 5,700 m), two to four days in Mexico City at 7,300 feet (2,225 m) should be followed by two to three days at the well-equipped Tlamacas Lodge on Popocatepetl at 13,000 feet (4,000 m) before ascending to the 17,887-foot (5,452-m) summit.

One-Stage Ascent

Ascending to 10,000 to 12,000 feet (3,000 to 3,700 m) without stopping would require rest with minimal activity at that elevation for three to four days before heavy work is begun. The risk of altitude illness after such an ascent would be high. This method would be the least satisfactory way to acclimatize and would be no faster than spending the three or four days at 6,000 to 8,000 feet (1,800 to 2,400 m).

Gradual Ascent

Only a few hours are required to go by car from the Peruvian coast to passes more than 16,000 feet (4,900 m) high in the Andes. In areas such as the Himalaya, however, long approach marches are often required to reach high elevations (although commercial airline flights to landing strips at relatively high elevations are now available to trekkers). During such gradual ascents, acclimatization and some physical conditioning would be achieved. At altitudes above 14,000 feet (4,300 m) ascents should be limited to 500 to 1,000 feet (150 to 300 m) per day, and every third day should be a rest day. To ascend to altitudes greater than 14,000 feet (4,300 m) and begin climbing immediately would be foolhardy and dangerous.

Other Considerations

The altitude at which individuals sleep strongly influences the occurrence of altitude illness. Skiers and climbers who sleep below 8,000 feet (2,400 m) can ascend to 14,000 feet (4,300 m) with only minor altitude discomfort. Sleeping above 8,000 feet (2,400 m) increases the risk of altitude illness, particularly acute mountain sickness and high altitude pulmonary edema.

Acclimatization is lost at about the same rate it is gained; therefore, acclimatization to significant altitude requires continuous exposure. The amount of acclimatization achieved by weekend sojourns above 10,000 feet (3,000 m) is negligible. An acclimatized individual can spend a few days at sea level and return to high altitude without much loss of tolerance. However, if the stay at sea level is longer than one or two weeks, altitude problems occur just as frequently as during the initial ascent.

Prolonged high altitude exposure at yearly intervals has been observed to provide some benefits in succeeding years, although the benefit may consist largely of greater knowledge of methods for coping with altitude. Individuals over twenty-five years old are less likely to develop acute mountain sickness or high altitude pulmonary edema than younger persons. Physical fitness does not confer any protection against acute mountain sickness and does not facilitate acclimatization, even though physical training before ascent to high altitudes clearly allows more effective climbing. Individuals who can not carry loads up and down steep hills for days on end at sea level should not expect to be able to do so when they get to high altitude.

Apart from acetazolamide, no artificial aids to acclimatization are known. Breathing a low-oxygen mixture several times daily is of no value. No vitamin or supplemental iron is beneficial.

ALTITUDE TOLERANCE

Climbers who have reached the summit of Everest without oxygen have enjoyed certain physiologic advantages that can not be entirely predicted by sea level studies or performance. These include an unusual ability to perform extreme and sustained physical work for long periods of time; highly developed mountaineering skills that permit efficient, fast climbing with minimal energy expenditure; a high pulmonary diffusing capacity; a normal or increased ventilatory response to hypoxia; effective muscular function during severe hypoxia; and the ability to think usefully despite severe hypoxia.

Summit of Mount Everest

The barometric pressure on the summit of Everest, as measured for the first time in 1981, was 253 mm Hg, or about one-third sea level atmospheric pressure. The pressure was 17 mm higher than had been predicted, apparently due to the greater thickness of the atmosphere around the equator. The pressure may vary by the equivalent of 100 to 300 feet (30 to 90 m) due to weather-related changes in atmospheric pressure. At the summit of Everest the oxygen pressure in the blood is about 28 to 32 mm Hg, or approximately one-third that of sea level.

ACUTE MOUNTAIN SICKNESS

Acute mountain sickness, often abbreviated to AMS, is a term applied to a common set of symptoms related to rapid ascent to high altitudes. It afflicts those who ascend too high, too fast, and is invariably relieved by descent. The primary cause is probably the direct effect of low oxygen on the brain, but changes in the circulation of blood in the brain—low oxygen saturation dilates cerebral blood vessels—may be important. Dilatation occurs despite the constricting effect of the low carbon dioxide levels produced by increased pulmonary ventilation.

A normal response to ascent is a temporary increase in urine volume. Symptoms of mountain sickness occur most often in people who retain fluid at altitude, and, broadly speaking, those people have the least increase in ventilation and the lowest oxygen levels.

Any explanation of the cause of acute mountain sickness has to account for the fact that this disorder grades uninterruptedly into high altitude cerebral edema, with which there is overt swelling of the brain; for the fact that acute mountain sickness is associated with water retention; and for the fact that symptoms of acute mountain sickness are prominent in people with high altitude pulmonary edema, in whom oxygenation is far lower than would be expected from altitude alone. One hypothetical explanation for the symptoms of acute mountain sickness is that rapid ascent causes generalized water retention and redistribution, but in susceptible people greater amounts of fluid collect in the tissues at the base of the brain. In a few individuals, sometimes because they have unusually low oxygenation due to concurrent pulmonary edema, this fluid accumulation becomes more severe and they develop cerebral edema.

The development of symptoms of acute mountain sickness depends upon the rate of ascent, the elevation attained, and—most significantly—individual susceptibility. Symptoms usually start twelve to twenty-four hours after arrival and begin to decrease in severity on about the third day. Common symptoms are headache, which tends to be at the back of the head and is worse on awakening in the morning, dizziness, fatigue, dry cough, loss of appetite, nausea and vomiting (particularly in children), disturbed sleep, and a general feeling of being unwell (malaise) that has been compared to "flu" or a hangover. Urine volume is decreased (table 21-3).

A few individuals have an unsteady gait (ataxia), an important sign of a more severe disorder that is progressing to high altitude cerebral edema. If such persons begin to stumble and fall, become drowsy and apathetic, and become unable to look after themselves, they should be considered to have cerebral edema. They often have accompanying pulmonary edema with breathlessness at rest and rales (bubbling or crackling sounds) that can be heard when listening to their lungs. Such individuals are in great danger, and treatment by descent—and with supplemental oxygen, if available—is urgently needed.

Acute mountain sickness can be prevented by gradual acclimatization at intermediate altitudes. It occurs with increasing frequency during unbroken as-

---

TABLE 21-3.
Symptoms and Signs in 154 Trekkers in Nepal with Acute Mountain Sickness

Mild	Moderate	Severe
65 percent	30 percent	5 percent
Headache relieved by analgesics	Headache not relieved by analgesics	Altered consciousness, ataxia, papilledema
Loss of appetite, nausea, malaise	Vomiting, reduced urine volume	Rales, cyanosis, dyspnea at rest

From Hackett, P. H., Rennie D., 1979: Râles, peripheral edema, retinal hemorrhage, and acute mountain sickness. *Amer. J. Med.* ;67:214.

cents to higher altitudes. After rapid ascents from near sea level to between 8,000 and 10,000 feet (2,400 to 3,000 m), occasional individuals have symptoms. After rapid ascents from near sea level to 14,000 feet (4,300 m), almost everyone has symptoms. In 1975, sixty-nine percent of trekkers who flew from Katmandu to 9,275 feet (2,825 m) and started hiking to the Mount Everest base camp at 17,500 feet (5,350 m) experienced acute mountain sickness (table 21-4). Two years later, an educational prevention campaign by the Himalayan Rescue Association had reduced the incidence to forty-three percent. Children are very susceptible to acute mountain sickness. They frequently become very sleepy and develop striking cyanosis of the lips and tongue at high altitude.

None of the symptoms of acute mountain sickness are diagnostic. They also occur in people who are exhausted, are dehydrated, are hypoglycemic, are hypothermic, are suffering from carbon monoxide poisoning, have a severe hangover, are on drugs (prescription or recreational), or are developing an infection. Usually the individual's history indicates the diagnosis. The presence of a high fever suggests infection; an appreciably raised temperature does not occur with acute mountain sickness.

TABLE 21-4.
Incidence of Acute Mountain Sickness

Group Studied	Sleeping Altitude	Rate of Ascent*	Percent with AMS	Percent with HAPE or HACE
Skiers in Colorado, Utah, etc.	2,400–2,800 meters	1–2 Days	15 percent	0.01 percent
Mount Everest trekkers	3,000–5,200 meters	1–2 days (flew In) 10–13 days (walked in)	47 percent	1.6 percent
Mount McKinley climbers	3,000–3,500 meters	1–7 days	30 percent	2-3 percent
Mount Rainier climbers	3,000 meters	1–2 days	67 percent	0 percent

*Days taken to go from sea level to a high-level camp (sleeping altitude).

Abbreviations: AMS = acute mountain sickness; HAPE = high altitude pulmonary edema; HACE = high altitude cerebral edema

From Hackett, P. H.: Personal communication.

Attendants should not try to become too clever at diagnosis if the person appears at all ill. Anyone who has recently ascended to high altitude and is symptomatic should be assumed to have acute mountain sickness. If the individual is getting worse in spite of rest, he must be removed to a lower altitude. Supplemental oxygen may be given, but is not a satisfactory substitute for descent. Lower altitude will benefit the individual, whatever the cause of his illness, and also will help confirm the diagnosis.

Acute mountain sickness, like all altitude illnesses, is associated with disordered thinking. Decisions have to be made for the affected individual, and he may have to be forced to accept them. Difficulties have been encountered when the sufferer has been a physician. Clear-thinking associates have been too ready to defer to an ill and confused individual who had a medical degree.

Carbon monoxide poisoning from cooking in small, sealed tents aggravates altitude-induced hypoxia, frequently results in severe symptoms of acute mountain sickness, including coma, and has caused quite a few deaths. This possibility must always be considered, even though the treatment—rapid descent and oxygen—is the same as that for high altitude cerebral edema.

Individuals with acute mountain sickness should avoid heavy exertion, although light outdoor activity is preferable to complete rest. Sleep is definitely not helpful because respirations are slower during sleep, which may make symptoms worse. At night, sedatives should be avoided since they also decrease respirations. Affected persons should drink extra fluids and eat a light, high-carbohydrate diet. Aspirin can be taken for headache. Tobacco and alcohol should be avoided.

Sojourners at high altitude must appreciate that acute mountain sickness gives plenty of warning, must look for and recognize mild symptoms early, and must avoid progression to severe illness by resting and not ascending further. In particular, sleeping at higher altitude must be avoided until symptoms have disappeared. When acute mountain sickness is severe, individuals may be forced to rest by their illness.

By far the simplest and surest therapy is an immediate descent on foot of 2,000 to 3,000 feet (600 to 900 m). In the unlikely event that a plentiful supply of oxygen is at hand, two liters a minute may be given through a mask that covers the nose and mouth. To obtain full benefit from oxygen, it should be used continuously for at least fifteen minutes. Oxygen is of no value if it is inhaled for only a few minutes a few times a day. If the supply is adequate, which is rare on treks, oxygen can be used for twelve to forty-eight hours, particularly at night for sleeping (0.5 to 1 liter per minute). If severe symptoms persist despite oxygen (or if oxygen is not available), descent to a lower altitude results in prompt relief.

A form of therapy for acute mountain sickness that is becoming fashionable is the Gamow Bag, a lightweight, portable, hyperbaric bag made of coated nylon. This bag, which weighs only 14.5 pounds (6.6 kg), was devised in 1987 and currently is being manufactured in quantity. One version is 7 feet (2.1 m) long and 21 inches (53 cm) in diameter, has a zippered entrance, and can be inflated with air (not oxygen) with a foot pump to 103 torr (2 psi) above ambient atmospheric pressure. Fifteen pump strokes per minute deliver 44 liters of air, or 8.8 liters of oxygen.

Although, to date, enthusiastic anecdotal reports have been more common than controlled trials of the Gamow Bag, it is probably as effective as giving oxygen. At 14,000 feet (4,300 m) the altitude for a person inside the bag can be calculated to be "lowered" to about 7,900 feet (2,400 m); at 20,000 feet (6,000 m), where the atmospheric pressure is about 352 torr, the pressure in the bag can be increased to the equivalent of about 13,000 feet (4,000 m), where the atmospheric pressure is about 103 torr higher. An expedition or trek going above 12,000 to 15,000 feet (3,700 to 4,600 m) in places where evacuation is likely to be problematic probably should take along such a bag. Information from carefully controlled studies, particularly information about problems ranging from bursting the bag to difficulties with a comatose person's airway, is needed. Significantly, a person being treated in such a bag can not simultaneously descend to a lower and safer altitude.

Occasionally, an individual who has recently arrived at high altitude becomes unusually drowsy or very weak. He may rest in a semisleeping condition, becoming increasingly cyanotic and beginning to hallucinate or behave in an irrational manner. Improvement can be achieved quickly by awakening the individual, helping him walk around in the open air, and encouraging him to breathe deeply. Because his respirations are decreased during sleep, the oxygen concentration in the blood can fall to low levels, but the oxygen content increases rapidly when the individual is awake, active, and breathing deeply.

Some temporary relief from the symptoms of acute mountain sickness can be achieved by voluntarily taking ten to twelve deep breaths every four to six minutes. However, if overdone, this maneuver can cause dizziness and tingling of the lips and hands due to "blowing off" too much carbon dioxide.

Acetazolamide (Diamox) has been found to have a considerable prophylactic effect against acute mountain sickness. When taken before ascent, it not only reduces the severity of acute mountain sickness but seems to speed acclimatization. A physician should provide the prescription because this drug is contraindicated in the presence of certain kidney, eye, or liver diseases. The usual dose is 250 mg twice daily, or a 500-mg sustained-action capsule once a day, beginning one day before ascent and continuing for two to five days after arrival. Side effects include tingling of the lips and fingertips, blurring of vision, and alteration of taste, but these symptoms subside when the drug is stopped. The best drugs for acute mountain sickness after it has developed are aspirin for the headache, compazine for the nausea, and, if symptoms are moderate or severe, dexamethasone every six hours for a day or two.

HIGH ALTITUDE CEREBRAL EDEMA

In a small proportion of people with acute mountain sickness (see table 21-3), usually at altitudes above 12,000 feet (3,700 m), the symptoms become steadily worse. The ataxia, which can be diagnosed early by having the individual try to walk along a straight line, becomes so bad that he can not stand or can not get into his tent or sleeping bag. He can not get dressed, tie his shoelaces, or handle a knife and spoon; he simply lies helplessly. Mental dysfunction can range from confusion, loss of memory, and inability to exercise proper judgment to hallucinations, psychotic behavior, and coma. A victim who has had worsening headache, vomiting, and lassitude for several days may retire to his tent to sleep, and lapse into coma. His companions become aware of his condition only when they can not wake him up. Indeed, he may not respond even to painful stimuli. Occasionally the individual may have weakness or paralysis of a limb; rarely he may have a seizure. He almost always looks pale and blue (cyanotic), and often rales (bubbling and crackling sounds) can be heard in the lungs, indicating concurrent pulmonary edema. The optic nerve is usually swollen (papilledema), which is an indication of cerebral edema, an abnormal accumulation of fluid in the brain. Cerebral edema has been found in the few individuals who have been autopsied, though small hemorrhages also have been seen.

High altitude cerebral edema can cause death or, more rarely, permanent brain damage. Early diagnosis and treatment are important. Trip leaders must check the condition of party members, particularly in the morning, when signs and symptoms may be more severe, but also in the evening after arrival at a higher altitude. Any confusion or ataxia combined with a severe persistent headache is indicative of cerebral edema. Individuals with such findings should be given oxygen and forced to descend. Assistance must be provided during descent because ataxia may progress rapidly and the individuals may fall and be injured. Two young climbers who lapsed into coma at 13,700 feet (4,200 m) but were promptly tobogganed down the mountain on skis rapidly regained consciousness at 10,700 feet (3,200 m), indicating that even a small descent can be effective if accomplished promptly. Some individuals appear to be unusually susceptible to this disorder and have suffered more than one episode. Once high altitude cerebral edema has occurred, even if recovery is rapid at a lower altitude, further ascent is not advisable.

Persons who are unconscious after descent must be hospitalized as soon as possible. The intravenous mannitol and diuretics usually administered for cerebral edema at sea level should probably not be employed for two reasons: cerebral edema may not always be present, and these agents may reduce the circulation of blood to the brain and impede recovery. Dexamethasone is beneficial, has the advantage of not decreasing blood flow to the brain, and should be administered promptly, either intravenously or by mouth if the victim is still conscious.

High altitude cerebral edema may occur in the absence of acute mountain sickness or high altitude pulmonary edema. However, many individuals with severe pulmonary edema may be unconscious, some may exhibit all of the signs and symptoms of cerebral edema, and a few may not have a cough or shortness of breath. (Presumably the extra hypoxia caused by pulmonary edema leads to cerebral edema.) For this reason, the heart rate and respiratory rate should be determined, and the lungs should be examined carefully in all persons with central nervous system abnormalities at high altitude. To look further for pulmonary edema, a chest x-ray should be obtained as soon as a medical facility has been reached.

Other neurologic disorders may occur at high altitude in the absence of cerebral edema. Strokes occur rarely (see Chapter Fifteen, "Neural Disorders"). More commonly, the problem, which may include blindness, is arterial spasm in the brain and is transient.

Case Study One

A twenty-two-year-old experienced climber was a member of an expedition to Makalu. Three years earlier he had developed mild confusion and stumbling at 17,500 feet (5,350 m), but these symptoms disappeared after descending to 14,500 feet (4,450 m). On Makalu he spent twelve days climbing to 16,400 feet (5,000 m), where he stayed for two days. On successive days he carried loads to 17,500, 18,500, and 20,000 feet (5,350, 5,650, and 6,100 m). At 20,000 feet (6,100 m) he noticed that he was dizzy and had poor balance on delicate pitches. He slept at 20,000 feet (6,100 m) and then carried a load to 21,000 feet (6,400 m). That evening he felt very sleepy and dozed off between the courses of his evening meal. He was not short of breath and had no headache. During the night, he was observed to be snoring loudly and could not be awakened. The following morning he was unconscious. His eyes were open and staring, and he frequently made involuntary, convulsive movements. Over the next several days he was carried down to 14,750 feet (4,500 m), where he became conscious but was confused and hallucinating. He crawled aimlessly around his tent and could not recognize his own sleeping bag. He still made convulsive movements and frequent facial grimaces. Eighteen days after his collapse he became mentally clear for the first time. A month afterward retinal hemorrhages persisted. He could not perform delicate hand and foot movements and was unable to maintain his balance. Abnormal reflexes were present, indicating persistent nervous system injury.

This young man had a serious episode of high altitude cerebral edema with residual nervous system abnormalities, but he did survive. Others have not been so fortunate. Apparently, the longer a person with high altitude cerebral edema remains at high altitude, the more severe and prolonged are the symptoms, and the greater is the risk of permanent nervous system damage or death.

HIGH ALTITUDE PULMONARY EDEMA

High altitude pulmonary edema is the most dangerous of the common types of altitude illness. It usually occurs in the context of acute mountain sickness and makes it worse, sometimes leading to high altitude cerebral edema. High altitude pulmonary edema results when the alveoli of the lungs fill with fluid that has oozed through the walls of the pulmonary capillaries. As more alveoli fill with fluid, oxygen transfer from air to the red blood cells in the pulmonary capillaries is blocked. A drop in the concentration of oxygen in the blood results, eventually causing cyanosis, impaired cerebral function, and finally death, essentially from suffocation.

High altitude pulmonary edema is not the result of heart failure or pneumonia, although prior to the recognition of this disorder in 1960, most episodes in climbers were incorrectly diagnosed as pneumonia. The cause lies in the pulmonary circulation. High altitude, sleep hypoxia, hypoxia from any other cause, and heavy exercise are all associated with a rise in pulmonary artery pressure. Normally, constriction of the smallest pulmonary arteries (called arterioles) protects the capillaries from excessive pressure and high flow rates. In individuals susceptible to high altitude pulmonary edema, arteriolar constriction may not be uniform throughout the lungs. Arterioles in some areas constrict, but arterioles in other areas do not. In the areas where no constriction occurs, high pressure and flow are transmitted directly to the capillaries. A shearing effect seems to make the capillary walls highly permeable, and they leak fluid into the alveoli of the lung.

Some individuals are unusually susceptible to high altitude pulmonary edema and have had repeated episodes of this disorder. Such subjects may have an abnormal rise in pulmonary artery pressure at high altitudes, particularly during exercise. This abnormal rise in pressure appears to be the first event leading to high altitude pulmonary edema.

When severe enough to cause physical incapacity, high altitude pulmonary edema has usually followed rapid ascents by unacclimatized individuals who engaged in heavy physical exertion after arrival at high altitudes. Very rapid ascents may result in high altitude pulmonary edema even in acclimatized individuals. However, this disorder rarely occurs below 8,000 feet (2,400 m).

The incidence of high altitude pulmonary edema and cerebral edema vary widely with the terrain and the ease of descent (table 21-3). A climber living in Seattle can be up and down Mount Rainier (14,410 feet, or 4,400 meters) in a weekend. Since that climber will be climbing fast, the probability of acute mountain sickness will be high, but he will be able to descend at once if symptoms become bad. On much larger and higher Mount McKinley (20,300 feet, or 6,200 meters), deep snow, heavier packs, severe weather, and longer distances to be traveled restrict mobility, slow ascent, and reduce the incidence of acute mountain sickness, but also make rapid descent far harder.

The chance of developing symptomatic high altitude pulmonary edema after a rapid ascent to 12,000 feet (3,700 m) is about one in two hundred (0.5 percent) in individuals more than twenty-one years old, but may be six to twelve times higher in individuals ten to eighteen years old. (Episodes of high altitude pulmonary edema producing only mild or no symptoms and spontaneously subsiding without specific treatment may also occur, but their incidence and related features are unknown.) Probably no one is completely immune; high altitude pulmonary edema does occur in experienced mountaineers. Acclimatized individuals who live at high altitude may develop high altitude pulmonary edema if they descend to a lower elevation for a few days and rapidly ascend again.

Symptoms of high altitude pulmonary edema usually begin one to four days after arrival at a high elevation and consist of undue shortness of breath with moderate exertion, a sense of tightness in the chest or a feeling of impending suffocation at night, weakness, and marked fatigue. The individual with pulmonary edema is typically much more tired than other members of the climbing party. Since the hypoxia of altitude is made much more severe by the fluid in the alveoli, the symptoms of acute mountain sickness, such as headache, loss of appetite, nausea, and vomiting, are frequently prominent, particularly in children. Coughing is an important early sign, although it is probably more frequently caused by drying of the throat than pulmonary edema. The cough is usually dry and intermittent at first, but with pulmonary edema the cough becomes persistent, and white, watery or frothy material is coughed up. Later the sputum may be streaked with blood. In rare instances, high altitude pulmonary edema may be manifested first by disturbances of consciousness or coma with little or no shortness of breath.

The pulse rate is usually rapid (110 to 160 beats per minute), even after several hours of rest, and is associated with rapid respirations (20 to 40 per minute). The lips and nail beds are cyanotic, and the skin may be pale and cold. Bubbling or crackling sounds (rales) may be heard when listening to the lungs with the unaided ear or with a stethoscope. Sometimes rales are heard on one side only. The symptoms and signs often become worse during the night (table 21-5).

An important indication of the severity of high altitude pulmonary edema is the level of mental acuity. Confusion, delirium, and irrational behavior are signs of a pronounced reduction in the oxygen supply to the brain and are indicative of severe pulmonary edema. If the subject becomes unconscious, death may follow within six to twelve hours unless prompt descent, oxygen, or hyperbaric therapy is initiated.

TABLE 21-5.
Analysis of Thirty-three Cases of
High Altitude Pulmonary Edema in Climbers

	Average	Range
Age	30 years	20-43
Altitude of occurrence	13,670 feet (4,166 m)	8,600–24,000 feet (2,630–7,315 m)
Duration of ascent	3.9 days	1–11 days
Interval before onset of symptoms	3 days	1–11 days
Pulse rate	115/min	96–170
Duration of edema	5.2 days	2–10 days
Prior episodes of pulmonary edema	4 (12%)	
Deaths	9 (27%)	
Most common features	Cough (24); shortness of breath (20); fatigue (16); confusion, mental changes (16); gurgling in chest (14)	

Grading the severity of high altitude pulmonary edema may be useful (see table 21-6). Persons with a disorder of grade-one severity usually have only mild symptoms such as fatigue or exertional dyspnea. Listening to the chest usually discloses fine rales. If an x-ray of the chest is taken, small infiltrates may be present, particularly in the right midlung field. Individuals with grade-one pulmonary edema usually recover after descending to a lower altitude for two to three days. Subjects with more severe grades of high altitude pulmonary edema should be considered medical emergencies and require more vigorous treatment.

TABLE 21-6.
Classification of High Altitude Pulmonary Edema

Grade	Signs and Symptoms	Pulse	Resp.	Chest X-ray
I Mild	Minor symptoms. Dyspnea on moderate or heavy exertion. May have rales.	<110/min	<20/min	Minor infiltrates, <25 percent of one lung field.
II Moderate	Dyspnea, weakness, fatigue on ordinary effort. Headache, dry cough, and rales.	110–120	20–30	Infiltrates in 50 percent of one lung field, usually RML.
III Serious	Dyspnea, weakness, headache at rest. Anorexia. Persistent productive cough. Rales easily heard.	120–130	30–40	Infiltrates in half of both lung fields.
IV Severe	Stupor or coma. Hallucinations. Can not stand. Severe cyanosis. Rales prominent. Copious sputum, often bloody.	>130/min	>40/min	Infiltrates in >50 percent of both lung fields

Trip leaders and physicians must actively look for the early signs of high altitude pulmonary edema, particularly during the first week of climbing above 8,000 feet (2,400 m). Young, ambitious, physically fit climbers may conceal symptoms. A useful method of detecting early high altitude pulmonary edema is to evaluate each party member at the end of each day's climbing after the individual has rested quietly for fifteen to twenty minutes. His climbing performance should be evaluated; symptoms of undue fatigue, weakness, or shortness of breath should be sought. The heart rate and respiratory rate should be determined, and the chest should be examined by the ear or stethoscope for crackling or bubbling sounds during inspiration. Unusual fatigue, a resting heart rate greater than 110 beats per minute, a resting respiratory rate of greater than 16 per minute, or rales in the chest may indicate the presence of high altitude pulmonary edema. If these signs and symptoms persist through the night, the person should be taken to a lower altitude, preferably while he is in good enough condition to walk under his own power. High altitude pulmonary edema may progress very rapidly, particularly during the night, and frequent examination of subjects with mild signs is necessary. Any worsening of the condition is an indication for prompt descent.

The most important method of treatment is descent to a lower altitude. If the individual can not walk, litter evacuation may be necessary. A descent of as little as 2,000 to 3,000 feet (600 to 900 m) often results in prompt improvement. After arriving at a lower altitude, the subject should rest for two to three days. Physical activity increases the severity of high altitude pulmonary edema, and several days are required for the fluid to be absorbed from the lungs.

If oxygen is available, it should be administered without delay. Rescue parties, particularly helicopter evacuation units, should carry oxygen to the subject and begin using it at once. Deaths have occurred during evacuation when oxygen has not been carried. However, descent to a lower altitude is essential even if oxygen is available. If immediate descent is impossible and a Gamow Bag is available, it should be used.

Oxygen should be given at a flow rate of four to six liters per minute for the first fifteen minutes, after which the flow rate can be reduced to two liters per minute to conserve oxygen. A snugly fitting face mask (rather than nasal prongs) is essential for administration. (Lightweight oxygen cylinders and attachments are available from Nageldinger, 1 Mahan Street, West Babylon, NY 11704.)

In mild cases, improvement is usually rapid after oxygen is begun. However, administration should be continued for at least six to twelve hours if possible. Oxygen should be continued after arrival at a lower elevation. Twenty-four to forty-eight hours of low-flow oxygen therapy (two liters per minute) may be required for prompt and complete recovery. Oxygen should not be given for less than fifteen minutes; continuous low-flow oxygen for six to twelve hours is more beneficial than intermittent short periods at high flow rates.

As soon as the subject reaches a medical facility, a chest x-ray should be obtained. Diagnostic pulmonary densities may persist for several days after apparent recovery. Residual weakness and fatigue may persist for one to two weeks.

Many drugs have been employed in the treatment of high altitude pulmonary edema, but probably the only ones that have been of benefit are furosemide (Lasix), morphine, and nifedipine. Furosemide has been used to remove fluid from the lungs, but the only type of pulmonary edema in which fluid can be removed from the lungs by a diuretic is that due to heart failure. (In heart failure, the drug lowers the pressure in the left ventricle and thereby lowers the pulmonary capillary pressure. The lower capillary pressure stops the movement of fluid into the alveoli and permits absorption of the edema fluid.) Since high altitude pulmonary edema is not due to heart failure, a diuretic would not be expected to be helpful. In some individuals a diuretic can cause a large urine output, resulting in a drop in blood volume and collapse. A person who is able to walk and to descend with minimal assistance can be converted into a litter case. Nevertheless, in severe high altitude pulmonary edema, diuretics are worth trying. The role of acetazolamide in the treatment of early or mild high altitude pulmonary edema is unknown and needs to be studied. Morphine may be helpful, particularly for individuals who are very apprehensive and have marked shortness of breath, but should be given only by a physician. Recent studies suggest that nifedipine, which relaxes the pulmonary arterioles and reduces pulmonary artery pressure, may be effective. This drug also should be given only by a physician. (See Editor's Note at the end of this chapter.)

Measures for preventing high altitude pulmonary edema are identical to these for preventing acute mountain sickness: gradual ascent and acclimatization. Heavy physical exertion should be avoided for the first few days after a rapid ascent to high altitude. A low salt intake is recommended.

Individuals with a prior history of this disorder must be particularly careful, and preventive measures can not be stressed too strongly. Such persons may be helped by acetazolamide, which should be started on the day before ascent and continued for three to five days after arriving at high elevations. Subjects who have the rare congenital abnormality in which the right pulmonary artery is absent are very susceptible to high altitude pulmonary edema and may develop this disorder at altitudes below 8,000 feet (2,400 m).

In the central Peruvian Andes, more than 300,000 people live at altitudes exceeding 12,000 feet (3,700 m) and travel to the sea coast and jungle frequently. In the 1960s, twenty to forty cases of high altitude pulmonary edema in high altitude residents reascending to high altitude were seen annually at one Andean hospital located at 12,400 feet (3,780 m). As people became aware of the problem, preventive measures were instituted. For susceptible subjects, treatment with acetazolamide was started prior to ascent and oxygen was administered for six to twelve hours after arrival. Exercise was forbidden for the first two days after arrival. If signs or symptoms of high altitude pulmonary edema were present, the individual was put to bed and given low-flow oxygen at home. As a result of these measures, high altitude pulmonary edema has become a rare occurrence in this hospital.

Case Study Two

A thirty-eight-year-old, healthy, experienced mountaineer was climbing in the Cordillera Blanca of Peru. In three days he climbed with a heavy pack from 9,000 to 14,000 feet (2,700 to 4,300 m) over a series of ridges, one of which was 16,000 feet (4,900 m) high. On the evening of the third day he was more tired than other members of the party and had periodic respirations. The following day he engaged in little activity but on the fifth day climbed steeply with a heavy pack to a higher camp. He was far more short of breath than other members of the party. Upon arrival at the 16,000-foot (4,900-m) camp he was tired and listless and could not eat. He began to cough and one of his companions stated that he "obviously had fluid in his lungs." He was comfortable only in a seated position. Because he was thought to have pneumonia, he was given penicillin. His breathing rapidly became more labored and his cough more severe and frequent. His companion, who was not a physician, wrote in his diary, "the next few hours his breathing became progressively more congested and labored. He sounded as though he were literally drowning in his own fluid with an almost continuous loud bubbling sound as if breathing through liquid." During the night the victim's breathing became far worse and he lost consciousness. He died at dawn on the second day of his illness. His companion's diary stated, "a couple of hours after his death, when we got up to carry on the day's activities, I noticed that a white froth resembling cotton candy had appeared to well up out of his mouth." An autopsy disclosed severe pulmonary edema.

At the time of this incident, high altitude pulmonary edema had not been recognized. Prompt evacuation to a lower altitude would have been life-saving.

Case Study Three

A thirty-year-old salesman from the San Francisco Bay area was an avid skier, skiing nearly every weekend from late November to the middle of April in the Lake Tahoe area. A late snowfall in May enticed him to ski over the Memorial Day weekend. He drove to Mammoth Lakes (8,000 feet, or 2,400 meters), where he spent the next three nights. He skied the next two days on Mammoth Mountain between 8,000 and 11,000 feet (2,400 and 3,400 m). On the afternoon of the second day at Mammoth he noted increasing shortness of breath, fatigue, and weakness. He continued to ski even though he barely could climb up the loading ramp to the chairlift. That night he developed a cough and more intense shortness of breath, and he noted gurgling sounds in his chest. Early the next morning he was coughing up bloody sputum, and a physician was called. He was given an injection of penicillin and advised to drive home. The following day, eighteen hours after arrival at sea level, he still felt weak and short of breath and saw his family physician. He had a respiratory rate of twenty-four per minute and a heart rate of ninety-two. Persistent crackling sounds were present in the lower portion of the right lung. A chest x-ray disclosed fluid in the lower portions of both lungs. After he was hospitalized and treated with oxygen, he improved rapidly and was discharged four days later after complete clearing of the pulmonary fluid.

This study illustrates several important aspects of high altitude pulmonary edema:

1. Two days of skiing between 8,000 and 11,000 feet (2,400 and 3,400 m) and three nights of sleeping at 8,000 feet (2,400 m) were sufficient to produce pulmonary edema in this physically fit man. Shorter periods of skiing, or sleeping at a lower elevation, might have prevented the episode.
2. He continued his physical exertions on the second day of skiing in spite of his symptoms, a common occurrence in individuals who develop severe high altitude pulmonary edema.
3. His symptoms became worse at night, a frequent event probably caused by lower blood oxygen concentrations during sleep.

HIGH ALTITUDE RETINAL HEMORRHAGE

Hemorrhage (or bleeding) into the retina, the layer of sensitive light receptors in the eye, occurs commonly at altitudes above 14,000 feet (4,300 m) and has been found in thirty to one hundred percent of climbers at an elevation of 17,600 feet (5,365 m). Such bleeding is rare below 14,000 feet (4,300 m). In most instances the hemorrhages cause no visual difficulty, are painless, and can be found only by examining the retina with special instruments. Occasionally the hemorrhages are larger, involve the central part of the retina, and cause clouding of vision or the inability to see in certain directions with one eye. Individuals with such large hemorrhages should descend to a lower elevation since further exposure to high altitude can worsen the condition. The hemorrhages usually clear up completely four to six weeks after descent. Only rarely have minor visual defects been permanent.

The hemorrhages are probably related to dilatation and increased blood flow in the blood vessels of the retina due to reduced blood oxygen concentrations. The high pressure may produce small openings in these thin-walled vessels, resulting in bleeding.

Whether to descend after the discovery of small retinal hemorrhages that cause no visual difficulty is a decision that each individual climber must make for himself or herself.

HIGH ALTITUDE SYSTEMIC EDEMA

Swelling of the feet and hands may occur after ascent to high altitude, particularly in women. Swelling of the face and eyelids may be troublesome in the mornings. Urine output is usually low despite an adequate fluid intake, and a weight gain of eight to twelve pounds may occur within a few days. High altitude systemic edema may not be associated with symptoms of acute mountain sickness. Recurrent episodes are common. Although this condition sometimes is a nuisance, it is harmless and clears up within a few days after returning to sea level. A copious urine output and rapid loss of the extra weight usually signal its disappearance after descent.

The edema results from retention of salt and water by the kidneys, but the cause is not understood. Prolonged exercise at sea level may also result in water retention, but the edema is less severe.

Salty foods, salt tablets, or sodium-containing antacid tablets should be avoided because an increased sodium intake aggravates the condition. A diuretic such as furosemide taken once or twice daily for three to six days usually eliminates the excess fluid. Acetazolamide may be given if symptoms of acute mountain sickness are severe and persistent.

HIGH ALTITUDE DETERIORATION

Acclimatized persons can live a normal life span at elevations up to approximately 17,000 feet (5,200 m). Above this altitude even acclimatized individuals experience a slow, progressive deterioration in physical fitness and persistent symptoms of acute mountain sickness. The causes are not clear, but chronic hypoxia is the probable culprit.

Dehydration is common because fluid losses are increased and the sense of thirst is diminished. Loss of appetite and progressive weight loss may occur. The concentration of red cells in the blood may increase to almost twice the usual sea level values, which greatly increases the viscosity of blood. This concentrated, viscous blood flows slowly, almost like syrup, and can cause poor perfusion of vital organs such as the brain. Such viscous blood also has a greater tendency to clot within blood vessels, which can result in serious disorders such as a stroke or a pulmonary embolus.

High altitude deterioration can be minimized by spending as little time as possible at extreme altitudes and periodically descending to lower altitudes for several days for recovery. An adequate fluid intake is essential. The urine volume must be greater than 500 cc every day, preferably two to three times greater, and urine color should be clear or light yellow, not deep yellow or orange. Efforts must be made to eat an adequate amount of food in spite of a poor appetite. An adequate caloric intake is needed more than specific nutrients. Nutritional deficiencies do not develop in healthy individuals during the short periods expeditions are at high altitudes. Inhaling oxygen through a face mask during sleep at a flow rate of two liters per minute is beneficial. The value of drugs is unknown. Prolonged stay at high altitude may perhaps be further extended by removing some blood and replacing it with fluid to reduce viscosity, but such extreme measures are not justified when simple descent would solve the problem painlessly.

CHRONIC MOUNTAIN SICKNESS

The basic disturbance in chronic mountain sickness is failure by the body's chemical receptors to react to lower blood oxygen concentrations and stimulate faster, deeper respirations. As a result, aeration (or ventilation) of the lungs is inadequate for blood oxygenation. An individual with chronic mountain sickness is deeply cyanotic, sleepy and lethargic, and has edema of the feet, legs, and abdomen due to heart failure. The cure is descent to sea level, and the individual can never return to high altitude. However, chronic mountain sickness has been observed only in persons who have lived at a high altitude for many years. It apparently never occurs in climbers, even after weeks at high elevations.

THROMBOSIS, STROKES, AND PULMONARY EMBOLISM

At high altitude, blood has an increased tendency to clot (thrombose) in veins and arteries. Factors (in addition to altitude and hypoxia) contributing to this tendency include dehydration, long periods of immobility in tents during bad weather, an increased number of red cells in the blood, and possibly an increase in the factors that promote clotting.

Blood clots in the leg veins may detach and be carried to the lungs, where they obstruct the pulmonary arteries (pulmonary embolism). Warning signs of thrombosis of the leg veins are swollen, painful, tender legs and feet, particularly after long periods of immobility. (See Chapter Ten, "Respiratory System Disorders.") Blood may clot in arteries in the brain and cause a stroke. Temporary or permanent paralysis, commonly limited to one side of the body, is the usual result. (See Chapter Fifteen, "Neural Disorders.") Any of these disorders is a serious problem that may cause death or serious disability and is an indication for prompt descent, oxygen therapy, and hospitalization. Recurrent episodes are likely upon return to high altitude.

PREEXISTING MEDICAL PROBLEMS AT HIGH ALTITUDE

Medical conditions aggravated or complicated by high altitude include:

1. Chronic lung disease with low arterial oxygen saturation
2. Pulmonary hypertension
3. Congenital absence of a pulmonary artery
4. Cyanotic congenital heart disease
5. Previous stroke or pulmonary embolus
6. Pregnancy
7. Heart failure
8. Severe angina
9. Anemia
10. Sickle cell disease

Though these conditions are not likely to be problems for mountaineers, anyone with one of these disorders should consult his physician before going to higher elevations. Ideally, the physician should be able to turn to epidemiologic studies of the effect of ascent at any given speed to any altitude on large groups of people of any sex, age, lung and heart function, and training. By comparing the subject with the experience of those in the relevant group, the physician should be able to provide advice based on information better than guesswork. For example, studies have demonstrated that even moderate altitudes can be dangerous for individuals with the sickle cell trait.

However, almost none of these data actually exist. As a result, physicians are in a very difficult position and often are forced to be exceedingly conservative, which usually means recommending that the subject not go to high altitudes. Since this opinion may require the subject to give up an activity that has great meaning, it is a pity that it may be decided on a "better safe than sorry" principle. No good evidence indicates that acute exposure to high altitude is dangerous to either mother or fetus, for example, but in today's litigious climate, advising a pregnant woman that she would not be harmed by ascent to high altitudes would be risky.

A special problem arises when symptomless men are instructed by their trekking companies or trip leaders to get a physician to certify their fitness to trek or climb at high altitude.

No evidence exists that altitude threatens the normal heart in any way, but five to six percent of symptomless men fifty years old have abnormal coronary arteries. Testing in doctors' offices is notoriously poor at identifying coronary artery disease in men at sea level, and no one knows how good such testing is for predicting how hearts will do at high altitude. Reported deaths from coronary artery disease are very rare at high altitudes, though 35 million people, two percent of whom have coronary artery disease, visit altitudes above 8,000 feet

(2,450 m) each year in the United States alone. Indeed, the minimal value of such testing can easily be demonstrated, because most of the abnormal findings turn out to be erroneous.

The situation is quite different for symptomatic persons—for example, those with angina. The pain typical of this condition comes on sooner at high altitude, and such individuals, in concert with their physicians, must experiment cautiously to determine their exercise tolerance at increasing altitudes. However, subjects who tolerate exercise poorly at sea level can not expect to perform better at high altitude.

Mountaineers search for adventure and try to "get away from it all." They must remember that they are also getting away from prompt, sophisticated medical care, which means that each individual must assume full responsibility for himself.

NUTRITION AT ALTITUDE

Maintenance of an adequate food and water intake is particularly difficult at high altitudes. Appetites are poor, and high altitude climbers usually eat and drink much less than they need. Much of the fatigue and weakness experienced at high altitudes is due to inadequate nutrition, dehydration, and possibly potassium loss accompanying very high energy expenditure. British Himalayan parties have reported that the average caloric intake during approach marches was 4,200 Kcal (kilocalories) per day, but intake fell to 3,200 Kcal between 19,000 and 22,000 feet (5,800 and 6,700 m) and to 1,500 Kcal above 24,000 feet (7,300 m). The American party that first ascended the west ridge of Everest attributed a large part of its success to continuous conscious efforts to consume adequate amounts of food in spite of a lack of appetite.

Impairment of food absorption in the gastrointestinal tract has been suggested as a cause for the weight loss, which reportedly can not be prevented by forced feeding. The tastelessness of the freeze-dried foods carried by most expeditions may be more significant. The 1983 German-American Everest Expedition purchased all of its food supplies from community grocery stores and had no problems with weight loss. One member even gained weight!

Climbers often go hungry at high altitude rather than eat food that they do not crave. Menus should consist largely of foods known to be enjoyed by all the party members, but foods to satisfy individual tastes must also be carried. Diets should contain large amounts of sweets, which are usually consumed in large quantities at high altitudes. Fatty foods or highly condensed rations may not be tolerated.

On prolonged expeditions where fresh vegetables and fruits are not available, possible vitamin C deficiency can be prevented with ascorbic acid. However, most packaged drinks such as lemonade or orange juice contain vitamin C. Furthermore, about six months are required for signs of vitamin deficiency to appear in individuals who previously were in good nutritional condition. If vitamin intake appears inadequate, one or two multivitamin tablets per day can be taken. Higher vitamin intakes, or special vitamins such as E or B complex vitamins, are of no benefit at high altitudes (or anywhere else). Vitamin requirements are only minimally increased by the rigors of an expedition, and a standard diet contains much more vitamins than are required. Any excess is simply excreted in the urine. Excess vitamin A and D—possibly others—are definitely harmful.

FLUID BALANCE AT ALTITUDE

Almost everyone is dehydrated at high altitudes as the result of inadequate fluid intake and increased fluid losses. This problem is discussed under Fluid Balance in Chapter Two, "Basic Medical Care and Evacuation."

ACKNOWLEDGMENTS
The author has relied heavily on Dr. Herb Hultgren's earlier version of this chapter, and this distinguished high altitude physiologist and physician will still recognize much of his own work. The author also, over the years, has relied on numerous conversations with his good friend and co-investigator Dr. Peter Hackett. Along with all those who have an interest in high altitude physiology and altitude disorders, he is deeply indebted to Dr. Charles Houston.

ADDITIONAL READING
Hackett PH, Rennie D, Levine HD: The incidence, importance and prophylaxis of acute mountain sickness. *Lancet* 1976;2:1149.
Hackett PH, Roach RC, Sutton JR: High Altitude Medicine, in Auerbach PS and Geehr EC, eds.: *Management of Wilderness and Environmental Emergencies, Second Edition.* St. Louis, CV Mosby, 1989, pp 1–34.
Houston C: *Going Higher: The Story of Man and Altitude.* New York, C.S. Houston and American Alpine Club, 1983.
Houston C, Dickinson J: Cerebral form of high altitude illness. *Lancet* 1975;2:758.
Hultgren HN: Treatment and prevention of high altitude pulmonary edema. *Amer Alpine J* 1965;14:363.
Mosso A: *Life of Man on the High Alps.* Kiesow E, trans. London, T. Fisher Unwin, 1908.
Rennie D: The great breathlessness mountains. *JAMA* 1986;256:81.
Rennie D: Will mountain trekkers have heart attacks? *JAMA* 1989;261:1045.
Sutton J, Houston C, et al: Effect of acetazolamide on hypoxemia during sleep at high altitude. *New Eng J Med* 1979;201:1329.
West JB: Human physiology at extreme altitudes on Mount Everest. *Science* 1984;223:784.
West JB, Lahiri S, Gill M, et al: Arterial oxygen saturation during exercise at high altitude. *J Appl Physiol* 1962;17:617.

Editor's note: Since this chapter was completed, an investigation of the effectiveness of nifedipine for preventing high altitude pulmonary edema and an editorial on that subject have been published, as has an investigation of the effectiveness of the Gamow Bag for treating acute mountain sickness. Following are citations to those publications and an older publication about nifedipine:

Bartsch P, Maggiorini M, Ritter M, et al: Prevention of high-altitude pulmonary edema by nifedipine. *New Eng J Med* 1991;325:1284.

Oelz O, Maggiorini M, Ritter M, et al: Nifedipine for high altitude pulmonary oedema. *Lancet* 1989;2:1241.

Reeves JT, Schoene RB: When lungs on mountains leak: Studying pulmonary edema at high altitudes. *New Eng J Med* 1991;325:1306.

Robertson JA, Schlim DR: Treatment of moderate acute mountain sickness with pressurization in a portable hyperbaric chamber (Gamow™) Bag. *J Wild Med* 1991;2:268.

CHAPTER TWENTY-TWO

COLD INJURIES

The common disorders produced by cold are hypothermia and frostbite. Hypothermia is a decrease in the core temperature of the body that impairs intellectual, muscular, and cardiac function. Frostbite is a localized injury characterized by freezing of the tissues. Preventing and treating these disorders requires knowledge of the way heat is lost or gained and the body's responses to cold.

MECHANISMS OF HEAT EXCHANGE

Heat is lost or gained from the environment by four routes:

- Radiation
- Evaporation
- Convection
- Conduction

Radiation

Radiation, by far the largest source of heat loss in temperate climates, is a form of direct energy emission, much as infrared radiation. Heat is exchanged directly with the environment and can be quantitated by the formula:

$$J_Q = EK(T_S^4 - T_A^4)$$

in which J_Q = heat gain or loss; E = emissivity, which varies with skin color; K = Stefan-Boltzmann constant; T_S = skin surface temperature; and T_A = air temperature. As this formula indicates, heat loss is determined by the difference in temperature between the skin and the atmosphere or surrounding objects such as rocks, trees, snow, or ice (fig. 22-1). Radiant heat loss increases as the environment grows colder.

In an environment that is warmer than the skin surface temperature (about 95°F, or 35°C), radiant heat is absorbed by the body. The inability to lose heat by radiation in such environments can contribute to heat illness.

Clothing has little effect on heat loss by radiation. The heat radiates from the body to the clothing and from there to the atmosphere. Efforts to develop clothing

RADIATION

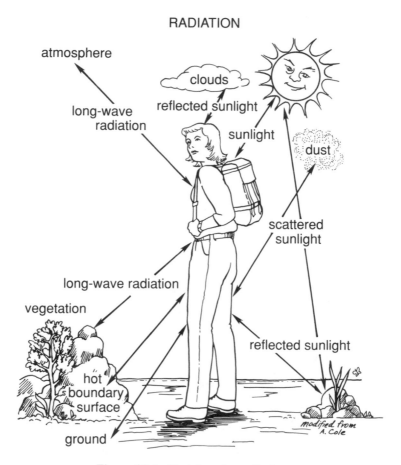

Figure 22-1. Heat loss by radiation.

materials that reflect heat back to the body have met with little success. However, radiant heat loss becomes a major problem only in extremely cold situations (below −20° to −30°F or −29° to −35°C). If clothing adequately limits heat loss by other routes, particularly convection, the body can compensate for the increased radiant heat loss encountered in most cold wilderness environments.

Evaporation

Perspiration is continuously being produced in small amounts, even in cold climates. This "insensible" perspiration evaporates from the skin, extracting approximately 575 calories of heat for each cubic centimeter lost. Additional heat is lost from the respiratory passages as inspired air is warmed to body temperature and moistened to 100 percent relative humidity. In temperate conditions, twenty to thirty percent of all heat loss results from evaporation, about two-thirds of which takes place on the skin.

Heat and water losses from the lungs become much greater at high elevations, where breathing is deeper and more rapid to compensate for the lower quantity of oxygen in the atmosphere. As much as four liters of water and 2,300 kilocalories (1,000 calories = 1 kilocalorie, or 1 Calorie) of heat can be lost daily through the lungs at high altitudes.

Heat loss from the respiratory tract can not be reduced in any practical manner. Mouth breathing increases fluid and heat loss somewhat, but the amount is insignificant in comparison with the quantity of heat lost through other sources. Outdoor enthusiasts must be aware that this heat and water loss is occurring, must eat enough food to regenerate the heat, and must drink enough liquids to replace the water.

Heat loss from insensible perspiration also can not be effectively limited. Vapor barrier systems, which consist of a layer of material impermeable to water vapor (usually plastic) between layers of insulation, have been tried. Since the barrier prevents water vapor loss, the air beneath the barrier quickly becomes saturated, perspiration can not evaporate, and heat loss by that route should be eliminated. However, perspiration does not cease, and the clothing underneath the barrier becomes saturated with water. Wet clothing is hazardous because it no longer limits convective heat loss, and evaporative heat loss is greatly increased.

No vapor barrier system works well at temperatures above freezing because too much water accumulates. Even at lower temperatures the only vapor barrier system widely used is in footwear (Korean, or "Mickey Mouse," boots.) Although such boots do keep feet warm, application of antiperspirants to the feet and frequent sock changes are needed to avoid injury by perpetual wetness.

Convection

Air in contact with skin is warmed to the skin's temperature. When the warmed air is displaced, cool air that replaces it is also warmed. Since the heat that warms the air comes from the skin, body heat is lost as the warmed air moves away.

Convective heat loss is an almost continuous process, but the amount of heat required to warm air (the specific heat of air) is so small that little heat is lost by this route in temperate climates. In a cold atmosphere, convective heat loss is greater because more heat is required to warm the colder air. However, the greatest convective heat losses occur when the air is moving. Even a mild breeze greatly increases heat loss because the layer of warm air next to the skin is constantly being replaced with cooler air.

The amount of heat extracted by moving air increases as the square of the velocity, not in direct proportion to its speed. A wind of eight miles an hour removes four times as much heat, not twice as much, as a wind of four miles an hour. A strong wind can remove tremendous amounts of heat.

The increased heat loss that occurs with moving air is called "wind chill." The accompanying chart (table 22-1) illustrates the additional cooling produced by wind in a cold environment. For instance, a temperature that poses little threat in still air, such as 15°F (−9.5°C), can be life-threatening in a wind of 20 to 25 miles

TABLE 22-1.
Wind Chill Chart

WIND (MPH) (KPH)	EQUIVALENT TEMPERATURE (DEGREES FAHRENHEIT) (DEGREES CELSIUS)													
CALM	35	30	25	20	15	10	5	0	-5	-10	-15	-20	-25	-30
	2	-1	-4	-7	-9	-12	-15	-18	-21	-23	-26	-29	-32	-34
5 MPH	33	27	21	16	12	7	1	-6	-11	-15	-20	-26	-31	-35
8 KPH	1	-3	-6	-9	-11	-14	-17	-21	-24	-26	-29	-32	-35	-37
10 MPH	21	16	9	2	-2	-9	-15	-22	-27	-31	-38	-45	-52	-58
16 KPH	-6	-9	-13	-17	-19	-23	-26	-30	-33	-35	-39	-43	-47	-50
15 MPH	16	11	1	-6	-11	-18	-25	-33	-40	-45	-51	-60	-65	-70
23 KPH	-9	-12	-17	-21	-24	-28	-32	-36	-40	-43	-46	-51	-54	-57
20 MPH	12	3	-4	-9	-17	-24	-32	-40	-46	-52	-60	-68	-76	-81
32 KPH	-11	-16	-20	-23	-27	-31	-36	-40	-43	-47	-51	-56	-60	-63
25 MPH	7	0	-7	-15	-22	-29	-37	-45	-52	-58	-67	-75	-83	-89
40 KPH	-14	-18	-22	-26	-30	-34	-38	-43	-47	-50	-55	-59	-64	-67
30 MPH	5	-2	-11	-18	-26	-33	-41	-49	-56	-63	-70	-78	-87	-94
48 KPH	-15	-19	-24	-28	-32	-36	-41	-45	-51	-53	-57	-61	-66	-70
35 MPH	3	-4	-13	-20	-27	-35	-43	-52	-60	-67	-72	-83	-90	-98
56 KPH	-16	-20	-25	-31	-33	-37	-42	-47	-51	-55	-58	-64	-68	-72
40 MPH	1	-4	-15	-22	-29	-36	-45	-54	-62	-69	-76	-87	-94	-101
64 KPH	-17	-16	-26	-30	-34	-38	-43	-48	-52	-56	-60	-66	-70	-74

per hour (32 to 40 kilometers per hour).

Because convective heat loss can increase so enormously, it is the major cause of terrestrial hypothermia in the wilderness. Fortunately, clothing can greatly reduce this type of heat loss. Insulating clothing such as down or wool forms myriads of small pockets in which air is trapped—the essence of thermal insulation. Windproof outer garments prevent displacement of the air within and between layers of clothing.

Convection also is a major route of heat loss in cold water. The water next to the skin extracts heat and is warmed, but any movement, such as swimming, displaces the warmed water, which is replaced by more cold water. Because the specific heat of water is so high, tremendous amounts of heat can be lost through convection, much more than can be generated by physical activity, even by strong, excellently conditioned swimmers. Individuals accidentally immersed in cold water can stay warmer by holding still to reduce water movement and limit heat loss than they can by swimming to generate heat. (Unless the shore or a boat is a very short distance away, active swimming should be avoided.) Positions that limit the area of the body surface exposed to water also help reduce heat loss. Two or more persons should huddle together to limit their contact with water (fig. 22–2).

Figure 22-2. Methods for reducing the body surface area exposed to cold water.

Conduction

Heat is conducted from the body when it is in contact with water, snow, rocks, or any cold object that is a good conductor. Air is not a good conductor. Water is an excellent conductor, and conductive heat loss is a major contributor to hypothermia during immersion in cold water.

Conductive heat losses can become significant in the wilderness when a person is seated or lying on ice, snow, or a cold rock. One cause of conductive heat loss is lying or sleeping on the ground without adequate insulation. Foam pads eliminate most of the conductive heat loss by this route. (Air mattresses, which allow air to circulate freely, provide less insulation than foam pads.) Although conductive heat loss alone is rarely a major cause of hypothermia, heat loss by this route can aggravate large convective heat losses and should be avoided.

Conductive heat losses can become large when clothing is wet.

PHYSIOLOGIC LIMITATION OF HEAT LOSS

Physiologic mechanisms for limiting heat loss are largely limited to constriction of blood vessels in the skin and in the arms and legs. (Humans evolved in a tropical climate, and the body's mechanisms for increasing heat loss are much better developed than those for reducing heat loss.) Vasoconstriction reduces cutaneous blood flow, which allows the tissues to cool. Since the skin temperature is lower, less heat is lost by radiation and by convection.

As a result of their long, narrow shape, the arms and legs have a greater relative surface area than the body and tend to lose heat more readily. The narrowing of blood vessels in the extremities reduces blood flow and heat loss and also tends to keep the heart and brain supplied with warm blood so they can function after the rest of the body has become significantly chilled.

PREVENTING HYPOTHERMIA

A human's greatest protection against the cold is his intellect. At ambient temperatures below about 82°F (28°C), an unclothed human body loses more heat to the environment than its heat-generating processes can produce and its heat-preserving mechanisms can retain. Almost everywhere they live, humans are dependent upon intellectually devised clothing and shelter to insulate them from the environment and reduce heat loss to levels for which metabolism and physiology can compensate.

Informed, intelligent behavior is even more essential in the severe cold of high altitudes and high latitudes. Threatening situations must be recognized in time for effective countermeasures; preparation is even more essential. Clothing adequate for such climates can rarely be improvised. Even when available, such clothing must be worn properly. Shelter often can be improvised, but a skier with a snow shovel is far more capable of improvising a satisfactory shelter than a skier without one.

Water and Food

Avoiding hypothermia in a cold climate requires water, food, and clothing. Failure to replace normal water losses through the kidneys, skin, and lungs, or abnormal losses by other routes, results in dehydration, which decreases the blood volume and, in a cold environment, impairs heat production by exercise. Dehydration can be accompanied by weakness, fatigue, dizziness, and even a tendency to faint when standing, which impede efforts to deal rationally with a threatening environment.

Dehydration contributes to other problems. Constriction of peripheral blood vessels so that more of the smaller volume of blood goes to vital organs increases the risk of frostbite. Severe shock may develop following minor injuries. Clots tend to form in the legs and can result in pulmonary embolism. (See Chapter Ten, "Respiratory System Disorders.")

In a dehydrated state the sensation of thirst is diminished or absent, and a conscious effort to consume adequate fluids must be made. With mild exertion, water intake should be at least two quarts per day; with heavier exertion or at high altitudes, three to five quarts are needed. In a world of snow and ice, fuel is required to melt snow for drinking water. Eating snow does not provide an adequate volume of water, and body heat is lost in warming ingested snow to body temperature.

An adequate fluid intake is indicated by urine that has a light yellow color and a volume of at least one liter every twenty-four hours. Few wilderness users would measure urine volume, but they should be able to appreciate a reduced frequency for voiding, particularly the absence of a need to void after a night's sleep. They certainly can recognize the deep yellow or orange color of concentrated urine indicative of dehydration. When voiding into snow, orange "snow flowers" are an ominous sign.

Food is needed for physical activity and heat production. Eating small amounts of food at frequent intervals helps prevent depletion of energy stores during the day. Experienced outdoor enthusiasts often seem to be munching almost continuously and have developed mixtures of nuts, dried fruits, candies, and other high-calorie food known by names such as "gorp" or "trail mix."

In a survival situation, experience has demonstrated that food is one of the most important ingredients of success. Any source of food, even wild animals such as birds or rodents, which may have to be eaten uncooked, is preferable to the fatigue and depression that result from not eating and that can contribute significantly to hypothermia.

Clothing

Clothing for cold climates must not only protect from the cold, it must be able to compensate for changes in temperature and heat production. The best clothing systems are composed of multiple layers. The outer layers can be opened or removed when the environmental temperature or heat production increases; additional layers can be added as the temperature falls or the person becomes inactive.

In a multilayered clothing system each succeeding layer must be larger than the one beneath. If the layers are the same size, the outer layers compress the deeper layers and reduce their insulation value. Each layer must be large enough to provide a quarter-inch air space between it and the layer beneath. The outer layer should be windproof.

Sweating must be avoided. Sweat moistens the clothing, greatly reducing its insulation value, and more heat is lost as the perspiration evaporates. The outer layers must be opened or taken off as soon as activity begins, not after the individual has become hot and begun to perspire. These layers must be put back on or closed as soon as activity ceases, not after the individual has become cold and requires more heat to warm him again.

Clothing Materials

Wool is the oldest and one of the best insulating materials for cold-weather clothing. It is one of the few materials that maintains its insulating properties when wet. Its only disadvantage is its somewhat greater weight.

Goose down is the best available insulating material for its weight—when it is dry. When wet, down mats together and loses most of its insulating properties. However, when precipitation is in the form of dry snow, which is typical of high altitudes, down is the insulating material of choice.

The various polyester fibers provide insulation similar to down and retain their insulating properties when wet. Their disadvantages are their greater weight (about fifty percent heavier) and their bulk or lack of compressibility.

Polypropylene provides a greater sensation of warmth because it transports moisture from the skin to the surface of the fabric, where it evaporates without cooling the skin. To be effective, polypropylene undergarments must be worn next to the skin, not over cotton underwear. Polypropylene retains most of its insulating properties when wet.

When the body is cooled, the blood vessels in the hands and feet constrict, reducing heat loss through those tissues, but also reducing their temperature and commonly causing severe discomfort. The most effective way to prevent cold extremities is to keep the body warm, a lesson some wilderness users seem to have great difficulty learning.

For the hands, mittens are much warmer than gloves. Radiant heat is lost from the surface of protective garments; the larger the surface area, the more heat that is lost. Because the fingers are such narrow cylinders, increasing the thickness of gloves to more than one-quarter inch increases the surface area to such an extent that the increased heat loss eliminates any benefit from the increased insulation. Because mittens do not have such a large relative surface area, their thickness can be increased to a much greater extent without a concomitant increase in heat loss.

One of the warmest types of footgear yet devised is the U.S. Army double vapor barrier boot known as the white Korean boot. However, this type of footwear is too soft for kicking steps in hard snow and is difficult to fit with crampons. For the severely cold climates typical of high altitudes, double or triple boots are best for climbers. The outer boot is usually constructed of hard, protective plastic, and the inner boots are made of softer insulating material. Older double boots were made of leather, which is entirely adequate but is heavier than plastic. Leather "breathes," which allows moisture to escape, and leather can expand to accommodate the swelling of feet and ankles due to an upright position or altitude. It remains the best material for single boots in moderately cold climates.

The voluminous blood flow to the head is a potential source of major heat loss. In cold weather, effective headgear, such as wool caps, is essential. Balaclavas that cover the neck and lower face are desirable for severe conditions. Hoods do not fit closely enough to be as effective, but do provide additional protection when worn over caps, particularly if the hood is insulated.

RECOGNIZING HYPOTHERMIA

Hypothermia can usefully be divided into two forms: mild and severe. A person with mild hypothermia has a body temperature that is lower than normal but is not so incapacitated that he can not stand or walk with assistance. Usually his temperature is above 90°F (32°C).

A person with severe hypothermia is intellectually impaired, usually can not walk, and may be unconscious. His body temperature is typically below 90° (32°C), although the temperature at which such severe impairment appears varies significantly (table 22-2).

TABLE 22-2.
Stages of Hypothermia

Mild Hypothermia

98°–95° *(37°–35°C)*	Sensation of chilliness, skin numbness; minor impairment in muscular performance, particularly in fine movements with the hands; shivering begins.
95°–93°F *(35°–34°C)*	More obvious incoordination and weakness; stumbling; slow pace; mild confusion and apathy.
93°–90°F *(34°–32°C)*	Gross incoordination with frequent stumbling, falling, and inability to use hands; mental sluggishness with slow thought and speech ; retrograde amnesia.

Severe Hypothermia

90°–86°F *(32°–30°C)*	Cessation of shivering; severe incoordination with stiffness and inability to walk or stand; incoherence, confusion, irrationality.
86°–82°F *(30°–28°C)*	Severe muscular rigidity; semiconsciousness; dilatation of pupils; inapparent heart beat or respirations.
Below 82°F *(Below 28°C)*	Unconsciousness; eventually death due to cessation of heart action at temperatures approximating 68°F (20°C) or below.

Temperature is not a practical basis for recognizing severe hypothermia in the wilderness because obtaining a temperature is so difficult. Profoundly hypothermic individuals usually have their jaws so tightly clamped that oral measurements are impossible. Rescue personnel uniformly refuse to try rectal measurements, particularly in a threatening environment. Such reluctance is probably fortunate, because moving the individual to take such measurements would precipitate ventricular fibrillation (see below) much of the time.

Mild Hypothermia

The key to early recognition of mild hypothermia is awareness of the risk of hypothermia and the speed with which it can develop. Even in the summer, cold, wet conditions can be dangerous, particularly when a wind is blowing. Anyone who is physically active and generating heat but still feels cold, must realize he is going to become even colder when that activity ceases. If he can not produce enough heat to warm himself while exercising, he certainly can not do so when resting and must have more clothing or shelter to provide protection from the environment or an external heat source.

Close observation of one another by members of a group is a vital element of hypothermia prevention. Every member of a party must be responsible for observing everyone else.

Feeling cold is the most typical early symptom of hypothermia. Painfully cold hands or feet are common. As body temperature continues to fall, muscular coordination is lost. Fine movements can not be performed with the hands, but if the individual is walking and not using his hands, such loss may not be detectable. The first sign of incoordination may be slowing of pace or stumbling, particularly on rough ground or loose rocks. As hypothermia becomes more severe, stumbling becomes worse and the individual may fall. Characteristically he lags behind, which should provide an unmistakable warning for the rest of his group. If he is left unattended, subsequent deterioration in his condition will go unobserved. Shivering, which usually appears when body temperature has dropped two to four degrees, may further impair his ability to walk over rough terrain.

The intellect is also impaired as hypothermia develops. Personality changes, particularly irritability, are typical. A common early sign is refusal to admit that anything is wrong. Some individuals are apathetic and unconcerned about their deteriorating condition. Mental sluggishness may be manifested by slow thought and speech. Confusion and retrograde amnesia subsequently indicate a greater decline in body temperature.

A mnemonic for remembering the signs of mild hypothermia is "umbles." The person fumbles, mumbles and grumbles, stumbles and tumbles. At this point the presence of hypothermia should be obvious, unless the other members of the group are hypothermic also. Failure to institute corrective measures can result in progression to severe hypothermia.

Severe Hypothermia

Severe hypothermia should be defined by the person's condition, not by a specific body temperature. However, the signs typical of severe hypothermia usually appear when body temperature has fallen to about 90°F (32°C) or below.

As body temperature approaches this level, shivering gradually disappears, an easily recognizable indicator of severe hypothermia. Muscular incoordination becomes so severe that the individual usually can not walk without assistance. As his temperature drops further, he becomes unable to even stand without support.

Intellectual impairment is greater, but the impairment may be subtle. A common and important sign of severe hypothermia is neglect or carelessness about protection from the cold. Coats and pants are left unzipped; hoods are not pulled up; caps or mittens are not worn. Sleeping bags or blankets are not snug around the head; fires are neglected. Individuals who seemed to be acting quite sensibly have made gross errors in judgment that have caused problems for an entire group. A pattern typical of hypothermia is that an individual appears to be capable of cooperating with other members of the group but does not do so.

Eventually confusion and irrationality progress to incoherence, semiconsciousness, and finally total unconsciousness and a failure to respond to any stimuli.

As a subject begins to lose consciousness, he may develop a sensation of extreme warmth and, if unattended, may actually remove his clothing or climb out of a sleeping bag. Such bizarre behavior is not uncommon, and its occurrence in urban surroundings has aroused suspicion that the person has been assaulted, particularly when the person has been female. Sometimes the individual's clothing has been neatly folded, an unlikely occurrence during an assault.

As the severely hypothermic individual's mental function deteriorates, his other body functions also slow drastically. A comatose subject's breathing may be so slow and shallow that it appears absent. His heart rate slows dramatically and can become so weak that it can not be palpated.

Unquestionably, a number of individuals with severe hypothermia, but who were actually still alive, have been pronounced dead and have been denied medical assistance. In the wilderness, few hypothermic individuals should be declared dead unless their measured body temperature has fallen to environmental levels. Only after unsuccessful rewarming can death be certain.

No one should be considered cold and dead until he has been warm and dead!!!

TREATING MILD HYPOTHERMIA

The treatment of mild hypothermia is simple. Recognizing its presence is much more critical.

Decreasing heat loss by convection can be achieved by putting on more clothing: sweaters, caps, mittens, jackets, parkas, windpants, or whatever is available. Protection from the wind by parkas or windpants, rocks or trees, natural shelters such as caves or even crevasses, or manmade shelters such as cabins or snow caves reduces convective heat loss, or "wind chill." Replacing wet clothing with dry clothing restores insulation and reduces evaporative heat loss. The warmer environment provided by a fire—or just body heat within a windproof shelter—reduces radiant heat loss.

Heat production can be increased significantly. Shivering is an involuntary muscle activity that generates heat at a rate equivalent to walking fast. Much more heat can be generated by vigorously exercising the large muscles in the legs and back. Such exercise is even more useful if it helps a hypothermic person get out of a hostile environment. However, if escape from the predicament is not possible, then purposeless exercise, such as repeatedly stepping up onto a stone or log, can generate heat. A metabolic energy source—food—is needed if increased heat production is to be maintained.

Heat-producing exercise can not be continued indefinitely. Nor can enough heat be produced by exercise to compensate for the large quantity of heat lost in cold water or in a snowstorm if the individual is inadequately protected.

Once hypothermia has been corrected, measures to prevent its recurrence are essential. Obviously, returning a rewarmed person to the same environment with no additional protection would have the same result. Hypothermia would probably recur even faster because his energy stores would have been depleted.

TREATING SEVERE HYPOTHERMIA

Severe hypothermia is a complex disorder for which the simple measures that effectively treat mild hypothermia are inadequate. Two major problems must be managed. Ventricular fibrillation must be avoided while the individual is being rewarmed with external heat sources.

Ventricular Fibrillation

Ventricular fibrillation is a life-threatening condition in which the thousands of muscle fibers that make up the heart contract independently. Since all of the muscle fibers must contract together for the cardiac chambers to squeeze out blood, no blood is pumped when the fibers are not synchronized. The effect would be the same if the heart were not beating at all.

The hypothermic heart is extremely prone to ventricular fibrillation. It has appropriately been compared to a mouse trap, ready to snap with the slightest bump or jolt—often without a recognizable precipitating event. Individuals have begun fibrillating in hospital emergency rooms even though the possibility of that event was well recognized and every effort to avoid it was being made.

Severely hypothermic individuals can not be placed in a basket stretcher and carried out of the wilderness. The unavoidable jarring and bouncing associated with evacuation over rough terrain would almost inevitably provoke fibrillation. Although profound hypothermia prolongs the time an individual can survive the absence of effective blood circulation without sustaining significant neurologic damage, that time is limited to about one hour.

A severely hypothermic individual in ventricular fibrillation who can not be evacuated by helicopter, or in less than an hour by stretcher, is in a hopeless situation. He must receive CPR to avoid neurologic damage, but CPR can not be administered while he is being carried on a stretcher. Cardioversion (defibrillation with electrical shocks) is almost never effective until the heart has been warmed to about 90°F (32°C).

Individuals with severe hypothermia in the wilderness must either be evacuated by helicopter or rewarmed on the spot. Leaders of major rescue organizations have realized that essentially none of the severely hypothermic individuals carried out of the wilderness by hand without rewarming have survived. They now try to rewarm such individuals where they are found.

Rewarming

Severely hypothermic persons require external heat sources for rewarming because their metabolism is slowed to such a low level that they can not generate enough heat to rewarm themselves, unless they are well-protected from the environment.

Theoretically, the most effective rewarming methods would rewarm the core of the body first—"central rewarming." Since the heart would be among the first tissues rewarmed, it would be protected from fibrillation. In hospitals, central rewarming can be achieved with heated peritoneal or pleural dialysis fluids, heated gastric lavage, or heart-lung machines for individuals without effective cardiac function.

However, experience has demonstrated that central rewarming is not essential for most individuals who have functioning hearts. Hospitals in which hypothermia is a common problem, such a those in Anchorage, Alaska, rely primarily on external rewarming with recirculating water mattresses or electrical heating blankets. Heated, humidified gases (aerosols) provide some central rewarming, but the amount of heat transported by such systems is quite small.

The development of wilderness rewarming techniques has met with limited success, but the need for such rewarming has only recently been recognized. Three general procedures are currently followed:

- Protection from the environment
- External rewarming
- Central rewarming

Protection from the environment can be achieved by placing the individual in a tent and in a sleeping bag. To avoid moving the individual and precipitating ventricular fibrillation, a hole can be cut in the floor of the tent before it is set up over the subject. An insulating pad should be gently slipped under him, and he can be carefully slid into a sleeping bag. (The sleeping bag only protects the person; his body is producing so little heat that the sleeping bag does not rewarm him.) The air within the tent can be warmed and humidified by boiling water on portable stoves.

External rewarming transfers so little heat that all available techniques must be employed. Folded sheets or blankets soaked in hot water and placed in plastic bags, hot-water bottles, or similar warming devices placed along the sides of the neck, chest, abdomen, and in the inguinal areas, where the body wall is thin, is one of the more effective methods. (Obviously, if enough warming instruments are available, they can be placed anywhere.)

Placing a normothermic individual in the sleeping bag with a hypothermic person transfers a minimal amount of heat through body-to-body contact.

Now that the need for rewarming in the wilderness has been recognized, the development of more effective techniques can be anticipated. Perhaps a small, gasoline-driven electrical generator could be used to power warming devices.

Central rewarming can also be achieved in a wilderness situation but requires specific equipment and individuals familiar with the techniques. Nonetheless, some methods are simple, and proficient individuals should be members of cold-weather rescue teams.

The most widely used method employs heated air saturated with water vapor. The quantity of heat carried by the air is quite small, because so little heat is required to raise the temperature of air (fig. 22-3). Furthermore, the depth and rate of respirations are greatly reduced with severe hypothermia, and the volume of inhaled air is less than half of normal. However, physicians who have used this system consider the benefits greater than can be explained by the small amount of heat the system is capable of transferring.

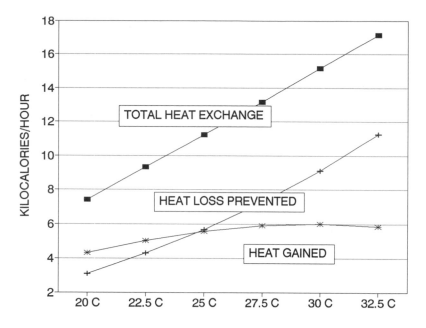

Figure 22-3. Maximum calculated heat exchange (heat gained and heat loss prevented) from inhaling a humidified aerosol heated to 104°F (40°C) at an environmental temperature of 5°F (–15°C). Actual heat exchange would be lower. (Respiratory tidal volume assumed to be 2.0 1/min, 2.5 1/min, 3.0 1/min, 3.5 1/min, 4.0 1/min, and 4.5 1/min at core temperatures of 20°C, 22.5°C, 25°C, 27.5°C, 30°C, and 32.5°C.

The air must be saturated with water or the evaporation of water from the respiratory tract would extract more heat from the body than the heated air could supply. Most of the heat transferred to the body results from condensation of the water vapor. In a cold wilderness environment, a heated aerosol also eliminates the small heat loss from the respiratory tract.

If an endotracheal tube is inserted and the individual is ventilated at a normal volume of five to six liters per minute, the heat gain does increase. However, the tubing must be modified to increase "dead space" and carbon dioxide retention in order to avoid severe respiratory alkalosis, which also predisposes to ventricular fibrillation. At altitudes above 10,000 feet (3,000 meters) heated, humidified oxygen may be more useful.

Severely hypothermic individuals are inevitably dehydrated, and all benefit from correction of the dehydration. Since most are unable to ingest fluids orally, rehydration fluids must be given intravenously. If two liters of rehydration fluids were heated to 104°F (40°C) and administered over a period of two hours to an individual with a temperature of 77°F (25°C), 30 Kcal (kilocalories) of heat per hour would be transferred to the subject. The peripheral veins of a dehydrated, severely hypothermic person are collapsed, and accessing a vein requires experience.

Gastric lavage—introducing heated fluids through a tube inserted into the stomach and replacing the fluids as they cool—is a technique for central rewarming that has been employed in hospitals. Since this technique is simple and is associated with little risk of significant complications, it could be adapted for use outside of the hospital.

Other techniques are being explored. Norwegian investigators are evaluating a system in which the hands and feet are warmed. These tissues, which have a generous blood supply close to the surface, serve as "heat exchangers." Initial results are encouraging, but investigation is incomplete.

In a hospital, the temperature of severely hypothermic individuals being rewarmed with noninvasive techniques increases at a rate of 0.9°F to 2.7°F (0.5°C to 1.5°C) per hour. In the wilderness, rewarming would be slower. Rescuers must be prepared to spend many hours—perhaps one or more days—rewarming a person before moving him. Stoves and abundant fuel for heating water must be available so heating devices can be renewed as they cool.

Cardiopulmonary Resuscitation (CPR)

CPR is essential for profoundly hypothermic subjects who have no effective blood circulation, and who can survive for only about an hour without sustaining significant neurologic damage, particularly when evacuation is prolonged. However, the probability of success is so limited that any risks to rescuers or other members of the party can not be justified. CPR should be initiated in the wilderness only by a team of experienced individuals in a safe, relatively protected environment. If a hostile environment poses a major threat to the team, CPR should be postponed or abandoned entirely.

Individuals with a detectable heartbeat, no matter how slow, should not receive CPR or assisted ventilation because ventricular fibrillation would almost certainly result. Three minutes or longer should be spent trying to detect a carotid pulse before assuming a severely hypothermic person has no effective cardiac activity.

A portable EKG monitor or similar device to detect cardiac activity in subjects with severe hypothermia may be necessary, and such units should probably be carried by rescue groups. (In a wilderness environment, portable EKG monitors can not be relied upon for distinguishing between abnormalities such as asystole, ventricular fibrillation, or baseline artifacts, but do reliably indicate presence of a heartbeat by portraying QRS complexes.) Hypothermic subjects with a functioning heart commonly have a reduced blood pressure, and blood pressure measurement may be further hindered by the absence of Korotkoff sounds.

CPR should be given at one-half the usual rate to severely hypothermic persons. Such individuals have such a slow metabolism that they need limited amounts of oxygen and are producing little carbon dioxide. A slower rate of ventilation avoids excessive carbon dioxide loss and respiratory alkalosis. A slower rate of cardiac compression provides a longer interval for the heart to be filled with blood by the slow circulation.

CPR should be instituted immediately following a witnessed cardiac arrest or fibrillation, particularly when transportation to a hospital is expected to require more than a few minutes. CPR probably should be administered for individuals with unwitnessed cardiac arrest who appear resuscitatable, but each situation can be expected to be so unique that more definitive recommendations are not possible. CPR should not be initiated if the subject can be transported to a hospital in minutes.

CPR should not be initiated for fibrillating hypothermic subjects considered unsuitable for resuscitation due to their situation, or for individuals with extremely low body temperature, associated severe illness or injuries, a noncompressible chest, prolonged cardiac inactivity, or drowning with more than one hour of witnessed submersion.

The role of drugs in preventing fibrillation is unclear; perhaps no role exists. Bretyllium is the only antiarrhythmic drug demonstrated to be effective at low body temperatures. Anecdotal evidence indicates that lidocaine is not effective at body temperatures below 90°F (32°C). Other agents have not been evaluated.

FROSTBITE

Frostbite is a cold injury produced by freezing of the tissues. The hands and feet, the ears, and the face, particularly the tip of the nose, are most commonly injured. The hands and feet are farthest from the heart, and their blood supply is further reduced by vascular constriction when the body is cold. The ears are thin and have a meager blood supply; the rims are often frozen. Portions of the face, particularly the tip of the nose, are often exposed.

Constriction of blood vessels in the extremities to conserve heat for the central portions of the body can be so rigorous that circulation to those areas almost ceases. Cold also damages the endothelial cells that line blood vessels, causing plasma to leak through their walls. Loss of plasma causes the blood to sludge inside the vessels, further impairing circulation.

As circulation is diminished, the tissues begin to freeze. Ice crystals form within and between the cells and grow by extracting water from the cells. However, freezing does not necessarily kill cells. In laboratories, cells frozen for long periods of time can be thawed and grown in cultures.

The ultimate damage from frostbite results from the damage to vascular endothelial cells. When the tissues are warmed, blood exposed to these damaged cells clots and completely obstructs the circulation. The result is identical to the effects of thrombosis in arteriosclerotic arteries: the tissue supplied by that artery dies (is infarcted).

Prevention

Frostbite can occur in any environment in which the temperature is below freezing, but is usually associated with hypothermia. When a contributing condition can be identified, impaired circulation is most common. Immobility contributes to impairment of the circulation, particularly in soldiers under fire in wartime or in substance abusers, but boots that are too tight, or encircling, tightly fitting garments, are common offenders.

On rare occasions frostbite can result from unprotected contact with cold metal or liquids, most commonly gasoline or ethyl alcohol, that remain liquid at temperatures far below the freezing temperature of water.

Frostbite is best prevented by avoiding the conditions by which it is produced, particularly hypothermia. Clothing that keeps the trunk warm also keeps the extremities warm by eliminating the need for blood vessel constriction to preserve heat. "If your feet are cold, put on a sweater" is excellent advice. Also essential is footgear that does not constrict the circulation, such as the white Korean (or "Mickey Mouse") boot.

Cigarette smoking constricts the blood vessels in the skin and aggravates local cold injuries such as frostbite.

Diagnosis and Prognosis

The early signs of frostbite are cold and pain and pallor in the affected tissues. Some individuals suffer little pain, and pain disappears as the tissues begin to freeze. As freezing progresses, the tissues become even whiter and all sensation is lost. As frostbite extends deeper, the tissues become quite hard. With extensive frostbite, such as an entire hand or foot, the tissues often have a dull purple color.

Frostbite of the face, tip of the nose, or ears can be recognized by pain and the pallor of the affected tissues.

The extent and severity of frostbite are notoriously difficult to judge accurately while the tissues are still frozen or immediately after thawing. However, a few hours after thawing, prognostic signs begin to appear. Minor frostbite ("frostnip") that involves only the tips of the fingers or toes, the tip of the nose, or small areas of the face or ears produces redness and swelling that lasts for a few days but leaves no permanent damage.

With more severe injuries, blisters develop after rewarming and may cover entire digits. If the blisters contain clear fluid, the underlying tissues can be expected to recover. If the blisters do not cover the tips of the digit, the uncovered area usually will be lost. When the blisters are filled with bloody fluid, much of the underlying tissues can not recover. The most severe frostbite injuries are not followed by blisters and retain a deep purple color.

After a week or ten days the dead, frostbitten tissues develop a thick, black covering called an "eschar." Eventually, usually after four to six weeks, the dead tissue, including entire fingers or toes, separates spontaneously.

Treatment

The preferred treatment for frostbite is rapid rewarming in a water bath. However, opportunities for such therapy are rare because most frostbite injuries have thawed before the individual arrives at a site where rewarming can be performed. Climbers or cross-country skiers have to be evacuated before they can be rewarmed, and thawing of the frostbitten tissues during evacuation may be unavoidable. Individuals with frostbite in urban settings, who vastly outnumber those with frostbite in the wilderness, delay an average of twelve hours before seeking medical care.

Rewarming can be carried out best in a hospital, where the person can be kept warm and supplies for rewarming and later care are available. Treatment in a wilderness environment should be attempted only when the following conditions can be met:

- The person does not need to use the frostbitten extremity until healing is complete. Specifically, he does not need to walk on a foot that has been frostbitten and thawed. The greatest damage from frostbite occurs when frozen tissues are thawed and refrozen. Far less damage is produced by walking on a frozen foot.
- The person can be kept warm during rewarming and afterward for as long as recovery requires. If the person's body is cold, the blood vessels in his extremities will be constricted. Rewarming in such circumstances leaves badly injured tissues without an adequate blood supply at the time it is most needed.
- Adequate facilities for prompt rewarming, including abundant supplies of warm water and accurate methods for maintaining the temperature of the rewarming bath, are available.

Even if the frostbitten extremity has thawed, rewarming probably still has beneficial effects if administered within twenty-four hours of injury. After longer intervals, rapid rewarming has little or no benefit.

During rewarming the water temperature should be maintained between 100°F and 108°F (38°C and 42°C). Higher temperatures damage the tissues. The water must not feel uncomfortable to an uninjured person's hand. A large water bath permits more accurate temperature control and warms the frozen extremity more rapidly, often resulting in less tissue loss, particularly when freezing has been deep and extensive.

The extremity should be stripped of all clothing and any constricting bands, straps, or other objects that might impair the circulation. The injured member should be suspended in the center of the water bath and not permitted to rest against the side or bottom.

During rewarming, hot water must be added to the bath periodically to keep the temperature at the desired level. (A frozen hand or foot acts essentially like a block of ice and cools the water.) The injured extremity should be removed from the bath and not returned until the water has been thoroughly mixed and the temperature measured.

An open flame should not be used to keep the water warm. The frostbitten extremity may come in contact with the heated area and be seriously burned because sensation in the tissues has been lost.

Rewarming usually requires thirty to sixty minutes; it should be continued until the tissues are soft and pliable, or until no further changes in color are seen.

During rewarming, the frostbitten tissues usually are quite painful. Aspirin and codeine, morphine, or meperidine may be needed during or after rewarming for pain.

Following rewarming, the individual must be kept warm and the injured tissues must be elevated and protected from any kind of trauma or irritation. Bedclothes should be supported by a framework to avoid pressure or rubbing on the injured area. To avoid infection, blisters should not be ruptured.

The subject should be evacuated immediately. Healing requires weeks to months, depending upon the severity of the injury. Subsequent care in the field should be directed primarily toward preventing infection. Cleanliness of the frostbitten area is extremely important. Soaking the extremity in disinfected, lukewarm water to which a germicidal soap has been added may be helpful. A small amount of dry, sterile cotton or gauze should be placed between fingers or toes to avoid maceration. Antibiotics should not be given routinely, but if infection appears to be present, ampicillin or cloxacillin should be administered every six hours until a physician's care is obtained.

Smoking should be strictly prohibited because it reduces the already deficient blood supply to the damaged area. Movement of the extremities should be encouraged, but should be limited to movements that can be carried out without manipulation or assistance from others. Most individuals with frostbite need continuing reassurance and emotional support.

Surgery has little or no role in the immediate therapy for frostbite. Unfortunately, surgeons with no experience with this injury are occasionally so alarmed by the appearance of frostbitten extremities that they insist upon immediate amputation. Tragic mutilations have occurred; other individuals have refused amputation and recovered with minimal or no tissue loss.

With essentially no exceptions, surgery must be delayed until demarcation of the dead tissues is complete and unmistakable. At that time minor surgical debridement of infected eschars or incision of constricting eschars that completely surround a digit and are obstructing circulation may be needed. However, surgery is usually not required until long after the initial injury, and then only to complete the separation of frostbitten tissues or to reconstruct hands or feet. "Frozen in January; amputate in June" is a maxim that emphasizes the need to delay surgery as long as possible.

Individuals who have suffered frostbite usually have increased sensitivity to cold and are more susceptible to cold injury in previously frostbitten limbs because the blood vessels in these injured tissues have been permanently damaged.

TRENCH FOOT

Trench foot is a nonfreezing cold injury that in essence has been a problem only in military campaigns. In the 1982 Falkland Islands fighting, fourteen percent (70 of 516) of the hospitalized British battle casualties had trench foot. Only soldiers with the most severe trench foot injuries were hospitalized; estimates of the number with lesser injuries ranged as high as 2,000.

Trench foot results from wetness and cold that is uninterrupted for many days or weeks. The feet do not have to be immersed in water; simply being wet will produce the disorder. Symptoms rarely appear in less than four or five days, and even then only in severely cold, windy weather—as was encountered in the Falklands.

The disorder was first described during the Napoleonic campaigns, particularly the retreat from Moscow, but received its name during World War I from the men who spent weeks with their feet in the cold water that flooded the trenches. The British had more than 115,000 casualties from trench foot and frostbite in that conflict. Similar injuries in individuals who spent weeks with their feet in cold water in rafts or lifeboats after their ships had been sunk or their aircraft had crashed led to the name "immersion foot." Other names exist for this disorder, but trench foot is the most clearly and widely recognized.

The cold induces intense vasoconstriction, which deprives the feet of an adequate blood supply. (The separate roles of cold and poor circulation in producing injury have not been distinguished.) After five to seven days (or longer) the feet become red, swollen, and quite painful. British soldiers with trenchfoot in the Falklands screamed in pain when putting on their boots in the morning (although they stormed into battle anyway!).

Treatment is simple. It consists of keeping the subject warm with his feet dry, elevated, and protected from bedclothes. Nothing more. Nerve damage can cause persistent pain so severe that amputation is required, but such injuries are rare. The British had no immediate amputations in the Falklands. Sensitivity to cold is usually lifelong and can disqualify soldiers for continued military service.

Prevention of trench foot is also simple. World War I commanders ordered their troops to dry their feet and put on dry socks every day, which reduced their trench foot casualties to very low numbers, even though the men were returned immediately to flooded trenches.

Outdoor enthusiasts, particularly participants in water-based activities, must be aware of the potential for injury in wet, nonfreezing weather. They must carry dry socks and must take time to dry their feet, change their socks, and dry their boots. However, they should encounter many fewer distractions while attending to such precautions than do soldiers in combat.

CHAPTER TWENTY-THREE

HEAT AND SOLAR INJURIES

HEAT ILLNESS

Normal Heat Loss

Normal human body temperature is maintained within a narrow range by sensitive temperature control centers in the hypothalamic area of the brain that function like a thermostat. Heat produced within the body is dissipated to the environment so that a temperature between 97°F and 100°F (36°C and 38°C) is maintained.

Largely through muscular activity most individuals generate 2,000 to 5,000 kilocalories of heat per day; the rate depends upon their size, physical activity, and state of nutrition. The body must get rid of this heat to prevent an increase in its temperature that could have devastating effects. If no heat were lost, the body temperature of a relatively sedentary individual weighing 154 pounds (70 kilograms) producing only 2,000 kilocalories per day would climb approximately 62°F (34.4°C) to 160°F (71.4°C) in twenty-four hours. (The temperature would climb at that rate as long as he was alive!)

Humans lose heat largely through their skin. Although the lungs are the principal route of heat loss (panting) for hairy animals, and at high altitudes deeper, more rapid breathing of cold, relatively dry air causes significant heat loss in humans, in temperate or hot climates much less heat is lost through the lungs.

The skin acts much like the radiator of a liquid-cooled engine. Blood is warmed as it passes through exercising muscles, just as the liquid circulating around the cylinders of an engine is warmed. When the warmed blood circulates through the skin, heat is lost to the surrounding atmosphere, just as heat is lost from the radiator of an engine. The thermostat on the engine increases the flow of coolant through the radiator when the engine is hot; comparable mechanisms increase blood flow to the skin by dilating cutaneous blood vessels when exercise heats the body.

However, the radiator for an engine is cooled only by air passing over it. Heat is lost from the skin in this way (convection), but in a hot climate by far the largest heat loss from the skin is through the evaporation of perspiration. Evaporative skin cooling is highly effective because such a large amount of heat is required to change water from a liquid to a vapor. The evaporation of one cubic centimeter (1 cc) of water at a skin temperature of 95°F (35°C) requires 577 calories, enough to reduce the temperature of 1,000 cc of water approximately 1°F (or 577 cc of water 1°C). Most of this heat is extracted from the body through the skin.

Evaporative cooling is limited. The maximal sweating rate for individuals not acclimatized to heat is about 1,500 cc per hour. Evaporation of that much perspiration would eliminate the heat produced by running six miles at a pace of ten minutes per mile, which is not a particularly fast pace. Acclimatization takes about one week, results in an increased tolerance for exercise in a hot environment, and is produced by mechanisms that increase the maximum sweating rate but reduce salt loss. Water deprivation does not accelerate or contribute to the acclimatization process.

Exertional and Nonexertional Heat Illness

Heat illness results from the inability of the body to get rid of heat it has produced. Two distinct disorders have been identified. Exertional heat illness results from an increase in heat production so large that all of the heat can not be dissipated even though the heat-losing mechanisms are functioning well. Nonexertional heat illness results from impairment of heat-losing processes by disease and can occur even though heat production is low or normal.

Heat illnesses occurring in healthy individuals participating in vigorous wilderness activities would essentially all be exertional disorders, and nonexertional heat illness is not considered in this discussion.

The most common cause for an elevated body temperature (hyperthermia) is infection, and the increased temperature is called a fever. This form of hyperthermia results from a change in the body's temperature control mechanism that resets the "thermostat" at a higher level. Even though the best treatment is that needed for the underlying condition, a fever can be controlled with drugs such as aspirin. Such drugs have no effect upon the elevated temperature associated with heat illness.

Preventing Exertional Heat Illness

The only way exertional heat injuries can be prevented is by recognizing climatic conditions in which heat can not be dissipated and sharply curtailing physical activity. Those conditions are an environmental temperature of 95°F (35°C) or higher and a high relative humidity.

The average skin temperature is 95°F (35°C), slightly lower than core temperature. At environmental temperatures above this level heat can not be lost by convection because the air temperature is higher than skin temperature. Heat can not be lost by radiation because the environment is hotter than the skin surface. (Heat would be gained by radiation.) The only way heat can be lost in such circumstances is by evaporation. (Mechanisms of heat loss are described in Chapter Twenty-two, "Cold Injuries.")

In an atmosphere with a high relative humidity evaporation is greatly diminished, and heat can not be lost by that route. If the environmental temperature is greater than 95°F (35°C), heat can not be lost effectively by any route! In the southeastern United States, where hot, humid conditions are common in the summer, experienced residents know that a person dripping with perspiration is in danger of heat illness. If perspiration were evaporating and cooling him, it would not accumulate on his skin. To avoid heat illness, heat production must be reduced to the lowest possible level. Vigorous exercise must cease. In tropical areas, where temperatures and humidity are usually high, the midday siesta is a sensible way to minimize the risk of heat illness during the time when the threat is greatest.

The most frequent causes of exertional hyperthermia in the United States have been distance running (including jogging) and football practice in late summer, the latter combining vigorous physical activity, a uniform that inhibits evaporation of sweat, and a hot, often humid environment. Recognition of the hazard associated with these activities has led to scheduling them in the early morning, when temperatures are lower, and other modifications. Wearing plastic or rubberized suits while exercising in order to lose weight is another dangerous practice. Such suits increase body temperature, sometimes to high levels, because they do not allow perspiration to evaporate. Fortunately, this practice has been largely abandoned in recent years, probably more from the realization that only water—not fat—was being lost than from recognition of the danger of heat illness.

Water Replacement

Staggering quantities of water must be consumed to replace perspiration losses in desert conditions. In 1964, during U.S. Army maneuvers in the deserts of southern California, where daytime temperatures of 100°F to 110°F (38°C to 43°C) were expected, participants were required to drink eight quarts of water every day. Not a single case of heat illness occurred, which was considered almost miraculous at the time. Each Israeli soldier operating in the Sinai Desert during the 1967 war with Egypt was allotted ten liters of water a day. No heat illness, which is punished by court martial in that army, occurred among the Israelis; but the Egyptians, who received only three liters of water each per day, suffered many fatalities due to heat illness.

Thirst alone does not ensure an adequate fluid intake. Individuals must make a conscious effort to consume the quantities needed. During desert operations, military commanders are held responsible for ensuring that their men meet daily intake requirements. In the past, an augmented salt intake also has been considered essential for preventing heat illness. Soldiers in the California desert were required to take three to five grams of salt—six to ten tablets—every day. However, increased knowledge about daily salt requirements has led to abandoning that recommendation. The diet of residents of most developed nations contains enough salt for stressful heat conditions.

Heat Syncope and Heat Exhaustion

Heat illnesses range in severity from very mild to lethal. Typical patterns of illness have been given specific names, but the various types of heat injury must be recognized as different manifestations of the same basic disorder. Mild heat illnesses have the potential for becoming severe and must be treated with care.

Heat syncope and heat exhaustion are similar, relatively mild forms of heat illness to which dehydration contributes significantly. In an effort to increase heat loss the blood vessels in the skin dilate to such an extent that the blood supply to the brain is diminished. Reduction in blood volume by dehydration contributes to the lower cerebral blood flow. The result is a disorder essentially identical to ordinary fainting (syncope) except for its cause. Initially the subject feels faint and is usually aware of a rapid heart rate. Nausea, vomiting, headache, dizziness, restlessness, or even brief loss of consciousness are not uncommon. The presence of sweating and the skin color are variable.

These two disorders have been distinguished on the basis of body temperature, which is normal with syncope but elevated to 102°F to 104°F (39°C to 40°C) with heat exhaustion. (No sharp division between heat exhaustion and heat stroke is possible. Some physicians consider anyone with an elevated temperature and evidence of brain dysfunction, such as dizziness or brief unconsciousness, to have heat stroke—an approach that appears wise in view of the dire consequences of that disorder.)

Heat syncope should be treated just like fainting. If the individual recognizes preliminary symptoms, he should lie down, or at least sit down, to avoid injury. His feet should be elevated. He should try to get to a cooler environment and should at least be protected from direct sunlight. He should be given fluids, particularly fluids containing salt, and should not engage in vigorous activity for at least the rest of that day. Only after he has completely restored his body fluids and has a normal urine output should he cautiously resume exercise in a hot environment.

An individual with heat exhaustion should be treated in the same way, but his body temperature must be closely monitored. If his temperature is above 104°F (40°C), or continues to climb after he has been taken out of the sun and is at rest, he should be actively cooled (see Heat Stroke, below). Individuals with heat exhaustion have an even greater fluid deficit that must be corrected than persons with heat syncope. Such persons must be very careful about resuming physical activity and probably should be examined by a physician beforehand.

Heat Stroke

Heat stroke (also called "sunstroke") is the most severe form of heat illness. Fatalities are common, as are permanent residual disabilities. The onset typically is very rapid and is characterized by changes in mental function. Confusion and irrational behavior are most frequent, but incoordination, delirium, and unconsciousness often follow. Convulsions occur commonly. The pupils may be dilated and unresponsive to light.

The rectal temperature is almost always above 104°F (40°C) and is commonly above 107°F (42°C), which is the upper limit for most clinical thermometers. (A rectal thermometer reading to 113°F (45°C) is usually needed to measure the temperature of most individuals with heat stroke, but would not be carried unless severe heat stress had been anticipated, in which case effective preventive measures should have been instituted.) If the temperature is not measured for some time after the onset of the illness, it may have fallen.

The skin feels hot. If the subject has been actively exercising, he is usually covered with perspiration at the time he collapses. Later he may have dried, particularly if cooling has been instituted. The hot, dry skin long associated with heat stroke is typical of individuals with the deranged heat loss of nonexertional heat illness, not those with exertional heat illness. However, sweating does decrease during exercise and can fall to quite small volumes, particularly when exercise has been prolonged and the individual has become dehydrated.

Pulse and respiratory rates are increased. Shock is usually present.

Treatment should be instituted as rapidly as possible. Heat stroke is one of the few true medical emergencies in which a delay of only a few minutes may significantly alter the outcome. If the subject is unconscious, an open airway must be maintained. Shock should be treated by elevating the feet and by any other methods that are feasible.

Cooling should be started immediately. The subject should be moved to the coolest spot possible; he must be shaded from sunlight. In a hospital emergency room, a person with heat stroke is cooled by removing his clothing, covering him with wet sheets, and placing large fans to blow directly across his body from two directions. In the wilderness, similar methods should be devised. Clothing should be removed, the extremities and trunk should be covered with wet towels or clothing, and the body should be fanned to increase air circulation and evaporation. Immersion in water would be useful. Any reasonable method for cooling the person should be employed.

In a wilderness environment that produced heat stroke, ice or snow would not be available. In an urban environment, they probably should not be used. A person with heat stroke should be cooled by evaporation and transported to a hospital immediately. Alcohol sponging should not be used. Isopropyl alcohol may be absorbed through the skin, particularly by children.

During cooling, the extremities should be massaged to help propel cooled blood back into the organs of the body and head. Oxygen should be administered if available.

After body temperature has been reduced to 102°F (39°C), active cooling should be slowed to avoid hypothermia, but the subject must be closely monitored to ensure that his temperature does not climb back to higher levels. Rebound is particularly common three to four hours after cooling. Aspirin is not effective, may aggravate complications, and should not be administered.

As soon as possible the subject should be evacuated to a hospital, particularly if he has been unconscious for more than a few minutes. The complications of heat stroke include failure of essentially every organ system—particularly the heart, liver, and kidneys—blood-clotting abnormalities, gastrointestinal ulceration with bleeding, biochemical alterations, and extensive brain damage. Unconsciousness of more than two hours' duration is a poor prognostic sign that is usually followed by permanent disability or death.

HEAT CRAMPS

Heat cramps are severe, spasmodic contractions of one or more muscles, most commonly the leg muscles. Cramps may last up to fifteen minutes or even longer, and the muscles are usually painful for several days afterward.

Cramps usually can be stopped almost immediately by stretching the muscle. For example, the calf muscle can be stretched by extending the leg and pulling the foot upward. Kneading or pounding the muscle is ineffective and probably contributes to the residual soreness.

Cramps usually appear in the most heavily worked muscles and may be produced, in part, by an excessive water intake without accompanying salt, resulting in dilution of the salt in the extracellular fluid. Cramps are more common in circumstances that tend to cause salt depletion; they can be prevented to a large extent by consuming large quantities of salt and water.

INJURY BY SOLAR RADIATION

Sunlight is beneficial (it plays a major role in Vitamin D synthesis), but excessive exposure is harmful. Sunburn is well recognized; less well known are the degenerative changes associated with repeated overexposure that can eventually lead to cancer. Three hundred thousand new cases of skin cancer are diagnosed every year in the United States, and the incidence is increasing.

Melanoma is the most aggressive form of skin cancer, and the incidence of this malignancy has almost tripled in the last four decades, a rate of increase greater than that of any other malignancy. Approximately 32,000 new cases and 6,500 deaths from melanoma are predicted in the United States in 1991, and this tumor has become the most common cancer in whites between the ages of twenty-five and twenty-nine. Sunlight is the most significant environmental element causing this tumor. Intermittent exposure, particularly early in life, appears to increase risk more than cumulative exposure. Three or more episodes of blistering sunburn during childhood or adolescence is currently thought to predispose individuals to melanoma.

Much of the energy in solar radiation has shorter (ultraviolet) or longer (infrared) wavelengths than visible light. Most biologic damage is caused by ultraviolet radiation with wavelengths less than 400 nanometers (nm) (1 centimeter = 10^7 nanometers = 10^8 Ångstroms) (fig. 23-1).

Even when a person is shielded from the direct rays of the sun, much ultraviolet radiation can still reach him due to atmospheric scattering. This "sky radiation" may contribute half of total ultraviolet radiation and tends to be greater when high, thin cirrus clouds are present. Indeed, total ultraviolet radiation can be greater on an overcast day than on a cloudless day. Such radiation is particularly insidious because it is so inapparent.

Ultraviolet exposure at high altitudes is greater than at sea level because the atmosphere is thinner and filters out less sunlight, particularly in the harmful wavelengths. Snowfields and glaciers reflect about seventy-five percent of the incident ultraviolet radiation; in a cirque or bowl, reflection can increase the radiation even more. Individuals participating in water sports are exposed to direct radiation and large quantities (up to 100 percent) of reflected radiation. High altitude sail boarding can result in great ultraviolet exposures.

SPECTRAL DISTRIBUTION OF SUNLIGHT

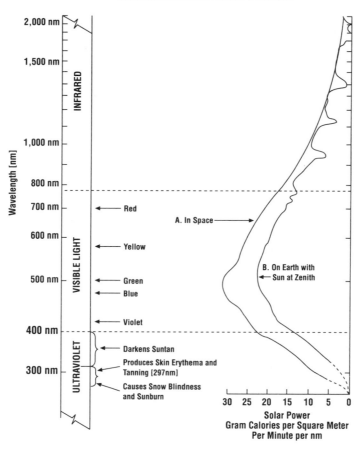

Figure 23-1. Quantity of light of different wavelengths in sunlight.

Sunburn

Individuals vary widely in their sensitivity to sunlight. Redheads are particularly sensitive. Blue-eyed blondes are more susceptible to sunburn than brunettes. Individuals of northern European ancestry are more sensitive than Mediterranean, Indian, black, or other peoples whose skin contains more protective pigment (melanin). Children are more susceptible than adults.

Sensitivity to sunlight may be increased by drugs such as sulfonamides and their derivatives (trimethoprim-sulfamethoxazole—Bactrim® and Septra®); oral antidiabetic agents; phenothiazine tranquilizers (Thorazine®, Compazine®,

Phenergan®, and Sparine®); thiazide diuretics (Diuril®); most tetracyclines, particularly doxycycline (Vibramycin®), which is used to prevent traveler's diarrhea; and barbiturates. Many other substances increase sensitivity to sunlight, including biothionol, which is used in soaps; many first aid creams and cosmetics; green soap; many plants and grasses, such as fig leaf, certain meadow grasses, wild parsnip, and celery; dyes used in lipstick; and coal tar and its derivatives.

Excessive exposure to ultraviolet radiation with a wavelength of 290 to 320 nm damages the skin. Mildly excessive exposure produces redness and slight swelling; greater exposure causes pain and blistering. Severe burns may be associated with chills, fever, or headache. Sunburn of the lips is often followed by painful *Herpes simplex* infections ("fever blisters" or "cold sores"). Years of exposure produce precancerous changes.

Ultraviolet radiation with wavelengths in the range of 320 to 420 nm increases pigmentation and increases the thickness of the outer layer of the skin. The resulting suntan is protective because the pigment and the thickened skin reduce the penetration of harmful ultraviolet radiation. Until recently 320 to 420 nm radiation was considered harmless and beneficial, but recent investigations have indicated these wavelengths may produce skin damage also.

Preventing Sunburn

The best way to prevent sunburn is through gradually increasing exposure to sunlight, which permits natural tanning and thickening of the skin. For many redheads and some other light-skinned individuals, adequate tanning is impossible. Such persons may benefit from the use of trioxsalen (Trisoralen®), but this is a potent drug that must be taken only under the close supervision of a physician, preferably a dermatologist.

Protective creams or lotions that contain sunscreens are the most convenient methods for protecting exposed skin from sunlight. They should be applied liberally and frequently, particularly when sweating or wiping the neck and face tend to remove the preparation. The nose, cheeks, neck, and ears are most frequently sunburned; the lower surfaces of the nose and chin are commonly burned by reflected radiation.

Many products currently marketed in the United States to prevent sunburn contain sunscreens that filter out ultraviolet radiation of the wavelengths 290 to 320 nm, but allow some radiation of longer wavelengths to pass through. The sunscreen that is best known and has been used longest is para-aminobenzoic acid (PABA). However, PABA containing products can cause contact dermatitis (see Chapter Twenty, "Allergies"), particularly in young children, which has led to the development of products that contain other sunscreens and to a separate category of sunscreens for children. Avobenzone, which is sold under the trade name Parsol 1789®, is the only agent put through the FDA New Drug Application procedure and demonstrated to effectively block 320 to 420 nm radiation.

Price has little relation to the effectiveness of sunscreens. Investigators for the Consumers Union, publisher of *Consumer Reports,* found equally effective adult sunscreens to range in price from $0.66 to $4.28 per ounce. Their article entitled "Sunscreens," published in *Consumer Reports* (June 1991;56:400), contains a thorough description of available products. Copies are available from Consumers Union Reprints Department, 101 Truman Avenue, Yonkers, NY 10703-1057.

The sun protection factor (SPF) value indicates how much longer an individual can tolerate direct sunlight when protected by a product that contains a sunscreen than with no protection. When protected by a sunscreen with an SPF of twelve, a person whose skin would begin to turn red after five minutes of unprotected sun exposure could stay in the sun for twelve times longer, or sixty minutes, before his skin would begin to redden (assuming the sunscreen was not removed by wiping or sweating).

Two-thirds of the day's ultraviolet radiation is received during the four hours in the middle of the day; protection from solar injury is needed primarily during this interval. Preparations with an SPF rating of fifteen provide protection for that long for most individuals. Preparations with a higher SPF have no real value and are usually more expensive. If longer protection is needed, it is best obtained by reapplying the original preparation, because lotions and creams, regardless of their SPF, are removed by wiping or moisture after four hours. Even the so-called "waterproof" preparations, although more resistant to moisture, are not completely impervious to perspiration or water from other sources and are lost during this interval.

A group of protective agents that block out all ultraviolet radiation contain opaque pigments such as titanium dioxide (A-Fil®) or zinc oxide (Zincofax Cream®). Red Veterinary Petrolatum® (R.V.P., from the Paul B. Elder Co.) is also effective. Such agents are used on the nose, lips, and ears, which are easily sunburned and are not covered by clothing. (Products containing benzophenones, such as Uval® and Solbar®, also screen out all ultraviolet radiation but were developed primarily for individuals with skin diseases that require such complete protection. These agents are easily removed by sweating and are not suitable for protection during recreational sun exposure.)

Treating Sunburn

If prevention has been neglected or has been inadequate, the application of cold, wet dressings soaked in a boric acid solution (one teaspoonful per quart of water) or a one to fifty solution of aluminum acetate may relieve discomfort. Soothing creams may be helpful if swelling is not severe. Anesthetic sprays or ointments are effective but can produce significant allergic reactions. Steroid preparations, such as 0.25 percent hydrocortisone ointment or an aerosol containing prednisolone, help reduce inflammation and may reduce pain if applied early. However, steroid preparations probably slow healing and repair, may increase susceptibility to infection, and must be used sparingly. Extensive or unusually severe sunburn must be treated as a second-degree burn.

Skin Cancer

Repeated sun exposure over a period of many years for individuals who are not darkly pigmented produces degenerative skin changes that are cosmetically unattractive and commonly lead to cancer. Degenerative skin changes are particularly likely in persons who spend much time in intense sunlight, such as ski patrol members, lifeguards, and river boating enthusiasts. Tanning clearly provides incomplete protection.

Individuals who spend much of their time in sunlight must reduce the severity of such changes by conscientiously applying sunscreens whenever they are exposed, regardless of the risk of sunburn. However, the best protection is clothing, particularly long-sleeved shirts and wide-brimmed hats that shade the face.

Snow Blindness

The surface of the eye (cornea and conjunctiva) absorbs ultraviolet radiation just like the skin. Excessive exposure can result in sunburn of these tissues, producing snow blindness (photophthalmia). Any source of ultraviolet radiation—the sun, ultraviolet lamps, or electric welding equipment—may produce photophthalmia. During the period of exposure no sensation other than the intensity of the light serves to warn the subject.

Symptoms may not develop until eight to twelve hours after exposure. The eyes initially feel irritated or dry, but as symptoms progress, they feel as though they are full of sand. Moving or blinking the eyes becomes extremely painful. Even exposure to light may cause pain. Swelling of the eyelids, redness of the eyes, and excessive tearing occur. A severe case of snow blindness may be disabling for several days and may even lead to ulceration of the cornea, permanently damaging the eye.

Preventing Snow Blindness

Snow blindness can and should be prevented by consistently wearing protective goggles or sunglasses. Any lens transmitting less than ten percent of the erythemal band of sunlight (below 320 nm) is satisfactory. Glasses should be large and curved or have side covers to block the reflected light coming from below and from the sides. When ultraviolet radiation exposure is high, as it would be on a concave high altitude snowfield, goggles are safer, even though they may be less comfortable and tend to fog. If only glasses are available, a sunscreen should be applied to the eyelids to prevent burning. Spare goggles or glasses should be carried, but emergency lenses can be made of cardboard with a thin slit or pinhole to see through. The eyes may be covered alternately so that only one eye at a time is exposed to the sunlight.

Eye protection is just as necessary on a cloudy or overcast day as it is in full sunlight. Snow blindness can occur during a snowstorm if the cloud cover is thin.

Treating Snow Blindness

Snow blindness heals spontaneously in a few days. The pain, which may be quite severe, may be relieved temporarily by cold compresses and a dark environment. Early and frequent (hourly) applications of an ophthalmic preparation containing an anti-inflammatory steroid help relieve the pain, lesson the inflammatory reaction, and shorten the course of the illness. The patient must not rub his eyes. Local anesthetics should not be employed because they rapidly lose their effectiveness and may lead to damage of the delicate corneal surface.

CHAPTER TWENTY-FOUR

ANIMAL BITES AND STINGS

All animal bites are associated with a high risk of serious infection. The mouths of all animals—including humans—contain innumerable bacteria, many of which are introduced into the wound when a bite is inflicted. Human bites tend to produce particularly virulent infections.

All bite wounds should be treated as contaminated soft-tissue injuries. They must be washed copiously with soap and water, and an antimicrobial agent such as povidone-iodine should be applied. Under no circumstances should the wound be sutured. It must be left open with a sterile dressing and must be watched closely for signs of infection.

Because the mouths of animals contain so many bacteria, treatment for tetanus (toxoid injection) should be administered if the individual has not had a recent booster.

RABIES

Rabies is a viral infection; its catastrophic effects result from encephalitis (infection of the brain). Rabies has been known and justifiably feared since antiquity. Only two humans with rabies are known to have survived (in the 1970s), and they had severe residual neurologic damage.

Rabies Within the United States

Within the United States, human rabies has been controlled to a large extent by vaccinating domestic animals. Dog rabies has diminished from 5,688 cases in 1953 to 95 cases in 1986. Human rabies has concomitantly declined from approximately 350 cases in the 1940s to fourteen cases since 1980. Ten of those fourteen infections were acquired outside of the United States.

Essentially, all animals are susceptible to rabies and capable of transmitting the infection, but transmission by rodents has not been documented. Currently, most confirmed animal rabies is in skunks, foxes, bats, and raccoons. In one study, dogs and cats were found to be responsible for sixty-four percent of the bites for which therapy was administered, but constituted only thirteen percent of the infected animals. In contrast, skunks, foxes, and raccoons were responsible for only thirty-three percent of the therapy, but made up eighty-three percent of the infected animals (fig. 24-1).

Bat rabies is endemic in all areas of the continental United States, both urban and rural, and poses an unequivocal threat to spelunkers. Bats were the source of infection for three of the four individuals who contracted rabies within the United States since 1980.

In an infected animal, the virus involves the salivary glands and is present in the saliva. Transmission of the infection occurs when a wound is contaminated with the saliva of the rabid animal. The virus can not penetrate intact skin but can pass through an intact mucous membrane such as the lining of the mouth, nose, or eyelids. The infection can be transmitted by licking alone. Infection has been transmitted by breathing aerosolized rabies virus in a medical laboratory and in at least one cave inhabited by rabid bats.

The average incubation period between the time of the bite and the appearance of a clinically evident infection is thirty-five days. (Three Asian immigrants to the United States have developed infections by virus strains found only in their home-land as much as six years after any possible exposure.) The virus appears to travel along nerves at a relatively constant speed to reach the brain. Bites on the extremities allow more time for treatment than bites about the face, which are particularly dangerous and must be treated urgently.

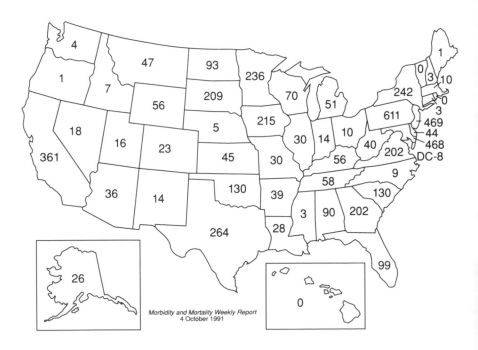

Figure 24-1. Nonhuman rabies cases in the U.S., 1990.

Treating a Bite by a Rabid Animal

The treatment for rabies is known as immunotherapy or immunoprophylaxis, terms that mean the infection is prevented by immunization before encephalitis develops. Treatment must be initiated immediately after the bite is inflicted. Therapy begun after the subject begins to show signs of rabies is ineffective.

The treatment of any animal bite has three components:

- Diagnosis of rabies in the attacking animal
- Treatment of the bite wound
- Immunotherapy

If the attacking animal is a domestic pet that has been vaccinated for rabies within the past year and can be captured, it should be confined under observation for ten days following the bite. If the animal is healthy at the end of that time, it is safe to assume the animal did not have transmissible rabies at the time the bite was inflicted, and immunotherapy is not required.

Within the United States all other animals should be killed and their heads should be shipped to a laboratory where the brain can be examined to determine whether rabies virus is present. Public health services are responsible for maintaining reliable laboratories and for transporting the heads.

If the animal can not be killed or captured, or if the contact occurs in an underdeveloped country, the animal must be assumed to be rabid regardless of the manner in which it was behaving. Rabies in animals follows a highly variable course. The notorious "mad dog" foaming at the mouth is almost never seen. Unprovoked attacks are the most common indication of rabies. Occasionally the only sign of rabies is the absence of fear of man, which may even appear to be a show of friendliness. Animals such as skunks, which usually scurry away from any threatening situation, may actually pursue humans.

The only exceptions to this caveat would be those few areas where rabies does not occur. Hawaii, for example, is considered to be free of all forms of wildlife rabies. (All animals brought into the islands are quarantined for six months, regardless of their vaccination history, to prevent the introduction of this infection.)

Treatment of the bite wound is a vital part of the care for persons exposed to rabies. The severity and speed of onset of any infection is dependent to a significant extent upon the number of organisms (viruses or bacteria) introduced. Washing saliva out of the wound reduces the number of viruses that can enter the tissues.

The wound should be thoroughly washed with large quantities of soap and water and should be flushed with povidone-iodine. Immediate washing is of such urgency that it should be instituted without delay. Someone else should catch or kill the attacking animal. If soap and water are not available, anything on hand—even a favorite whiskey—should be used.

Immunotherapy for rabies consists of administering serum from an individual already immune to rabies—rabies immune globulin—followed by vaccine to build up immunity to the rabies virus during the incubation period between the bite and the appearance of signs of the disease. Twenty international units per kilogram of body weight (20 IU/kg) of rabies immune globulin of human origin should be injected, one-half around the wound and the remainder into the deltoid (shoulder) muscle opposite the bite. In addition, one milliliter (1 cc) of human diploid cell rabies vaccine should be injected into the deltoid muscle on the day of the bite (day zero) and on days three, seven, fourteen, and twenty-eight. The injections must be made into the deltoid muscle. The only two reported individuals world-wide who developed rabies following immunotherapy received gluteal injections.

The rabies vaccine currently used in the United States, human diploid cell vaccine (HDCV), is prepared from viruses grown on human diploid cell cultures and is largely free of the serious side effects that were common with older vaccines.

Rabies in Underdeveloped Countries

Rabies remains a scourge in many underdeveloped countries. In India 40,000 to 50,000 human rabies deaths a year have been reported; other underdeveloped countries are thought to have comparable rates of human infection. Outside the United States, Canada, and Western Europe, domestic animals are not vaccinated for rabies, and the risk of infection by pets or other animals is high.

Any bite or contact with saliva from an animal in an underdeveloped country should be considered exposure to rabies. In a recent study from Nepal, ten of fifty-one bites were inflicted by monkeys leaping for food held by tourists visiting the Swayambunath Temple. Thirty-six bites were by dogs.

Individuals exposed to rabies while visiting underdeveloped countries can not depend upon local physicians or institutions for reliable treatment. In most of these areas Semple vaccine is used to treat rabies because it is inexpensive. This vaccine, which is prepared by treating infected sheep brains with formalin, varies considerably in its potency and effectiveness and is associated with a high incidence of side effects, some of which are disastrous.

U.S. citizens exposed to rabies must go immediately to the nearest American, Canadian, or British embassy. These embassies have physicians on their staffs or available to them and have means for obtaining reliable vaccine within twenty-four hours or less. U.S. embassies are required to provide this service. The embassies of all three countries have always welcomed the opportunity to assist citizens of any of the three nations in an emergency.

Human Vaccination for Rabies

In April 1987 vaccination of humans for rabies was approved by the Federal Drug Administration (FDA). The schedule calls for three one-tenth of a milliliter (0.1 cc) intradermal injections of vaccine on days zero, seven, and twenty-one or twenty-eight. (The volume injected is one-tenth that administered after a bite, and the injections are intradermal, not intramuscular.)

If a vaccinated individual subsequently has contact with a rabid animal, he still must be treated with vaccine. However, rabies immune globulin is not needed, and only two vaccine injections (1 cc injected into the deltoid muscle) on day zero and day three after exposure are required.

The Centers for Disease Control (CDC) divides individuals at risk of developing rabies into three groups. Group I has the highest risk and consists of rabies laboratory workers. The CDC recommends that such individuals be vaccinated and have serological testing to determine their level of immunity or booster injections every six months.

Group II has a lower but significant risk and includes spelunkers, as well as veterinarians, animal control workers, and fish and game wardens in areas of high rabies incidence. For these individuals the CDC recommends vaccination and serologic testing or boosters every two years.

Group III, which has a definite but still lower risk, includes travelers staying more than thirty days in areas with a high incidence of rabies, as well as veterinarians and animal control workers in areas of low rabies incidence, and veterinary students. For these individuals the CDC recommends vaccination without subsequent serologic testing or boosters. (The recommendations for travelers have been questioned by a group of physicians in Nepal, who calculated the incidence of animal exposure requiring immunoprophylaxis in tourists and foreign residents in that country to be only one in 123,000 days, or 337 years, and considered the low but definite risk of severe reaction to the vaccine to be greater.)

POISONOUS SNAKE BITES

Poisonous snake bites are unquestionably serious, potentially deadly accidents. Nonetheless, the danger from a single bite has been greatly exaggerated, particularly in the United States, where an average of less than fifteen people die each year as the result of bites by poisonous snakes. Less than one percent of poisonous snake bites in this country are lethal. In other parts of the world, where many snakes have a much more toxic venom, treatment is less successful, and sophisticated medical care is not available, poisonous snake bites are a more serious problem.

Unfortunately, the treatment of poisonous snake bites remains a subject of controversy and confusion. (Even the material used to treat snake bites is variously referred to in the English literature as antivenom, antivenin, or antivenene.) The authoritative publication of untested personal opinions or the results of poorly designed and inadequately controlled animal experiments, aided by a sensationalist press, have produced widespread misinformation.

Families of Poisonous Snakes

The world's poisonous snakes have been divided into three families. Within the family Elapidae are the North American coral snakes (eastern, western, and Sonoran), the Indian krait of India and Pakistan, the tiger snake of Australia, the death adder of Australia and New Guinea, the Indian cobra (which occurs in most of Southeast Asia, including Indonesia and Formosa, and reportedly is responsible for more deaths than any other species), the mamba of East Africa, and the ringhals of South Africa.

The Viperidae include the puff adder, found in most of Africa and southern Arabia; the saw-scaled viper, which ranges from northern and western Africa to northern India; the Palestine viper of the Middle East; and the Russell's viper, found from West Pakistan to Formosa.

The Crotalidae are of major importance in North America. They include all of the North American rattlesnakes as well as the copperheads and cottonmouth moccasins, the fer-de-lance and neotropical rattlesnakes found from Mexico to Argentina, the jararaca of tropical South America, and the habu, which occurs in the Ryukyu Islands of Japan with closely related species in Formosa and the southeastern part of the People's Republic of China.

Identification of U.S. Poisonous Snakes

The poisonous snakes of the United States are the rattlesnakes, the copperheads and cottonmouth (or water) moccasin, and the coral snakes. In the United States, poisonous snakes, except for coral snakes, are pit vipers and have a characteristic triangular head and heavy body. The body markings are rarely sufficiently unique for species identification by inexperienced individuals.

These snakes are called "pit vipers" because they have a small pit located between the eye and the nostril, a feature found only in these poisonous species (fig. 24-2). This pit is an infrared sensing organ instrumental in detecting the small, warm-blooded animals these snakes eat. The pit vipers are also characterized by single scales reaching across the undersurface of the body posterior to the anus. Most other snakes have double scales (fig. 24-3).

If fangs are present, a snake is undoubtedly poisonous, but searching for fangs is hazardous. The fangs may be folded back against the roof of the mouth, which makes them difficult to identify. One or both fangs may be broken off; three or four are occasionally found. Rattles are of obvious significance, but the absence of rattles is not, because they get broken off. The Catalina Island rattlesnake sheds its rattles with its skin and never has more than one.

Coral snakes are small, thin, brightly colored snakes with small heads and are quite different from pit vipers. They can be identified by the adjacent red and

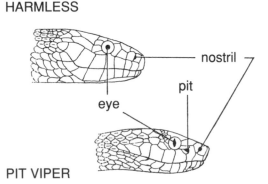

Figure 24-2. Comparison of the heads of pit vipers and nonpoisonous snakes.

POISONOUS   NONPOISONOUS

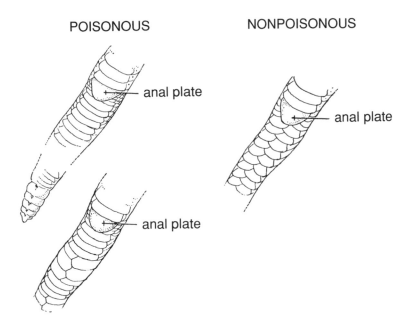

Figure 24-3. Comparison of the scales on the undersurface of tails of
poisonous and nonpoisonous snakes.

yellow bands. The nonpoisonous king snakes and other harmless species with
similar coloration have adjacent red and black bands. A helpful mnemonic is:
"Red and yellow—kill a fellow. Red and black—venom lack."

Poisonous snakes from other parts of the world do not closely resemble their
American counterparts. The vipers do have rather large heads and heavy bodies
and tend to resemble the pit vipers, but they lack pits.

Elapids have small heads and thin bodies like the coral snakes, but few have
such brilliant coloring. Except for a few species with distinctive hoods (mostly
cobras), they have an appearance similar to many nonpoisonous snakes. The
poisonous snakes of Australia, including the innocent-sounding brown snake and
the more appropriately named death adder and tiger snake, are elapids; many of
the poisonous snakes of Africa, including the notorious black mamba, are elapids.
To individuals accustomed to the heavy-bodied American crotalids or pit vipers
these snakes appear harmless, but their venoms are vicious. Travelers who are not
knowledgeable should avoid all snakes in areas inhabited by these reptiles.

Snake Venoms

The venoms of all poisonous snakes contain similar toxins; classifying snakes
according to a single target for their toxins is misleading and can result in inadequate medical therapy.

Vascular toxins damage the walls of blood vessels; others inhibit blood clotting; the combination of the two results in bleeding into the tissues at the site of the bite as well as spontaneous bleeding from the gums, nose, or gastrointestinal tract. The damaged blood vessels allow proteins and fluid to leak into the tissues, which produces swelling at the point where the bite occurs. Such fluid loss in combination with the destruction of red blood cells and blood proteins reduces the circulating blood volume and leads to shock, a consistent feature of severe envenomation by snakes of all species.

The ultimate effect of neurotoxins is paralysis, most importantly respiratory paralysis. However, abnormal sensations such as tingling or prickly feelings and partial paralysis of the eyelids are more common. Although pit vipers have been described as having predominantly hemolytic toxins, one of the characteristic early symptoms following the bites of some rattlesnakes is numbness and tingling of the lips and a metallic taste, both of which result from the effects of the toxin on neural tissues.

Crotalid venoms do tend to have higher concentrations of hemolytic toxins; elapid and viperine toxins tend to have higher concentrations of neurotoxins. However, more than a dozen different venom components have been identified. Different species within the same family have venoms of different composition. Venom concentrations also vary; some, like that of the copperhead, are rather weak, while others, like that of the Mojave rattlesnake, are concentrated and quite potent. Additionally, larger snakes are able to inject a larger volume of venom than smaller snakes. The concentration of the venom, the concentrations of its individual components, and its total volume are different in the same snake at different times of the year.

Because the venom of a copperhead is so mild, persons bitten by these snakes require little more than supportive therapy. Antivenin is almost never needed for adults bitten by a single snake. In a compilation of more 400 copperhead bites in eastern North Carolina, only two deaths could be found. In both instances, the unfortunate victims had been bitten simultaneously about the head by three or more snakes.

In contrast, the eastern diamondback rattlesnake, a large species that is more aggressive than most snakes, produces a venom that is only moderately toxic, but the volume is so great that bites by this snake require vigorous treatment. In the United States this species is responsible for more poisonous snake bite deaths than any other. Most of the bites occur in Florida.

The Mojave rattlesnake is small but has a very potent venom with a high concentration of neurotoxins. The effects of envenomation by this species tend to be delayed, commonly do not become fully apparent until twelve to sixteen hours after the bite, and often are much more severe than indicated by the initial reaction. Bites by this species must be treated aggressively from the outset.

Diagnosis of Envenomation

Any snake that inflicts a bite should be precisely identified if possible. Many people are injured by unnecessary treatment for the bites of nonpoisonous snakes. More significantly, a bite by a Mojave rattlesnake may produce very little reaction in the hours immediately after it occurs, when treatment is most effective. Only if the species of snake is known can optimal therapy be started without delay. Preferably the snake should be killed and brought to a medical center with the person who was bitten so that the exact species can be determined.

In some areas of the world broad-spectrum antiserum is not available (for some species it is not effective) and specific antiserum must be administered. If the snake can not be precisely identified, specific therapy may be impossible.

Inspecting the bite occasionally helps in determining that the snake is poisonous. Typically, the fangs of a pit viper produce two small puncture marks, which are a reliable indication that the snake was a member of this family. However, characteristic fang marks are distinctly uncommon. The target is usually moving and the snake's strike is rarely accurate. Only one fang may strike, or the fangs may only graze or scratch the skin. The snake may have had one fang broken off; occasional snakes have three or even four fangs. The fang marks may be hidden among the marks from the other teeth if the snake has embedded his fangs so deeply that the other teeth have also penetrated the skin. Although only the fangs have entered the skin, a U-shaped row of teeth marks from the bottom jaw may be present.

Even though an attacking snake can be positively identified as poisonous, the individual it has bitten does not require specific treatment unless envenomation has occurred (venom has been injected). Poisonous snakes attack humans in sheer terror, not for food. Sometimes snakes strike without opening their mouths or extending their fangs. Occasionally venom is only sprayed on the surface of the skin. Even when the fangs pierce the skin, no venom or only a very small quantity may be injected.

Approximately twenty percent of the individuals with rattlesnake bites transported to the University of Southern California–Los Angeles County Medical Center over a period of years had not been envenomated. About two-thirds of these had fang wounds that only scratched the skin or had penetrated too superficially for venom to be injected. In the remaining one-third, the fangs had penetrated deeply but no venom had been injected. Reportedly, about fifty percent of cobra bites are not associated with envenomation; for sea snake bites the incidence of nonenvenomation is about eighty percent.

If the subject has been bitten but not envenomated, the bite should be treated like any other animal bite. It must be thoroughly cleaned. Since the wound is a puncture wound, bleeding should be encouraged and tetanus prophylaxis should be administered.

Crotalid Envenomation

The reaction following the bite of a crotalid (pit viper) is one of the best indications that the snake was poisonous and is the only indication that envenomation has occurred and treatment may be needed. This reaction begins within minutes after the bite, typically is severe following an eastern diamondback rattlesnake bite, but is usually less marked after other pit viper bites. The reaction may be deceptively mild following the bite of a Mojave rattlesnake and almost nonexistent after a massagua or pygmy rattlesnake bite.

The earliest symptom is pain or burning at the site of the bite, although some people experience relatively little pain. Shortly afterward the area begins to swell as fluid pours into the tissues. Bleeding usually produces a purple or green discoloration, but this change may take several hours to appear.

If no further symptoms develop, the envenomation is mild, and antiserum therapy is rarely needed. However, the individual should be taken to a hospital, even though he has only a mild reaction. Evidence of more severe envenomation may take several hours to develop.

Numbness or a tingling sensation about the mouth or tongue—sometimes extending into the scalp or involving the fingers and toes, and often associated with a metallic or rubbery taste—commonly follows the bite of eastern diamondback and some western rattlesnakes.

Following moderate envenomation, the swelling and discoloration extend further from the site of the bite, large blisters that contain clear or bloody fluid appear, and the regional lymph nodes, particularly in the armpit or the inguinal crease, become enlarged and tender. Severe envenomation is heralded by the development of a systemic reaction. The subject becomes weak and dizzy and develops signs of shock, particularly cold, clammy skin and a weak pulse.

Prehospital Care for Urban Crotalid Bites

Most of the poisonous snake bites within the United States occur in situations where hospitalization is less than two hours away. The average interval between bite and hospitalization has been reported to be thirty-five minutes. When a subject can be hospitalized in such a short time, the only treatment needed is limiting the spread of the venom and immobilizing the extremity. No other measures, particularly incision and suction, should be attempted.

Tourniquets have been recommended to help reduce spread of the venom, but rarely are applied correctly and commonly do more harm than good. Tourniquets that obstruct the flow of arterial blood to an extremity are too painful to be tolerated by a conscious person for more than a few minutes. If left on for an hour or more, they cause gangrene. Tourniquets that obstruct only the flow of venous blood also produce discomfort after a period of time and can increase bleeding or extravasation of blood at the site of the bite.

A properly applied tourniquet should only obstruct lymphatic flow. The tourniquet should be made from a band at least one inch wide and should not be so tight that a finger can not be inserted beneath it without difficulty. Such tourniquets can easily be applied too loosely or become too tight as swelling spreads up the limb. Because applying such tourniquets correctly seems almost impossible, many individuals have recommended that tourniquets not be applied at all.

Wrapping the bitten extremity snugly and immobilizing it with a splint is a treatment technique devised for inhibiting the spread of venom of Australian elapids. This procedure has proven effective in experimental studies and in clinical use only for those species and has not undergone controlled testing following crotalid bites, although it has been used for a few individuals.

Any kind of fabric, including an elastic bandage, is satisfactory. With most snake bites, venom is injected only into the subcutaneous (superficial) tissue, not into the underlying muscle. A snug fabric wrapping that compresses the subcutaneous fat and blood vessels eliminates most blood and lymph flow from those tissues and effectively immobilizes the venom without compromising blood flow to the limb. The wrap is not tight enough to interfere with arterial flow, and although it compresses the superficial veins, venous blood can still return through the deep veins.

An inflatable splint can be useful for this purpose because this device can both immobilize the extremity and apply pressure. The pressure in the splint must be rather high, approximately 50 to 60 mm Hg. Any available splint can be used and does not have to be as carefully applied as a splint for a fracture.

The immobilized extremity should be kept at the same level as the heart, and the person should be transported to a hospital with as little effort on his part as possible. Movement, even just walking, increases the circulation of blood and speeds the movement of venom away from the bite to the rest of the body. Furthermore, the effects of activity are frequently worse than would be expected from this consideration alone. The person should be lying still if possible. No drugs, including alcohol, should be administered; no other treatment should be attempted.

Because the venom is immobilized at the site of the bite by this type of wrapping, greater local damage is produced by pit viper venom. Therefore, wrapping should not be applied unless envenomation is known to be moderate or severe—the bite was inflicted by a large snake, and pain and swelling appear at once—and a hospital is many hours or days away.

After the individual reaches the hospital, the wrapping should not be removed from the extremity until preparations have been made to administer antivenin. If significant envenomation is known to have occurred, antivenin should be started before the wrapping is removed.

Prehospital Care for Wilderness Crotalid Bites

Few snake bites occur in truly remote wilderness situations, perhaps because people in such circumstances are more aware of the presence of poisonous snakes and try to avoid them. Hiking boots that cover the ankles prevent many bites. Furthermore, snakes, like all cold-blooded animals, must avoid extremes of heat or cold and are much less common at altitudes where temperatures drop to low levels at night.

The prehospital care for snake bite in a remote area is basically the same as that for an urban environment: immobilization and transportation (with as little exertion by the person who has been bitten as possible) to the nearest medical facility. However, in a truly remote situation where evacuation would require many hours or days, and the bite has been inflicted by a pit viper, incision and suction may be considered. This form of therapy is an ineffectual, stopgap measure. Under ideal conditions, incision and suction removes less than twenty percent of the venom. The risk of infection or damage to underlying tissues is considerable. However, after severe envenomation, particularly of a child or elderly adult, even that small benefit may be significant.

The following conditions must be met before incision and suction is attempted:

1. The individual must be three hours or more from the nearest medical facility, and incision and suction must not delay evacuation.
2. The snake must have been clearly identified as a pit viper, and significant envenomation must have been manifested by pain and swelling.
3. Incision and suction can be initiated less than ten minutes after the bite, preferably sooner.
4. The necessary equipment is available, and a member of the party is familiar with its use.

The following procedure should be carried out:

1. A tourniquet should not be used because the hazards are significant and it is almost never applied correctly.
2. The skin should be washed and swabbed with an antiseptic.
3. The fang marks may be enlarged slightly with a sharply pointed scalpel blade (number eleven Bard-Parker) by pushing the tip of the blade through the punctures into the subcutaneous fat—no deeper. Larger incisions should not be made.
4. Suction must be applied with an extractor. Rubber bulbs or oral suction are not adequate. Suction should be applied for thirty minutes for adults and up to an hour for children.
5. After suction has been discontinued, the limb should be immobilized.

A person by himself in a remote area has no choice but to walk out. If a companion is present, the companion should make sure the person is warm and comfortable and then go for help, preferably a helicopter. If the party is large enough, the subject can be carried out. Jostling on a makeshift stretcher probably stimulates blood flow and venom absorption less than walking the same distance.

Antivenin Therapy

Antivenin against the venom of the attacking snake is the only specific treatment for poisonous snake bite. However, the antivenin currently available is prepared in horses, and many individuals are allergic to horse serum. As a result, the administration of antivenin can be hazardous and should not be attempted by anyone other than a physician, and even then only in situations (such as a hospital emergency room) where potentially lethal allergic reactions can be treated. Recent investigations have disclosed that allergic reactions of some type, mostly mild but occasionally severe, occur in seventy percent of antivenin recipients who were not previously allergic to horse serum.

A few individuals carry single vials of antivenin when traveling in snake-infested areas so that they can be prepared to treat themselves should they be bitten. This practice is dangerous for the following reasons:

1. A person who is bitten by a snake and who needs crotalid antivenin requires at least five to fifteen vials—sometimes as many as forty—not one.

2. Carrying antivenin could impart a false sense of security that could lead to inadequate precautions to avoid poisonous snakes.
3. If the antivenin were administered and a major allergic reaction occurred, the individual or others in his party would not be able to provide effective therapy.

The antivenin most widely available in the United States is a polyvalent, or general-purpose, crotalid antivenin made by Wyeth Laboratories that is effective against all North American pit vipers. A specific *Micrurus fulvius* antivenin, which should be used for bites by coral snakes, is made by the same company.

Coral Snake Bites

The coral snakes are the only elapids native to the United States. These snakes have a range largely restricted to the coastal states from southern North Carolina to Texas. The eastern coral snake inhabits this area from Mississippi eastward; the western coral snake is found in Louisiana and Texas. The Sonoran coral snake is found in a limited portion of southern Arizona.

These North American elapids are shy and rarely seen; bites are even less common. Reportedly, children may play with these snakes for hours without being bitten. Envenomation appears to occur in less than forty percent of the bites that are inflicted. Coral snake bites make up less than two percent of all U.S. snake bites.

Fatalities from coral snake bites apparently have not occurred since the development of specific *Micrurus fulvius* antivenin. This antivenin is effective for bites of the eastern coral snake *(Micrurus fulvius fulvius)* and the western coral snake *(Micrurus fulvius tenere)*. It is of little value for bites by the Sonoran coral snake *(Micruroides euryxanthus)*, but envenomation by this species is usually not very severe.

Coral snakes tend to bite and hang on, sometimes chewing for as long as a minute, which contrasts strikingly with the lightning attack of pit vipers. The bites are rarely associated with the local reaction—severe pain and swelling—typical of crotalid bites. Puncture marks from the fangs usually can not be identified, particularly if the person was intoxicated and can not provide a reliable account of the bite, which is a common occurrence. Some pain may be present and may radiate up the limb. Often the first sign of elapid envenomation is painful enlargement of the regional lymph nodes. With severe envenomation, numbness and weakness of the limb appear within one to two hours, sometimes less. Later signs and symptoms include drowsiness, apprehension, weakness, tremors of the tongue or other muscles, difficulty swallowing, nausea, and vomiting. Pronounced weakness of the eye or eyelid muscles may occur; pupils may be pinpoint in size. Breathing may be labored. Convulsions may occur. Eventually, in inadequately treated, severely envenomated persons, unconsciousness and paralysis are followed by death in shock from respiratory and cardiac failure.

Antivenin is the only effective therapy for coral snake bites and should be administered as quickly as possible without waiting for signs and symptoms of envenomation. The limb should be wrapped to immobilize the venom and should be splinted. The individual should be rapidly transported to a hospital with as little effort on his part as possible. Incision and suction or other forms of nonhospital treatment are of no value.

Bites by Exotic Poisonous Snakes

Bites by snakes that are not native to the United States occasionally occur among collectors, amateur and professional herpetologists, and exhibitors. The treatment for such bites is essentially identical to that for coral snake bites: immobilization of the venom by wrapping the limb, splinting, and transportation to a medical center. Incision and suction has no value in treating such bites.

Antivenins for bites by exotic species of snakes, as well as the names of physicians experienced in treating such bites, may be available through zoos. Poison control centers and university-associated herpetologists also can be valuable sources of information and assistance. The Antivenin Index in Oklahoma City (405-271-5454) maintains a twenty-four-hour service to assist in locating antivenins and provide advice about the treatment for snake bites. Another source of information is the Poisondex central office in Denver (800-332-3073).

In other countries, such information and antivenins may not be so easy to obtain. The nearest hospital would probably be the most reliable source of information and assistance, particularly in areas where snake bites are common.

Other Considerations

If a person who has been bitten by a poisonous snake in a wilderness area can not be evacuated for several days (after which evacuation may not be needed), antibiotics may be needed to combat wound infection. A tranquilizer every four to six hours may help keep the individual quiet and allay anxiety, but must not be given to a stuporous or unconscious person. Pain should be controlled with moderate analgesics; strong analgesics may have harmful effects and should not be administered. Alcohol, which increases absorption of the venom and the subject's physical activity, must be avoided.

Most snake bite fatalities result from shock, regardless of the species of snake or whether the venom is primarily hemolytic or neurotoxic. This complication should be anticipated and treated.

Every person with a poisonous snake bite is different, and the treatment for each must be individualized. Children and elderly persons tolerate poisonous snake bites poorly and require more vigorous treatment. Bites occurring in the spring, when the snake has just emerged from hibernation and its venom is more concentrated, are more severe than bites occurring at other times of the year. Bites about the head or trunk are more dangerous than bites on the extremities and require more aggressive treatment.

Avoiding Poisonous Snakes

Poisonous snakes and their bites are best avoided, not treated. Several simple measures could prevent almost half of all envenomations:

- Poisonous snakes should not be teased or handled, even after they are dead. Reflex strikes with envenomation can occur for several hours after death.
- Unprotected hands should not be inserted under logs or stones or into cracks or crevices that have not first been visually inspected.
- Snakes are nocturnal animals. After dark, special care must be taken to avoid them. Walking barefoot or collecting firewood after dark are two activities that contribute to poisonous snake bites.
- Snakes rarely strike higher than the ankle. Loosely fitting long pants and hiking boots that cover the ankles prevent many bites.

SPIDER BITES

Almost all spiders produce toxic venoms, but their fangs are too small and weak to penetrate the skin, the venom is too weak, or the volume of venom is too small to pose a significant threat for humans. The black widow *(Latrodectus mactans)* is the only spider found in the United States that is capable of routinely producing serious illness by its bite. The "tarantula" native to the U.S. Southwest bites only after extreme provocation. Its weak and ineffective fangs can only penetrate thin skin, such as that on the sides of the fingers; the effects of the bite are no worse than an insect sting.

In other parts of the world are spiders that can cause severe, even fatal poisoning in humans. Other species of *Latrodectus* produce effects similar to the black widow. The bites of large, hairy tarantulas found in areas such as Brazil or Peru can have similar results. The Sydney funnel web spider, reportedly limited in distribution to the area within 100 miles of Sydney, Australia, is capable of inflicting a bite that can be lethal for healthy young adults.

Some spiders, such as the brown, or violin, spider *(Loxosceles reclusa)* inflict bites that occasionally cause extensive damage at the site, but usually have less severe generalized effects. The jumping spider *(Phidippus)* is the most common biting spider in the United States. Bites by this spider, trapdoor spiders, orbweavers, and spiders of the *Chiracanthium* species, such as the garden spider, commonly produce local reactions that ulcerate and less often produce systemic symptoms. However, individuals with these bites almost never require hospitalization. Spiders usually cling to the site of the bite. (If the spider can not be found, some other arachnid, such as a bedbug, should be suspected.) Anyone who has been bitten should take the spider to be identified.

Rarely, an individual may be bitten repeatedly by a relatively harmless spider or insect and develop an allergy to the toxin produced by that species. Subsequent bites can produce severe, even fatal allergic reactions. Fortunately such events are rare. The treatment for such reactions is identical to the treatment for allergic reactions to insect stings.

Black Widow Spider Bites

The female black widow typically is coal black and has a prominent, spherical abdomen that may be as large as one-half inch (1.25 cm) in diameter. This appearance is so distinctive that finding the characteristic markings on the undersurface of the abdomen is rarely necessary. The typical markings consist of red or orange figures that usually resemble an hourglass, but may be round, broken into two figures, or have some other configuration. Markings of the same color but in varying patterns are sometimes present on the back, although only the undersurface markings are considered characteristic. In some southwestern states black widow spiders have irregular white patches on their abdomens. Different species of *Latrodectus* in other countries have a similar appearance. (The male is smaller, has a brown color, and is harmless.)

The black widow weaves a coarse, crudely constructed web in dark corners, both indoors and out. Almost half the black widow bites reported in the medical literature in the first four decades of this century were inflicted on the male genitalia by spiders on the underside of outdoor toilet seats. However, this spider is timid and would rather run than attack an intruder.

Thirty to forty years ago five to ten deaths a year resulted from black widow spider bites, although they were limited almost entirely to small children or elderly individuals in poor health. Recognition and treatment of such bites has improved so much that deaths are rare within the United States. (Bites in children weighing thirty pounds or less would still have a mortality of about fifty percent if untreated.) In healthy adults, black widow spider bites cause painful muscle spasms and prostration for two to four days, but complete recovery essentially always follows. Antivenin treatment is not recommended for adults.

The bite may feel like a pin prick, may produce a mild burning, or may not be noticed at all. Small puncture wounds, slight redness, or no visible marks may be found at the site of the bite. Within about fifteen minutes painful muscle cramps develop at the point of the bite and rapidly spread to involve the entire body. The characteristic pattern of spread is by continuity. From a bite on the forearm the cramps would spread to the upper arm, to the shoulder, and over the chest to involve the rest of the body, including the legs. The abdominal muscles are characteristically rigid and hard, although the abdomen is not tender. Weakness and tremors are also present.

A typical subject is anxious and restless. A feeble pulse and cold, clammy skin suggest shock; labored breathing, slurred speech, impaired coordination, mild stupor, and rare convulsions (in children) suggest disease involving the brain. Bitten individuals are often covered with perspiration; dizziness, nausea, and vomiting are common. If the spider or its bite have not been observed, the signs and symptoms may lead to an erroneous diagnosis of an acute abdominal emergency.

Symptoms typically increase in severity for several hours, occasionally as long as twenty-four hours, and then gradually subside. After two or three days essentially all symptoms disappear, although a few minor residua may persist for weeks or months.

Treatment consists of efforts to relieve the painful muscle spasms and antivenin for small children. No treatment at all should be directed to the site of the bite, with the possible exception of applying an ice cube to relieve pain. Incision and suction is damaging and useless and should not be performed.

Essentially nothing can be done outside a hospital; small children must be hospitalized. Antivenin, produced in the United States by Merck Sharp & Dohme, and the drugs to control spasms are rarely available anywhere else. The antivenin is prepared in horses and should not be given to persons allergic to horse serum. It is usually not administered to healthy adults between the ages of sixteen and sixty, and only to individuals of small body size with severe symptoms who are twelve to fifteen years old. Instructions with the vial of antiserum should be followed.

Muscle spasms may be relieved by periodic injections of 10 cc of a ten percent calcium gluconate solution or 10 cc of methocarbamol, but these are rarely available outside a hospital. A tranquilizer (diazepam) may help relieve less severe muscle spasms; hot baths are occasionally helpful. Strong analgesics are helpful but rarely provide complete pain relief.

Brown Spider Bites

The brown, or violin, spider *(Loxosceles reclusa)* more recently labeled the "brown recluse spider," has received attention as the cause of "necrotic arachnidism." Following the bite of this spider, a blister appears, and is surrounded by an area of intense inflammation about one-half inch (1.25 cm) in diameter. Pain is mild at first but may become quite severe within about eight hours. Over the next ten to fourteen days the blister ruptures and the involved skin turns dark brown or black. Eventually the dead, black tissue drops away, leaving a crater that heals with scarring.

A few individuals have large skin losses that require grafts to cover the defect. Some children have lost considerable portions of the face. Such events have attracted great notoriety for this spider, even though much smaller wounds are far more typical. Bites are attributed to *Loxosceles reclusa* (incorrectly) well outside of its habitat, which is limited to the southeastern and south-central portion of the United States and ends at the Texas–New Mexico border.

Generalized symptoms that may appear within thirty-six hours of the bite include chills and fever, nausea and vomiting, joint pain, and a skin rash or hives. With severe reactions, red blood cells are broken down (hemolysis) and platelets are destroyed (thrombocytopenia), which can result in a significant anemia and bleeding tendency. Rare fatalities have occurred, mostly in children.

Essentially nothing can be done for such bites in a wilderness situation unless appropriate injectable medications are carried along. If the person can be hospitalized within less than eight hours, the site of the bite can be surgically excised. Such therapy should be reserved for bites from spiders clearly identifiable as *L. reclusa,* so the spider must be captured (intact if possible) and brought to the hospital to be identified. After eight hours the area involved may be too large to be excised. Corticosteroids may also be administered. One recommended program is 4 mg of dexamethasone, administered intramuscularly every six hours until the reaction starts to subside, and then in tapered doses. Others include injection of hydrocortisone beneath the bite and the administration of dapsone. Nothing is very satisfactory.

SCORPION STINGS

Scorpions are found throughout most of the United States, but the species lethal for man, *Centruroides,* are limited to Arizona, New Mexico, Texas, southern California, and northern Mexico. In these areas scorpions are a significant problem. Sixty-nine deaths resulted from scorpion stings in Arizona between 1929 and 1954. During the same period, only twenty deaths resulted from poisonous snake bites. With improved medical management of the complications of scorpion stings, no deaths have occurred in Arizona for twenty years.

Scorpions are eight-legged arachnids that range in length from three to eight inches (7.5 to 20 cm) and have a rather plump body, thin tail, and large pinchers. They are found in dry climates under rocks and logs, buried in the sand, in accumulations of lumber, bricks, or brush, and in the attics, walls, or understructures of houses or deserted buildings. The problems with scorpions in Arizona are clearly related to their tendency to live in the vicinity of human habitation where children are frequently playing.

Stings can be avoided by exercising care when picking up stones, logs, or similar objects under which scorpions hide during the day. Since scorpions are nocturnal, walking barefoot after dark is inadvisable. Shoes and clothing should be shaken vigorously before dressing in the morning, particularly when camping outdoors.

The lethal species of scorpions are often found under loose bark or around old tree stumps. They have a yellow to greenish yellow color and can be distinguished from other species by a small, knoblike projection at the base of their stingers. Adults measure three inches (7.5 cm) in length and three-eighths inch (1 cm) in width. One subspecies has two irregular dark stripes down its back.

The sting of a nonlethal scorpion has been described as similar to that of a wasp or hornet, although usually somewhat more severe, and should be treated in an identical manner. (Scorpion venom is not identical to insect venom, and individuals allergic to insect stings usually are not allergic to scorpion stings.) Lethal scorpion stings are more painful, but fatalities have been limited almost entirely to small children.

Initially the sting of a scorpion of one of the lethal species produces only a pricking sensation and may not be noticed. Nothing can be seen at the site of the sting. (Swelling and red or purple discoloration are indications that the sting has been inflicted by a nonlethal species.) Pain follows in five to sixty minutes and may be quite severe. The sting site is quite sensitive to touch and is the last part of the body to recover. Tapping the site produces a painful tingling or burning sensation that travels up the extremity toward the body. (Apparently stings by other species of scorpions can occasionally produce a similar sensation.) Sensitivity may persist as long as ten days, although other symptoms usually disappear within ten hours.

Individuals who have been stung typically are extremely restless and jittery. Young children writhe, jerk, or flail about in a bizarre manner that suggests a convulsion. Their movements are completely involuntary. However, in spite of their constantly moving bodies, the children can talk. Although they appear to be writhing in pain, they usually state that they do not hurt. Convulsions have been described, but the true nature of these events is questionable. Visual disturbances such as roving eye movements or a fluttering type of movement known as nystagmus are common. Occasionally a child complains that he can not see, but nothing abnormal can be found when examining his eyes, and sight returns spontaneously in a few minutes. Children under six years of age may develop respiratory problems such as wheezing and stridor, and a few may need assisted respiration.

Persons who have been stung typically have an elevated blood pressure, which may be an important diagnostic sign since hypertension is rare in children. The blood pressure usually returns to normal within four to six hours and becomes life-threatening only in infants.

Elderly individuals with preexisting health problems and small children stung by one of the lethal scorpion species should be taken to a hospital. Only a medical facility of that sophistication has the equipment and supplies necessary to monitor these individuals and deal with any complications that may arise. An ice cube applied to the site of the sting may help reduce pain, but no other therapy is possible outside a hospital. In locations such as the Grand Canyon, where prompt evacuation is not possible, diazepam can be given to children for control of the involuntary movements.

Other countries have species of lethal scorpions much more deadly than those in the southwestern United States. Mexico reportedly has had as many as 76,000 scorpion stings resulting in 1,500 deaths in a single year. The stings of such scorpions must be treated with antivenin, which is rarely obtainable outside a hospital, particularly by someone who does not speak the country's language. Death from the stings of such scorpions is usually the result of sudden, very severe high blood pressure. Adrenergic blocking agents such as propranolol may be an effective method for treating such stings and probably should be carried by visitors to the countries where such lethal species of scorpions exist.

ALLERGIC REACTIONS TO INSECT STINGS

Between fifty and one hundred deaths result annually from allergic reactions to Hymenoptera stings (bees, wasps, hornets, and fire ants) in the United States, more than the deaths from rabies, poisonous snakes, spiders, and scorpions combined. Approximately one of every two hundred people in the United States has experienced a severe reaction to such stings. Potentially fatal reactions can be prevented or successfully treated in individuals known to have such allergies, but many deaths still occur in persons whose allergic status had not been previously recognized. The problem of allergies and the severe, potentially lethal allergic reactions known as "anaphylactic shock" are discussed in Chapter Twenty, "Allergies."

An individual allergic to insect stings usually experiences milder allergic reactions before having a potentially fatal reaction. Two types of nonlethal reactions occur: local reactions and systemic reactions.

Local reactions are characterized by severe swelling limited to the limb or portion of the limb that is the site of the insect sting. Almost all insect stings are associated with some swelling, but the area of swelling is usually three inches (7.5 cm) or less in diameter. With severe local reactions, a major portion of an extremity, such as the entire forearm, is swollen, and may be painful, associated with itching, or mildly discolored.

Systemic reactions occur in areas of the body some distance from the site of the sting. Most typical are hives, which may be scattered over much of the body. Generalized itching or reddening of the skin may also occur. Persons with more severe reactions may have hypotension (low blood pressure) and difficulty breathing. (Clearly, the last two reactions could be fatal if severe.)

Investigators of insect hypersensitivity reactions have recommended that individuals who have had a systemic reaction to an insect sting undergo skin testing with Hymenoptera venoms. (If the results of skin tests are inconclusive, more sophisticated measurement of venom-specific IgE antibodies by the radioallergosorbent procedure can be carried out.) About half of the people who have had a systemic reaction and also have a positive skin test would be expected to have a severe, possibly fatal reaction if stung again. Desensitization with purified insect venoms—not whole-body extracts—is recommended for these individuals. (In one recent study of children who had experienced an anaphylactic reaction following a sting, only nine percent of subsequent accidental stings led to severe reactions. None of the reactions were more severe than the original reactions, which led to the conclusion that immunotherapy was unnecessary for such individuals.)

Desensitization can be a drawn-out, uncomfortable procedure but also can be life-saving. Starting with very small quantities, increasingly larger amounts of the insect venoms are injected subcutaneously until the allergic reaction is "neutralized." The individual is still allergic to the Hymenoptera venoms, but the antibodies responsible for producing the allergic reactions are "used up" by the repeated injections of the material with which they react. Generally, even after successful desensitization, injections must be continued at approximately monthly intervals for years or indefinitely. If the desensitization injections are stopped, the former allergic condition often reappears.

Desensitization must be carried out under the close supervision of a physician experienced with the procedure. Severe, life-threatening allergic reactions to the desensitization injections may occur, and a physician must be on hand to deal with them. However, a physician who is standing by watching for a reaction can treat it effectively. Allergic reactions to insect stings in a wilderness environment without a physician in attendance are a far greater threat.

Desensitization, or even skin testing, is not recommended for individuals who have large local reactions because these are rarely followed by systemic reactions. However, carrying epinephrine (adrenaline) is recommended for individuals who have had either type of reaction.

For individuals experiencing an anaphylactic reaction, 0.3 cc of a 1:1,000 solution of epinephrine should be injected subcutaneously as soon as symptoms are detected. Second (and sometimes third) injections are often needed at intervals of twelve to fifteen minutes.

Rock climbers and some other wilderness users who have systemic allergic reactions to insect stings have a unique risk of fatal reactions because they are subject to stings in locations, such as rock walls, where they can not be immediately treated by others and only with difficulty by themselves. Such persons should seriously consider desensitization now that purified venom preparations, which make that procedure so much more reliable, are available. They also must be prepared to treat an anaphylactic reaction at any time.

FIRE ANT STINGS

Both the black fire ant *(Solenopsis richteri)* and the red fire ant *(Solenopsis invicta)* appear to have entered the United States in the early twentieth century through the port of Mobile, Alabama. These insects were originally expected to occupy most areas where the average minimum annual temperature was higher than 10°F (−12°C), but discovery of hybrids that are more tolerant of cold indicates that these insects will ultimately infest one-quarter of the U.S. land area. As recently as 1950, fire ants were limited to the western half of southern Alabama and the adjacent eastern part of southern Mississippi. In 1989 they were found in most of South Carolina, Georgia, Alabama, Florida, Mississippi, and Louisiana; the southeastern two-thirds of Texas; and parts of Missouri and North Carolina. They are expected eventually to occupy the rest of Texas, most of California (sparing only the northern and central Sierra Nevada), and the coastal areas in Oregon and Washington.

In infested urban areas, thirty to sixty percent of the inhabitants are stung by fire ants every year. Stings are more common among children, on the legs, and during the summer. The ant grabs the skin with powerful mandibles and, if undisturbed, stings repeatedly, rotating its body so it can reach different sites. Almost everyone stung by an ant develops a wheal-and-flare reaction (a pale bump that itches and is surrounded by a thin rim of skin that has turned red). This reaction resolves in about thirty to sixty minutes, but within twenty-four hours evolves into a sterile pustule (a pimple or small boil). The skin over the pustule sloughs in two to three days. No therapy is effective for the pustule, but scratching can lead to infection that may require antibiotic therapy.

Between one-fourth to half of the individuals who have been stung develop large local reactions that are red, swollen, firm, and "itch like crazy." In extreme cases, compression of nerves or blood vessels develops, and a few individuals have required amputation. Elevation of the extremity, steroid therapy, and antihistamines can largely prevent such extreme reactions. Topical steroid ointments such as 0.25 percent hydrocortisone, local anesthetic creams, and oral antihistamines reduce the itching associated with more common, less severe reactions.

About one-half to one percent of stings are followed by anaphylactic reactions, and at least thirty-two deaths have resulted. Most of the individuals had been stung less than five times. Anaphylactic reactions can occur hours after a sting. Such reactions should be treated in the same manner as any other anaphylactic reaction. (See Chapter Twenty, "Allergies.")

No method for controlling the population of fire ants over a large area is currently available. Avoiding contact with the insects is virtually impossible for individuals who live in infested areas. Those who develop anaphylaxis following a sting should be desensitized. Whole-body extracts of fire ants, unlike whole-body extracts of other Hymenoptera, contain substantial (although variable) quantities of venom and are effective for desensitization. Thousands of residents of infested areas are receiving such therapy. Anyone who has had an anaphylactic reaction to the sting of one of these insects should at least consult a physician about desensitization.

MEDICATIONS

Dosages for medications recommended in this text are provided only in this appendix. The precautions that must be observed with the administration of these agents are included with the dosages. In this way, anyone using the drug is warned of risks without the need to repeat such a warning each time the drug is discussed in the text. (Rare individuals may have unpredictable adverse reactions to any drug, even aspirin. Warnings about such idiosyncratic reactions are not included.)

The doses listed are those that can be safely administered to a young or middle-aged adult in good health. The doses of some drugs for children or elderly individuals are quite different. The doses for individuals with liver or kidney disease are also quite different. Administration of the stated doses of these drugs to such persons could have deleterious, possibly even lethal, effects.

For some medications a range of doses is given, indicating the dose should be adjusted for the patient's weight or for the severity of his disease.

Essentially all drugs have two types of names: a generic name and one or more trade names. (Drugs also have names based on chemical structure and official names listed in the *United States Pharmacopoeia* or *National Formulary,* but these are rarely used.) Generic names, assigned by the American Medical Association–United States Pharmacopeia Nomenclature Committee, are widely used. Some generic names are similar to chemical or official names; many are not.

In the United States, a drug has only a single generic name even though it may be produced by a number of companies. In contrast, a drug produced and sold by more than one manufacturer is given a different trade name by each maker. (A few pharmaceutical manufacturers sell their products only under generic names.) Trade names are registered trademarks that can be used only by the manufacturer that has created them. Drug trade names are devised to be more easily remembered than generic names so that physicians will prescribe that specific manufacturer's product. Some are similar to generic names; many are not.

In this text, medications have been listed by their generic names with some of the better-known trade names in parentheses to help with identification. For some agents—aspirin or penicillin, for instance—generic names are more familiar and are the only ones listed. Many generic names are unfamiliar to people who are not medical professionals, but are known by pharmacists and by most physicians through whom these drugs must be obtained. Generic names used in countries other than the United States may be totally different, even in other English-speaking nations. (U.S. generic names are assigned by a U.S. committee.)

Drug prices are provided so that the costs of therapy with similar medications can be compared (the cost to a pharmacy for enough oral penicillin for one day of therapy is $0.30 to $0.82 per day; the cost for one day of therapy with an oral cephalosporin is $2.19 to $8.10 per day, up to twenty-seven times as high), and to demonstrate the differences between generic and proprietary products (enough Flagyl® for one day of therapy costs a pharmacy $3.25; the cost for the same amount of the generic product, metronidazole, is $0.13 to $1.66 per day, as little as one twenty-fifth as much). Even the prices of generic products vary remarkably. Some variation results from differences in packaging—a bottle of 100 capsules would be expected to cost less than 100 individually wrapped capsules—but no explanation is apparent for other cost variations. (Metronidazole is listed iden-

---

TABLE A-1.
U.S. and Metric Equivalents

Volume

U.S.	Metric
1 ounce	29.57 cc
(16 Ounces=1 Pint)	
1 pint	473 cc
(2 Pints=1 Quart)	
1 quart	946 cc
(4quarts=1 gallon)	
1 gallon	3,785 cc
1.057 quarts	1 liter
(1,000 cc=1 liter)	

Weight

U.S.	Metric
1 grain	64.8 milligrams
(1,000 Milligrams [mg]=1 Gram)	
1 ounce	28.35 grams
(16 ounces=1pound)	
1 pound	453.6 grams
(1,000 grams=1 kilogram)	
2.20 pounds	1 kilogram

Abbreviation: cc = cubic centimeters = milliliters (ml)

tically by different manufacturers at prices for 100 tablets ranging from $4.34 to $54.50.)

Selection of a particular preparation when so many are available presents problems to pharmacists as well as consumers. One reliable method is to consult the *Orange Book,* published by the Federal Drug Administration (FDA), which specifies generic products that have been tested and demonstrated to be bio-equivalent to the original, proprietary products (which have been extensively tested for effectiveness and safety), and to purchase the cheapest of generic bio-equivalent drugs. Most hospital pharmacies—as well as others—have copies of this publication.

Most of the costs cited are from the *1991 Drug Topics Redbook,* a listing of the products of most pharmacologic manufacturers. The prices are the costs to pharmacies, but retail prices should be proportional. Generic prices are printed in italics. (For recently developed medications still protected by patent, no generic products are available.) For agents that must be taken at regular intervals for a number of days, primarily antimicrobial agents and drugs for treating peptic ulcers, the cost of one day's therapy is listed in parenthesis after the cost of the drug. (Although the cost per dose may be higher, the total cost of a medication taken only once daily may be cheaper than that of an agent that must be taken more frequently.)

MEDICATIONS FOR THE RELIEF OF PAIN

Drugs that relieve pain are known as analgesics or local anesthetics. Analgesics can be classified as mild and strong. The mild analgesics are aspirin, acetaminophen, ibuprofen, and codeine. Moderate analgesia is provided by codeine combined with acetaminophen or aspirin. The commonly used strong analgesics are morphine and other opiates, so called because they were originally derived from opium, and meperidine (Demerol®). The strong analgesics are called narcotics, but that is a vague term that has no basis in chemical or pharmacologic properties. (*Narcotic* is defined as any drug that numbs, soothes, or induces a dreamlike state.)

The major hazard associated with strong pain-relieving drugs is cerebral depression that impairs respiration. No one with a known or suspected head injury or neurologic illness should be given strong pain medications.

Addiction is *not* a major hazard of strong analgesics—possibly not even a significant hazard—for individuals receiving such analgesics for legitimate reasons. Almost everyone who undergoes major surgery—thousands of people every day—receives strong analgesics postoperatively to control pain. Subsequent addiction is almost nonexistent. Many of the drugs effective for the relief of severe pain also produce euphoria, which is clearly beneficial for the victim of a major accident or illness. Addiction results when these drugs are taken for euphoria alone.

Codeine and the strong analgesics (and many other agents) are classified as "controlled substances" in the United States, and their distribution is regulated by the Drug Enforcement Agency, an arm of the U.S. Treasury Department, not the Public Health Service. They are difficult to obtain for anyone who is not a licensed physician (or a habitual drug user). Problems with the regulatory agency, particularly for individuals who are not physicians, can be lessened by precise records that detail the total amount of such agents on hand, where they are stored, the security of that location, persons authorized to remove the agents from storage, the names of individuals treated, and the time, place, quantity, and reason for administering the drugs.

To minimize the risk of addiction to strong analgesics, the following precautions should be observed:

1. Strong analgesics should not be administered except when clearly needed for the relief of pain (or the few other conditions for which some are effective, such as treatment of the pulmonary edema of heart failure with morphine).
2. A less potent analgesic should be substituted for a stronger agent as soon as pain has diminished to a level at which the milder drug can provide relief.
3. If therapy with a strong analgesic must be continued for more than seven days, a switch from one of the opiates (morphine and others) to meperidine or vice versa helps prevent addiction.
4. Strong analgesic administration should not be continued for more than twelve to fourteen days except in extraordinary circumstances, but such circumstances could occur in the wilderness. Evacuation of a person with a painful fracture from a remote area such as Antarctica or the Himalaya could well take more than two weeks. Failure to provide analgesia, even if addiction resulted, could be devastating.

If a potent analgesic is needed, one should be used and should be given in adequate quantities to relieve pain. A person with severe pain desperately needs the rest and relief that these drugs alone can provide. Halfway measures, such as inadequate doses or inadequate drugs, are of almost no value at all.

Aspirin

Aspirin is a mild analgesic that is as effective for the relief of minor pain as any available single drug except the strong analgesics. No other mild analgesic is as effective except acetaminophen, ibuprofen, and codeine. Aspirin is often not highly regarded because it is so familiar.

All aspirin is the same; all brands sold in the United States are identical in quality and effectiveness even though the prices differ as much as 1,000 percent. Combination with other compounds offers no significant analgesic benefits.

An apparently unrelated action of aspirin is its ability to reduce fever, which is a major reason it provides symptomatic relief for colds. More significantly, aspirin is valuable for the reduction of high fevers that threaten brain damage.

PRECAUTIONS

Aspirin is poisonous when taken in large quantities. In the United States it is by far the most common cause of poisoning in children. Aspirin, particularly flavored "children's" aspirin, must be inaccessible to children, like all medications.

Aspirin is a strong gastric irritant. A recent study at a major university medical center found that more than ninety percent of the individuals hospitalized for gastrointestinal bleeding had been taking aspirin. This drug should not be used by persons with peptic ulcers or related disorders, including severe indigestion. The addition of buffering agents or antacids does not increase analgesic potency but can reduce the gastric irritation that aspirin commonly produces. However, for this purpose, enteric coating is more effective.

Aspirin should not be used in circumstances in which it might mask a fever that could be the first indication of an infection. (Codeine is probably the best substitute in this situation.)

DOSE

650 mg (10 grains) orally every four hours.

COST

325 mg: $3.30 to $20.85/1,000.
Buffered: $8.50 to $17.20/1,000.
Enteric coated: $9.25 to $15.90/1,000.

Acetaminophen

Acetaminophen (Tylenol® and others) is a mild analgesic just as effective as aspirin for relieving minor pain and for reducing fever. However, acetaminophen has much less tendency to cause stomach irritation. The increased dose in "extra strength" preparations has no benefit for individuals who are not unusually large.

PRECAUTIONS

Acetaminophen in large quantities (10 to 15 gm) produces severe liver damage. (At one time it was the drug most commonly used for suicide in Great Britain.) Unless treatment for an overdose is initiated within a few hours after the drug has been ingested, it is totally ineffective. This medication should be used with caution for individuals known to have liver disease. Many over-the-counter preparations for colds or sinus problems include acetaminophen, but this information is provided only in the list of contents in very small print. Such preparations should not be combined with acetaminophen alone.

DOSE

325 to 650 mg orally every three to four hours.

COST

320 mg: $6.48 to $14.61/1,000.

Ibuprofen

Ibuprofen (Motrin®, Nuprin®, and others) is a nonsteroidal anti-inflammatory agent and prostaglandin antagonist that is sold primarily as a mild analgesic. Its analgesic properties are essentially the same as those of aspirin or acetaminophen. Its greatest value has been for dysmenorrhea (painful menstrual cramps) because its antagonism to prostaglandins tends to make the uterine muscle relax. (The anti-inflammatory effects make this drug useful for arthritis, but that is not an acute disorder that requires care in wilderness circumstances.)

PRECAUTIONS

Ibuprofen is a gastric irritant, like aspirin, although some patients who can not tolerate aspirin have no problems with ibuprofen. It should not be taken by persons with a history of peptic ulcer or severe indigestion. All individuals receiving this drug must be aware of its potential to produce gastrointestinal ulceration and bleeding and must be alert for signs or symptoms of those disorders.

Ibuprofen also has a tendency to cause fluid retention. Whether it would aggravate symptoms of acute mountain sickness or high altitude pulmonary edema has not been studied, but it should be used with caution in circumstances in which those disorders could appear.

DOSE

For dysmenorrhea: 400 to 600 mg orally every four hours. (Tablets may contain 200, 300, 400, 600, or 800 mg; most tablets sold over the counter are 200 mg.)

COST

200 mg: $3.30 to $7.61/100; $24.50 to $36.44/1,000.
400 mg: $4.88 to $14.50/100; $60.63 to $77.95/1000.
600 mg: $6.50 to $23.35/100; $75.94 to $105.90/1,000.
800 mg: $7.88 to $27.48/100; $124.00 to $181.90/1,000.

Codeine

Codeine is an opium derivative that can augment the analgesia provided by other mild analgesics.

The analgesic effect of codeine alone is no stronger than that of aspirin or acetaminophen, but the analgesia produced by combining codeine with one of these two agents is twice that of either alone. Most codeine sold in the United States is in combination with one of these two drugs.

Codeine is legally classified as a "controlled substance" in the United States because it is an opium derivative, not because it is an addicting drug of abuse. In almost all other countries, including developed countries with sophisticated drug regulations such as Canada and Great Britain, codeine is sold over the counter. Codeine has almost none of the euphoric effect of other narcotics, and addiction is essentially nonexistent.

Codeine is a useful substitute for other mild analgesics when masking a fever might delay recognition of an infection.

PRECAUTIONS

Symptoms of indigestion or heartburn occur frequently in individuals who have such symptoms with other drugs, alcohol, or spicy foods. Some individuals experience nausea, and a small number may vomit. Constipation is common following codeine administration.

Codeine, like all opium derivatives, causes spasm of the muscles controlling outflow from the biliary system (sphincter of Oddi) and should be used sparingly for patients with liver disease, gallstones, acute cholecystitis, or acute or chronic pancreatitis.

DOSE

32 to 64 mg (1/2 to 1 grain) orally, usually in combination with 625 mg of aspirin or acetaminophen.

COST

Codeine sulphate: $18.98 to $35.91/100.
Codeine phosphate: $42.28/100.
Aspirin, 325 mg, with codeine, 30 mg: $67.50 to $90.00/1,000.
Acetaminophen, 320 mg, with codeine, 30 mg: $44.99 to $93.06/1,000.

Morphine

Morphine is a potent analgesic that has been so widely used for so long, and so effectively relieves severe pain, that it has been called "God's own medicine." It is one of the oldest and most valuable agents in the armamentarium of a physician.

In addition to its analgesic properties, morphine has a strong sedative effect that helps calm injured persons and limit thrashing about, which could aggravate wounds or hinder evacuation. This sedation and morphine's euphoric effect also help relieve the anxiety that follows an accident.

PRECAUTIONS

Morphine, like all sedatives, depresses brain function. **Therefore, morphine must never be given to a patient with a central nervous system injury or disease,** even a mild disorder, because morphine would usually further impair cerebral function. After the administration of morphine or a related drug, determining whether subsequent changes in the patient's condition were the result of progression of his disorder or the effects of the drug would be impossible. A person who is unconscious does not require analgesia.

Since the brain controls respiration, morphine also depresses respiratory function. It must be used cautiously for patients with chest injuries or pulmonary diseases, particularly at higher altitudes. However, relieving the pain of a severe chest injury may allow a patient to cough and breathe more deeply (in the absence of an accompanying brain disorder).

Morphine causes nausea and vomiting in some individuals; it is constipating for almost everyone and can contribute to the development of fecal impaction. This drug may cause spasm of the muscles controlling outflow from the urinary bladder, resulting in urinary retention requiring urethral catheterization, particularly following abdominal injuries. Like codeine, morphine causes spasm of the muscle controlling biliary outflow and should be used with caution for patients with liver, gallbladder, or pancreatic diseases. Meperidine produces such spasm much less frequently and should be used when these patients need a potent analgesic.

Morphine is addicting, should be used only when specifically needed for the relief of severe pain, and should be discontinued when less potent drugs can provide adequate analgesia.

Oral administration can produce satisfactory analgesia if enough of the drug is given (orally administered morphine is only one-third to one-sixth as effective as the injected drug), but absorption is slower and thirty to sixty minutes are required for the drug to take effect. More rapid onset can be obtained with sublingual tablets held under the tongue until dissolved. Rectal suppositories also are effective, particularly for individuals who are nauseated. Following intramuscular injection, analgesia can be expected after ten to fifteen minutes; the onset following intravenous injection is almost immediate. The intravenous route of administration should be used for patients in shock, preferably by individuals with previous experience with intravenous drug administration. The drug must be injected slowly over a period of several minutes, and the injection should be stopped if pain relief is achieved before the full dose is administered.

DOSE

For individuals weighing 150 pounds (70 kg) or more, 16 mg intramuscularly, 12 to 16 mg intravenously, or 20 to 30 mg orally every four hours. For individuals weighing less than 150 pounds (70 kg), 12 mg intramuscularly, 9 to 12 mg intravenously, or 15 to 20 mg orally every four hours.

COST

10-mg tablets: $18.54/100.
15-mg tablets: $13.78 to $23.52/100.
20-mg suppositories: $10.85 to $17.50/12.
20-ml vial for injection, 15 mg/ml: $10.95 to $13.73.

Meperidine

Meperidine (Demerol®) is a synthetic analgesic first introduced in 1938. It is not an opium derivative, as are codeine and morphine. The analgesia provided by meperidine is equal to that of morphine, but meperidine does not have as much sedative and euphoric effect, and the overall relief from severe pain may not be as satisfactory as that obtainable with morphine. For individuals with less severe injuries, the absence of sedation and euphoria may be desirable.

PRECAUTIONS

Meperidine was developed as a potent analgesic because it was thought to have fewer side effects than morphine. However, **meperidine definitely depresses cerebral function, must not be given to patients with central nervous system injuries or diseases, and must be used very carefully for patients with respiratory disorders.**

Meperidine does cause fewer problems with biliary outflow than morphine; it appears to cause nausea and vomiting, constipation, or urinary retention less commonly, but such problems do occur.

Meperidine is definitely addicting, but addiction may take longer to develop and may occur less frequently because meperidine produces less euphoria. Precautions to avoid addiction must be observed. For patients who require a potent analgesic for longer than seven to ten days, switching from morphine to meperidine at that time may help avoid addiction.

DOSE

100 mg orally or intramuscularly, or 75 to 100 mg intravenously, every three to four hours.

COST

100-mg tablets: $18.75 to $39.90/100.

30-ml vial for injection, 50 mg/ml: $9.86.

Demerol®: 100-mg tablets: $105.17/100; 30-ml vial for injection, 50 mg/ml: $15.52.

Dibucaine Ointment

Dibucaine (Nupercainal®) is a local anesthetic that is neither a narcotic nor related to procaine or cocaine and can be used by individuals allergic to those agents. Although the ointment can provide temporary relief from the pain and discomfort of many minor disorders, it is used most commonly for hemorrhoids and related anal problems.

PRECAUTIONS

Few precautions are necessary, although no more than one ounce of the one percent ointment should be used in a single twenty-four-hour period. Allergy to this agent may develop, usually produces a rash covering the area to which the ointment has been applied, and commonly causes more discomfort than the condition for which this medication was being used.

COST

One-ounce tube: $0.70 to $1.64.

Lidocaine

Lidocaine (Xylocaine®) is an injectable local anesthetic that is widely used for dental procedures and for minor surgery, including suturing lacerations. (The same agent is also used to prevent some cardiac rhythm abnormalities, but that use is not considered here.) Epinephrine may be added to lidocaine solutions to constrict blood vessels at the site of injection, reduce the speed of absorption, and prolong local anesthesia. Lidocaine ointment is available and should be used in the same manner as dibucaine ointment.

The concentrations of solutions for injection range from one-half to two percent; a one percent solution appears most useful for wilderness circumstances, although the higher concentrations provide more of the agent in a smaller volume.

PRECAUTIONS

For the uncommon individuals who are allergic to lidocaine this drug must not be used. Adverse reactions include anaphylaxis (see Chapter Twenty, "Allergies") and convulsions.

During injections of lidocaine, repeated aspirations should be made with the syringe to ensure the drug is not being injected into a blood vessel.

DOSE AND ADMINISTRATION

The usual injection consists of 5 to 10 cc of a one percent solution, although more is occasionally needed. The solution should be injected into and just beneath the skin first and into deeper tissues after the skin has been anesthetized. Before each injection the plunger of the syringe should be pulled back to ensure the needle is not in a blood vessel. Anesthesia is almost immediate, usually persists for thirty to forty-five minutes, and can be tested by pricking the injected area with the tip of a sterile needle.

COST

50-ml vial for injection, one percent without epinephrine: $1.25 to $3.75; $18.44 to $21.75/25.

Xylocaine®: 5-ml ampule for injection, one percent with epinephrine—$14.38/10; 10-ml vial for injection, one percent with epinephrine—$6.94/5.

MEDICATIONS FOR SLEEP OR SEDATION (TRANQUILIZERS)

Conventional sleeping medications should not be taken at altitudes above 10,000 feet (3,000 m). Under the influence of these drugs, respirations can be slowed to such an extent that the blood oxygen level falls significantly, aggravating the symptoms of acute mountain sickness. Acetazolamide is the drug of choice for promoting sleep at higher elevations.

Benzodiazepines

The benzodiazepines are a group of drugs with almost identical pharmacologic properties, but chlordiazepoxide (Librium®) and diazepam (Valium®) are most commonly used as tranquilizers, and flurazepam (Dalmane®) is most commonly used for promoting sleep. Diazepam (Valium®) also is used to relieve muscle spasm, particularly in the back muscles.

The benzodiazepines are safe although questions have been raised recently about triazolam (Halcion®). Lethal overdose is rare unless some other drug, usually alcohol, is taken along with very large quantities of the benzodiazepine.

PRECAUTIONS

Unusual drowsiness may persist the day following ingestion of any of these drugs.

Like the strong analgesics, benzodiazepines depress brain function and should not be given to individuals with head injuries or central nervous system disease.

Benzodiazepines potentiate the depressive effects of alcohol.

DOSE

To induce sleep: flurazepam (Dalmane®), 15 or 30 mg, orally at bedtime.

For sedation or as a tranquilizer: chlordiazepoxide (Librium®) or diazepam (Valium®), 5 to 10 mg orally two to four times per day.

As a muscle relaxant: diazepam (Valium®), 5 to 10 mg orally two to four times per day.

COST

Flurazepam: 15 mg—$10.13 to $28.25/100; 30 mg—$10.80 to $31.58/100.
Dalmane®: 15 mg—$45.00/100; 30 mg—$48.96/100.
Chlordiazepoxide: 5 mg—$1.20 to $6.56/100; 10 mg—$1.20 to $16.50/100.
Librium®: 5 mg—$28.20/100; 10 mg—$41.09/100.
Diazepam: 5 mg—$2.10 to $23.50/100; 10 mg—$2.87 to $39.75/100.
Valium®: 5 mg—$48.49/100; 10 mg—$81.74/100.

Others

Diphenhydramine (Benadryl®) is an antihistamine but has recently been approved by the FDA for use as a sleeping medication, particularly for elderly individuals who may become excited after taking barbiturates. Other medications capable of inducing sleep have significant disadvantages, or would rarely be needed or available in wilderness situations. Barbiturates are not as safe as benzodiazepines and are particularly dangerous when combined with alcohol. They produce greater cerebral depression and have a greater tendency to cause a "hangover" characterized by lassitude and somnolence. Chloral hydrate is rarely used any more because better agents are available.

Glutethimide (Doriden®) and methaqualone (Sopor® and others) are not as effective as benzodiazepines for legitimate uses and have been abused so extensively they have fallen into disrepute. Glutethimide has the singular disadvantage of not being removable by dialysis so that an overdose can not be effectively treated.

ANTIMICROBIAL AGENTS

The antimicrobial agents include antibiotics and sulfonamides, which are used to treat established infections, and antiseptics such as povidone-iodine, which kill microorganisms on contact.

Bacteria are classified as positive or negative according to their reaction with the gram stain; as cocci (spheres), bacilli (rods), or spirochetes (spirals); and as aerobic if they are able to grow in the presence of oxygen or anaerobic if they can not. This classification is used in the discussion that follows.

The Penicillins

Penicillin, the first antibiotic to be discovered, is still widely used and is effective. Slight modifications to penicillin have been made, and this entire group of drugs is referred to as "the penicillins." The penicillins actively kill bacteria and are called bacteriocidal; some antibiotics just keep them from multiplying and are called bacteriostatic. Organisms susceptible to the penicillins include streptococci ("strep" throat, cellulitis, impetigo); staphylococci (boils, abscesses, wound infections); pneumococci (conjunctivitis, pneumonia); Neisseria (gonorrhea, meningitis); and the spirochete that causes syphilis. Except for ampicillin and similar agents, the penicillins have little effect against the organisms likely to cause gastrointestinal infections such as traveler's diarrhea, dysentery, or typhoid fever.

Of the available penicillin preparations, phenoxymethyl penicillin (penicillin V) is most suitable for oral administration because it is resistant to destruction by acid in the stomach. Aqueous crystalline penicillin G is usually used for intravenous administration. Procaine penicillin G is used for intramuscular administration because it is less painful and persists longer. Benzathine penicillin G is also administered intramuscularly, is absorbed much more slowly, and its action lasts much longer, albeit at lower blood concentrations. It is rarely used to treat infections other than syphilis.

Some staphylococci produce an enzyme, called penicillinase, that destroys penicillin. Penicillinase-resistant penicillins that are effective against such organisms have been developed. Cloxacillin and dicloxacillin are penicillinase-resistant penicillins that are effective when administered orally. Nafcillin and methicillin are penicillinase-resistant but are usually administered intramuscularly and intravenously. Infections caused by staphylococci should always be treated with penicillinase-resistant agents unless they have been proven to be sensitive to other antibiotics.

PRECAUTIONS

The penicillins are essentially nontoxic, but allergic reactions occur in about ten percent of the patients receiving them. Most of these reactions consist of skin rashes, a low fever, or other minor problems, but a few individuals develop severe anaphylactic reactions that may be lethal within minutes. (See Chapter Twenty, "Allergies.")

Anyone who has suffered an anaphylactic reaction to any of the penicillins must never be treated with any of them again. The danger of a potentially lethal reaction is significant. A history of previous minor allergic reactions is not predictive of such a life-threatening event, but such individuals should avoid penicillins if possible.

If signs of anaphylaxis develop in a patient receiving a penicillin, the drug should be discontinued immediately. The patient should be warned of his allergy to penicillin and must tell his physician or anyone who subsequently cares for him. He should wear a bracelet or a tag warning of his allergy. Participants with allergies to penicillin on a wilderness outing should inform other members of the party and must make preparations in advance to have other antibiotics available.

DOSE

Phenoxymethyl penicillin: 500 to 1,000 mg orally every six hours.

Procaine penicillin G (Wycillin®): 375 to 3,000 mg (3 gm) or 0.6 to 4.8 million units per day intramuscularly in equal doses every six to twelve hours.

Aqueous crystalline penicillin G: 375 to 12,500 mg (12.5 gm) or 0.6 to 20 million units per day intravenously in equal doses every two to six hours.

Ampicillin: 500 to 1,000 mg orally every six hours.

Cloxacillin: 500 to 1,000 mg orally every six hours.

Dicloxacillin: 250 to 500 mg orally every six hours.

Nafcillin: 1.0 to 2.0 gm intravenously or intramuscularly every two to six hours.

COST

Phenoxymethyl penicillin: 500 mg—$7.50 to $10.25/100 ($0.30 to $0.82 per day).

Wycillin®: 1,500 mg (1.5 gm) or 2.4 million units—$2.33/preloaded syringe ($4.66 to $18.64 per day).

Aqueous crystalline penicillin G: 3 gm or 5 million units—$108.25/10 vials ($10.83 to $43.30 per day).

Ampicillin: 500 mg—$9.95 to $33.39/100 ($0.40 to $2.67 per day).

Cloxacillin: 500 mg—$36.50 to $79.00/100 ($1.46 to $6.32 per day).

Dicloxacillin: 250 mg—$12.60 to $42.02/100; 500 mg—$46.35 to $75.63/100 ($0.50 to $3.03 per day).

Nafcillin: 6-ml vial for injection, 500 mg—$20.00/10 ($16.00 to $96.00 per day).

The Cephalosporins

The cephalosporins are a group of antibiotics that are chemically and therapeutically similar to the penicillins. The organisms against which the first-generation cephalosporins and the penicillins are effective are essentially the same. Second- and third-generation cephalosporins are effective against a wider spectrum of organisms. However, the cephalosporins are considerably more expensive than the penicillins.

Cephradine (Anspor® and Velosef®), cephalexin (Keflex®), cefazolin (Kefzol® and Ancef®), and cephalothin (Keflin®) are first-generation cephalosporins used to treat staphylococcal infections. Cephradine and cephalexin can be administered orally; cefazolin and cephalothin are administered intramuscularly or intravenously. Cefoxitin (Mefoxin®) is a second-generation cephalosporin that is usually administered intravenously and can be a useful alternative to either clindamycin or chloramphenicol for treating anaerobic bacterial infections such as peritonitis. Ceftriaxone (Rocephin®) is a third-generation cephalosporin administered intramuscularly and intravenously that is particularly useful for treating meningitis.

PRECAUTIONS

Ten percent of individuals allergic to penicillin are also allergic to the cephalosporins. Anyone who has had a severe reaction to penicillin, particularly an anaphylactic reaction, should not be treated with cephalosporins.

In general, the cephalosporins enter the cerebrospinal fluid poorly and except for ceftriaxone should not be used for treating meningitis.

DOSE

Cephradine (Anspor®, Velosef®): 500 mg orally every six hours.

Cephalexin (Keflex®): 500 mg orally every six hours.

Cefazolin (Kefzol®, Ancef®): 500 to 1,000 mg (1 gm) every six hours intramuscularly or intravenously.

Cephalothin (Keflin®): 1,000 to 2,000 mg (1 to 2 gm) every six to eight hours intramuscularly or intravenously.

Cefoxitin (Mefoxin®): 1,000 to 2,000 mg (1 to 2 gm) every six to eight hours intramuscularly or intravenously.

Ceftriaxone (Rocephin®): 1,000 mg (1 gm) every twelve or twenty-four hours intramuscularly or intravenously.

COST

Cephradine: 500 mg—$54.75 to $120.60/100 ($2.19 to $4.82 per day).

Anspor®: 500 mg—$164.30/100 ($6.57 per day).

Velosef®: 500 mg—$158.29/100 ($6.33 per day).

Cephalexin: 500 mg—$28.43 to $160.74/100 ($1.14 to $6.43 per day).

Keflex®: 500 mg—$202.52/100 ($8.10 per day).

Cefazolin: powder for injection, 500 mg—$18.00 to $30.30/10; 1,000 mg (1 gm)—$35.25 to $60.80/10 ($7.20 to $24.32 per day).

Kefzol®: powder for injection, 500 mg—$1.44 each; $22.92/10; 50-ml vial for injection, 500 mg—$24.00/10; 1,000 mg (1 gm)—$38.40/10 ($9.17 to $15.36 per day).

Ancef®: powder for injection, 500 mg—$35.29/25; 1,000 mg (1 gm)—$70.59/25; 50-ml vial for injection, 500 mg—$89.60/24; 1,000 mg (1 gm)—$121.60/24 ($5.65 to $20.27 per day).

Cephalothin: powder for injection, 1,000 mg (1 gm)—$70.31/25; 10-ml vial for injection, 1,000 mg (1 gm)—$4.38 each; 50-ml vial for injection, 1,000 mg (1 gm)—$200.84/24; 2,000 mg (2 gm)—$265.86/24 ($8.44 to $44.31 per day).

Keflin®: powder for injection, 1,000 mg (1 gm)—$32.40/10; 2,000 mg—$57.60/10 ($9.72 to $23.04 per day).

Mefoxin®: powder for injection, 1,000 mg (1 gm)—$85.25/10; 2,000 mg (2 gm)—$169.88/10; 50-ml vial for injection, 1,000 mg (1 gm)—$261.30/24; 2,000 mg (2 gm)—$464.40/24 ($25.58 to $77.40 per day).

Rocephin®: powder for injection, 1,000 mg (1 gm)—$30.46 each ($30.46 to $60.92 per day).

Erythromycin

Erythromycin is effective against pneumococci, streptococci, mycoplasma, and most staphylococci, but is used primarily for individuals who are allergic to penicillin. As a penicillin substitute it probably should not be used for severe staphylococcal infections.

PRECAUTIONS

Very few adverse reactions to erythromycin occur, and those that do appear are mild.

DOSE

500 mg orally every six hours.

COST

500-mg: $15.95 to $28.62/100 ($0.64 to $1.14 per day).

Clindamycin

Clindamycin is another antibiotic with antibacterial effects similar to those of penicillin and is a suitable substitute for individuals allergic to penicillin. In addition, clindamycin is effective against staphylococci and a number of anaerobic organisms, particularly *Bacteroides fragilis,* one of the most common of the anaerobic organisms that cause peritonitis.

PRECAUTIONS

Approximately two to twenty percent of patients being treated with clindamycin develop diarrhea. Usually the diarrhea is mild, and treatment can be continued. However, rare individuals develop a life-threatening colitis from overgrowth of toxin-producing bacteria in the colon. Copious fluids and electrolytes are lost, and large amounts of blood and mucus appear in the stools. Clindamycin must be discontinued at once if this type of diarrhea appears, the lost fluids must be restored—intravenously if necessary—and metronidazole should be given orally every eight hours for ten days.

DOSE

300 mg orally every six hours.
300 to 600 mg intramuscularly or intravenously every eight hours.

COST

150-mg tablets: $82.49 to $103.90/100 ($6.60 to $8.31 per day); 6-ml vial for injection, 900 mg/ml: $360.00 to $429.69/25 ($2.40 to $5.73 per day).

The Aminoglycosides

The aminoglycosides are a group of antibiotics that include streptomycin, tobramycin, neomycin, and gentamicin. Streptomycin is now used only for tuberculosis or bubonic plaque. Neomycin use is limited to preparations from which it can not be absorbed, such as ophthalmic ointments. Tobramycin and gentamicin are effective against a large number of gram-negative bacilli and are used for severe infections such as peritonitis. Due to their toxicity these antibiotics should not be used for relatively minor infections. They are ineffective against anaerobic bacteria.

PRECAUTIONS

The aminoglycosides are excreted by the kidneys and can damage them. Patients with renal disease should not receive aminoglycosides or should receive them in smaller doses.

The aminoglycosides can cause damage to the inner ear and the auditory and vestibular nerves, resulting in deafness, ringing or buzzing in the ears, loss of balance, or vertigo.

The aminoglycosides should not be injected directly into a body cavity or be given rapidly by vein. Respiratory arrest due to a form of nerve block can result.

DOSE

Gentamicin: 1.7 mg per kg of body weight intramuscularly, followed by 1.0 mg per kg every eight hours.

Tobramycin: 3 to 5 mg per kg of body weight intramuscularly every eight hours.

COST

Gentamicin: 2-ml vial for injection, 40 mg/ml—$1.50 to $3.18; $26.04 to $58.00/25 ($43.12 to $9.54 per day).

Tobramycin: 2-ml vial for injection, 20 mg/ml—$85.63/25; 2-ml vial for injection, 80 mg/ml—$170.63/25.

The Tetracyclines

The tetracyclines (Achromycin® and others) are effective for infections produced by a broad spectrum of organisms that includes rickettsia and some viruslike organisms as well as a large number of gram-positive and gram-negative bacteria. However, the tetracyclines are bacteriostatic drugs, and a number of more effective agents have replaced them for the treatment of many infections. Currently, the disorders for which tetracycline is the antibiotic of choice are certain mycoplasmal and rickettsial infections, urinary tract infections caused by susceptible gram-negative organisms, and cholera.

Doxycycline (Vibramycin®), a longer-acting tetracycline, has been recommended for preventing and treating traveler's diarrhea, but such use may allow resistant strains of bacteria to emerge and may be associated with severe sunburn because this agent increases sensitivity to ultraviolet light.

PRECAUTIONS

Tetracycline therapy may cause mild diarrhea due to the suppression of the bacteria that normally predominate in the intestines and their replacement by other organisms. The diarrhea is rarely severe and usually stops after administration of the drug has been terminated.

Nausea and vomiting sometimes occur in patients receiving tetracyclines.

All tetracyclines increase sensitivity to ultraviolet light and predispose individuals receiving them to severe sunburn.

Tetracycline can permanently stain the dental enamel in young children; it should not be administered to children and pregnant women whenever other agents are available.

Tetracycline and penicillin tend to be antagonistic; the two drugs should not be administered together. Tetracycline also is inactivated in the stomach by food and antacids and should be given before meals.

DOSE

Tetracycline: 250 to 500 mg orally every six hours.

Doxycycline: 50 to 100 mg orally every twelve hours.

COST

Tetracycline: 250 mg—$2.20 to $6.11/100 ($0.09 to $0.49 per day); 500 mg—$3.90 to $11.04/100 ($0.16 to $0.44 per day).

Achromycin®: 250 mg—$6.82/100 ($0.27 to $0.54 per day); 500 mg—$13.29/100 ($0.53 per day).

Doxycycline: 50 mg—$4.30 to $29.45/50 ($0.17 to $2.36 per day); 100 mg—$5.80 to 48.90/50 ($0.23 to $1.96 per day).

Vibramycin®: 50 mg—$154.05/100 ($3.08 to $6.16 per day); 100 mg—$274.99/100 ($2.74 to $5.48 per day).

Chloramphenicol

Chloramphenicol (Chloromycetin®) is a potent antibiotic with such a wide spectrum of antibacterial activity that it could be one of the most valuable antibacterial agents but for one flaw. In about one of every 25,000 to 50,000 patients receiving this drug, lethal bone marrow suppression occurs. Furthermore, this reaction is totally unpredictable.

Some investigators have claimed that the death rate due to adverse reactions to chloramphenicol is no greater than the death rate caused by reactions to penicillin. Nonetheless, administration of chloramphenicol is usually limited to a few specific life-threatening conditions that include: (1) bacterial meningitis in patients allergic to penicillin and ceftriaxone, or when only oral therapy can be given; (2) severe anaerobic infections for which clindamycin is not effective; (3) infections by gram-negative bacilli that do not respond to other antibiotics; and (4) severe rickettsial infections.

PRECAUTIONS

In view of the severe bone marrow depression that can result from chloramphenicol therapy, this drug must be used only for those specific infections for which it is indicated.

DOSE

250 to 1,000 mg (1 gm) or 12.5 mg per kg of body weight, orally or intravenously, every six hours.

COST

Chloramphenicol: 250 mg—$26.34 to $37.75/100 ($1.05 to $6.04 per day).
Chloromycetin®: 250 mg—$85.79/100 ($3.43 to $13.73 per day).

Ciprofloxacin

Ciprofloxacin (Cipro®) is one of the antimicrobial agents known as quinolones. It is effective against a broad spectrum of bacteria and is particularly useful for urinary tract and gastrointestinal infections.

PRECAUTIONS

Ciprofloxacin should not be administered to children less than eighteen years old or pregnant women. In animal studies, high doses given to immature animals produced permanent cartilage damage.

DOSE

500 mg orally every twelve hours, preferably two hours after eating.

COST

500 mg: $255.47/100 ($5.11 per day).

Polymyxin B, Bacitracin, and Neomycin Ophthalmic Mixture

This antibiotic mixture (Neosporin®) is available as an ophthalmic ointment and as an ophthalmic solution (drops). It is used to treat conjunctivitis caused by a wide variety of organisms.

PRECAUTIONS

Some individuals are allergic to one or more of the components of this mixture and should not be treated with it.

A similar ointment produced for use on other tissues, such as skin, is called simply Neosporin® Ointment. This preparation must not be confused with the ophthalmic ointment because it may contain minor impurities that could be irritating or injurious to the eye even though they would not harm less sensitive tissues.

The antibiotics used in this preparation are valuable for treating infections only in locations where the agents are not absorbed by the body. They must never be taken internally.

DOSE

A small amount of the ointment or one or two drops of the solution should be installed behind the lower lid every three to four hours.

COST

Neosporin Ophthalmic Ointment®: 3.75 gm—$11.68.
Neosporin Ophthalmic Drops®: 10 ml—$11.68.

Trimethoprim-Sulfamethoxazole

Trimethoprim-sulfamethoxazole (Bactrim®, Septra®, TMP-SMX, or "trimethoprim-sulfa") is a combination of two agents, one of which is a sulfonamide. Sulfonamides are useful for treating many gastrointestinal and urinary tract infections because they can be administered in preparations that produce high concentrations of the drugs in these organs. Additionally, some organisms resistant to antibiotics are readily destroyed by sulfonamides.

PRECAUTIONS

Sulfonamides in general are not very soluble in water and tend to precipitate in the urine, in effect forming small kidney stones that can cause significant damage. In order to prevent such damage, patients receiving these drugs must consume large quantities of fluids to maintain a high urinary volume (at least one to one-and-one-half liters per day).

Some patients are allergic to sulfonamides and should not be treated with them. This preparation should not be taken by individuals with glucose-6-phosphatase deficiency. (This disorder, which must be diagnosed by a physician, usually causes mild anemia and is aggravated by certain drugs, particularly some sulfonamides.)

Sulfonamides cross the placenta, are excreted in milk, and can have harmful effects on a fetus or newborn. They should be administered during the last months of pregnancy and to nursing mothers only by a physician.

DOSE

160 mg of trimethoprim and 800 mg of sulfamethoxazole (one double-strength tablet) orally every six to twelve hours.

COST

Trimethoprim-sulfamethoxazole, double strength: $10.93 to $14.90/100 ($0.22 to $0.60 per day).

Septra®: standard—$52.12/100; double strength—$85.54/100 ($1.71 to $4.17 per day).

Bactrim®: standard—$56.56/100; double strength—$92.83/100 ($1.85 to $4.52 per day).

Silver Sulfadiazine Cream

Silver sulfadiazine cream is a sulfonamide in an ointment (Silvadene®, SSD Cream®, and others) that is applied to burns to help control bacterial infections. It is effective against a wide variety of organisms, particularly the organisms that most commonly infect burns.

PRECAUTIONS

Since silver sulfadiazine is a sulfonamide, the precautions described for trimethoprim-sulfamethoxazole should be observed.

DOSE

A thin layer of the cream should be applied sterilely to the burn twice a day if the burn is exposed. Dressings covering a burn should not be removed just to apply the cream if no evidence of infection can be found.

COST

Silver sulfadiazine cream: one percent—$4.94 to $6.44/50 gm.
Silvadene®: one percent—$5.50/50 gm.
SSD Cream®: one percent—$4.50/50 gm.

Chloroquine

Chloroquine is used primarily for malaria and is highly effective for both prevention and treatment, except for chloroquine-resistant *falciparum* malaria for which mefloquine is the prophylactic agent of choice. Chloroquine is also effective to some extent in the treatment of amebiasis.

PRECAUTIONS

In the dosages used for preventing or treating malaria, chloroquine has few serious side effects. Therapeutic doses may cause minor gastrointestinal disturbances. Skin rashes or itching occasionally occur. However, these symptoms often do not require interruption of therapy or prophylaxis and rapidly disappear when administration is ended.

DOSE

Prevention: 0.5 gm orally once weekly on the same day of the week, starting two weeks before entering a malaria-endemic area and continuing for five weeks after leaving.

COST

250 mg: $2.04 to $6.95/100.

Mefloquine

Mefloquine is administered for preventing or treating chloroquine-resistant *falciparum* malaria.

PRECAUTIONS

Individuals allergic to mefloquine or related agents, particularly quinine or quinidine, should not take this drug.

Because dizziness occasionally follows mefloquine ingestion, individuals taking it must be careful with activities such as driving a car, piloting an aircraft, or using machinery in which injury could occur. Psychiatric reactions such as anxiety, depression, restlessness, or confusion rarely occur with mefloquine, and the drug should be stopped if these appear.

The safety of mefloquine during pregnancy has not been established, so the drug should not be taken by pregnant women.

DOSE

250 mg once weekly beginning one week before entering an area in which chloroquine-resistant *falciparum* malaria is known to exist and continuing for four weeks after leaving the area.

COST

Lariam®: 250 mg—$133.10/25.

Metronidazole

Metronidazole (Flagyl® and others) is a drug used to treat a variety of parasitic infestations and bacterial infections. Its principal use in wilderness circumstances is for treating giardiasis and amebiasis.

PRECAUTIONS

Alcoholic beverages taken during therapy with metronidazole can cause severe vomiting and should be avoided while the drug is being taken and for one day afterward.

Metronidazole should not be administered during the first trimester of pregnancy and should be given only by a physician to anyone with concomitant disease, particularly liver, blood, or neurologic disorders.

Metronidazole should not be given to children except to treat laboratory-diagnosed amebiasis.

DOSE

For giardiasis: 250 mg orally three times a day for five to ten days.

For amebiasis: 750 mg orally three times a day for five to ten days.

COST

Metronidazole: 250 mg—$4.34 to $55.45/100 ($0.13 to $1.66 per day for giardiasis; $0.39 to $4.98 for amebiasis).

Flagyl®: 250 mg—$108.22/100 ($3.25 per day for giardiasis; $9.75 per day for amebiasis).

Benzalkonium Chloride

Benzalkonium chloride (Zephiran®) is a cationic quaternary ammonium surface-acting agent that is a highly effective antiseptic. Aqueous solutions of benzalkonium and povidone-iodine are the only agents readily available that are capable of killing bacteria in the depths of a wound without killing or seriously damaging the tissues.

PRECAUTIONS

When used as intended, benzalkonium chloride has very little toxic effect. However, serious results, including collapse, coma, and death, can result if the solution is ingested.

Alcoholic solutions (tinctures) as well as aqueous solutions are available, but the aqueous are more suitable for wound antisepsis and do not burn or sting as do the tinctures.

Solutions of benzalkonium chloride must be kept in glass bottles.

DOSE

Benzalkonium chloride is used as a 1:750 solution for disinfecting intact skin prior to needle puncture or for cleaning minor wounds. For washing out deep or dirty wounds, the solution should be diluted with disinfected water to about 1:3,000, and copious quantities should be used, particularly for bites inflicted by a possibly rabid animal.

COST

Benzalkonium chloride: 50 percent—$6.55 to $15.95/500 ml.

Aqueous Zephiran®: 17 percent—$320.00/gal (3,785 ml); 1:750—$65.49/gal (3,785 ml).

Povidone-Iodine

Povidone-iodine, an iodophor, is a loose complex of iodine with poly-vinylpyrrolidone that was patented in 1956 and subsequently has become widely available as a ten percent solution under the trade names Betadine®, Povidine®, Pharmadine®, and others. These preparations offer two significant advantages for wilderness use: they can be kept in polyethylene containers instead of glass, and they are effective disinfectants in dilute solutions so that less must be carried.

Povidone-iodine retains the strong bacteriocidal activity of iodine but eliminates many of the disadvantages, such as skin irritation, staining of the skin, and the odor of iodine. A 1:100 dilution of a ten percent solution has been found to have much greater bacteriocidal action than the original stock solution, and 1:1,000 dilutions are almost equally effective.

PRECAUTIONS

Rare individuals are allergic to iodine; a chronic skin rash is the usual manifestation. Such individuals should not use povidone-iodine.

Povidone-iodine has been recommended for water disinfection, but no substantiating data has been provided. The 1:10,000 dilution that would result has been found to have no significant antimicrobial activity. At the present time these agents can not be considered reliable for water disinfection.

DOSE

For skin disinfection prior to injections the undiluted stock solution is suitable and convenient. For rinsing a larger wound, the original stock solution should be diluted several hundred times and the wound thoroughly rinsed with large quantities of the solution, particularly following the bite of a possibly rabid animal.

COST
Povidone-Iodine solution: $2.75 to $4.80/pint; $14.50 to $27.60/gallon.
Betadine® Surgical Scrub: $11.60/quart.

MEDICATIONS AFFECTING THE HEART, BLOOD VESSELS, AND RESPIRATORY SYSTEM

Acetazolamide

Acetazolamide (Diamox®) inhibits the enzyme carbonic anhydrase, which catalyzes the reversible combination of carbon dioxide with water to form carbonic acid. This drug promotes renal bicarbonate excretion and tends to reduce the respiratory alkalosis (increase in blood pH) resulting from carbon dioxide loss at high altitudes by faster and deeper breathing.

Acetazolamide reduces the severity of acute mountain sickness symptoms in individuals who must ascend from sea level to 12,000 to 14,000 feet (3,700 to 4,300 m) without adequate time for acclimatization. It may not eliminate such symptoms entirely. In addition, acetazolamide promotes acclimatization.

A significant effect on high altitude pulmonary edema has not been demonstrated.

Perhaps the greatest benefit from acetazolamide is relief of sleep problems at high altitude. Elimination of episodes of severe hypoxia during sleep may be responsible for better tolerance of high altitude during waking hours.

PRECAUTIONS
Acetazolamide is a sulfonamide, although it does not have any antibacterial actions. Persons allergic to sulfonamides may be allergic to this drug.

Persons with liver or kidney disease should not be treated with acetazolamide, and the drug should not be given during the last months of pregnancy or to nursing mothers.

Some individuals develop tingling sensations in the lips and fingertips, blurring of vision, and alterations of taste when taking this drug. These sensations disappear when the medication is stopped.

DOSE
To prevent acute mountain sickness: 250 mg orally every twelve hours starting one to two days before ascent and continuing for three to five days after arrival.

To promote sleep at high altitude: 250 mg orally at bedtime.

COST
Acetazolamide: 250 mg—$5.25 to $13.19/100.
Diamox®: 250 mg—$30.74/100.

Dexamethasone

Dexamethasone (Decadron® and others), a synthetic glucocorticoid, is a potent steroid that is used extensively to treat a wide variety of disorders, but its value in the wilderness is quite limited. The ability of this agent to reduce the edema associated with the spread of malignant tumors from other organs to the brain led to therapeutic trials for high altitude cerebral edema. In the wilderness, its value is largely limited to the treatment of severe acute mountain sickness and high altitude cerebral edema.

Dexamethasone is not as effective as acetazolamide for preventing acute mountain sickness because it does not promote acclimatization. Symptoms of acute mountain sickness relieved by dexamethasone therapy tend to recur when treatment is stopped. Dexamethasone should be used only when preventive measures have been neglected or have been impossible (e.g., in emergency rescue situations) and symptoms have developed.

PRECAUTIONS

Significant side effects from dexamethasone administered for the short time periods required to evacuate individuals with acute mountain sickness or high altitude cerebral edema, which should be the principal form of therapy, are essentially nonexistent. The primary risk is relying on dexamethasone alone and not evacuating the affected individual to a lower altitude.

Prolonged therapy with dexamethasone is associated with major side effects, but such prolonged therapy should never be needed for altitude problems.

DOSE

4 mg orally or intramuscularly (if the individual is unconscious) every six hours.

COST

Dexamethasone: 4 mg—$18.76 to $45.14/100.
Dexamethasone sodium phosphate: 5-ml vial for injection, 4 mg/ml—$1.20 to $4.50.
Dexamethasone acetate: 5-ml vial for injection, 8 mg/ml—$6.95 to $29.93.
Decadron®: 4 mg—$125.97/100.

Nifedipine

Nifedipine (Procardia® and Adalat®) is a member of a new class of drugs, the calcium channel blockers, used primarily to treat angina associated with coronary artery disease. Because this drug lowers pulmonary artery pressure, it has been given to some individuals with high altitude pulmonary edema. The initial results have been promising, and investigators have recommended administration of nifedipine for high altitude pulmonary edema; but further studies are needed.

PRECAUTIONS

Nifedipine administered for the time required to evacuate an individual with high altitude pulmonary edema would produce few side effects. However, the proven therapy for high altitude pulmonary edema is descent to a lower altitude. Oxygen may be helpful and should be administered during descent. Until further studies have proven nifedipine's value, dose and cost information is not provided.

Nitroglycerin

Nitroglycerin relaxes the walls of small blood vessels, permitting them to dilate and increase the flow of blood. This compound—which is the explosive—is most commonly used to treat angina pectoris (severe chest pain associated with inadequacy of the blood supply to the heart) but dilates all small arteries and can be used to increase the blood flow to other organs or tissues. As the result of dilatation of cerebral arteries, throbbing headaches frequently follow the use of nitroglycerin.

PRECAUTIONS

The most serious side effect of nitroglycerin therapy is a drop in blood pressure due to the dilatation of blood vessels. Fainting or—even worse—aggravation of the cardiac damage could result. Therefore, a patient receiving this drug must be closely attended. He should lie down with his head lowered if symptoms of faintness or dizziness appear.

The tablets should be kept in their original brown bottle and should not be kept longer than six months after purchase as they begin to lcse their potency. Cotton wads should not be kept in the bottle, which must be kept tightly stoppered.

DOSE

0.4 mg (1/150 grain) or 0.8 mg sublingually at the onset of an attack. If the pain persists, additional tablets may be taken at fifteen- or thirty-minute intervals for a total of four tablets during one hour. The tablets may be chewed but must not be swallowed. About three minutes is required for the medication to take effect.

COST

Nitrostat®: 0.4 mg sublingual—$5.21/100.

Digoxin

Digoxin is one of the digitalis preparations, which are the oldest and most valuable drugs available for the treatment of a variety of heart disorders. Digitalis strengthens the contraction of the heart muscle, permitting more effective cardiac function for patients in heart failure. Digitalis preparations also help restore normal cardiac rhythm for patients with many types of abnormal rhythms. (These drugs are not beneficial and may be quite harmful for persons with normal hearts.)

PRECAUTIONS

Loss of appetite, nausea or vomiting, or slowing of the heart rate to less than sixty beats per minute are indications of digoxin toxicity. If such signs appear in a patient receiving this drug, the dose must be reduced.

Digoxin must be given with great care to anyone who has taken any digitalis preparation within the previous week. These drugs are excreted slowly over a period of several days or longer. An overdose could result if treatment were restarted shortly after it had been discontinued without an appropriate reduction in the quantity of the drug administered.

A number of digitalis preparations, such as digitoxin, have similar names. These preparations must not be confused because the therapeutic doses are significantly different.

DOSE

Initially: 0.25 mg orally every two hours for a total of 1.5 mg.
Maintenance: 0.25 mg orally once daily at the same time of day.

COST

Digoxin: 0.25 mg—$4.07 to $4.93/100; $8.70 to $27.90/1,000.
Lanoxin®: 0.25 mg—$9.40/100.

Epinephrine

Epinephrine (adrenaline) is a hormone secreted by the medulla of the adrenal gland. It is used to treat spasm of the bronchi due to anaphylactic shock or severe asthma, or to relieve the spasm and respiratory obstruction of laryngeal edema. Adrenaline is effective when injected or when applied directly to the involved tissues. It is destroyed by the acid and digestive enzymes in the stomach and is ineffective when administered orally.

PRECAUTIONS

Epinephrine must be administered very slowly and carefully to elderly individuals or to persons with heart disease of any kind, high blood pressure, thyroid disease, or diabetes. It also should not be given to persons in shock from blood loss. Epinephrine is a powerful cardiac stimulant; its effect on individuals with these disorders could be lethal.

Repeat injections of epinephrine should not be given until the obvious effects of a previous injection have disappeared. An overdose of epinephrine could cause severe problems for persons with normal hearts.

The epinephrine preparation must be discarded without being used if it has turned brown or contains a precipitate.

DOSE

Subcutaneously: 0.3 cc to 0.5 cc of a 1:1,000 solution (3 to 5 mg) every fifteen to thirty minutes.

Inhalation: Prepared aerosols contain different amounts of epinephrine, but most will deliver 3 to 5 mg with two careful, deep inhalations.

COST

Ampules for injection, 1 ml of 1:1,000 solution—$36.88 to $87.50/100.
Aerosol for inhalation, 15 ml—$5.25 to $9.00.
Epi-pen®: $23.92 each.
Ana-Kit®: $96.20/6.

Aminophylline

Aminophylline is closely related to caffeine chemically and pharmacologically but does not have as much stimulating effect on the central nervous system. This drug is used to treat asthma because it relaxes the bronchial walls and permits the bronchi to dilate, relieving respiratory difficulty. At high altitudes, aminophylline can prevent the interruption of sleep by Cheyne-Stokes respirations, but acetazolamide is preferable for that purpose.

PRECAUTIONS
Aminophylline in therapeutic doses has few toxic effects.

DOSE
500 mg (suppository) inserted well up into the rectum.

COST
500-mg suppository—$5.40 to $6.90/10.

Phenylephrine

Phenylephrine hydrochloride, a decongestant well known in the United States as Neo-Synephrine®, is present in many other preparations. This agent causes the blood vessels in the nasal mucosa to contract, reducing their volume, but also reducing the amount of fluid collected in the tissue (edema) around the vessels.

As a nasal spray, phenylephrine is used to shrink the swollen mucosa of the nose for patients with colds, hay fever, or sinusitis. This agent not only relieves obstruction to the passage of air, but also relieves obstruction and promotes drainage from the small canals opening into the sinuses.

PRECAUTIONS
Administration of the nasal spray should be repeated ten minutes after the first application. Initially the spray only reaches the mucosa over the more prominent structures in the nasal cavity. Not until this portion of the mucosa has been shrunk can a subsequent application extend into the recesses where the small canals draining the sinuses open.

After the effects of the nasal spray have worn off, swelling of the nasal mucosa and airway obstruction recur. Such rebound symptoms are often worse than the initial symptoms. With each subsequent application, the duration of the spray's effects tends to become shorter. For this reason, use of the spray perhaps should be limited to the hours when decongestant action is needed to promote restful sleep. An oral decongestant should be used in conjunction with the spray to obtain more complete and longer-lasting results.

DOSE
0.25 to 0.50 percent solution sprayed into each nostril and repeated after a ten-minute interval. Administration may be repeated every three to four hours.

COST
Phenylephrine: 0.25 percent, 1 pint—$2.82 to $6.29.
Neo-Synephrine®: 0.25 percent, 15-ml spray—$2.96, 15-ml pump—$3.65; 0.50 percent, 15-ml spray—$3.25.

Oxymetazoline

Oxymetazoline, a decongestant that is equally effective and much longer acting than phenylephrine, lasts up to twelve hours after a single application. (Because the onset of its action is slower, some individuals have gained the impression that oxymetazoline is not as effective as phenylephrine.) A 0.05 percent solution is contained in a number of preparations, such as Afrin® and Dristan®

long-acting nasal spray, but some drugstore chains sell identical preparations under their own label at a price forty to fifty percent below that of the established brands.

PRECAUTIONS

The precautions listed for phenylephrine should be followed for oxymetazoline, particularly for individuals with symptoms of sinusitis. However, rebound following oxymetazoline does not seem to be as severe as that following phenylephrine.

DOSE

One or two sprays in each nostril every twelve hours.

COST

Oxymetazoline spray: 0.05 percent, 15 ml—$1.30 to $2.25, $20.40/12; 30 ml—$1.80 to $2.75.

Afrin®: 15 ml—$3.85; 30 ml—$6.18.

Pseudoephedrine

Pseudoephedrine (Sudafed® and others) is a systemic decongestant. The drug acts through the nerves supplying the blood vessels in the mucosa of the upper respiratory tract, causing those vessels to contract. Excess fluid in the mucosa (edema) is reduced, the mucosa shrink to normal thickness, and obstruction to the passage of air is relieved. This drug also shrinks the mucosa lining the small canals that drain the sinuses and the eustachian tubes that drain the middle ears, allowing air or fluid to move through these structures and helping to avoid aerotitis media, aerosinusitis, or infectious sinusitis.

PRECAUTIONS

Pseudoephedrine should be given to individuals with high blood pressure, heart disease, thyroid disease, or diabetes only by a physician.

Pseudoephedrine acts as a mild stimulant and makes some individuals restless or jumpy, which can inhibit restful sleep. Reducing the dose of the drug by taking only part of a tablet usually relieves these side effects.

DOSE

60 mg orally every six to eight hours.

COST

Pseudoephedrine: 60 mg—$1.65 to $8.18/100.

Sudafed®: 30 mg—$9.01/100.

Triprolidine with Pseudoephedrine

This combination of an antihistamine with a systemic decongestant (Actifed® and others) is one of the most popular for controlling the symptoms of allergic reactions, such as hay fever, or for colds.

PRECAUTIONS

The precautions that must be observed are those for both the antihistamines and pseudoephedrine.

DOSE
   One tablet every eight hours.

COST
   Triprolidine with pseudoephedrine: $2.10 to $12.50/100.
   Actifed®: $11.86/100.

ANTIHISTAMINES

Antihistamines are a group of drugs that block the effects of histamine, a substance released during allergic and inflammatory reactions and considered responsible for many symptoms of allergy. In addition, some of these agents can prevent or reduce symptoms of motion sickness.

Chlorpheniramine and Triprolidine

Chlorpheniramine and triprolidine are two widely used antihistamines administered to relieve the symptoms of hay fever and similar allergies. They may also provide some relief with colds. Chlorpheniramine is present in Alka-Seltzer Plus Cold Tablets®, Allerest®, Chlor-Trimeton®, Coricidin®, Co-Tylenol®, Novahistine®, Sinarest®, Teldrin®, Tuss-Ornade®, and many others. Some of these products are available in delayed release forms that extend drug action after a single administration for as long as twelve hours. Triprolidine is not as widely used as other antihistamines but is combined with pseudoephedrine in Actifed®, one of the most widely used combinations of an antihistamine with a decongestant (see above).

PRECAUTIONS
   All antihistamines have a tendency to cause drowsiness, although individual susceptibility to this effect varies. Anyone who has taken an antihistamine must be very careful about engaging in activities for which drowsiness could be a hazard, particularly driving a car.

DOSE
   Dose depends upon the preparation being used.

Diphenhydramine and Terfenadine

Diphenhydramine (Benadryl® and others) is a highly effective antihistamine for treating allergies. However, its tendency to make recipients drowsy is so pronounced that it has been approved by the FDA as a sleep medication.

   Terfenadine is better known as Seldane®, a recently developed antihistamine that has a greatly reduced tendency to produce drowsiness, although this agent is not completely free of that side effect. Some individuals find that terfenadine is not as effective as other agents. It is much more expensive.

PRECAUTIONS
   All antihistamines have a tendency to cause drowsiness, although individual susceptibility to this effect varies. Anyone who has taken an antihistamine must

be very careful about engaging in activities for which drowsiness could be a hazard, particularly driving a car.

DOSE

Diphenhydramine: 50 mg orally at bedtime (for sleep) or every six to eight hours (for allergies).

Terfenadine (Seldane®): 60 mg orally every twelve hours.

COST

Diphenhydramine: 50 mg—$1.40 to $16.99/100.

Benadryl®: 50 mg—$20.38/100.

Seldane®: 60 mg—$71.40/100.

Dimenhydrinate, Meclizine, and Cyclizine

Dimenhydrinate (Dramamine®), meclizine (Bonine® and Antivert®), and cyclizine (Marezine®) are antihistamines used primarily to control motion sickness. All should be taken about one hour before embarking on a trip. An advantage of meclizine is that a single dose is effective for twenty-four hours. All are fairly effective against allergies.

PRECAUTIONS

All antihistamines have a tendency to cause drowsiness, although individual susceptibility to this effect varies. Anyone who has taken an antihistamine must be very careful about engaging in activities for which drowsiness could be a hazard, particularly driving a car.

DOSE

Dimenhydrinate: 50 mg orally every four hours.

Meclizine: 25 to 50 mg orally every twenty-four hours.

Cyclizine: 50 mg orally every four to six hours.

COST

Dimenhydrinate: 50 mg—$1.15 to $9.52/100.

Dramamine®: 50 mg—$15.42/100.

Meclizine: 25 mg—$1.55 to $9.64/100.

Bonine®: 25 mg—$43.71/100.

Antivert®: 25 mg—$36.81/100.

Marezine®: 50 mg—$20.53/100.

MEDICATIONS FOR GASTROINTESTINAL DISORDERS

Paregoric

Paregoric (camphorated tincture of opium) is a mixture of several compounds, the most important of which is morphine. This mixture is used to control diarrhea through the immobilizing action of opium derivatives on the lower gastrointestinal tract.

PRECAUTIONS

The problems related to using any drug to control diarrhea are discussed in Chapter Twelve, "Gastrointestinal Disorders."

Paregoric is classified as a controlled substance due to its opium content. Addiction to paregoric does occur rarely, but not from reasonable use.

DOSE

One teaspoonful (5 ml) orally every two hours or after each bowel movement.

COST

2 mg/5 ml—$3.12 to $12.91/480 ml.

Diphenoxylate with Atropine

Diphenoxylate with atropine (Lomotil®) is a combination of two compounds that is used to control diarrhea through slowing of intestinal mobility.

PRECAUTIONS

The most important complications resulting from the administration of diphenoxylate are those from using any drug to control diarrhea.

This drug is chemically very similar to meperidine, although lacking its analgesic and euphoric properties. Addiction is at least theoretically possible, and diphenoxylate is classified as a controlled substance.

DOSE

Two tablets four times a day is the maximum recommended dose. Smaller amounts should be used if they are effective.

COST

Diphenoxylate with atropine: $2.28 to $7.25/100; $10.50 to $79.95/1,000. Lomotil®: $36.41/100.

Loperamide

Loperamide (Imodium®) helps control diarrhea by reducing intestinal mobility. The suspension is now available over the counter.

PRECAUTIONS

The most important complications associated with the administration of loperamide are those resulting from using any drug to control diarrhea, as discussed in Chapter Twelve, "Gastrointestinal Disorders."

DOSE

Two 2-mg capsules followed by one 2-mg capsule after each unformed stool, not to exceed eight capsules in any twenty-four-hour period.

COST

Imodium®: 2-mg tablets—$57.96/100; 1-mg/5-ml suspension—$5.68/120 ml.

Prochlorperazine

Prochlorperazine (Compazine®) was one of the first tranquilizers and is quite similar to chlorpromazine (Thorazine®), which is better known. Although these agents were major therapeutic advances, they have largely been replaced by more effective drugs, and the principal use of prochlorperazine currently is for treating severe nausea and vomiting.

PRECAUTIONS

Prochlorperazine must not be given to individuals who are comatose or whose consciousness is significantly impaired.

Prochlorperazine must not be given to children younger than two years old and in wilderness situations probably should not be given to preteenage children.

Individuals who are vomiting repeatedly may be unable to retain oral medications, and rectal suppositories must be substituted.

DOSE

5 to 10 mg orally three or four times a day as needed.

25 mg rectally (suppository) every twelve hours as needed.

COST

Prochlorperazine: 5 mg—$7.80 to $46.46/100.

Compazine®: 5 mg—$41.80/100; 10 mg—$62.70/100; 25-mg suppositories—$24.75/12.

Antacids

Antacids are preparations that contain combinations of aluminum hydroxide, calcium carbonate, magnesium carbonate, magnesium hydroxide, and magnesium trisilicate. They are administered to neutralize acids in the stomach in the treatment of peptic ulcers and for relief of symptoms of indigestion. Some of the preparations are flavored. Alkets® are considered by some to be the most effective. Titralac® and Robalate® are effective but may be more difficult to find. Other well-known antacids—Alka-Seltzer®, Alka-2®, Amphojel®, Gaviscom®, Gelusil®, Maalox®, WinGel®, Rolaids®, and Tums®—may be considered if none of the first three is available.

PRECAUTIONS

Magnesium-containing antacids sometimes produce a mild diarrhea, but this side effect rarely requires treatment or interruption of therapy. These drugs are absorbed from the gastrointestinal tract in minimal amounts, if at all, and have no effects on the rest of the body. They are of no value in preventing acute mountain sickness.

Antacids should not be taken indiscriminately over long periods of time. Prolonged consumption of antacids and calcium-containing foods such as milk can lead to calcium deposits in the kidneys and impaired renal function.

DOSE

The dose depends upon the preparation being used but usually consists of one or two tablets as often as required for the pain or distress of an ulcer or indigestion.

Antispasmodics

Antispasmodics reduce the amount of acid produced by the stomach as well as reducing peristaltic activity, both of which are desirable in the treatment of indigestion, peptic ulcer, or acute pancreatitis. Some of the better-known antispasmodics are Donnatal®, Pamine®, Pro-Banthine®, and tincture of belladonna. Many others of equal effectiveness are available.

PRECAUTIONS

Antispasmodics produce blurring of vision and dryness of mouth as their most common side effects. Following ingestion of one of these drugs, a person might not be able to participate in activities requiring visual acuity, such as driving a car.

Individuals with a history of glaucoma should not be treated with these drugs. Blurring of vision by antispasmodics results from dilatation of the pupil and immobilization of the muscles that focus the eyes. Dilatation of the pupils in this manner can seriously aggravate glaucoma, a condition characterized by increased intraocular pressure.

Some antispasmodics have a significant constipating effect and should not be used alone. A generous fluid intake and the use of antacids that have a laxative action, as most do, counteracts this tendency.

These drugs also have a tendency to immobilize the urinary bladder, resulting in urinary retention that requires urethral catheterization. Although this complication would be rare in wilderness users, therapy may have to be discontinued for several days and then resumed at a lower dose if it occurs.

DOSE

The dose depends upon the preparation being used. The drugs are usually given half an hour before meals and at bedtime. A double dose may be given at bedtime if the patient tends to be awakened at night by ulcer pain.

Preparations for intramuscular injection are available for treating patients with acute pancreatitis for whom oral therapy is undesirable.

H_2 Blockers

The cells that secrete acid in the stomach are stimulated by several agents, one of which is histamine, or "H_2". The H_2 blockers inhibit the secretion of acid in the stomach by blocking the sites at which histamine attaches to the walls of the acid-secreting cells. These agents were first introduced in 1976 and were a major advance in the treatment of peptic ulcers, drastically decreasing the need for surgical treatment for this disorder.

PRECAUTIONS

These drugs have few side effects, particularly as they would be used in a wilderness setting. Their safety in children and nursing mothers has not been established.

DOSE

Cimetidine (Tagamet®): 300 mg orally with meals and at bedtime, 400 mg in the morning and at bedtime, or 800 mg at bedtime are all treatment regimens that have proved successful. Probably the first or second should be used while ulcer symptoms are present, and the last can be used to prevent their recurrence.

Ranitidine (Zantac®): 150 mg orally in the morning and at bedtime, or 300 mg at bedtime.

Famotidine (Pepcid®): 40 mg orally at bedtime while ulcer symptoms persist, then 20 mg at bedtime to prevent recurrence.

COST

Tagamet®: 200 mg—$68.33/100; 300 mg—$71.45/100; 400 mg—$120.06/100 ($2.40 to $3.57 per day).

Zantac®: 150 mg—$140.38/100; 300 mg—$245.60/100 ($2.46 per day).

Pepcid®: 20 mg—$121.76/100; 40 mg—$235.24/100 ($1.22 to $2.35 per day).

Sucralfate

Sucralfate (Carafate®) helps peptic ulcers to heal (and helps prevent new ulcers) by, in essence, forming a film that coats the surface of the ulcer and keeps out gastric acid and digestive enzymes. This agent is absorbed from the gastrointestinal tract in only minuscule amounts.

PRECAUTIONS

Because sucralfate is not absorbed it is quite safe, and no contraindications have been established.

DOSE

1 g orally four times a day on an empty stomach; after ulcer symptoms have disappeared the dose can be reduced to 1 gm twice a day.

COST

Sucralfate: 1 gm—$13.56/30 ($1.78 per day).
Carafate®: 1 gm—$57.50/100 ($2.30 per day).

Misoprostil

Misoprostil (Cytotec®) is a synthetic prostaglandin E_1 analog that inhibits the secretion of gastric acid but also stimulates the secretion of mucus and bicarbonate, which help protect the gastric and duodenal mucosa from the erosive actions of acid and digestive enzymes. It is principally used to prevent ulcers in individuals receiving nonsteroidal anti-inflammatory drugs (NSAIDs)—of which aspirin is the most common.

PRECAUTIONS

Misoprostil must not be used during pregnancy because it frequently causes abortions; in a wilderness situation the resulting bleeding and other problems could be disastrous. The safety of this drug for nursing mothers and children has not been established.

DOSE

100 to 200 mcg orally with meals and at bedtime.

COST

Cytotec®: 100 mcg—$34.62/100; 200 mcg—$59.66/100 ($1.38 to $2.39 per day).

THERAPEUTIC PROCEDURES

ADMINISTERING MEDICATIONS

Oral Medications

The oral route is the easiest, most convenient, and safest method for administering drugs, but it has two major disadvantages: the time required for a drug to be absorbed and variations in the rate and completeness of absorption. Acid and enzymes in the stomach completely inactivate some therapeutic agents, which must be given by another route.

Individuals who are not fully conscious may aspirate oral medications and must never be given them.

Oral therapy is much less effective for a person who is vomiting. Even if the drugs are not expelled, emptying of the stomach is greatly retarded and the onset of action by the agent is markedly delayed because orally administered drugs are usually absorbed only in the small intestine.

With the exception of agents that are irritating to the stomach, such as aspirin or ibuprofen, oral medications should be taken at least half an hour before meals. The stomach empties more slowly and irregularly when it is filled with food, which delays onset of a drug's actions. Food interferes with the absorption of some medications.

Intramuscular Injections

The intramuscular route for administering drugs avoids the vagaries of intestinal absorption but is associated with several hazards. The most significant is the risk of an overdose. An excessive dose or the wrong drug given orally can be partially retrieved by making the person vomit. No such safety valve is available for medications that have been injected.

Intramuscular injections are associated with a slight risk of injecting the drug directly into a blood vessel inside the muscle, which would produce higher and more toxic blood concentrations of the agent than the slower absorption from a true intramuscular site.

Intramuscular injections are usually not absorbed well by individuals who are in shock or who are hypothermic. If several injections of an agent were given and the medication was not absorbed until the person recovered, all of the agent would be absorbed at once, producing an overdose and possibly serious toxicity.

The needle used for an intramuscular injection may injure nerves, blood vessels, or other structures if the site for the injection is not carefully chosen (fig. B-1).

The most common complication of intramuscular injections is an infection produced by bacteria introduced with the needle. Although the needle may be free of bacteria, the skin through which it passes can not be completely sterilized. Thorough cleansing of the skin and avoiding needle contamination usually limits the quantity of bacteria introduced to a number that the body's defenses can destroy.

The following steps should be followed in administering any therapeutic agent intramuscularly:

1. The skin over the injection site should be cleaned with soap and water, swabbed with alcohol (or a disinfectant such as Betadine®), and permitted to dry.
2. The label on the drug container should be read closely to ensure that the proper medication in the correct dose is being administered.
3. A syringe of appropriate size should be fitted with a twenty-five-gauge needle.
4. The rubber top of the vial through which the needle is to be inserted should be swabbed with alcohol or a disinfectant.
5. The drug should be extracted by inverting the vial, inserting the needle through the rubber top, injecting a volume of air equal to the volume of fluid to be removed, and withdrawing the medication. While the needle is still in the vial, air bubbles or excess medication should be expressed from the syringe.
6. The label on the container must be reexamined to ensure that no mistakes have occurred. Such errors are far easier to prevent than to correct.

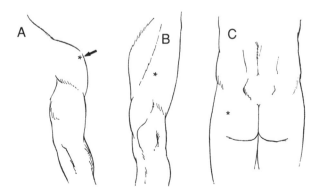

Figure B-1. Sites for the administration of intramuscular injections (A, shoulder; B, thigh; C, buttock).

7. Without touching the injection site, a mound of skin and muscle should be pinched up so that the needle does not strike the underlying bone, and the needle should be inserted with a jab.
8. Before the medication is injected, the plunger of the syringe must be pulled back to make certain the needle is not in a blood vessel. If blood is pulled back into the syringe, the needle must be removed and inserted in a different location.
9. The contents of the syringe should be injected slowly to minimize discomfort, but the needle should be withdrawn quickly.

Subcutaneous Injections

Subcutaneous injections are absorbed more slowly than intramuscular injections, which is an advantage with a few agents, such as epinephrine. The technique for subcutaneous injections is the same as for intramuscular injections, but the needle should be inserted at an angle so that it stays in the subcutaneous fat and does not enter the muscle. Injections can be made wherever a significant amount of fat is present beneath the skin.

Intravenous Medications

Intravenous drug administration is required in a few medical emergencies, may be the only effective way to administer drugs to individuals who are in shock, and is the most effective method to treat some severe infections because higher blood concentrations of a therapeutic agent can be attained, and a more constant blood concentration of the drug (without the swings associated with intermittent intramuscular or oral administration) can be maintained.

However, intravenous injections may be hazardous because high drug concentrations in the blood can develop quite rapidly. If a medication is injected too rapidly, severe complications—even death—can result. As with intramuscular injections, once an agent has been injected intravenously it can not be recovered—no safety valve is available. If the person has an allergic reaction to the drug, little can be done to reverse the process. Such injections must be given only when necessary; specified rates of injection must be closely observed.

If the injections are intermittent, as are the periodic injections of morphine to provide analgesia for a person in shock, the large veins located in the fold of the arm at the elbow should be used. Preparation of the injection and the injection site should be the same as for intramuscular injections. After the needle has been inserted into a vein, a small amount of blood should be withdrawn to dilute the drug and make certain the needle is in the proper location. Subsequently, the drug should be injected slowly, but continuously, over a period of two to three minutes.

The technique for administering intravenous medications over a long period of time is the same as for intravenous fluid administration (see below). Intravenous antibiotics are administered by injecting the antibiotic directly into a bottle of intravenous fluids, or the plastic container holding the antibiotic can be attached directly to the intravenous catheter.

Intravenous Fluid Therapy

Intravenous fluid therapy is required to replace normal and abnormal fluid losses for individuals who are not able to take fluids orally, to administer blood or plasma following a severe hemorrhage, and for the intravenous administration of some medications.

Currently, catheters are used in most U.S. medical centers for the administration of intravenous fluids because they rarely puncture the vein walls after they have been inserted, as do sharp needle tips, and do not become dislodged as easily.

The technique for administering fluids intravenously is basically simple. Individuals planning outings to wilderness areas where intravenous fluids might be required should learn the technique beforehand from a nurse or physician.

Although minor details in the way intravenous fluids are administered by different individuals vary, the basic technique is as follows:

1. The protective cap should be removed from the container of fluids to be administered, the tubing on the dispensing apparatus should be clamped below the drip chamber, and the apparatus should be inserted into the proper opening. The drip chamber—a small reservoir that keeps air bubbles from being carried into the subject's vein by the fluid—should be half filled by squeezing it repeatedly. (Compressing the drip chamber forces air out of the tubing between the chamber and the fluid container. When the pressure is released, the chamber expands and draws fluid back into the space previously occupied by air.) After the chamber is half full, the tubing should be filled by briefly releasing the clamp. The container (with its tubing) should be suspended two to three feet above the person who is to receive them.

2. The person should be placed in a supine position and a tourniquet that blocks venous but not arterial blood flow should be placed around the upper arm. (The pulse must be palpable at the wrist.) The subject should open and close his fist several times to engorge the superficial veins with blood. Letting the arm hang down for a few minutes or covering it with a warm, moist towel helps make the veins more prominent if they are small or obscured by subcutaneous fat.

3. A large, prominent vein in the lower arm, preferably on the inner, flat surface, should be selected and the overlying skin should be cleaned with soap and water and swabbed with alcohol or a disinfectant. After the skin has dried, the subject's arm should be held in one hand with the thumb stretching the skin tight over the vein into which the catheter is to be inserted. (Intravenous catheters consist of an outer thin sheath—the catheter—that has a hub into which the intravenous tubing is inserted, and an inner metal needle that protrudes beyond the tip of the catheter and has a handle but no hub.) The apparatus should be held almost parallel with the vein with the bevel of the needle upward (fig. B-2). The needle should be inserted through the skin, into the vein, and threaded up the vein for about one inch. A slight "give" can be felt as the vein is entered and blood flows back into the needle.

Figure B-2. Technique for inserting a needle for intravenous therapy.

4. After the needle has been threaded into the vein, the hub of the catheter should be grasped securely to ensure that it is not pulled out, and the needle should be extracted. The end of the intravenous tubing should be inserted into the hub of the catheter, the clamp on the tubing should be released, and the tourniquet should be removed from the subject's arm.

5. Once the fluids are flowing satisfactorily, the catheter should be anchored with tape, and the last eight to ten inches of tubing should be formed into an "S" or "U" and taped to the person's arm. Such loops absorb any accidental pulls on the apparatus and prevent dislodging of the catheter. If the individual is not fully conscious or is thrashing about, his arm should be anchored in some manner while fluids are being given.

6. Usually the clamp on the tubing should be partially closed so that the fluid is flowing at about 200 cc per hour (approximately fifty drops per minute). However, plasma administration following a severe hemorrhage or fluid replacement for disorders such as cholera often have to be made at much faster rates. Occasionally fluids must be given at more than one site in order to achieve the needed speed of administration. (Intravenous lines and the rate at which they are running need to be checked at least every two hours.)

7. Swelling at the site of the catheter indicates that the vein has been punctured and fluids are infiltrating into the tissue. The catheter must be withdrawn, discarded, and another catheter inserted at another site. No effort should be made to reinsert a catheter in the original vein until all swelling has disappeared, which requires several hours. The swelling usually produces little or no discomfort and requires no specific treatment. Such events are much less common when fluids are given through a catheter than when fluids are administered through a needle.

8. If the fluid fails to flow when the tubing is unclamped, the catheter may be obstructed. Changing its position slightly may move the tip away from the wall of the vein and restart the flow. Squeezing the tubing may force out small clots or plugs of tissue blocking the catheter. If the tourniquet on the upper arm has not been removed, or a similar venous obstruction (by tight clothing, for instance) is present, the fluid can not flow. Occasionally such measures are not successful in starting or restarting flow, the catheter must be withdrawn, and a new catheter must be inserted at another site.

9. When more than one container of fluids is to be given, a dispensing apparatus can be inserted into the second container, the tubing filled as described, and a large needle placed on its tip. The tubing should be clamped and the needle inserted into an injection port in the tubing to the first container. When the first container has emptied, its tubing should be clamped above the injection port, and the clamp on the second tubing should be released. The tubing from the first container can then be inserted into a third container of fluids if one is to be administered. This technique eliminates the need to clamp the tubing to the subject precisely as the last fluid runs out of the first container but before the drip chamber empties,

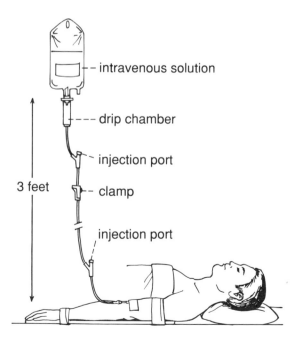

- - intravenous solution

- - - drip chamber

- injection port

3 feet   - - clamp

injection port

Figure B-3. Apparatus for administration of intravenous fluids.

and frantically trying to insert the dispenser into a second container before blood clots in the catheter and obstructs it.

10. If intravenous fluids are expected to be given for several days, they can be administered slowly to keep the catheter open for fluid administration the following day. (At a rate of 100 cc per hour, or about twenty-five drops per minute, about twenty-four hours would be required to administer 2,500 cc of fluid.) After forty-eight to seventy-two hours the catheter should be removed and another catheter inserted at another site if it is still needed.

11. The veins used for intravenous fluid therapy usually clot after the catheter is withdrawn and are not suitable for subsequent use. In situations where intravenous fluid therapy at more than one site is anticipated, the first catheters should be placed near the person's wrists and subsequent catheters placed higher up the arms as the veins become obstructed.

12. The veins on the back of the hands should not be used for intravenous therapy if other sites are available as these areas are quite sensitive. However, for individuals who are in shock or hypothermic, or who are obese, particularly if they have darkly pigmented skin, such veins may be the only ones that can be found.

13. Occasionally, veins for intravenous therapy are impossible to access, particularly in obese people or individuals who are in shock, hypothermic, or severely dehydrated. In such circumstances, fluids can be administered by inserting the needle beneath the skin of the back, abdomen, or upper thighs and letting the fluid infiltrate the subcutaneous space. Absorption from such sites is erratic, and administration may produce some discomfort, but when fluids are needed, this route is better than not giving fluids at all. Medications should not be administered in this manner.

NASOGASTRIC INTUBATION

Nasogastric intubation is a highly desirable—almost essential—element in the care of individuals with intestinal paralysis (paralytic ileus). All of the serious disorders associated with severe, acute abdominal pain produce such paralysis; the effects are most severe with intestinal obstruction or disorders causing peritonitis.

Large quantities of air are swallowed with food or liquids, including saliva. Gas is always present in the gastrointestinal tract, and swallowed air is the source of most of it. If the stomach is paralyzed, its contents—including gas—can not be expelled into the intestine, and it quickly becomes ballooned with air. The distended stomach impinges on the diaphragm and interferes with respiration; it also presses on the veins in the abdomen and impedes the return of blood from the lower body to the heart.

Large quantities of fluids—digestive juices, partially digested food, and other liquids that have been consumed—pool in the paralyzed stomach with the air and eventually lead to vomiting. Loss of the fluids and electrolytes can produce or aggravate dehydration, and pneumonia or respiratory obstruction may result if the vomitus is aspirated.

A tube inserted through the nose and esophagus into the stomach permits the air that is swallowed to escape and prevents most of these problems. The tube is uncomfortable because it causes a sore throat, but it usually does not cause gagging or related symptoms.

The use of nasogastric suction is not without hazard since fluids are removed from the stomach as well as air. If these fluids are not replaced intravenously with a balanced salt solution or saline, salt and water depletion inevitably result. If fluids for intravenous therapy are not available, the nasogastric tube should be used only to remove air that has collected. After the air has escaped, the tube should be clamped and reopened only when significant quantities of air have reaccumulated.

The technique for nasogastric intubation is as follows:

1. The tube, at least a size-eighteen French, should be chilled and the tip lubricated with a bland jelly, mineral oil, or at least water before it is inserted.
2. The subject should be sitting up and should have cold water, crushed ice, or snow to swallow.
3. The tube should be inserted through one nostril, along the floor of the nasal cavity, to the back of the throat. Then the person should be instructed to swallow. As he swallows, the tube should be thrust further so that the tongue and muscles of the throat can guide it into the esophagus. Several attempts are usually necessary. When the tube does enter the esophagus the individual should be told to keep swallowing. With each swallow the tube should be thrust further down until a length equal to the distance from the person's nose to his stomach (which should have been previously marked) has been inserted.
4. After the tube is in place, a small amount of air should be injected through it with a large syringe or bulb syringe. If the tube is in the stomach, bubbling sounds made by the injected air can be clearly heard. If the tube has coiled in the back of the person's throat or turned on itself in his esophagus and has not entered the stomach, such sounds are not heard, and the tube must be partially withdrawn and reinserted.
5. Rarely the tube may enter the trachea, causing the individual to cough and sometimes to be unable to talk. If the tube is withdrawn promptly, no harm is done, but he may be understandably reluctant to undergo further attempts at intubation.
6. After the tube is in place it should be taped to the person's nose or forehead to prevent its being expelled or swallowed entirely. Air and fluid in the stomach can be withdrawn with a syringe equipped with an attachment to fit the tubing. After the stomach is emptied, the tube should be attached to a suction apparatus constructed by suspending a bottle filled with water several feet above the subject's body, as shown in the accompanying diagram. (A lower bottle can collect the drainage.)
7. Nasogastric tubes have a tendency to become obstructed by mucus or particles of food. Therefore, the tube should be flushed with a small amount of a salt solution (or water if a salt solution is not available) every two

hours. (The fluid used to irrigate the tube must be subtracted from the total volume lost through the tube when calculating the subject's fluid requirements.)

8. The total volume of fluid lost through the nasogastric tube must be carefully measured and recorded. All of the fluid lost in this manner should be replaced intravenously with a balanced salt solution or saline.

URETHRAL CATHETERIZATION

Following a prolonged period of unconsciousness or after severe trauma, particularly injuries in which the lower portion of the body is paralyzed, the urinary bladder may be severely distended. Due to stretching of the bladder muscles and pressure against the opening of the bladder, the individual may be unable to void. As his bladder becomes more distended, it becomes painful. To relieve the distension a catheter must be inserted into the bladder through the urethra. The discomfort from this procedure is surprisingly small, usually much less than that from a distended bladder.

Urethral catheterization is rarely required for females, whose much shorter urethra offers far less resistance to voiding. If urethral catheterization is needed for a female, it must be carried out by someone with enough knowledge of female anatomy to correctly identify the urethral opening.

Rarely, an individual with a distended bladder repeatedly voids a small amount but does not completely empty his bladder. For such individuals distension requires longer to develop but can become much more severe because it is less obvious. Since the individual is voiding, the primary symptom is the severe discomfort from the distended bladder.

Usually about eight to ten hours are required for the bladder to become distended. Urethral catheterization can often be avoided if the person can be induced to void before that much time has elapsed. Having him stand up and walk around for a few minutes or placing his hand in warm water is frequently helpful in achieving this goal.

The greatest risk from urethral catheterization is infection, but meticulous care to avoid contamination of the catheter greatly reduces this hazard.

The following procedure should be followed for urethral catheterization:

1. Everything needed must be assembled before the procedure is begun. Any break to obtain a forgotten item invites contamination and infection. The required supplies consist of a sterile urinary catheter (size-sixteen or -eighteen French), sterile rubber or plastic gloves or sterile instruments to handle the catheter, sterile lubricating ointment, and alcohol swabs. A sterile towel on which to place the items is a great convenience and helps avoid contamination. The sterile wrapper from the gloves may be an appropriate substitute. A receptacle to collect the urine should also be on hand, particularly if the volume of urine must be measured.

2. The glans must be cleaned with alcohol, a disinfectant, or just soap and water, and the catheter must be removed from its container without being

contaminated. The circumstances and assistance available should determine which is done first, but the glans should not touch any nonsterile objects after it has been cleaned. For women, the labia should be spread and the opening of the urethra and surrounding mucosa should be cleansed in a similar manner. The labia must not be allowed to close until the catheter has been inserted into the bladder.

3. A small amount of a sterile lubricant should be applied to the catheter tip, and, with the individual in the supine position, the catheter should be inserted into the urethra and gently threaded upward until urine begins to flow from the open end. In men, this maneuver is facilitated if the penis is pulled upward to straighten the urethra and eliminate any folds in the mucosa lining this passage. After the urine has ceased to flow, the catheter should be gently withdrawn.

4. Most individuals require only a single catheterization and are subsequently able to void without difficulty. However, subjects with paralysis of the lower portion of their bodies usually have to be catheterized every eight hours to prevent overdistention of the bladder and possible renal injury. For such persons, an indwelling (Foley) catheter should be inserted. This type of catheter has a small balloon just below the tip. After the catheter has been inserted, this balloon can be inflated by injecting fluid with a syringe and needle into the nipple provided for this purpose on the external end of the catheter. The balloon must be deflated by clipping off the end of this nipple before the catheter is withdrawn. A catheter of this kind can usually be left in place for three to five days. To reduce the risk of infection, the subject may be given trimethoprim-sulfamethoxazole.

TUBE THORACOSTOMY

Tube thoracostomy is a severely hazardous procedure. The possible complications include infection, puncture of the heart or a major blood vessel, laceration of the lung, or even penetration of the diaphragm and laceration of the liver or spleen, all of which would probably be disastrous in a wilderness situation. This procedure must be attempted only when the following conditions can be met:

1. The subject is dying as the result of impaired respiratory function due to air or fluid in the chest, which would almost always be the result of traumatic injury.
2. All of the required equipment is available: flutter valve, trochar or means for inserting the tube, and the necessary tubing. A local anesthetic and means for preventing infection are also desirable.
3. The person performing the procedure has been instructed by a physician.

In spite of the hazards it presents, this procedure, properly performed, may be life-saving for individuals with a tension pneumothorax, particularly at high altitudes. Tube thoracostomy should be performed as follows:

1. If possible, the subject should be sitting up with his arms forward, propped in this position if necessary. If he can not sit up, he should have his head and chest higher than the rest of his body, and the side of the chest in which the tube is to be inserted should be uppermost.
2. If the person's condition allows time, the attendant should scrub his hands and arms with soap or Betadine® and a brush for ten minutes—by the clock!
3. A wide area of the individual's chest above the nipple on the injured side should be similarly scrubbed. Subsequently this area should be swabbed with iodine followed by alcohol or Betadine®, or just alcohol if nothing else is available.
4. If sterile rubber gloves are available, they should be put on after the attendant's hands have been scrubbed and the subject's chest has been scrubbed and swabbed with an antiseptic.
5. The rib at the same level as the nipple or at its upper margin should be identified. A point just lateral to the nipple (just beyond the edge of the breast for females) and at the upper margin of the rib should be selected for the thoracostomy.
6. The point selected should be anesthetized by infiltration with a local anesthetic (lidocaine). The infiltration should extend down to the rib and over its upper border.
7. A flutter valve (Heimlich valve) should be attached to one end of the chest tubing before the thoracostomy is begun. The valve must be checked to be certain it is not attached backward.
8a. If a trochar is available, a small nick about one-quarter inch (6 mm) in length should be made in the skin with a sterile scalpel blade to facilitate its insertion. The trochar should be pushed firmly through the chest wall until it stops against the rib. Then the tip should be moved upward slightly until it passes over the top of the rib, thus avoiding the blood vessels that course along the bottom of every rib. The chest wall is one-and-a-half to two-and-a-half inches (4 to 6.5 cm) thick, depending upon the individual's muscularity and the amount of fat present.
8b. If a trochar is not available, a one-inch (2.5-cm) incision should be made with a sterile scalpel and carried down to the rib. The bleeding that accompanies this incision can safely be ignored. The rib should be palpated with a sterile finger to ensure that its upper margin is located.
9a. After the trochar passes over the top of the rib, it should be pushed into the chest cavity. A gush of air or fluid should be encountered as the pleura is entered. The tubing with flutter valve attached should be passed through the trochar so that two to three inches of tubing extends beyond the trochar into the chest. While holding the tubing to make sure that it is not pulled out, the trochar should be withdrawn. (Leaking of air around the tubing is prevented by the muscles and other tissues of the chest wall.)
9b. With a pair of forceps or with a scalpel—carefully—the muscle above the rib and the underlying pleura should be punctured. A gush of air or blood should be encountered. Puncturing the pleura is usually painful in spite of the local anesthetic and the subject may require reassurance. A sterile

finger can briefly palpate the inner surface of the pleura to ensure that the chest has been entered. Then the tubing should be inserted, using the finger in the incision to guide it into position, with about two inches extending into the pleural cavity.

10. Usually the subject experiences marked relief of his respiratory difficulties immediately. If he does not, the tube should be checked to make certain it has been inserted to the proper depth and is not obstructed.

11. The tube should be anchored to the chest wall with tape so that it can not be pulled out or forced farther into the chest. A sterile bandage should be placed around the opening in the chest wall.

12. After the tube is in place, air and perhaps a little blood can be seen to pass through the valve whenever the person coughs. With severe lung injuries such emissions can be seen during quiet respiration. The valve should collapse during inspiration to prevent air from being sucked into the chest.

13. If a large amount of fluid or blood is being lost through the tube, a sterile receptacle of some type should be attached to the end away from the person's body, preferably with a second length of tubing, in order to measure the volume of the loss and prevent soiling the subject's clothing, sleeping bag, or other items (fig. B-4).

14. Most individuals must be evacuated with the tube in place. However, small lung punctures usually seal within one to four days, at which time air no longer flutters the valve on the end of the chest tube. When no air has been seen for six hours or more, the tube can be clamped, and the subject watched closely for several hours to determine whether respiratory distress returns. If he remains in satisfactory condition, the tube should be left

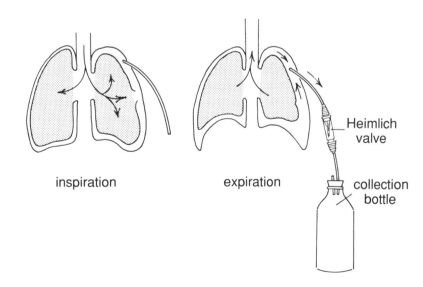

Figure B-4. Pulmonary function with a pneumothorax treated by tube thoracostomy. (Adapted from *Surgery of the Chest,* 3d ed.)

clamped for twenty-four to forty-eight hours. If no air passes from the tube when the clamp is released at the end of this time, the tubing may be withdrawn to reduce the risk of infection. If fluttering of the valve is seen, the entire procedure should be repeated forty-eight hours later. The individual must be closely attended during the time the tube is clamped so that the clamp can be released if respiratory difficulty develops.

INSTRUMENT STERILIZATION

Sometimes instruments must be sterilized in the field. At sea level, boiling instruments in water for fifteen minutes provides adequate sterilization, but equipment must be available for removing the items from the water without contaminating them. At higher elevations the boiling temperature of water is lower and the time required for sterilization is prolonged, but the additional time required is not easily determined. Boiling in a pressure cooker for fifteen minutes under fifteen pounds of pressure should be adequate at almost any altitude.

Scalpels, forceps, scissors, and similar metal instruments can be sterilized by washing them thoroughly, dipping them in alcohol, and lighting the alcohol. The instruments must be permitted to cool before they are used. (Blowing on the items to cool them produces contamination with bacteria from the nose and mouth.)

Regardless of the manner in which they have been sterilized, needles and syringes used for one individual must never be used to administer injections to another. The methods of sterilization in the field are too uncertain and the risk of transmitting infection is too great to chance in this manner. Most needles and syringes currently available are disposable—designed to be used only once and then discarded. Supplies of this type should be secured for wilderness outings. Items such as forceps and scalpels are also available in sterile, disposable kits that are convenient and relatively inexpensive.

Dressings and instruments should be wrapped in paper and autoclaved prior to an outing. Items protected in this manner remain sterile for several months if they are undisturbed and stay dry. If the items become wet, sterility is lost.

MEDICAL SUPPLIES

No wilderness party can be completely prepared for every medical problem. Only the supplies needed to care for common medical problems can be carried. The materials needed for severe accidents or major illnesses should be available at a base camp or similar central location.

No two individuals, whether physicians or not, can agree about the items that should be included in a wilderness medical kit. *(Because opinions vary so widely and often are so deeply entrenched, serious consideration was given to eliminating this appendix.—Ed.)* The following lists contain materials likely to be needed for acute medical disorders. "Personal Medical Supplies" lists items that probably should be carried by everyone on almost any outing. "Outing Medical Kit" suggests items that should be available in popular wilderness areas and on expeditions to remote areas. (Obviously, larger parties can carry a larger quantity and a greater variety of medical supplies.) The "Air-Drop Medical Kit" suggests items that could be available by air drop or similar means to victims of major accidents and possibly should be carried by major expeditions. Physicians should be consulted about the dosages and quantities of the items to be included.

Medications for preexisting disorders, such as diabetes or asthma, must be supplied by the individuals with such conditions.

Personal Medical Supplies

Acetaminophen, ibuprofen, or aspirin—50 or more
Aspirin and codeine—20 to 30
Meperidine, 100-mg tablets—10 or more
    or
Morphine, 10- or 15-mg tablets—10 or more
Adhesive pads (Band-Aids®), large—10 or more
Sterile gauze pads, four-inch squares—6 or more
Porous adhesive tape, two-inch width—1 roll
Moleskin, four-inch squares—4 to 6
Elastic bandage, three-inch width—1 or 2
Triangular bandage—2 or 3

Tweezers—1 per party
Sunscreen—generous supply
Wound antiseptic such as Betadine®—2 to 4 ounces
    or
Betadine® swabs—5 to 20
Personal medications—as needed

Outing Medical Kit

Medications (oral except where specified)
  Analgesics
    Aspirin and/or acetaminophen and/or ibuprofen
    Codeine (with aspirin or acetaminophen)
    Morphine (oral and injectable)
        or
    Meperidine (oral and injectable)
    Dibucaine ointment
  Antimicrobial preparations
    Penicillins
        Phenoxymethyl penicillin
        Ampicillin (oral and intramuscular)
        Cloxacillin
    Ciprofloxacin
    Tetracycline
    Trimethoprim-sulfamethoxazole
    Neosporin® ophthalmic drops
    Substitutes for members allergic to penicillin or sulfonamides
    Antimalarials appropriate for area
    Wound antiseptic(s)
  Gastrointestinal medications
    One or more antacids
    One or more motion-sickness agents
    One or more antispasmodics
    One or more laxatives
    One or more antidiarrheal agents
    One or more H_2 blockers
  Cardiac and respiratory agents
    Systemic decongestant
    Local decongestant spray, preferably long-acting
    Epinephrine
    Alupent Inhaler® or equivalent
    Acetazolamide
    Dexamethasone
  Others
    One or more antihistamines

One or more sedatives or tranquilizers
Sunscreens

Bandages and dressings
  Sterile gauze pads
  Nonadherent gauze pads
  Spenco Second Skin®
  Bandaging materials such as Kling
  Adhesive strips (Band-Aids®)
  Butterfly strips
  Sterile absorbent cotton
  Cotton swabs (Q-tips®)
  Eye pads
  Triangular bandages
  Porous adhesive tape, two-inch width
  Hypoallergenic tape
  Elastic bandages, two- or three-inch width
  Moleskin

Equipment
  Surgical forceps and tweezers
  Magnifying glass
  Penlight
  Scissors
  Scalpel with blades
  Syringes and needles
  Oral thermometer
  Stethoscope
  Sphygmomanometer
  Plastic oral airway(s)
  Tracheostomy device
  Tongue blades
  Inflatable lower leg splint
  Traction splint
  Hot-water bottle
  Snake-venom extractor
  Cervical collar

Items in personal medical kits

Air Drop Medical Kit

Items in outing medical kit
  Intravenous fluids (plastic containers)
    Balanced salt solution
    Five or ten percent glucose

Tubing and needles for administration
Intravenous antibiotics
Oxygen bottles, masks, valves, and tubing
Equipment for therapeutic procedures
Sterile gloves, lidocaine, syringes, and needles
Trochar, tubing, and valves for thoracostomy
Tubes, bottles, and syringes for nasogastric intubation
Catheters and lubricant for urethral catheterization
Leg and arm splints
Additional medications for known medical problems
Rescue gear
Rewarming gear
Ropes, carabiners, nuts or pitons, bolts, hammers, and pulleys
Ice axes, ice screws
Collapsible or wheel-equipped stretchers
Camping gear
Sleeping bags
Tents
Clothing
Food and potable water
Two-way radio

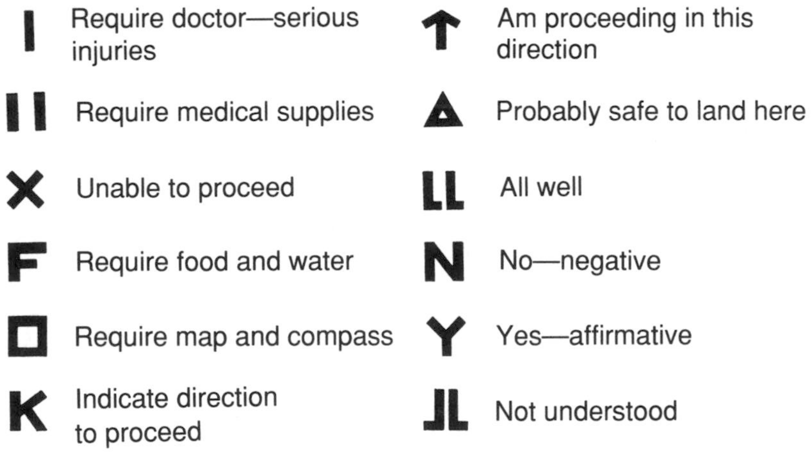

I Require doctor—serious injuries	**↑** Am proceeding in this direction
II Require medical supplies	**▲** Probably safe to land here
X Unable to proceed	**LL** All well
F Require food and water	**N** No—negative
□ Require map and compass	**Y** Yes—affirmative
K Indicate direction to proceed	**JL** Not understood

Figure C-1. Standard symbols for ground-to-air communication.

APPENDIX D

LEGAL CONSIDERATIONS

Few participants in wilderness activities would hesitate to provide medical care or to assist with the evacuation of an ill or injured individual, whether a member of their party or another. None of the following should raise doubts about that ethical—not legal—obligation. However, persons who do elect to render medical aid to others do have certain legal responsibilities as well as definite legal rights.

The following are general principles of the applicable laws in the United States and Canada. Each state, province, and nation makes its own laws, and they vary considerably. Anyone involved with such legal problems must obtain specific information about the law in the geographic area with which he is concerned.

PERSONAL LIABILITY

Almost no country has laws that require anyone to help a stranger in distress. An outdoor enthusiast can decline to provide medical assistance to anyone with legal impunity. Any obligation that exists in wilderness circumstances is ethical or traditional, not legal.

In contrast, a legal obligation to provide medical care or other assistance does exist if the individual has negligently caused the injury.

If medical assistance is provided, even though not required by law, it must be given reasonably and carefully. The diligence that would be exercised by an ordinarily prudent person under similar circumstances must be exercised. Anyone providing medical care is legally liable for harming the injured person if the injury could have been avoided by reasonable care. Additionally, more severe injuries or diseases are recognized to require closer attention and more extensive and sophisticated treatment.

The need for wilderness users to be familiar with first aid is well recognized. An outdoor enthusiast could be held liable for injuries resulting from lack of familiarity with techniques generally known to others, particularly if he had indicated in some manner beforehand that he had such knowledge. A physician is held to a higher standard. He must conduct himself as an ordinarily prudent doctor of medicine.

The circumstances in which assistance is rendered are also significant. The care legally required is that which is reasonable under the circumstances. The law takes into account the location of the victim, hazards for the person rendering aid, the equipment available, and the physical condition of the parties.

Finally, although a legal basis for claims sometimes does exist, lawsuits arising from voluntary medical assistance are rare. Few claims have followed voluntary assistance for individuals involved in wilderness accidents or illnesses.

ESTABLISHING DEATH

The problem of establishing that a person is dead is primarily medical, not legal. A death certificate signed by a physician is the customary method. If a physician is not available, a statement by persons who have actually seen the body and checked it for life usually suffices. If the body can not be found or recovered following accidents such as drownings or avalanches, the statements of those who witnessed the accident is ordinarily adequate. If no one saw the accident, death may still be established satisfactorily by circumstantial evidence, such as abandoned equipment, a deserted automobile or campsite, or the last statements of the deceased.

However, when such evidence can not be found, and only the disappearance of the missing person into a wilderness area can be documented, particularly if the wilderness area is one from which he could usually escape without difficulty, death might be impossible to establish. In such instances enough time must pass for legal "presumption" of death, usually seven years.

DISPOSAL OF THE BODY

The next of kin and local law enforcement agencies both have a legal interest in the body. The next of kin has the right to determine the disposal of the body (usually cremation or burial), where this shall be done, and what religious ceremony or other customs are to be followed. Law enforcement agencies must determine the cause of death to ensure that no crime has been committed and no public health hazard exists and must ensure that disposal of the body does not offend public sensibilities.

The next of kin and law enforcement officials may decide to leave the body in a remote, inaccessible location. Following a wilderness death, the members of a party are not legally obligated to retrieve or even to find the body.

ESTATE AND LIFE INSURANCE

Death occurring in the wilderness, even if the body is not recoverable, does not pose insurmountable problems in the administration of an estate or the settlement of life insurance claims. For administration of the estate, death must be proven, but the testimony of persons who actually saw the body is usually sufficient to establish the fact of death. If the deceased had life insurance, proof of death is a necessary condition for the payment of benefits. In general, proof of death that is adequate for administration of the estate will be sufficient for life insurance.

A different problem is associated with insurance that had a double indemnity clause, which pays twice the face amount of insurance if death is accidental. Often an exact cause of death must be ascertained. For example, after a fall, the question of whether death resulted from a heart attack that precipitated the fall might be raised. If a heart attack caused the fall, but injuries incurred in the fall killed the person, death usually would be considered accidental and the double indemnity provision would apply. If the individual died before the fall as the result of a heart attack, death would not have been accidental and the double indemnity provision would not apply. Deciding which occurred is not easy and may be impossible. For automobile accident deaths in which the victim has a heart attack and then crashes his car, double indemnity is commonly paid because injuries from the wreck can not be proven not to have caused the victim's death. (Many individuals survive heart attacks.)

The best method for answering such questions is to carefully examine the accident site and the victim, thoroughly question all witnesses to the accident, and write down the details as soon as possible. The body still may have to be evacuated for an autopsy to establish the cause of death.

GLOSSARY

Abrasion: A wound of the skin—and sometimes the underlying tissue—caused by scraping or rubbing.

Abscess: A localized collection of pus caused by infection and inflammation that destroy tissue. (Pimples and boils are small abscesses in the skin.)

Acidosis: An abnormally acidic condition of the blood that may be produced by a metabolic disorder such as diabetes mellitus or by severe accidental hypothermia.

Acute: 1. Appearing after or persisting for a relatively brief period of time. (This term does not indicate a specific time interval, but a short period of time in relation to the condition for which it is used. An acute onset would be minutes for some disorders, weeks for others.) 2. Requiring immediate or urgent attention.

Aerosinusitis: A painful condition of the paranasal sinuses produced by a rapid increase in external pressure (due to water submersion or a rapid descent from altitude) while the openings into the sinuses are closed and the pressure within the sinuses remains lower than external pressure.

Aerotitis: A painful condition of the middle ear similar to aerosinusitis but produced by pressure changes while the Eustachian tubes are closed.

Airway: Passages through which air enters and leaves the lungs.

Analgesia: The relief of pain.

Analgesic: A medication that relieves pain.

Anemia: A condition in which there is a reduced number of red blood cells in the circulating blood.

Angina Pectoris: Crushing or squeezing chest pain caused by a reduction in coronary artery blood flow due to arteriosclerosis.

Arrhythmia: An abnormal rhythm, usually referring to the heartbeat.

Arteriosclerosis: A disease of arteries characterized by deposits of material that narrow the lumens (most significantly) and also stiffens or "hardens" the walls.

Aspirate: 1. To inspire (air is aspirated into the lungs). 2. To draw in by suction (fluid is aspirated into a syringe).

Asthma: A disorder, typically allergic in origin, characterized by respiratory difficulty and caused by spasm of the muscles in small bronchioles that narrows their lumens.

Avulsion: An injury in which tissue is torn away or forcibly separated.

Bleb: A large blister.

Boil: An abscess located in the skin and subcutaneous tissue.

Bronchi: Air passages between the trachea and the bronchioles.

Bronchioles: Air passages between the bronchi and the alveoli, the smallest sac-like units of the lung.

Bronchitis: Inflammation of the bronchi and bronchioles, most often resulting from infection but also caused by cold injuries or burns of the bronchial mucosa.

Cardiac: Pertaining to the heart.

Cardiac Output: The volume of blood pumped by the heart during a specific period of time, usually one minute.

Carrier: A person who is immune to an infection but transmits it to others by carrying the organisms within his body.

Catheter: A tube introduced into an internal organ or structure. (A urethral or urinary catheter is passed into the urinary bladder.)

Central Nervous System: The brain and spinal cord.

Cerebral: Pertaining to the brain.

Cervical: Pertaining to the neck.

Cholera: An infection characterized by watery diarrhea so profuse that death from dehydration can result in less than a day.

Chronic: Appearing after or persisting for a relatively long time; opposite of acute.

Coma: A state of total unconsciousness.

Comatose: Totally unconscious.

Conjunctiva: The thin membrane that covers the white, visible surface of the eye and the inner surfaces of the eyelids.

Contusion: A bruise.

Convulsion: An intense, paroxysmal muscular contraction, commonly involving the entire body.

Crepitant: Producing crackling sounds or having a crackling sensation.

Cricothyroid: Area between the thyroid cartilage (Adam's apple) and the large cartilaginous ring (cricoid cartilage) just beneath.

Cricothyroidostomy: A surgical opening in the cricothyroid membrane that allows air to enter the trachea, created when the airway above that site is obstructed.

Cyanosis: A purple or bluish discoloration of the lips, nails, and skin that typically results from reduced oxygen in the blood.

Cystitis: An inflammatory disorder of the urinary bladder.

Debridement: Removal of foreign material and dead tissue from a wound.

Dehydration: Loss of excessive quantities of (body) water.

Delirium: A state of temporary mental confusion and clouded consciousness characterized by anxiety, tremors, hallucinations, delusions, and incoherence.

Diabetes Mellitus: A disorder of glucose metabolism that results in increased urinary output, glucose (sugar) in the urine, a tendency to develop severe infections, and other disorders, including accelerated arteriosclerosis and renal failure.

Diagnose: To distinguish one disease or injury from another; to identify an illness or injury.

Diagnosis: The identification of an illness or injury.

Dissociation: Separation of related psychologic activities into autonomously functioning units, as in the generation of multiple personalities (abnormal), or shutting out the emotional aspects of an injury scene while concentrating on the measures necessary to carry out a rescue (normal).

Dysentery: A bacterial infection of the gastrointestinal tract that results in diarrhea, mucus and pus in the stools, and fever.

Dysmenorrhea: Painful cramps associated with menstruation.

Dyspnea: Abnormal shortness of breath; awareness of the need to breathe.

Edema: An abnormal collection of fluid within body tissue. (Pulmonary edema is fluid within the lungs.)

Electrocardiogram: A recording of the electrical activity of the heart.

Electrolyte: One of the four major ions—sodium, potassium, chloride, and bicarbonate—in serum.

Embolism: Sudden obstruction of a blood vessel by an embolus, often resulting in death of the tissue supplied by that vessel.

Embolus: A clot or similar tissue carried by the blood stream from a peripheral site, such as a leg vein, through larger, more proximal vessels and the heart, until it is forced into a smaller artery, usually in the lung.

Encephalitis: An infection of the brain, most commonly caused by a virus and often spread by mosquitoes.

Endemic: Peculiar to or prevailing in or among a (specified) country or people.

Eosinophil: A white blood cell characterized by large red granules in its cytoplasm; eosinophils normally constitute two to four percent of all white blood cells.

Eosinophilia: An increased number of eosinophils in the blood; often indicative of a parasitic infestation or an allergic reaction.

Epididymitis: An infection of the epididymis, the structure in which sperm collect before being transported to the seminal vesicles.

Epilepsy: A neurologic disorder characterized by repeated convulsions.

Extrasystole: An abnormal cardiac rhythm in which a normally beating heart suddenly contracts after a shorter interval than usual; sometimes called "skipped beats."

Extravasate: To force a material such as blood out of its normal channel (a blood vessel) into surrounding tissue.

Exudate: Any substance, most commonly inflammatory cells and protein, that passes through blood vessel walls in living tissue and can be removed or extracted; most frequently associated with inflammation.

Fascia: A sheet or membrane of fibrous tissue separating or investing muscles or various other structures.

Fever: A higher than normal body temperature, most commonly the result of infection but also caused by other disorders.

Fibrillation: An abnormal cardiac rhythm in which cardiac muscle fibers contract independently of each other instead of in synchrony. When only the atrium is involved, the cardiac rhythm is completely irregular. If the ventricle is involved, the condition is lethal if not corrected within minutes because cardiac output falls to very low levels.

Flaccid: Completely lacking in muscle tone; totally relaxed.

Flatus: Gas or air expelled from the intestines.

Gangrene: Death of a part of the body, such as an arm or leg, usually as the result of an inadequate blood supply but sometimes due to infection.

Gasp Reflex: Involuntary tendency to gasp or inspire when suddenly immersed in cold water.

Generalized: Spread throughout the body; opposite of localized.

Glomerulonephritis: A renal disorder characterized by reduced renal function, low urinary volumes, and protein in the urine.

Gonorrhea: A sexually transmitted infection that typically produces painful urethral inflammation and a discharge in men but often produces no symptoms in women.

Hallucination: A sound, sight, or other sensation perceived as real in the absence of an actually existing object or source.

Heart Failure: Inability of the heart to pump out all of the blood returned to it, causing fluid to pool (edema) in the peripheral tissues or lungs, depending upon which ventricle is damaged.

Heart Valves: Valves that maintain the forward flow of blood within the heart.

Heimlich Maneuver: A maneuver for dislodging obstructing material, usually aspirated food, from the larynx or trachea.

Hematoma: A mass formed by clotted blood within tissue.

Hematuria: Blood (intact red blood cells) in the urine.

Hemoglobin: The oxygen-transporting pigment in red blood cells.

Hemoglobinuria: Hemoglobin in the urine, a reflection of disorders distinctly different from those that cause hematuria.

Hemorrhoids: Enlarged veins beneath the skin of the anus.

Hydrated: Containing water. (Normally hydrated means containing a normal amount of water.)

Hypertension: High blood pressure.

Hyperthermia: A higher than normal body temperature.

Hypoglycemia: A lower than normal concentration of glucose in the blood.

Hypothermia: A lower than normal body temperature.

Hypoxia: The presence of a lower than normal quantity of oxygen; can refer to body tissues, blood, or the atmosphere.

Immunization: The production of an immune condition by administration of an agent that stimulates a protective response.

Incubation Period: The period of time between infection by microorganisms and the onset of detectable signs or symptoms of the disease.

Infarction: The death of tissue caused by arterial obstruction.

Intramuscular: Within muscle; commonly used to indicate the site for injection of a medication.

Intravenous: Within a vein; commonly used to indicate the site for injection of a medication or fluids.

Intubate: To place a tube into a passage such as the trachea, usually to keep the passage open.

Jaundice: An accumulation of bile pigments in the blood, usually resulting from liver disease, that produces a yellow discoloration of the skin and eyes.

Ketosis: An accumulation of ketones in the blood, most commonly as the result of diabetes or starvation.

Laceration: A traumatic injury characterized by cutting or tearing.

Larynx: The upper part of the trachea; "voice box."

Lumen: The open passage within a tubular organ such as an intestine or a blood vessel.

Lymph Nodes: Collections of tissue that trap bacteria and debris and help retard the spread of infection or other disease processes.

Macerate: To reduce to a soft mass by soaking; to digest.

Malaise: A generalized feeling of discomfort or indisposition; feeling ill.

Malaria: A parasitic infectious disorder characterized by cyclic chills, fever and sweating, that is transmitted through the bite of female Anopheles mosquitoes.

Meningitis: Inflammation of the thin membranes that surround the brain and spinal cord, usually as the result of infection.

Metabolism: Processes in living organisms that use energy to construct compounds from assimilated materials or to break down such materials to release energy.

Necrosis: The death of tissue as the result of disease.

Neurologic: Of or pertaining to the nervous system.

Nontraumatic: Not caused or associated with physical injury.

Nutrient: Any component of food that aids growth, development, or replacement of tissues.

Osmosis: Diffusion of water through a semipermeable membrane.

Osmotic Pressure: Hydrostatic pressure created by diffusion through a semipermeable membrane.

Palpate: To feel or examine by touch.

Palpitation: A rapid or irregular heartbeat of which a person is aware.

Paralytic Ileus: Paralysis of the intestine that produces functional obstruction, most often caused by peritonitis.

Paresthesias: Abnormal sensations, commonly tingling or buzzing; sensations felt when a limb "goes to sleep."

Paroxysmal Tachycardia: An abnormal cardiac rhythm characterized by a heartbeat that is quite fast but entirely regular.

Pathogenic: Producing disease.

Penicillinase: An enzyme produced by some bacteria that inactivates penicillin and produces resistance to that drug.

Peptic Ulcer: A crater in the mucosa of the stomach or duodenum produced by the combined digestive action of gastric acid and digestive enzymes.

Peritonitis: Inflammation of the thin membrane lining the abdominal cavity as a result of infection or irritation by intestinal contents or blood.

Pharyngitis: Inflammation of the pharynx, the structures behind the mouth and nose; a "sore throat."

Pleurisy: Inflammation of the pleura, the thin membrane that covers the lungs and the chest wall.

Pneumonia: An infection of the lung.

Prognosis: A prediction or conclusion regarding the course and termination of a disease or injury.

Prone: Lying flat in a face-down position.

Prophylaxis: Preventive treatment for disease.

Proteinuria: Protein in the urine.

Pulmonary: Of or pertaining to the lungs.

Puncture Wound: A wound, usually produced by an object such as a nail or thorn, that is deep but has a narrow, constricted opening.

Purulent: Consisting of or containing pus.

Pustule: A pimple or small boil.

Pyelonephritis: An infection of the kidney.

Radial Pulse: The pulse felt at the wrist on the thumb side that is routinely used to determine heart rate.

Radiation of Pain: The sensation of pain experienced in an area other than the anatomical site of the injury or disease where it is produced.

Rales: Crackling or bubbling sounds heard when listening to the lungs in the presence of pulmonary edema.

Rebound Tenderness: The pain produced by releasing pressure with the fingers on the abdomen and allowing the abdominal wall to rebound; almost always an indication of an intra-abdominal condition that requires surgical treatment.

Renal: Of or pertaining to the kidneys.

Resorb: To reabsorb.

Respiratory: Pertaining to the lungs or their function.

Resuscitate: To revive; to restore to life or consciousness.

Rheumatic Fever: An inflammatory disorder associated with streptococcal infections in which the valves of the heart are damaged, often irreversibly.

Roughage: Food that is high in fiber and adds bulk to the gastrointestinal contents.

Salpingitis: An inflammatory disorder, usually infectious, that involves the fallopian tubes and may mimic appendicitis and other intra-abdominal disorders that require surgical therapy.

Shock: A condition characterized by low blood pressure, fast but weak pulse, pallor, "cold sweats," and mental impairment that commonly results from trauma or other disorders that produce severe bleeding.

Sign: Physical evidence of disease discovered by examination.

Sinus: A mucosa-lined space in the bones of the skull.

Sinusitis: An infection of one of the sinuses in the skull.

Soft Tissue: Nonosseous tissues of the body. (The joint ligaments and internal organs usually are not included.)

Somnolence: Oppressive drowsiness or sleepiness.

Spasm: An involuntary muscular contraction, usually painful.

Sphygmomanometer: A device for measuring blood pressure.

Spinal Canal: The canal within the vertebral column through which the spinal cord passes.

Sprain: An injury characterized by incomplete rupture of the supporting ligaments around a joint.

Stethoscope: A device that aids listening to body sounds, particularly those of the heart and lungs.

Strain: An injury characterized by stretching, with or without mild tearing, of a muscle or tendon.

Stress: An emotionally or physically disruptive or disquieting event or condition.

Stroke: The death of brain tissue caused by hemorrhage or arterial obstruction.

Subacute: Appearing after or persisting for a period of time that is intermediate between acute and chronic in duration. (See Acute.)

Subcutaneous: Beneath the skin.

Subdural: Beneath the dura, the fibrotic membrane covering the brain; most commonly used in reference to a hematoma.

Supine: Lying flat in a face-up position.

Suture: 1. To unite parts by stitching; to sew together the edges of lacerated tissue. 2. The joints between the bones of the skull.

Symptom: Any abnormal function, sensation, or experience that indicates the presence of disease.

Syncope: A brief episode of unconsciousness, usually not associated with a significant illness; fainting.

Syndrome: A group of signs and symptoms that occur together and comprise a disease entity.

Syphilis: A sexually transmitted infection that may produce no early symptoms but can be devastating years later if untreated.

Synergism: Two or more agents acting in combination to produce an effect greater than the sum of their independent effects.

Tachycardia: An abnormally fast heart rate.

Thoracostomy: A surgical procedure that creates an opening into the chest.

Thrombophlebitis: Thrombosis within veins that produces inflammation and pain.

Thrombosis: Clotting of blood, typically within a blood vessel.

Torsion: The twisting of an organ or tissue in such a manner that the flow of blood to the tissue is obstructed.

Toxic: Having a poisonous or noxious effect.

Toxin: A noxious or poisonous substance.

Trachea: The large air passage between the mouth or nose and the bronchi and lungs.

Tracheostomy: An opening created in the trachea through which air can flow; produced to bypass an obstruction above that site.

Trauma: 1. A physical force that injures the body; an injury produced by physical force. 2. Any external force that produces injury, including emotional trauma.

Traumatic: Of or pertaining to trauma.

Tuberculosis: A chronic infection, most often pulmonary, characterized by extensive tissue destruction and death if untreated.

Varicose Veins: Dilated, tortuous veins, most commonly in the legs.

Vascular: Of or pertaining to blood vessels.

Vertigo: A feeling that one's self or one's environment is whirling around; not synonymous with dizziness.

INDEX

THE MOUNTAINEERS, founded in 1906, is a non-profit outdoor activity and conservation club, whose mission is "to explore, study, preserve and enjoy the natural beauty of the outdoors...." Based in Seattle, Washington, the club is now the third largest such organization in the United States, with 12,000 members and four branches throughout Washington State.

The Mountaineers sponsors both classes and year-round outdoor activities in the Pacific Northwest, which include hiking, mountain climbing, ski-touring, snowshoeing, bicycling, camping, kayaking and canoeing, nature study, sailing, and adventure travel. The club's conservation division supports environmental causes through educational activities, sponsoring legislation, and presenting informational programs. All club activities are led by skilled, experienced volunteers, who are dedicated to promoting safe and responsible enjoyment and preservation of the outdoors.

The Mountaineers Books, an active, non-profit publishing program of the club, produces guidebooks, instructional texts, historical works, natural history guides, and works on environmental conservation. All books produced by The Mountaineers are aimed at fulfilling the club's mission.

If you would like to participate in these organized outdoor activities or the club's programs, consider a membership in The Mountaineers. For information and an application, write or call The Mountaineers, Club Headquarters, 300 Third Avenue West, Seattle, Washington 98119; (206) 284-6310.